FUNDAMENTAL COMPUTER PROGRAMMING USING FORTRAN 77

PRENTICE-HALL SOFTWARE SERIES
Brian W. Kernighan, advisor

FUNDAMENTAL COMPUTER PROGRAMMING USING FORTRAN 77

Jarrell C. Grout

Prentice-Hall, Inc. Englewood Cliffs, N.J. 07632

Library of Congress Cataloging in Publication Data

GROUT, JARREL C.
   Fundamental computer programming using Fortran 77.

   Includes index.
   1. FORTRAN (computer program language) 2. Electronic
digital computers—Programming. I. Title.
QA76.73.F25G76 1983   001.64'24   82-20421
ISBN 0-13-335141-6

Editorial/production supervision
  and interior design: *Aliza Greenblatt*
Cover design: *Jeannette Jacobs*
Manufacturing buyer: *Gordon Osbourne*

> *". . . to Him who is able*
> *to do exceeding abundantly*
> *beyond all that we ask or think,*
> *according to the power that works within us . . ."*
>
> *(Eph. 3:20 NASB)*

Printed in the United States of America
10 9 8 7 6 5 4 3 2 1

ISBN 0-13-335141-6

PRENTICE-HALL INTERNATIONAL, INC., *London*
PRENTICE-HALL OF AUSTRALIA PTY. LIMITED, *Sydney*
EDITORA PRENTICE-HALL DO BRASIL, LTDA., *Rio de Janeiro*
PRENTICE-HALL CANADA INC., *Toronto*
PRENTICE-HALL OF INDIA PRIVATE LIMITED, *New Delhi*
PRENTICE-HALL OF JAPAN, INC., *Tokyo*
PRENTICE-HALL OF SOUTHEAST ASIA PTE. LTD., *Singapore*
WHITEHALL BOOKS LIMITED, *Wellington, New Zealand*

Contents

Preface

This book is for people who want to learn computer programming and the FORTRAN 77 programming language. Its primary objective is to present the fundamental methodology of contemporary computer programming in a manner that is understandable and useful to learners. FORTRAN 77, the up-to-date standard version of the widely used Fortran language, is throughly described and illustrated to provide the means for applying the components of the methodology and practicing with them. The book meets the requirements of course CS1, Computer Programming I, of the ACM Curriculum '78 (*Communications of the ACM*, March 1979), but it is not limited to use by students of computer science; it is intended for anyone, at any age, who has at least the equivalence of a high school education and a desire to learn fundamental computer programming.

There are a number of features, in addition to readability, which distinguish this text from the other books that address the subjects of programming and FORTRAN 77 together. The major ones are listed and briefly described below.

1. There is a decided emphasis on program planning and problem-solving methods. In Chapter 2, an unusually comprehensive programming guide is presented and used to stress planning; then specific procedures for developing algorithms and program flowcharts are covered in depth. Subsequently, these are employed throughout the text to expand the learner's problem-solving skills. Top-down program design and stepwise refinement of algorithms are introduced in Chapter 2 and weaved into the text appropriately from there on. Chapter 2 is intentionally longer and more explanatory than corresponding chapters in most comparable books; yet toward the end of the chapter, the learner reads, studies, and runs a first simple program.

2. The creation of well-organized Fortran programs is encouraged and facilitated by the presentation, in Chapter 3, of a specific Fortran program organization method that emphasizes modularity at the design level and effective organization of whole programs at the coding level. The goal of the method is to make Fortran programs easier to design, document, read, understand, debug, and maintain—basically, the goal of structured

programming. This book can be used whether or not the method is adopted; its adoption, however, should be thoughtfully considered in the light of current good programming practices.

3. Well-designed input and output (i/o) is advocated, with specific i/o design instruction being given initially in Chapter 6. Printed output, especially, should be readable and understandable. Thus both explicitly formatted and implicitly formatted (i.e., list-directed) i/o are fully covered in the text; explicit formatting is not relegated to an appendix or treated as an afterthought as in many other books.

4. The GO TO problem is met head-on. Learners, and experienced programmers too, need to know when and when not to use the GO TO statement and how to use it properly when they do use it. The relevant instruction, with complete structured programming illustrations, is initiated in Chapter 4.

5. In every chapter except 1 and 10, there is at least one complete example program per chapter—completely planned, completely developed, and completely explained to the extent needed by the learner at that point. The programs are meant to be read and studied. They progress from the simple to the moderately difficult. Furthermore, they illustrate, among others, these fundamental programming techniques: linear and binary search, bubble sort (direct and indirect, numeric and alphabetic), report generation, program modification, program modularization, file building, file merging, and programming for on-line and interactive processing.

6. Programming language coverage is strictly American National Standard FORTRAN, X3.9-1978, commonly known as FORTRAN 77. The coverage is complete for the full language; no extensions are presented.

7. Instructions for using FORTRAN 77 to create good programs are integrated with the language presentation. By a good program, I mean one that is correct, well documented, readable, understandable, maintainable, produced on schedule, and reasonably efficient in terms of storage requirements and execution time.

This book can be used by individuals to learn programming and FORTRAN 77 independently; it can certainly be used to learn the same under a good teacher's guidance. Teachers should consider covering the material in one of the following three ways:

1. If the students have absolutely no background in computing, begin with Chapter 1 and cover most of the material through Chapter 11. The purpose of the first chapter is to introduce beginning students to computer

equipment, different types of computer programs, and the role of data in programming. One noteworthy point about Chapter 1 is that it provides a clear contrast between programs and data, thus alleviating a particular difficulty that beginners often have. If a time constraint occurs while going through the rest of the material, just touch lightly on or even bypass Chapter 10 on multidimensional arrays. The array chapters, 8 and 10, were purposely split to provide this flexibility and to allow the important subject of character data processing (chapter 9) to be considered sooner.

2.   If the students have completed an ''introduction to computers'' course, or the equivalence, cover Chapters 2 through 11.

3.   If the students have the background equivalence of an ''introduction to computers'' course and one programming course of any kind, Cover chapters 2 through 12.

Teachers, students, and independent learners alike, are encouraged to keep a copy of this book; it can serve as a long-term future reference text for computer programming and FORTRAN 77.

ACKNOWLEDGEMENTS

The late Dr. John Q. Hays, a long-time English professor and my friend, read a portion of the first draft and provided a valuable critique of my writing style. My wife Helen also read and critiqued parts of the manuscript for readability and style. My computer science colleagues Dr. John Anderson, Dr. Denis Hyams, Bill Herman, and Fred Fisher reviewed some of the early material and gave helpful recommendations. Dr. Brian Kernighan and Dr. Richard Austing performed technical reviews, providing a number of valuable suggestions. For several years, the students in my introductory computer programming classes participated in formulating the book by using versions of it in draft form. Notable contributions in the form of example program development were made in the early stages by my computer science students Brent Fodor, Chip Galloway, and Tammy Mays. Also, my non-computer science students Shiela Brookshire and Sandra and Logan Fitch reviewed significant portions of the material for readability. Stephen F. Austin State University supplied grant funds that partially supported the work leading ultimately to Chapter 3. Morris Lang, of the University Computer Center, provided a good deal of technical assistance. The *Journal of Data Education*, with prior permission from Prentice-Hall, Inc., published my initial report about the content of Chapter 3 in their October 1980 issue. An immeasurable amount of support in the way of prayers and words of encouragement came from my family. From my heart, I thank them all.

Let me also thank you for reading and using this book. Please make me aware of any suggestions you have for improvement. Be assured that I will respond to you.

Jarrell C. Grout
Nacogdoches, Texas

FUNDAMENTAL
COMPUTER
PROGRAMMING
USING
FORTRAN 77

Chapter

1

Computers, Programs, and Data

Before you begin to learn about computer programming, you need to have at least a fundamental familiarity with computers. It will also be helpful for you to know what a computer program is and how data are related to computers and computer programs.

If you already have this knowledge, you can probably bypass this chapter and go on to Chapter 2. If, however, you have no computer background of any kind, or if you just want to "brush up" on the concepts, you should read this chapter. It has been prepared to get you ready for computer programming by acquainting you as directly and summarily as possible with the background principles with which you need to be familiar.

1-1 WHAT COMPUTERS DO

Computers are just about the most useful machines around. Like virtually all machines, they were invented and have been developed to help people. Although they have been in widespread general use for only a relatively few years, the services they now perform are, without doubt, infinitely broader in scope than the early computer experimenters envisioned; their performance certainly far exceeds the early expectations.

It has been implied that computers are similar to human beings. In a limited sense, this is a valid analogy that can be used to help you begin to understand what computers do. In a very simplified way, then, human beings and computers are compared in the following statement:

Human beings act on the basis of knowledge and observation;
computers solve problems by means of instructions and data.

The essence of this statement is depicted in Figure 1-1. You can see from the diagram—as well as from the sentence above—that instructions are like knowledge, data are like observations, and problem solutions are like actions. Keep this in mind.

A *computer* is a machine that is capable of doing the following things without intervention by a human being: receiving and storing data and instructions, performing operations on the data as prescribed by the instructions, and displaying the results in a form understandable to human beings. This definition, which is the first of many that you should learn, provides a good starting point for finding out what can really be accomplished with a computer. I want to point out that although a computer can perform the activities described free of intermediate involvement by a person, it definitely takes a person to arrange for the data to be collected, come up with the instructions, get the operations started, and do something with the results. The computer is not the "thinker" in this process; it is the "workhorse."

By considering together the computer diagram of Figure 1-1 and the definition above, you can see that problem solving is the goal of computer use. The performance of certain tasks to accomplish this goal is the service for which the computer was invented. From the human view, these tasks can usually be characterized by one or more of such terms as "repetitive," "boring," "time consuming," "complex," and "impossible." If the computer can help us with tasks such as these, it must be an invention worthy of further study by just about everyone.

Problems that can be solved advantageously with the help of a computer exist all around us. From the need of a company to write checks with which to pay

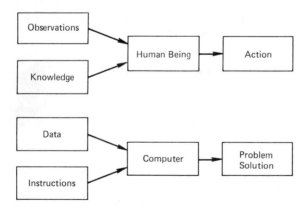

Figure 1-1. A Simplified Comparison of Human Beings and Computers

employees, to that of a scientist for analysis of some experimental data, to the individual problem of keeping personal budget records—they are everywhere. And computers are just about everywhere too.

1-2   KINDS OF COMPUTERS

There are two major classes of computers: analog and digital. In an *analog computer*, data are represented by continuously variable physical quantities such as electric current. In a *digital computer*, data are represented electronically in the form of distinct digits—ordinarily in the binary system. The digital computer is widely used throughout the world today and is usually the type meant when the term "computer" is mentioned. Similarly, from this point on, whenever I use the word "computer" I will be referring only to the digital computer because it is the type in which we are interested.

The primary characteristics that distinguish one digital computer from another are physical size and performance capabilities. Thus you will hear some referred to as "large-scale computers," others as "minicomputers," and still others as "microcomputers." Briefly stated, large-scale computers have broad capabilities and may occupy a fairly good-sized room; minicomputers ordinarily have a wide range of capabilities and can usually fit into a corner of a room; microcomputers are commonly small enough to set on the top of a desk, but they may be somewhat limited in capabilities. Figures 1-2, 1-3, and 1-4 illustrate these three kinds of digital computers.

Figure 1-2. A Large-Scale Digital Computer (*Courtesy of Honeywell Information Systems, Inc.*)

Figure 1-3. A Minicomputer (*Courtesy of Honeywell Information Systems, Inc.*)

Although photographs are useful for illustrating computers in a book like this, they can only convey a rather abstract, or at best incomplete, view for a person who has never seen an actual computer in operation. You might be surprised at how much you can later benefit—in terms of understanding and gaining confidence in your ability to use the computer properly—by observing a computer in action now. Therefore, I urge you to look for an opportunity to do just that. The first place to look is your university computer center, which probably has a large-scale computer and, perhaps, several minicomputers. Alternatively, or additionally, a nearby computer store will have a variety of microcomputers. Most likely, both the computer center and computer store will have explanatory literature that you can obtain; they may also have someone available who can describe the computer to you. If so, take advantage of it.

The means described above—involving physical size and performance capabilities for distinguishing among digital computers—has been convenient for the past few years. Technological advances, however, are resulting in significant physical size decreases in larger computers and capacity increases in weaker computers. That is, newer models of large-scale computers and minicomputers are smaller than previous models, and newer models of minicomputers and microcomputers are capable of performing a wider range of tasks than older models. Thus it is getting more and more difficult to distinguish by size and capability.

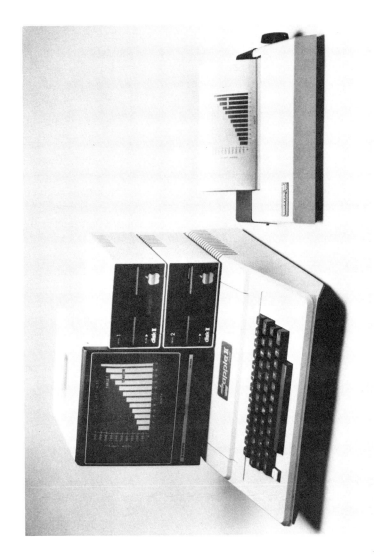

Figure 1-4. A Microcomputer (*Courtesy of Apple Computer, Inc.*)

For your purposes here, the ability to recognize that a particular digital computer is large-scale, mini, or micro is not too important. It is important, though, that you know some of the capabilities of the specific computer with which you are working. First, since you will be writing Fortran programs, you must know that your computer can process Fortran programs. Virtually all large-scale computers can, most minicomputers can, and many microcomputers can. Then you have to know some things about the components of the computer—what components are available, what functions each component performs, and how the components handle the data and instructions you provide.

1-3 COMPUTER COMPONENTS

Whether large-scale, mini, or micro, every digital computer has five primary components: input, memory, control, arithmetic-logic, and output. These, and their relationships with each other, are depicted in Figure 1-5.

As indicated in the figure, problem-solving instructions and problem data are entered into a computer through an input device. They are electronically transmitted to and stored in the computer's memory. The control unit fetches the instructions from memory in sequence, interprets them one by one, and sees to it that each is performed properly and completely before proceeding to the next one. The performance of an instruction, known as execution, leads toward the accomplishment of the overall goal: problem solution.

Execution basically involves transforming or moving data, and making decisions about which instruction is to be executed next. Arithmetic operations, for data transformations, and comparisons, for making decisions, are carried out by the arithmetic-logic component. Results are sent on to memory to be used or held, as needed, until internal processing is complete. Then the final solution data are transmitted from memory to an output device where they are displayed for human use or saved for later processing.

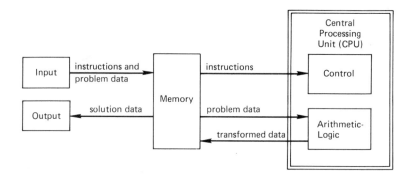

Figure 1-5. The Primary Components of a Digital Computer

Now, having been given an overview description of the functions performed by the components of a computer, you can begin to understand how a computer works. It will help you even more to consider the actual physical aspects of each of the components.

An *input device* must be capable of accepting instructions and problem data, and transmitting them to memory. Card readers have long been used for this purpose, but computer terminals with typewriter-like keyboards now have the most widespread use. Examples of the two are shown in Figures 1-6 and 1-7. Other input devices include typewriter terminals, mark-sense readers, magnetic tape units, magnetic disk units, and graphics terminals with coupled light pens.

In contrast to input devices, *output devices* must be able to accept solution data from memory and display them in a way that human beings can understand, or save them for later processing. The most common output devices are line printers, an example of which appears in Figure 1-8, and computer terminals having typewriter-like keyboards with video display screens. Yes, video display terminals are used for output as well as input. In fact, several devices—such as magnetic tape units, magnetic disk units, and graphics terminals—serve dual input and output purposes. Others besides line printers—such as card punches, paper tape punches, and graphical plotters—are strictly for computer output.

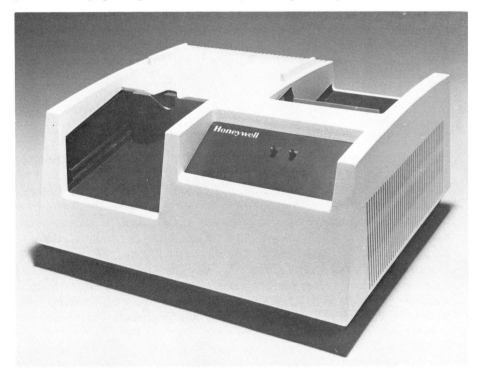

Figure 1-6. A Card Reader (*Courtesy of Honeywell Information Systems, Inc.*)

Figure 1-7. A Video Display Terminal (*Courtesy of Honeywell Information Systems, Inc.*)

Computer *memory* is an electronic device that is designed to hold data and instructions, in the form of groups of binary digits (1s and 0s), until they are needed by one of the other components. The device is made up of many small elements, each of which can electronically represent a binary digit. The memory size is limited by the number of elements it contains. Decimal digits, alphabetic letters, and other characters familiar to human beings can be represented by sequences of binary digits and thus sequences of these electronic elements. The sequences of elements are, in general, called *storage locations* and the memory itself is often called *storage*. Each storage location has associated with it an *address*, an actual number by which it can be referenced and its contents accessed by the other components. Everything you need to know about this for effective Fortran programming is explained in the next section.

The *control* and *arithmetic-logic* components of a computer are also electronic devices. Each has addressable binary storage elements similar to that of memory and each also contains electronic circuitry for performing its particular tasks. Physically, they appear together in one device called the *central processing*

Figure 1-8. A Line Printer (*Courtesy of Honeywell Information Systems, Inc.*)

unit (CPU). Instructions, coming from memory, are stored one by one in the CPU only long enough to be interpreted and executed individually. Data, also coming from memory, are stored in the CPU only long enough to be operated upon as directed by the instructions.

1-4 COMPUTER STORAGE

Whether in memory or CPU, data and instructions are stored in a manner that makes use of the binary number system. There are only two digits in the binary system: 1 and 0. These digits are called *bits*, a contraction of the words "bi(nary) (digi)ts." Formally defined, a bit is the smallest unit of information for computer storage. In the preceding section, I said that one memory element can electronically represent one binary digit. So, at any one time, one memory element can represent either the bit 1 or the bit 0.

One bit is some information, just as the decimal digit 2 or the letter W is some information, but it is not necessarily much information. What can you do if you want more information than one decimal digit or one letter provides? One thing is to attach more digits or letters (e.g., to 2, attach 12 to get 212; to W attach ATER to obtain WATER). The idea is this: The more decimal digits you can put together, the more individual numbers you can represent; the more letters you can put together, the more words you can create. In both cases you can have more information than you had before.

The same idea applies to bits. With one bit you have either 1 or 0. With two bits together you have 00 or 01 or 10 or 11. With three bits together: 000, 001, 010, 011, 100, 101, 110, or 111. And so on.

Given enough bits grouped together, you can use them to represent data in the forms that you are used to—decimal numbers and English words, for example. As an initial illustration, Table 1-1 contains the binary representation of the decimal digits 0 through 9. Notice that four bits or less are required to represent each of the decimal digits.

Table 1-1. DECIMAL DIGITS AND BINARY EQUIVALENTS

Decimal	Binary
0	0
1	1
2	10
3	11
4	100
5	101
6	110
7	111
8	1000
9	1001

Many computers are designed to conveniently allow 8 bits to be treated together as one unit of information. A group of bits like this is commonly called a *byte*. Specifically, a byte is a sequence of adjacent bits that is ordinarily operated on as the smallest addressable (locatable and accessible) unit of information for computer storage. Normally, then, you can expect a datum or an instruction to consist of at least one byte.

Consider the uses of an eight-bit byte. Table 1-2 illustrates the representation of decimal numbers in pure binary form, and Table 1-3 illustrates the representation of alphabetic letters by means of two binary coding methods known as ASCII (American Standard Code for Information Interchange—in 8-bit form) and EBCDIC (Extended Binary-Coded Decimal Interchange Code). As shown in the numeric illustration, 8 bits together can represent all the decimal whole numbers 0 through 255. Only a portion of the numbers in this range are included in the table because the purpose is to show you what can be done; the purpose is not to teach you the binary system. You need not know the binary system to write good Fortran programs. The knowledge, however, can be beneficial; it can help you understand, even more, how the computer works. I encourage you to take the time to do

Table 1-2. EIGHT-BIT BINARY REPRESENTATION
OF SELECTED DECIMAL WHOLE NUMBERS

Decimal	Binary	Decimal	Binary
0	00000000	240	11110000
1	00000001	241	11110001
2	00000010	242	11110010
3	00000011	243	11110011
4	00000100	244	11110100
5	00000101	245	11110101
6	00000110	246	11110110
7	00000111	247	11110111
8	00001000	248	11111000
9	00001001	249	11111001
10	00001010	250	11111010
11	00001011	251	11111011
12	00001100	252	11111100
13	00001101	253	11111101
14	00001110	254	11111110
15	00001111	255	11111111

a little outside research and learn it; then, as an exercise, fill in a portion of the gap in the binary numbers of Table 1-2.

Look at the alphabetic letter illustration in Table 1-3. To represent letters and other characters, an 8-bit byte is divided into two 4-bit portions. This method of division is a form of binary coding, and the two portions are referred to as the *zone* and the *numeric*. (In the table, a blank space between each set of zone and numeric bits is included for readability. The computer does not use blank spaces for this purpose.) For the letter A, as an example, the ASCII-8 form is 11000001. The leftmost 4 bits, 1100, make up the zone portion and the rightmost 4 bits, 0001, make up the numeric portion. Notice that the ASCII zone is the same but that the numeric varies in a definite pattern for the letters A−O; then, again, the zone is the same but the numeric varies in a definite pattern for the letters P−Z. A similar situation exists with the EBCDIC form except that it has three different zones with changes occurring at J and S. These two codes, the ASCII and the EBCDIC, are mentioned here because one or the other of them is used in virtually every computer to represent not only the alphabetic letters but many other characters as well.

Therefore, as you can see, one 8-bit byte can be used to represent all the letters in the alphabet (one at a time) and decimal whole numbers as large as 255. But what about all the other numbers you might have to work with? The ability to represent only 256 different whole numbers, including 0, is definitely not sufficient.

Fortunately, there is another, perhaps more conventional, unit of information that is ordinarily larger than a byte. It can be used to represent most of the other numbers you encounter. This unit of information is the computer word.

Again, a formal definition is in order. A *computer word* is a sequence of adjacent bits, normally more than that of a byte, which is ordinarily operated on as

Table 1-3. EIGHT-BIT BINARY CODED
REPRESENTATION OF ALPHABETIC
LETTERS*

Letter	ASCII-8	EBCDIC
A	1100 0001	1100 0001
B	1100 0010	1100 0010
C	1100 0011	1100 0011
D	1100 0100	1100 0100
E	1100 0101	1100 0101
F	1100 0110	1100 0110
G	1100 0111	1100 0111
H	1100 1000	1100 1000
I	1100 1001	1100 1001
J	1100 1010	1101 0001
K	1100 1011	1101 0010
L	1100 1100	1101 0011
M	1100 1101	1101 0100
N	1100 1110	1101 0101
O	1100 1111	1101 0110
P	1101 0000	1101 0111
Q	1101 0001	1101 1000
R	1101 0010	1101 1001
S	1101 0011	1110 0010
T	1101 0100	1110 0011
U	1101 0101	1110 0100
V	1101 0110	1110 0101
W	1101 0111	1110 0110
X	1101 1000	1110 0111
Y	1101 1001	1110 1000
Z	1101 1010	1110 1001

Example: My last name in ASCII-8 code could be
represented by the following sequence of 40 bits,
grouped in 8-bit units.

1100 0111　1101 0010　1100 1111　1101 0101　1101 0100
　　G　　　　　R　　　　　O　　　　　U　　　　　T

*ASCII, as developed by the American National
Standards Institute, is a 7-bit code. In actual use,
however, it is often augmented by one bit (either 1
or 0) to conform to an 8-bit byte. EBCDIC was
developed by IBM.

the usual addressable unit of information for computer storage. It is important for
you to know that computer word sizes vary among computers. A common size for
large-scale computers is 32 bits (4 bytes), but some have as few as 24 bits and others as many as 64 bits. Minicomputers frequently have 16-bit words. Most microcomputers have 8-bit words. The word size determines the extent to which
numbers can be represented.

Consider one of the most common sizes, the 32-bit word. In pure binary
representation of decimal numbers, the leftmost bit is often used to indicate the

sign of the number (i.e., whether it is positive or negative). That leaves 31 bits for the number itself. With 31 bits, the decimal whole numbers 0 through 2,147,483,647 can be represented. Considering both positive and negative values, this is a fairly wide range of numbers.

Without going into any more detail about the binary system, I must tell you that numbers containing decimal points and fractional digits (e.g., 3.14159) can also be conveniently represented by bits in a computer word. Then, summarily, I can say that at any one instant of time, one computer word can be used to store (represent at that time) one number, or several alphabetic letters, or several of the other characters that are often needed, or an instruction that causes the computer to perform an operation on one of the other items as a datum.

Thus the computer works with bits, whereas you and I work with decimal digits, the English language, and a few other symbols. To use the computer effectively it would be helpful for you to know something about bits and how the computer uses them, but you do not have to communicate with the computer in bits. You can communicate with the computer in one of a number of languages similar to the one you use to communicate with other people, but in the much more rigid form of a computer program. Most of the rest of this book is about writing computer programs in one of the human-oriented languages you can use.

1-5 COMPUTER PROGRAMS

Up to this point I have mentioned computer programs only a few times but I have actually given you a considerable amount of information about them. Computer programs are composed of instructions: the instructions that the computer uses to solve problems. They are similar in nature to recipes or lists of directions but they must be stated in a much more exacting way. Precisely, a *computer program* is a list of instructions written in a language the computer can accept and arranged in a sequence that will cause the computer to perform a particular task. In the context of this book, the single word ''program'' means the same thing as the term ''computer program.''

A computer can actually execute only the instructions that are in its elementary language—commonly called *machine language* and usually binary in form. You will be glad to know that programs written by human beings are rarely, if ever, written in this kind of language; rather they are almost always written in a programming language such as Fortran, Cobol, Basic, Pascal, or PL/I. Programming languages are far more closely akin to English than to binary. They allow programs to be prepared in a form that the computer can accept but cannot directly execute. In this form the programs are called *source programs*.

Figure 1-9 illustrates, in an overview sense, what usually happens when a source program and its problem data are loaded into a computer through an input device. The source program first undergoes a translation process, called *compilation*, that is accomplished by a program already stored in the computer—a *com-*

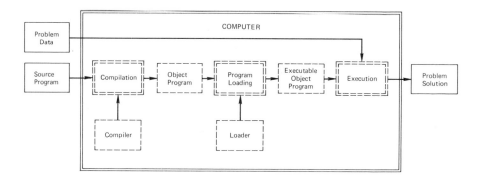

Figure 1-9. Computer Program Processing

piler. The compiler produces a machine language program called an *object pro-gram*. The object program can then be stored for later use or used immediately. Before direct execution can take place, the object program has to be positioned properly in the computer's memory. This is done by another previously stored pro-gram, called a *loader*, which performs a transformation and creates an executable object program. The executable object program is then executed on the problem data, ultimately yielding the problem solution.

Completed programs are normally stored in object form in the computer's memory or on a directly accessible input/output device such as a magnetic disk. Then, when they are needed to generate the solution for a particular set of problem data, they are simply loaded and executed with the data.

1-6 DATA

Data and programs are two different things. Often though, learners have a difficult time distinguishing between the two. Some people are never able to do so and they are therefore unable to learn to use the computer effectively. Don't let this happen to you.

You now know what a program is: very basically, a list of instructions for solving a problem. Problem *data*, on the other hand, are items of information that the instructions must have in order to be performed. The items of information are usually numbers or English words or a combination of the two.

Recall that very early in the chapter I compared computers to human beings and stated that instructions are like knowledge and data are like observations. As human beings we store in our minds the knowledge about how to act in a given situation. Then, when a specific instance of the situation occurs, we recall what we know about the situation; observe the necessary things—as directed by our knowledge—about what is taking place; and take action accordingly. A different occurrence of the same situation may cause different observations and result in our taking a different action even though our knowledge of that situation remains the same. For example, upon arrival at an intersection we may observe at one time a lighted sign which says WALK and at another time one that says DONT WALK. Regardless of our observation, our knowledge is essentially "When the WALK sign is lit, walk on across the street; when the DONT WALK sign is lit, stop and wait." Thus, given different observations we take different actions even though our knowledge remains constant.

Similarly, the computer stores in its memory a program that a human being has written to solve a specific problem. Then, given a particular set of problem data, it uses the program to operate on those data and derive a certain result. With different problem data, the program solves the same problem except with a different outcome. For example, the problem might be to add several numbers together to obtain a total. The program will consist of a few instructions to perform the addition. I offer the following set of English sentence instructions (an English language program) for your consideration:

1. Add the first two numbers to get a total.
2. Repeat instruction 3 below until all numbers have been added; then stop.
3. Add the next number to the total.

The data in this case consist of the actual numbers. What if there are three numbers: 2, 4, and 6? Aren't the instructions clear enough for you to follow them and obtain a total equal to 12? What if there are five numbers: 14, 20, 9, 1, and 7? Aren't the instructions clear enough for you to follow them and obtain a total equal to 51? Same set of instructions in each case, two different sets of data, and two different but correct results.

What if there were 5 other numbers, or 50 numbers, or 500, or 5000? Do you think the instructions, if followed exactly, would yield the correct answer? They would; the key word is "exactly." The computer can follow instructions exactly; you and I have difficulty doing so. Therefore my recommendation is that you learn, precisely, the difference between programs and data; then learn to write programs well so that you can make the computer do all the tedious work required to process the data correctly.

I want you to take note of two additional things about the set of instructions above. First, they are in English, a language that no currently existing commercially available computer can accept. So they do not constitute a computer program. A human being who knows a programming language could, however, develop a computer program from them. Second, this English language program will not work for all possible sets of data. For instance, it will not work if there is only one number. This does not make the program incorrect; it simply indicates that the program has limitations in regard to the problem data it can handle. All programs have limitations in regard to data or computation or some other factor. The programmer is responsible for stating the limitations and making sure that the program yields the proper results for all allowable problem data.

1-7 EXERCISES

1. Visit a computer store and obtain as much information as you can about a particular microcomputer that could be used as a personal computer. Find out if it has a Fortran compiler. If not, find out the names of the languages it can handle. Summarize the information you obtain in a two- or three-page handwritten article. (Popular brands of personal computers include Apple, Atari, Commodore, IBM, Radio Shack, Texas Instruments, and Xerox.)

2. Visit your university library and browse through the computer and data processing collections. Look for introductory material. Scan through, particularly, some of the popular computing magazines, such as *BYTE* or *Creative Computing*. Select a recently published introductory data processing text to check out and read. There are several available, six of which are listed below.

   Business Data Processing, by Elias M. Awad. Fourth edition published by Prentice-Hall, Inc., Englewood Cliffs, N.J., 1975.

   Introduction to Computers, by Gordon B. Davis. Third edition published by McGraw-Hill Book Company, New York, 1977.

   Principles of Business Data Processing, by V. Thomas Dock and Edward Essick. Third edition published by Science Research Associates, Inc., Chicago, 1978.

   Business Data Processing, by Mike Murach. Third edition published by Science Research Associates, Inc., Chicago, 1980.

   Introduction to Computers and Data Processing, by Gary B. Shelly and Thomas J. Cashman. Published by Anaheim Publishing Company, Brea, California, 1980.

   Data Processing: An Introduction, by Donald D. Spencer. Published by Charles E. Merrill Publishing Company, Columbus, Ohio, 1978.

3. Use either the ASCII or the EBCDIC code of Table 1-3 to represent your first and last names similar to the way I represented my last name at the bottom of the table.

4. Complete Table 1-2.

5. Revise the English language "program" given in Section 1-6 so that data sets containing only one number can also be successfully processed.

Problem-Solving Essentials

Concisely stated, a good program is one that is correct, well documented, readable, understandable, maintainable, produced on schedule, and reasonably efficient in terms of computer storage requirements and execution time. Performing the activities that lead to the solution of a problem in the form of a good program can be an exciting process. This chapter is designed to familiarize you thoroughly with the activities so that you can enjoy performing them successfully.

2-1   STEPS OF GOOD PROGRAMMING PRACTICE

Programming is more than writing instructions in a particular programming language—a lot more. It is a process that requires careful thought and planning; communicating and working with other people; an ability to understand, develop, and describe to others the procedures used to solve a problem; knowledge of how the computer works and of at least one computer language; and the ability to make sure that a program produces the results it is supposed to produce.

The steps that can be followed to meet these requirements are depicted together, in the form of a programming guide, in Figure 2-1. Each rectangular symbol in the diagram identifies one step of programming. The lines between the symbols indicate the performing sequence of the steps. The symbol containing the word START simply provides a convenient reference point for beginning the programming process.

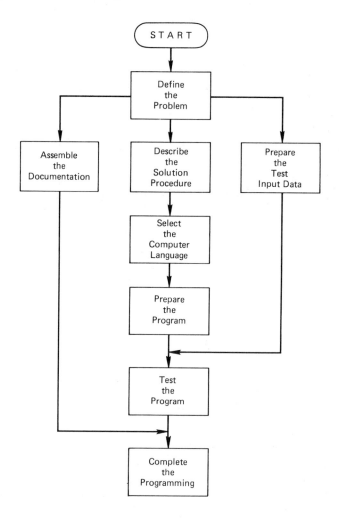

Figure 2-1. A Programming Guide

2-1-1 Define the Problem

Unless a problem is clearly defined, no attempt should be made to write a program. This seems obvious because, regardless of whether you use the computer or some other means, if you do not know what the problem is, you simply cannot describe a solution to it. Yet it is not uncommon to find beginners trying to write a program before they even understand the problem. The definition of a problem is complete for you only when you understand it fully.

To understand a problem completely it is necessary for you to have an initial problem description and also to know the answers to at least these two questions:

1. What problem data do you have to work with?
2. What solution data do you want to obtain?

The first question refers to the types of data having defined values that can be entered into the computer before it begins its work to solve the problem. In programming terminology these problem data are commonly called "input data" or just "input." The second question refers to the answers produced by the computer after it has performed its work on the problem. These answers are usually termed "computer output" or simply "output." It may be necessary for you to discuss the problem with a number of other people before the two questions are well answered.

After answering the questions, you can write a specific problem definition in your own words and then proceed to the next programming step. While learning to program, as you read this text, you will be shown by examples and suggestions how to answer these questions.

2-1-2 Assemble the Documentation

Documentation is the collection of formal records that describe the particular problem, the programmed solution, and the program use. Without this collection the program has no future and, in my opinion, should never be used.

As depicted in Figure 2-1, documentation assembly occurs in parallel with most of the other steps and is finished just prior to the completion of programming. This means that the records created at each other step are collected and organized to ensure that the program is fully described prior to the time it is released for productive use.

This phase of programming is often considered tedious and time consuming, and therefore it is frequently ignored or done without care. It need not be tedious; it is definitely time well spent. After all, you are creating a product that is probably intended for use by other people. When I do this I want my product to be used and enjoyed by other people for a long time. I hope its use will cause them to want to come back to me for additional products. If they understand it and enjoy using it, they will probably come back for more. Thus, to ignore documentation is to fail to provide an enduring, quality product that will make people ask for more.

The Fortran program organization method described in Chapter 3 serves to make the documentation assembly of Fortran programs a natural part of the programming process. With it, much of the documentation assembly occurs intrinsically.

2-1-3 Prepare the Test Input Data

In discussing the problem definition, I referred to "types of data." Here I mean the actual values of those data types that are to be used in testing the program. As indicated in Figure 2-1, you can begin to perform this step anytime after the problem has been defined. It should, however, be completed prior to the initiation of testing, because testing involves computer processing and computer processing requires both program and data.

Test data preparation actually consists of three activities: selecting and gathering of data values together, entering the values onto a computer-readable medium such as punched cards or magnetic disk, and determining the answers that are expected to be produced by the computer as the result of processing the program and test data together. Care must be taken to ensure that the values made available to the computer are correct. Otherwise, even if the program is correct, the answers produced will be wrong.

The data values that are used for testing may be real or "made-up" values. In either case, the test data should be representative of the complete range and combinations of possible input values—valid and invalid—to provide assurance that the program has been thoroughly tested prior to being implemented.

2-1-4 Describe the Solution Procedure

Beginning with this step, all others are accomplished in sequence. It is extremely important that the sequential order be maintained and that each step be completed before the next one is started.

A complete solution procedure can be specified formally in several different ways. Like the problem definition, it should be stated in a way that you, and perhaps other human beings, can directly see and understand before it is put into a form that the computer can use. If the problem is very complex, it may be necessary to analyze it further, breaking it down into segments that can be worked on independently. As a matter of fact, many computer professionals believe that it is advantageous to look first at a problem in an overview sense, then design the solution by breaking up the problem into independent parts at several different levels. At the highest level the solution is specified in terms of the overall problem; at the next level it is specified in terms of several independent subproblems that together form the complete problem; and at lower levels each subproblem is further divided into independent subproblems for which solutions are specified until, finally, a level is reached at which no further independent division is possible. It is then a fairly straightforward process to translate the independent solution procedures into a computer language.

In illustration of this process, consider the following problem that is not necessarily computer-oriented but is one encountered frequently by college students—one to which you can relate.

The concisely stated problem definition, as well as overview statement of the solution, is

```
Prepare for exam.
```

This might be divided, or refined, into two separate subproblems, or steps, such as:

```
Review.
Relax.
```

The first of these may be further refined to:

```
Study class notes.
Study textual material.
```

and the second to:

```
Take a hot bath.
Rest.
```

Then each of the above can undergo a final refinement into more precisely stated and detailed steps. The first, "Study class notes," becomes

```
Scan class notes.
Rewrite class notes.
```

The second, "Study textual material," turns into

```
Read assigned chapter.
Work assigned exercises.
```

The third, "Take a hot bath," may be broken down into several steps:

```
Draw hot bath water.
Undress.
Get into tub.
Wash and rinse.
Get out of tub.
Dry and dress for bed.
```

The fourth, "Rest," may then involve individual steps, such as:

```
Set alarm.
Get into bed.
Sleep.
```

Finally, all the separate, independent groups of detailed steps put together represent the complete solution procedure:

```
Scan class notes.
Rewrite class notes.
Read assigned chapter.
Work assigned exercises.
Draw hot bath water.
Undress.
Get into tub.
Wash and rinse.
Get out of tub.
Dry and dress for bed.
Set alarm.
Get into bed.
Sleep.
```

Although this is not specifically a computer-oriented but rather a human-oriented solution procedure, it is one that—with much more refinement—could be simulated by a computer.

The method of systematically developing a problem solution from overview level to detail level is known as *top-down design* or *stepwise refinement*. The individual computer solution procedures are translated into program units called *modules* that can be developed and tested together or separately. Formally, a module is a program unit that is discrete and identifiable with respect to compiling, combining with other units, and loading into the computer. An important guideline to follow in top-down design is that the individual solution procedures, and thus the modules, should be of a manageable size—small enough or short enough to be convenient to work with. It is accepted by many experts that a module is manageable if it contains 50 or fewer procedural instructions.

Most solution procedures for the problems of this text require no more than 50 procedural instructions. Thus most programs for these problems consist of only one module. However, the top-down design approach is followed as much as possible to help you begin to develop good programming habits. Then, in Chapter 11, modularity and top-down design in Fortran programming are covered more thoroughly.

Regardless of the approach taken to develop a solution procedure, the procedure must be described in a formal manner. It is common practice to use an algorithm or a program flowchart for the formal description. These topics are of such importance that a section of this chapter is devoted to each. Section 2-2 provides an introduction to algorithms and Section 2-3 discusses flowcharts.

2-1-5 Select the Computer Language

A computer language consists of a character set and clearly stated rules for organizing the characters into meaningful statements that human beings can use to communicate with computers. There are many, many different computer languages. There are only a few, however, that have widespread use. Some of the principal ones that are widely used are Cobol, PL/I, Basic, Pascal, and—of course—Fortran.

The actual language that should be selected in any given situation generally depends on the problem, the type of solution procedure, and the language knowledge of the programmer. Since one of the primary purposes of this text is to help you learn to write good programs in Fortran, there is no question about which language you and I will select. Fortran it is.

2-1-6 Prepare the Program

Program preparation involves three activities: translating the solution procedure into the selected language, adding job control statements, and then entering the resulting program and job control statements onto a computer-readable medium such as punched cards or magnetic disk. All three activities are accomplished manually.

The translation process is called *coding*. Many beginners and inexperienced people like to start coding as soon as they see the first draft of the problem definition, written or spoken, because the sooner they have some code, the sooner they can get on the computer. As you know by now, this is a mistake. It can lead to a wrong solution to the wrong problem, a wrong solution to the right problem, or a fine solution to the wrong problem. Rarely will it result in a correct solution to the complete problem.

You will be learning how to code in Fortran as you study the remaining chapters of this book. The physical result of coding a complete problem solution in Fortran is an executable program. An *executable program* is a collection of related program units that consists of exactly one main program and any number, including zero, of subprograms. A *main program* is a program unit that is executed only by being called on by the operating system of the computer. Its first statement should be a PROGRAM statement. A *subprogram* is a program unit that can be executed only by being called upon by another program unit. Its first statement must be a FUNCTION, a SUBROUTINE, or a BLOCK DATA statement. These and other Fortran statements are fully described in succeeding chapters.

Most of the executable programs you will write as you learn Fortran will consist only of main programs, but the ideas surrounding the use of subprograms will be mentioned when appropriate. By the time you get to Chapter 11, where subprograms are described in depth, you will find it natural to use them effectively.

After the executable program has been coded, *job control statements* are added to it to tell the operating system what to do with the program. Usually, you will want the system to compile and then execute, or run, your program. The job control statements required to accomplish these activities are computer dependent; that is, they are uniquely defined by the computer being used. Commonly, each job control statement has an identifying character such as / or ! or : in column one, and a keyword such as JOB or EXEC or RUN in the next few columns. Your computer center can supply you with information that tells you what job control statements are required and where they are placed, in relation to your program, in order to get the computer to process your program the way you want it to.

The entry of a coded program, with the appropriate job control statements, onto a computer-readable medium is most often accomplished by using a computer terminal or keypunch machine. It is common, though not essential, to use the same computer-readable medium for both the program and the input data and, therefore, to enter both onto the medium together. Computer terminals and keypunch machines are not difficult to use. They both have keyboards that are similar to typewriters and, even if you don't know how to type, you can hunt and peck as well as the next person. Your computer center has computer terminals or keypunch machines or some of each that you can use, as well as the instructions for using them.

Before you finish studying this chapter you will have an opportunity to examine, in detail, a complete Fortran program that solves a familiar problem. You can then prepare and run the program on the computer to get the "feel" of it. The program appears in Section 2-4.

2-1-7 Test the Program

To determine whether a program yields acceptable results, a test is performed. It involves one or more runs of the program using input data prepared specifically for that purpose. It is a planned activity and therefore the expected outcome for each test run should be known in advance. The prepared data should cover the full range of possible input values. This does not mean that all possible input values should be used; it does mean that values representative of all possible input values should be used. For example: smallest, largest, middle, negative, positive, odd, even, invalid, and so on.

Incorrectness in the results of a test run indicates the presence of one or more errors. Errors may occur in the input data, the job control statements, or the program. Errors in the first two are due, almost always, to carelessness. Don't be careless with input data or job control; check them both thoroughly—first.

Errors in a program are commonly called *bugs* and the process of eliminating such errors is called *debugging*. There are two types of bugs: syntactical and logical. *Syntactical* bugs, or errors in syntax, are caused by writing individual programming language statements incorrectly. They are due to either a lack of language knowledge or sloppiness on the part of the programmer. They are usually detected by the compiler, which then causes appropriate error messages (diagnostics) to be printed. Their presence in a program usually prevents the computer from completing compilation of the program. When this happens, the program cannot then be executed.

Because the compiler can help locate them, syntactical bugs can usually all be eliminated in one or two runs. A learner's program may initially contain a number of errors in syntax, whereas an experienced programmer's program should be free of them before the first run is made. Take the time to learn the programming language well and you can avoid having problems with syntax.

Logical bugs, or errors in logic, are mistakes in specifying the solution procedure. They are due primarily to inadequate design or incomplete checkout of algorithms and program flowcharts or writing a programming language statement syntactically correct but in a way that means something different to the compiler than the programmer intended.

Logical bugs are not always easy to locate. You should take every possible precaution to avoid creating them: follow the steps of good programming practice carefully, know your programming language well, and know the capabilities of your computer. However, when your program does have a logical bug you can usually trace it down by printing results periodically in your program and comparing those results to what you expect the computer to have at the points of printing. As implied, this is called a *trace*.

The final test runs, for all the test input data, must yield correct results. Only when correct test results are obtained can the program be certified. To certify a program means to endorse it as being capable of providing the correct solution to the problem it was written for, limited by the data represented by the test input.

2-1-8 Complete the Programming

Programming is completed only upon the performance of two more actions: organizing the documentation and then declaring that the program is available for its intended use.

By the time this step has been reached, all the documentation records should have been gathered together. Organizing them is then a matter of arranging them in an order that has meaning to the people who will be using the program or modifying it to meet changing needs later. I suggest the arrangement given in Figure 2-2. For preservation, I further suggest that the arranged records be placed in a documentation manual or booklet.

The final action, telling the program users that the program is complete and available, is the programmer's guarantee to the users that the program does what the documentation says it does. This action is not to be taken lightly. If you write a program, for yourself or someone else, complete the programming or throw the program away as a wasted effort.

1. Title Page
    Program name, programmer name, and date completed.
2. Table of Contents
    Major section headings and page numbers of the
    documentation manual.
3. Problem Definition
    A brief but complete narrative definition of the
    problem that is solved by the program.
4. Input Description
    Identification of all input data. Input layout
    forms, discussed in Chapter 6, can be used to show
    input formats.
5. Output Description
    Identification of output generated by the program.
    Output layout forms, discussed in Chapter 6, can be
    used.
6. Solution Procedure Description
    Complete algorithms or program flowcharts.
7. Program Listing
    Complete Fortran source program printout.
8. Program Test
    Narrative description of the test; identification
    of input test data values; complete test run output.

Figure 2-2. Fortran Program Documentation

2-1-9 Exercises

1. Develop a top-down design solution procedure for the problem "Dress for Church" (more formal than "Dress for Class"). (*Hint:* Dress half of your body independently of the other half or divide into inner garments and outer garments. State the final steps precisely.)

2. Assume that there is a traffic loop around your city that forms a perfect circle and coincides exactly with the city limits. Do a top-down design to find the approximate number of square miles within your city limits. Specify any resources you want to use (e.g., your automobile).

2-2 ALGORITHMS

An algorithm is a sequence of precisely stated rules that describes a problem solution in a finite number of steps. Algorithms are usually written first to be understood and performed by human beings. Then, when translated into a programming language such as Fortran, the computer can perform (or execute) them. Thus they represent the executable parts of programs.

Although you may not be aware of it, you often use algorithmic-like procedures. Figure 2-3 contains two such procedures. One is the recipe my wife uses for pie crust; the other contains directions for using my new camera flash attachment. There is no doubt in my mind that you can comprehend both the recipe and the flash directions because I know you are used to such things. Similarly, all you need to do in order to understand and be able to create algorithms is to get used to them.

1. A Recipe for Texas Pie Crust
   Mix together: 2 cups flour, ½ teaspoon salt, ½ cup oil, 5 tablespoons water.
   Roll between two sheets of wax paper on a damp cabinet.
   Place in pie pan and trim edges.
   For cream pies, poke fork-holes in bottom and bake at 450° F until golden.
   For other pies, add filling and cook until filling is done.

2. Photography with the Canon Speedlite 155A
   (Used by permission of CANON, U. S. A., Inc.)
   (a) Load the batteries.
   (b) Set the ASA film speed.
   (c) Mount the Speedlite 155A on the AE-1.
   (d) Turn on the main switch.
   (e) Set the AUTO/MANU switch.
   (f) Focus and press the shutter button.

Figure 2-3. Algorithmic-like Procedures

2-2-1 Algorithm Guidelines

First, you must ascertain the essential relationships between the input and output data. Primarily, these relationships consist of mathematical formulations and logical procedures. All may be stated, initially, in sentence form.

Next, solve the problem manually for your selected test data. Think about each of the processes you go through to solve it—step by step. This will help you understand the problem better and begin to visualize the solution procedure as a sequence of operational rules.

Then, begin to state the rules in sentences, one by one, trying not to omit any step you took manually. As you state them, be specific and as clear as possible, keeping in mind that they are the rules you or another person might follow later to solve the problem manually with different input data. After writing down all the rules, go through them with your data to determine if they yield the same results as those you obtained earlier.

I want to emphasize a point to you right now. There may be a number of different algorithms that solve the same problem. Your algorithm may contain different rules than those of your friend's algorithm, but as long as both of them result in the same correct solution, both are acceptable. Nevertheless, they should be developed according to the same guidelines so that they can be mutually understood and compared.

Since English allows many possible misunderstandings to occur, particularly in the form of ambiguities or double meanings, further refinement of the rules you have made is necessary if you are actually to produce an algorithm. (For an interesting ambiguity, take the second step of the Figure 2-3 pie crust recipe out of context.)

To accomplish the refinement, it will be helpful for us to adopt particular symbols and phrases. The symbols are used to specify operations required to perform an action, whereas the phrases, called *algorithmic primitives*, each specify in a very clear way one or more types of action to be taken. The proper use of these symbols and primitives, which are identified and described in Tables 2-1 and 2-2, not only aid refinement and clarity of algorithmic actions, but will also prepare you to learn a programming language.

Using the symbols and primitives, rewrite your sentence-form rules. Begin with a line that contains the phrase "ALGORITHM name," where name is an appropriate identifier for the algorithm. You may follow this line by one or more lines of commentary that describe the purpose of the algorithm, enclosing comments in braces (see Table 2-1) so that they can easily be distinguished from the rules of action. Then list the rules of action in sequence, following the suggestions given in the examples of the next section. At the point of completion of the algorithm, add a line which simply consists of the keyword "END." This is used to clearly identify the physical end of the algorithm.

Finally, take your selected test data and go through every step of the algorithm, obeying the rules exactly, to see if your algorithm yields the results you

Table 2-1. PRIMARY ALGORITHMIC SYMBOLS

Symbols	Meaning
←	Assignment: $a \leftarrow b$ is read "a is assigned the value of b"
=	Equality: $a = b$ is read "the value of a equals the value of b"
+	Addition
−	Subtraction or negation
*	Multiplication
/	Division
<	Less than: $a < b$ is read "the value of a is less than the value of b"
<=	Less than or equal to
>	Greater than
>=	Greater than or equal to
<>	Not equal to (inequality)
()	Left and right parentheses for enclosing expressions
{}	Braces for enclosing comments
'	Single quotation mark: Left and right quote marks are used to enclose literals (titles and column headings to be written)

Note: Other symbols, for which the meaning is absolutely clear and unambiguous, may also be used.

obtained manually. This necessary operation is the checkpoint for the algorithm. Its successful completion allows you to proceed to the next step of programming.

A summary list of the guidelines just discussed is given in Figure 2-4. Study the list now and in conjunction with the examples of the next section.

1. Determine the essential relationships between the input and output data.
2. Solve the problem manually for the selected test input data.
3. State the solution procedure rules in sentences, one by one, in sequence.
4. By using the recommended symbols and primitives appropriately, refine the rules to ensure that each is concisely and clearly defined.
5. Take your test data and work through the rules, step by step from start to finish, to make sure that the algorithm gives the same answers as your manual solution.

Figure 2-4. Algorithm Guidelines—Summarized

2-2-2 Algorithm Examples

Consider a simple example that illustrates the use of most of the primitives in Table 2-2. The problem is to read two numeric values, compare them, and write the larger and then the smaller of the two. It seems simple enough, but no problem is ever too simple that it should be approached carelessly—follow the guidelines.

Table 2-2. PRIMARY ALGORITHMIC PRIMITIVES

Primitive	*Meaning*
ALGORITHM name	Physical beginning of the algorithm; provides a means of referring to it.
Read values	Take values into memory (input).
variable ← expression	Assignment of the value of an expression to a variable.
If condition Then actions Else other-actions	Selection of actions to perform based on the truth or falsity of the condition. If it is true, perform the "Then" actions. If it is false, perform the "Else" other-actions. Then proceed in sequence. The Else clause is optional.
If condition action	A special case of selection representing the selection of an action to perform based on the truth or falsity of the condition. If true, perform the action. If false, do not perform the action, but proceed in sequence.
Go To label (direction)	Transfer to the rule with the given label and continue in sequence from there. "Direction" is either "Back" or "Ahead," to indicate where the labeled rule is located in relation to the Go To. A label can be any descriptive identifier (word, number, etc.).
Write values	Take values from memory (output) and display them for human use or save them for later computer use.
Stop	Terminate algorithm processing.
END	Physical end of the algorithm (no more rules).

Note: Other primitives, for which the meaning is absolutely clear and unambiguous, may also be used. Some other useful and important ones are given at appropriate points in the text.

Assume that I have already studied the problem, selected the test data, and begun documentation assembly. Then the algorithm guidelines are applied as follows.

1. The essential relationships are procedural relationships. The input values are also the output values except that the larger is to be written first. The procedure must distinguish between the larger and the smaller.

2. Although the problem is to be solved for only two values, it must handle any two values. Thus the test data consist of several sets of values representative of the possible values. If the selected test data consist of the six pairs of numbers (10, 5), (5, 10), (20, −20), (−20, 20), (15, 15), and (−15, −15), the input and output for the six different test "runs" can be depicted as follows.

Input		Output		
10,	5	10,	5	
5,	10	10,	5	
20,	−20	20,	−20	
−20,	20	20,	−20	
15,	15	15,	15	(Both are "larger")
−15,	−15	−15,	−15	(Both are "larger")

3.   One way of stating the rules in sentences is this:

```
Read the two values.
If the first value is larger than or equal to the second value,
write it and then write the second value.
Otherwise, write the second value and then the first value.
Stop.
```

4.   These rules must be refined until they are precisely stated and free of possible misunderstandings. To us, that means that each of the final rules must take the form of one of the algorithmic primitives. For refinement purposes, we give names to the two values, call them *a* and *b*, and attempt a first refinement which simply involves stating the above sentences more precisely.

```
Read a and b.
If a is larger than or equal to b, write a and then b.
Otherwise, write b and then a.
Stop.
```

Then proceeding with a further refinement that uses the adopted algorithmic primitives and contains explanatory commentary (in braces), we arrive at this final algorithm:

```
ALGORITHM Write:ordered
{ Two numeric input values, a and b, are compared and
then written in order—larger first and then smaller.}
Read a, b
If a >= b Then
   Write a, b          {a is larger}
Else
   Write b, a          {b is larger}
Stop
END
```

5.   To check the algorithm, we select a pair of test values and perform each rule, step by step, writing down the results of each, from the beginning to the end of the algorithm. This execution-checking process is called a *trace*. Separately, as we go, we also write down the output produced by the algorithm. For the first test pair (10, 5), then, the written results would be something like this:

Trace   **Output**
```
a = 10        {The result of                          10,    5
b =  5           Read a, b}
10 >= 5?  (true) Then
  Write 10, 5
Stop
```

Similarly, the fourth test pair $(-20, 20)$ would yield

Trace   **Output**
```
a = -20                                                20,  -20
b =  20
-20 >= 20?  (false)
Write 20, -20
Stop
```

So far, the algorithm yields correct results. It must, however, be checked for all selected test values before it is accepted. I leave this as a practice exercise for you.

Before leaving this initial algorithmic study, consider another algorithm that presents a valid solution to this same problem. It can be derived in a manner analogous to the one just developed. It is included here, in final form, to emphasize again that different algorithms may solve the same problem and to give you a look at the use of more algorithmic primitives.

ALGORITHM Write:ordered:alternative
```
{  Two numeric input values, a and b, are compared and
then written in order–larger first, then smaller.}
Read a, b
If a < b Then
  h ← a          {interchange a and b}
  a ← b
  b ← h
Write a, b
Stop
END
```

The trace and output for this algorithm, using the second data pair $(5, 10)$ is as follows:

Trace   **Output**
```
a = 5                                                  10,    5
b = 10
5 < 10?  (true) Then
  h = 5
  a = 10
  b = 5
Write 10, 5
Stop
```

For your own understanding and to make sure the alternative is correct, trace it for all the selected test sets.

2-2-3 *Exercises on Algorithms*

1. Give specific reasons why neither your favorite recipe nor the list of directions for using something you recently bought is an algorithm.

2. Take your favorite recipe or a list of directions and rewrite it so that it is as close to being an algorithm as possible.

3. Explain the difference between the symbols ← and = as used in algorithms.

4. Rewrite each of the algorithms in Section 2-2-2 so that the smaller input number is written out first.

5. Write the solution to Exercise 5 of Section 1-7 as an algorithm. The numbers are to be read as input data, one by one.

6. Develop an algorithm to find and write the area of a circle given the circumference as input data. As a check on the input data, include a test to make sure that the given circumference is not, for some unspecified reason, negative. If it is negative, the algorithm should cause an appropriate error message to be written out.

7. Study the algorithm below and determine what it does. In your study, perform a trace using at least these three sets of values for a, b, and c: (1, 2, 3), (2, 3, 1), and (3, 2, 1). (*Hint:* The algorithm is similar in nature to the first one in Section 2-2-2.)

```
ALGORITHM Study:1
{ Purpose and description to be supplied by student
after study.}
Read a, b, c
If a >= b Then
    If b >= c Then
        Write a, b, c
    Else If a >= c Then
        Write a, c, b
    Else
        Write c, a, b
Else If a >= c Then
    Write b, a, c
Else If b >= c Then
    Write b, c, a
Else
    Write c, b, a
Stop
END
```

8. Discuss the effect of replacing the interchange rules

    h ← a
    a ← b
    b ← h

   with

    a ← b
    b ← a

in the alternative algorithm of Section 2-2-2.

9.   Rewrite the algorithm of Exercise 7 employing an interchange technique such as the one mentioned in Exercise 8.

2-3   PROGRAM FLOWCHARTS

A *program flowchart* is a diagram that shows the sequence of operations in a program by means of symbols, interconnecting flowlines, and descriptive statements. Program flowcharts represent, primarily, the executable parts of programs. Thus they provide another means for formally specifying a solution procedure. They also serve as a convenient mechanism for interpreting programming language statements; particularly those involving decision making.

An algorithm can usually be translated directly into a program flowchart and, therefore, flowcharts are often used as the formal solution procedure specification in the documentation for a completed program. The primary reason for this may be that well-drawn flowcharts sometimes provide more of a "picture" of the solution procedure and, as someone has said: "A picture is worth a thousand words."

Flowcharts have disadvantages, however, some of which you will observe in this section and other parts of this chapter. For example, it is often necessary to use a more limited symbolism than is possible in algorithms and programs due to space limitations, and a given flowchart may require many more pages than the corresponding algorithm. For these and other reasons, some computing professionals avoid using flowcharts. Nevertheless, I believe that they are useful enough for communicating ideas and describing solution procedures that they deserve an exposition in this book.

Program flowcharts are not difficult to produce after an algorithm has been devised. All that is required is a knowledge of the symbols that can be used, of how to connect the symbols to represent the sequence of operations, and of what types of descriptive statements are needed. I also recommend the use of a flowcharting template—an inexpensive plastic device that can probably be purchased at your college bookstore.

The descriptive statements used in flowcharts occur inside the flowchart symbols and in commentary. They are analogous to the rules and commentary of algorithms. Thus, in flowcharts, we will make use of the notation given in Tables 2-1 and 2-2 in a manner similar to the way we are doing with algorithms.

The flowchart symbols most people use are the ones developed by a committee of experts and published as a standard by the American National Standards Institute. We will also use the standard, selecting only the symbols that are most useful for programs.

2-3-1   Flowchart Symbols and Guidelines

If you will look at Figure 2-5, you will see that there are only 10 symbols to learn. Take the time to learn them as you read this and you will have it easy later. Let's look at them together, top to bottom, left to right.

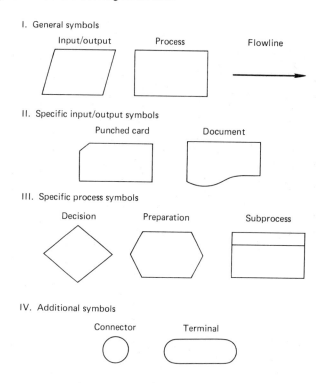

Figure 2-5. Program Flowchart Symbols

The first general symbol is the *input/output* parallelogram. It can be used to represent any input or output function; that is, the entry of data into memory for processing or the recording of information from memory onto an output medium. Keyterms to associate with this symbol are "read" and "write." The descriptive statement that goes into the symbol identifies the variables whose values are to be read into memory or written out of memory.

The rectangular *process* symbol, next in line, can be used to represent any processing function. For our purposes it will primarily be used for assignment operations.

Flowlines are the interconnecting lines that appear between the other symbols, linking them to show the sequence of executable operations. An alternative word for "flowline" is "arrow" because each flowline should have an arrowhead that points toward the next sequential symbol.

The specific input/output symbols are preferred over the general input/output symbol whenever it is known that the input or output medium is punched cards (the *punched card* symbol) or computer-readable/computer-generated pages (the *document* symbol). Again, the associated keyterms are "read" and "write."

Specific process symbols also clarify the picture presented by the flowchart more than the general process symbol does. The decision symbol represents a testing operation that may have more than one possible outcome. The descriptive statement in the symbol specifies the test being made. Then, based on the outcome of the test during execution, one of several different flowlines leading from the symbol will be followed. This is the only program flowchart symbol that can have more than one exit path. To direct the reader along the right path during execution, each different flowline must have beside it an indicator that designates the condition under which that path is to be followed. For example, it may be that one sequence of operations should be performed if it is true that the value of the variable x is less than the value of the variable y, and another sequence should be performed if it is false. This situation can be depicted by

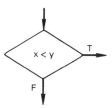

where the T and F mean True and False.

The *preparation* symbol represents the modification of a group of instructions that change the program itself, such as setting a switch or initializing a routine. We use this symbol beginning in Chapter 7 to signify entry into a special kind of loop called a Do-loop.

The other specific process symbol, *subprocess*, is used to represent a module called a subprogram. This symbol can be very useful in top-down design of Fortran programs. I will show you how to use it in Chapter 11.

Each of the symbols described above always has a flowline leading into it and at least one leading out from it. The last two symbols in the figure—*connector* and *terminal*—are different from the others in that they usually have a flowline leading in or a flowline leading out, but not both.

The connector can be looked upon as part of a flowline because it is used whenever a flowline cannot physically be continuous between two other symbols. This occurs whenever the flow must extend from one flowchart page to another or whenever, on one flowchart page, confusion might be caused if a flowline is drawn continuously between any other two symbols. Connectors are usually drawn in pairs: an *outconnector* to show the flow leading from another symbol and an *inconnector* to show the flow leading into another symbol. The descriptive statement within a connector consists of an identifier—a letter or number—for reference.

Corresponding inconnectors and outconnectors contain the same identifier. For example, the sequence

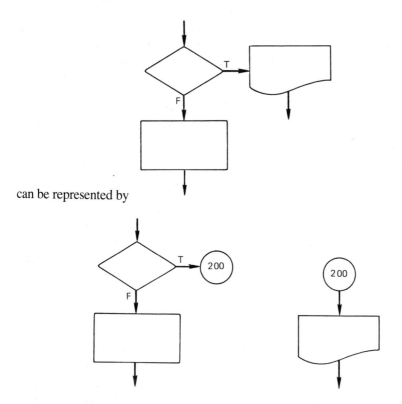

can be represented by

if the latter clarifies the solution procedure better.

The terminal symbol represents an extremity of some kind, particularly a starting or stopping point. All the program flowcharts in this text contain a *start* terminal to indicate the beginning point and name of the flowchart, and at least one *stop* terminal to indicate the ending point of execution of the flowchart. The start terminal does not directly correspond to any Fortran program instructions, but the stop terminals do.

A summarized set of guidelines for using the symbols discussed above is given in Figure 2-6. Examine the flowchart examples of the following sections in light of the guidelines.

1. Each flowchart page should have at least two columns, one of which is for annotation. The others are for the flowchart symbols.
2. Minimum annotation consists of describing the use of each input and output variable. Annotation should be thorough enough to clarify the solution procedure but not so detailed that it causes confusion.

Figure 2-6. Flowchart Guidelines—Summarized

3. The flowchart symbols should be drawn neatly with a template. Symbols should be aligned in columns and rows. Flow direction should, as much as possible, be left to right and top to bottom, clearly indicated by arrowheads on all flowlines. Flowlines should be horizontal and vertical, not angled or curved.

4. The first symbol in a flowchart should be a terminal containing the word START and a name for the procedure. Descriptive statements in other symbols should be concise and clear.

5. Labels, for reference, should be placed slightly above and to the left of the top center of a symbol.

6. For association of symbols appearing on different pages, page numbers should be placed slightly above and to the right of the top center of the symbols.

7. Specific symbols, rather than general symbols, should be used when possible.

8. Each symbol should have only one incoming and one outgoing flowline.

9. Finally, the flowchart should be checked for correctness.

Figure 2-6. (Continued)

2-3-2 Flowchart Examples

To illustrate the drawing of program flowcharts, I use the algorithms of Section 2-2. They are depicted in Figures 2-7 and 2-8.

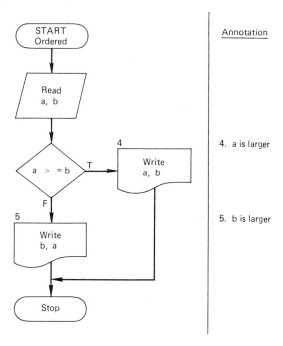

Figure 2-7. Flowchart to Find the Largest of Two Numbers (ALGORITHM Write:ordered) Two numeric values, a and b, are compared and then written in order—larger first and then smaller.

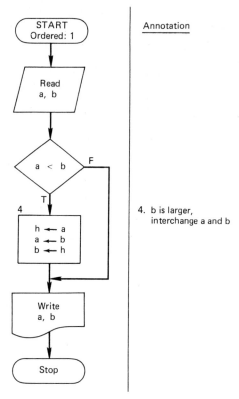

Figure 2-8. Flowchart to Find the Largest of Two Numbers (ALGORITHM Write:ordered:alternative) Two numeric values, a and b, are compared and then written in order—larger first and then smaller.

2-3-3 Exercises on Flowcharts

1. Using a flowcharting template, draw a complete flowchart, including annotation, for your answers to each of these exercises in Section 2-2-3: 2, 4, 5, 6, and 9.

2. Draw a flowchart for the algorithm of Exercise 7, Section 2-2-3.

2-4 A COMPLETE EXAMPLE: CONVERSION

To help you begin to use the programming guide and create solution procedures, an example problem is comprehensively presented and completely solved in this section. I purposely selected a fairly short and simple problem for this illustration.

2-4-1   The Problem Definition

Initially, the problem is stated as follows:

> Develop a table of kilometers and corresponding miles for integral values of kilometers from 1 to 10 inclusive.

You can probably solve this problem manually much faster than I can develop a computer program to do it. That, however, does not preclude it from being a good learning problem; it may even make it more useful in that respect.

The first thing to do is determine what problem data, or input data, we have to work with. Since we want to find out how many miles correspond to several given values of kilometers, we can say that the given kilometer values may be considered as input data. The problem statement does not indicate that there are any other defined values; therefore, all the possible input data have been identified.

Next, the solution data, or output, must be specified. Notice I said "specified." That means "stated explicitly." Since a table is called for, it will be helpful to depict the output in the following way:

```
KILOMETERS   MILES
     1       XXXXX
     2       XXXXX
     3       XXXXX
     .         .
     .         .
     .         .
    10       XXXXX
```

Observe that the table contains the actual kilometer values, but the mile values are represented symbolically by the groups of Xs. This type of layout will be useful later when the program is being coded. Also, notice the *ellipses* (series of periods) in each column. This type of notation is used, when appropriate, to indicate a continuation of similar but omitted terms.

To specify the output completely, a statement regarding the desired accuracy of the answers is needed. This can be determined by considering the nature and environment of the problem, and discussing it with the people who want to have it solved. For this example, I will arbitrarily say that it is sufficient to know the miles to the nearest hundredth.

2-4-2   The Documentation

The documentation, so far, should consist of the final problem definition and the table layout. The full documentation is described later in Section 2-4-8.

2-4-3   The Test Data Preparation

As identified in Section 2-4-1, the kilometer values (1, 2, 3, . . . , 10) can be considered as the total collection of possible input data for this problem. Values from this set must be selected for the test. To cover the full range, we will select 1, 5, and 10. Then, to avoid a possible error duplication with the similar values 1 and 10, we will include the value 9 in the test set. It is also always worthwhile to select some appropriate "invalid" values. In this case, believe it or not, we can select all numbers that are not one of the integers in our collection. Therefore, the full set of test input data consists of the kilometer values 1, 5, 9, and 10, and all other numbers except 2, 3, 4, 6, 7, and 8. You may even select one of those values if you have good reasons. Normally, for more complex problems, the test data will be only a very small portion of the possible data—but representative nonetheless.

We will postpone the entering of these values onto a computer-readable medium and the determination of the expected answers until we can accomplish these activities in conjunction with other appropriate steps. For instance, to find the answers for the selected data we must first find out how to transform kilometers into miles.

2-4-4 The Algorithm

The first thing to do here is determine the essential relationships between the input and output. A quick look in my dictionary at the definition of the word "kilometer" tells me that 1 kilometer is "approximately 0.62137 mile." Thus, since we only need to know the miles to the nearest hundredth for kilometers up to 10, we can multiply any kilometer value we have by 0.6214 to obtain the corresponding value in miles. Since this is the only relationship we need to know to complete the output table, there are no other mathematical relationships to determine.

Next, the problem must be solved manually for the selected test kilometer values 1, 5, 9, and 10. Remembering that the miles are to be found to the nearest hundredth, I manually construct the following partial table.

KILOMETERS	MILES
1	0.62
5	3.11
9	5.59
10	6.21

The solution to the problem for the invalid values selected is that we simply want to obtain no result corresponding to those values.

Now we want to begin to put statements of action together which, when taken in sequence, will result in a complete solution to the problem. We start by describing the overall solution procedure in a sequence of freely worded sentences. One sequence that describes the procedure is this:

```
Write down the column headings, ''KILOMETERS''
and ''MILES.''
Take the following actions for each given
value of kilometers, then stop.
   Find the corresponding value of miles as
   being equal to the value of kilometers
   multiplied by 0.6214.
   Write down the values of kilometers and miles.
```

I took the liberty of indenting the last two sentences to indicate that their actions are initiated by the sentence above them. Indentation is generally used in similar situations in algorithms and computer programs to provide for ready recognition of dependent and repeated actions, thus helping to make the algorithms and programs more readable and understandable.

As a "first try" at developing an algorithm, the foregoing sentences are fairly clear, providing an overview of the solution procedure. One immediately recognizable vagueness, however, is the lack of specification as to what the given values of kilometers are or how the values are to be obtained. Furthermore, the wordiness of the sentences tends to hide the specific operations required to perform each rule. Refinement is necessary.

The first sentence can be tranformed directly using the "Write values" primitive. Realizing that a table may be better understood if it also has a title, we devise a rule something like the following.

```
Write title:  'CONVERSION OF KILOMETERS TO MILES',
      and column headings:  'KILOMETERS', 'MILES'
```

The use of single quotation marks surrounding the title and column headings indicates that we want to write the surrounded characters "literally." Thus a group of characters enclosed in single quotation marks is termed a *literal*.

The second sentence of our first try implies that all the kilometer values must somehow be obtained and passed on to the other rules. It also says that after the other rules have acted on all the kilometer values, the performance of actions is to be terminated. There are a number of ways to describe these activities in an algorithm. In all cases, more than one primitive is required. Here is one way.

```
        kilometers ← 1
EOD. If kilometers <= 10 Then
        Actions to take on each value of kilometers
        kilometers ← kilometers + 1 {next kilometer value}
        Go To EOD. (Back)
      Stop
```

The first rule here establishes the initial value of 1 for the variable "kilometers." The second rule compares the value of kilometers to the number 10, allowing a group of actions to be performed when kilometers is less than or equal to 10, and a termination to occur whenever kilometers is greater than 10. The next-to-last rule in the indented group causes kilometers to be incremented to the next integer value; the final rule in that group then causes a return to the rule having the label "EOD.", where kilometers will again be compared to 10.

Consider, for a moment, the "EOD." label and the "Go To" rule. Labels provide a means for transferring to specific rules when necessary. In an algorithm, a label can be of any brief identifying form such as a number or a word or a descriptive term. Labels in Fortran programs take the form of numbers, but in algorithms I prefer to use terms that are descriptive of the rule to be performed. Here EOD was derived from the term end-of-data. It describes the type of test performed by the If rule. A label should also be set off from the rules so as to be clearly visible. Here I capitalized the letters EOD and used a period following EOD so that it is clearly recognizable as a label. In general, labels in algorithms and programs should be used sparingly—only when necessary—because too many labels can lead to confusion.

The Go To rule allows a repetition sequence, called a *loop*, to be established. Computers are capable of executing rules over and over, looping all day if necessary, and never making a mistake. You and I have trouble with such boring tasks. The Go To used above—Go To EOD.(Back)—clearly indicates that the direction of the rule labeled EOD. is "Back" toward the beginning of the algorithm from this point. The other form of the Go To phrase, Go To label(Ahead), points toward the other direction. The inclusion of a direction indication in the Go To mitigates the confusion that frequently surfaces in algorithms and programs that use such an unconditional transfer.

Referring back to our first try on the algorithm, we find that the final two sentences lead to the following two rules:

```
miles ← kilometers * 0.6214
Write kilometers, miles
```

These two rules, being the actions to take on each value of kilometers, follow immediately after the "If-Then" in the sequence of rules we just devised. The entire refined algorithm can now be written out. It is given, with statements to designate its beginning and ending points and descriptive commentary added, in Figure 2-9.

```
ALGORITHM Kilo:mile
     { Miles, corresponding to integral values of kilometers
     from 1 to 10 inclusive, are computed and printed.}
     Write title:   'CONVERSION OF KILOMETERS TO MILES',
          and column headings:   'KILOMETERS', 'MILES'
     kilometers ← 1
EOD. If kilometers <= 10 Then
          miles ← kilometers * 0.6214
          Write kilometers, miles
          kilometers ← kilometers + 1  {next kilometer value}
          Go to EOD. (Back)
     Stop
     END
```

Figure 2-9. Algorithm for Conversion of Kilometers to Miles

2-4-5   The Flowchart

Figure 2-10 contains a flowchart for the kilometers to miles conversion problem. You should compare it to the algorithm. Take note of these things.

1.   The descriptive statements in the flowchart reflect more limited symbolism than the algorithmic rules. This is due partly to the desire to be concise and partly to the space limitations of the flowchart. The limited symbolism requires that additional annotation be included to clarify the use of variables

such as *k* and *m*. If the annotation is not present, who can be sure what *k* and *m* represent?

2. Only the symbols that are referenced have labels. The placing of labels on unreferenced symbols tends to clutter the flowchart and confuse the reader. Numbers are used as labels for simplicity.

3. The numbers in the annotation column correspond to the labels on the flowchart symbols they refer to.

4. The flowlines and symbols together provide a clear picture of the decision and repetition processes.

5. The rule ''Go To EOD.(Back)'' is not specifically evident in the flowchart. It is represented, however, by the flowline leading from the last symbol back to the decision symbol.

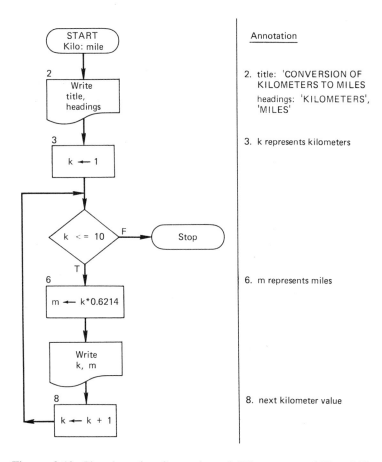

Figure 2-10. Flowchart for Conversion of Kilometers to Miles (Miles, corresponding to integral values of kilometers from 1 to 10 inclusive, are computed and printed.)

2-4-6 The Program

Figure 2-11 contains the Fortran code for the kilometer conversion problem. All together, the code constitutes one program unit—a main program—that I will simply refer to as the program. I purposely wrote the code on a Fortran coding form that identifies column numbers and other useful items. Whether you use a terminal or punched cards for entering your program into the computer, you will find it worthwhile first to write the code onto a printed coding form such as the one shown in the figure. Your college bookstore or computer center probably has a supply of the forms. When I write program code onto a form, I put a slash through the zeros and Zs so that they can be easily distinguished from the letter O and the number 2. You may also want to do this, particularly if someone else is going to do the key-entry for you.

As I stated earlier, algorithms and program flowcharts represent the executable parts of programs. Therefore, only a part of the program in Figure 2-11 corresponds directly to the algorithm and flowchart for the kilometer conversion problem. The other parts of the program are included to meet requirements of the Fortran language and provide explanatory information about the program. Since you already understand the problem as well as the solution procedure in two forms, I believe you can understand much about the program even though you haven't yet studied the Fortran language. Furthermore, I believe that if you understand this program fairly well now, you will find it easier to learn the Fortran language later. Reading good programs is a worthwhile exercise for people who want to learn to write good programs. Therefore, I will take the time here to go through the code, line by line, explaining as I go. Follow along as well as you can; you will understand more than you think you will.

Each line of code corresponds to one computer card, if cards are used, or one computer terminal entry line. The computer uses the lines of code one by one in sequence. Certain columns of a Fortran line of code have specific purposes, all of which are explained fully in Chapter 4. For example, an asterisk in column one indicates that the entire line is only a comment—not to be translated by the Fortran compiler or to be executed by the computer but to be understood by the human reader (you or me). The first line in the figure, then, is a comment that includes a brief descriptive title for the program.

The second line is also a comment. Since it is blank except for the asterisk in column 1, it is being used for spacing between lines so that the reading of the code will be easier. Notice that there are several other blank comment lines in the program. All of them serve the same purpose.

Line 3 contains a statement that identifies the name of the program: KIL-MIL. I chose this name to be as descriptive of the problem as possible considering that, because of Fortran limitations, it could contain no more than six letters. Lines 4 through 6 are self-explanatory comments.

The remainder of the program is divided into four labeled sections: (A) COMMENTARY, (B) DECLARATION, (C) I/O LAYOUT, and (D) ACTION.

This sectioning technique is my method of organizing a Fortran program unit. Its use and the reasoning behind it are explained thoroughly in Chapter 3. It is used in all program units in this book. Notice that the labeled section headers are all contained in comment lines.

The 11 lines beginning with the COMMENTARY header constitute a section that always contains only comments, all designed to describe the purpose and usage of the program. The dictionary portion identifies the symbolic names and their uses in the program. The uses of KILOS and MILES should be clear to you. We have to use an abbreviated term for kilometers (I selected KILOS) because we are limited, by Fortran, to six characters per symbolic name. The symbolic name PO is used to tell the computer which output device will be used to print the answers.

The DECLARATION section occupies the next six lines. It serves to describe, for the compiler, the characteristics of the symbolic names used in the program. The INTEGER statement specifies that KILOS and PO have whole number values, the REAL statement specifies that MILES has values containing decimal points and fractional portions, and the PARAMETER statement specifies that PO is to have the constant value 6.

As indicated above, and in the program, PO tells the computer which device is used to print the answers. In my computer, the device number for the line printer is 6. Your computer may use a different number for the line printer. If so, I suggest that you change the number in your copy of this book from 6 to your correct number. I believe, then, that the program will run on your computer with no other changes.

The I/O LAYOUT section, consisting of the next seven lines, tells the computer how the output data are to look when they are printed. Two FORMAT statements with numeric labels are used for this purpose. They are labeled so that they can be referenced by other statements when necessary. The contents of the FORMAT statements will be explained in detail later. For now, notice the colon in column 6 of each of the two lines between the two FORMAT statements. These are used to indicate a continuation of the FORMAT statement labeled 900; it actually occupies three lines in sequence.

Finally, we come to the part of the program that corresponds to the algorithm and program flowchart: the ACTION section. You can see that there is one Fortran statement for each algorithmic rule. The interpretation remains the same. Since you know the purpose of each algorithmic rule, you already know the meaning of each Fortran statement. In sequence, here is my explanation for you to compare with your own.

WRITE (PO, 900): Print the title and column headings. The output device is PO (number 6) and the FORMAT statement used in determining what the headings are to look like is labeled 900.

Figure 2-11. Fortran Program for Conversion of Kilometers to Miles

46

IBM

FORTRAN Coding Form

GX28-7327-6 U/M 050
Printed in U.S.A.

PROGRAM CONVERSION OF KILOMETERS TO MILES

PROGRAMMER JARRELL C. GROUT   DATE 7/7/79

PAGE 2 OF 2

PUNCHING INSTRUCTIONS	GRAPHIC		Ø	O	Z	1
	PUNCH		Zero	oh	Zee	One

```
900   FORMAT ('1',  'CONVERSION OF KILOMETERS TO MILES',
      :        /'0',  5X,  'KILOMETERS',  'MILES',
      :        /' ',  8X,  I3,  12X,  F5.2)
910   FORMAT (' ',  8X,  I3,  12X,  F5.2)
D.    ACTION
      WRITE (PO, 900)
      KILOS = 1
200   IF (KILOS .LE. 10) THEN
        MILES = KILOS * 0.6214
        WRITE (PO, 910) KILOS, MILES
        KILOS = KILOS + 1
        GO TO 200
      ENDIF
      STOP
      END
```

Figure 2-11. Fortran Program for Conversion of Kilometers to Miles -concluded

47

KILOS = 1: Assign the variable KILOS a value of 1.

200 IF (KILOS .LE. 10) THEN: Compare the current value of KILOS to the constant 10. If KILOS is less than or equal to 10, proceed to execute the statements immediately following, up to the ENDIF statement; otherwise, bypass those statements and continue execution with the statement after the ENDIF.

MILES = KILOS * 0.6214: Multiply the current value of KILOS by 0.6214 and assign the resulting value to the variable MILES. This and the following three statements are indented further to indicate that they are also inside the loop and are dependent on the IF statement.

WRITE (PO, 910) KILOS, MILES: Print the current value of KILOS and then the current value of MILES. Again, the output device is determined by the value of PO, but the FORMAT statement used to determine how the values of KILOS and MILES are to be printed is labeled 910.

KILOS = KILOS + 1: Add 1 to the current value of KILOS and then assign KILOS the new value. The new value replaces the current value becoming, then, the current value. (Notice that the = sign here is for assignment, not equality.)

GO TO 200: Transfer control of execution to the statement labeled 200, the IF.

ENDIF: A statement required in Fortran to designate the ending point of an IF-THEN sequence of statements. Its execution has no effect, but it must be present as the last statement in an IF-THEN statement group.

STOP: Terminate execution of the program.

END: A keyword that designates the physical end of the program unit. It indicates to the compiler that there are no more Fortran statements in this program unit. Every program unit must have an END statement as its last FORTRAN statement.

Now that you understand the coded program reasonably well, I want you to prepare it for a computer run. Use a computer terminal or a keypunch machine. Be sure to key-enter the program exactly as shown on the form except, if necessary, change the value of PO as described earlier. You will also need to determine the appropriate job control statements, prior to key-entry, and add them in the proper positions. Check with your instructor or computer center about job control.

Recall, from Sec. 2-4-4, that the algorithm itself generated the kilometer values and it therefore did not require any input data from outside. The same holds true for the program. Therefore, you do not have to key-enter any input data to go with this program.

2-4-7   *The Test*

The kilometer conversion program contains no bugs, but will your run of the program be bug-free? Take care and it will.

Once you have prepared the program, go ahead and run it on the computer. Even though you did not write the program, this exercise will help you get some experience with the key-entry equipment and the computer itself. Your instructor or computer center can help you make the run.

Take the time you need to prepare the program carefully. For our purposes, if you have completed this exercise by the time you finish reading Chapter 4, you will be doing just fine. Once you obtain your results from the computer, compare them to my results shown in Figure 2-12. Figure 2-12(a) contains the program listing—a computer printout of the Fortran program. You should always obtain a program listing when you compile a program. Program listings are useful for debugging and documenting.

```
*I. CONVERT KILOMETERS TO MILES
*
        PROGRAM KILMIL
*       PROGRAMMER:  JARRELL C. GROUT
*       DATE:  7/7/79
*
*  A. COMMENTARY
*
*           THIS PROGRAM DEVELOPS AND PRINTS A TABLE
*       OF KILOMETERS AND CORRESPONDING MILES FOR
*       THE INTEGRAL KILOMETER VALUES 1 THROUGH 10.
*
*           DICTIONARY.
*       KILOS:  KILOMETER NUMBER (1 THRU 10)
*       MILES:  NUMBER OF MILES (0.62 THRU 6.21)
*       PO:  PRINT-OUT DEVICE IDENTIFIER
*
*  B. DECLARATION
*
        INTEGER  KILOS, PO
        REAL  MILES
        PARAMETER  (PO=6)
*
*  C. I/O LAYOUT
*
    900 FORMAT ('1', 'CONVERSION OF KILOMETERS TO MILES',
       :        /'0', 5X, 'KILOMETERS', 8X, 'MILES',
       :        /' ')
    910 FORMAT (' ', 8X, I3, 12X, F5.2)
*
*  D. ACTION
*
        WRITE (PO, 900)
        KILOS = 1
    200 IF (KILOS .LE. 10) THEN
            MILES = KILOS * 0.6214
            WRITE (PO, 910) KILOS, MILES
            KILOS = KILOS + 1
            GO TO 200
        ENDIF
        STOP
        END
```
(a) Program Listing

```
            CONVERSION OF KILOMETERS TO MILES

            KILOMETERS        MILES

                1              .62
                2             1.24
                3             1.86
                4             2.49
                5             3.11
                6             3.73
                7             4.35
                8             4.97
                9             5.59
               10             6.21
```
(b) Output

Figure 2-12. Computer Results, Conversion of Kilometers to Miles

Figure 2-12(b) contains the output generated by the program. You should compare the printed answers to those expected to be printed, defined in Section 2-4-4 when I solved the problem manually for the selected test data. As you will find, the printed answers are correct. Recall also that we selected some invalid values for which we expected the program to produce nothing. Our success with invalid values is evident because Figure 2-12 contains the only answers that can be produced by the program.

If your results are different from mine, you have at least one error, perhaps a mistake in your job control statements or a bug in the program. First, make sure that your job control statements are correct; verify them with your instructor or computer center. Then compare each line of code you prepared to the code I gave you in Figure 2-11. Your code and mine must agree exactly except that your value of PO in the PARAMETER statement must be correct for the line printer on your computer. If your compiler has printed some diagnostics, try to interpret them and make appropriate corrections. Your mistake is probably due to improper key-entry of one or more characters. Try your best to find and correct every error before you make another run.

Listed and explained in Figure 2-13 are a few possible bugs to give you an idea of the errors that might be made. Even if you did not make any mistakes when you prepared the program (an accomplishment that deserves an ''A'') you might find it worthwhile to rerun the program after incorporating into it some of the errors in the figure. By doing so, you can observe the computer's reaction to the presence of bugs. Don't be hesitant about doing this. You cannot possibly harm the computer by running a program containing bugs.

1. Omission of an * from column 1 of a comment line. This turns a comment into a statement that the compiler cannot recognize, much less translate.

2. Misspelling a keyterm. The keyterms in this program are PROGRAM, INTEGER, REAL, PARAMETER, FORMAT, WRITE, IF, STOP, GO TO, and END. For example, you might misspell STOP as SPOT. The compiler will probably treat the misspelled term as an undefined variable and indicate that the statement is unrecognizable or incorrect in some way.

3. Omission of one or more necessary characters. If, for example,

   910 FORMAT (' ', 8X, I3, 12X, F5.2)

   is entered as

   91   FORMAT (' ', 8X, I3 12X, F5.2

   several bugs are present. From the left, the first bug is that instead of statement 910 you now have statement 91, a bug that is not directly detectable by the compiler. Next, a comma is omitted in the sequence I3 12X, again, a bug that may not be detected by the compiler. Finally, the right parenthesis is missing, a bug that will result in a diagnostic, by most Fortran compilers, indicating unbalanced parentheses. You will learn when and where characters can and cannot be omitted.

Figure 2-13. Some Possible Bugs for the Kilometer Conversion Program

4. Spelling a variable name two different ways. For example, spell KILOS correctly in all lines except the last one in which it is used:

    KILOS = KILO + 1

    KILO is completely different from KILOS as far as the computer is concerned. This is another bug that the compiler may not detect.

5. Keying-in an incorrect operator. For example, the line following statement 200 might have been entered as

    MILES = KILOS + 0.6214

    and the computer would have performed an addition—as directed—rather than a multiplication—as intended. This bug the computer will not see at all.

Figure 2-13. (Continued)

2-4-8   The Completion

Documentation for the kilometer conversion program is interspersed throughout Section 2-4. I believe you can see how it can be brought together and arranged, as described in Sections 2-1-2 and 2-1-8 and Figure 2-2, for placement in a manual or booklet. Therefore, once you have finished running the program on the computer, go ahead and put together a documentation manual for it. Then later, as you write other programs, always complete a documentation manual for each one. Never fail to complete your programming.

2-5   EXERCISES ON COMPLETE PROBLEMS

For one or more of the following exercises, use the "steps of good programming practice" (Section 2-1) to produce complete solutions in the form of algorithms and flowcharts. Complete all steps up to that point. Later, after you have studied Fortran, you can complete the programming.

1. Develop and print a table of ounces and corresponding grams for values of ounces from 0 through 10 inclusive, in increments of 0.1 (one-tenth ounce). There are approximately 28.35 grams in 1 ounce.

2. Develop and print a table of Fahrenheit and corresponding Celsius temperatures (to the nearest 0.1) for the integral Fahrenheit temperatures lowf (a variable) through highf (also a variable) inclusive. Use the relationship

    Celsius = (5/9) (Fahrenheit −32)

    The variables lowf and highf must be given values by input; a limitation, that must be checked, is that lowf <= highf.

3. Develop and print a table of square centimeters for values of square inches from lowin to highin in increments of 0.5 square inch. The values of lowin and highin are to be read in and a check must be made to ensure that lowin <= highin.

4. Temperature measurements from an experiment have been recorded onto a computer-readable medium. The experimenter needs to know, among other things, the temperature range (algebraic difference between the highest and the lowest temperature). The temperatures are to be read in one by one and "searched" for the highest and lowest, from which the range can then be found. Only one temperature is available at any one time. Solve the problem.

5. A class has taken an exam. The papers have been graded and the grades recorded on a computer-readable medium. The grades are integers, zero and above. Read, print, and accumulate the grades one by one, then compute and print the arithmetic average. Since the class size is unspecified, build a mechanism into your solution procedure to count the number of grades. (*Hint:* Use an invalid grade value—a negative number—to designate the end of the input grades.)

Chapter

3

Fortran Program Organization

Planning, the implicit emphasis of Chapter 2, is essential to programming. You have learned that you do not immediately begin to write program code as soon as you are given a problem to solve; you first go through several steps to help make sure that you are solving the right problem and will devise a program that produces a correct solution to the problem.

Organizing is also important in programming. In this chapter, I want to acquaint you with a particular method for organizing a Fortran program. It will help you understand the makeup of a program and provide a means for consistency in program design that goes right along with my overall objective of helping you learn to write good Fortran programs.

People have been writing Fortran programs since the late 1950s. Standards that specify the form and establish the interpretation of Fortran programs were published by the American National Standards Institute (ANSI) in 1966 and 1978 (see references 1 and 2 at the end of the chapter). The Fortran of this text is the one described in the 1978 ANSI publication. It is commonly called FORTRAN 77.

The published standard defines the allowable Fortran statements and prescribes an order for the statements in a program, but the order specification is extremely flexible, to the point of allowing wide variations in program organization. It is common, therefore, for Fortran programs written by different individuals to exhibit a lack of organizational consistency with respect to each other. This makes it difficult to compare one Fortran program with another, even if both were written to solve the same problem. It also makes it difficult for some students to learn to program in Fortran.

These difficulties are unnecessary, and can be alleviated by the use of a more

53

rigid specification of Fortran program structure than the standard prescribes. The specification does not have to restrict a programmer's creativity; rather, it may even improve one's potential for responsible creativity. The Fortran program organization method that is described in this chapter does just that. If used properly it makes Fortran programs easier to design, document, read, understand, debug, and maintain. You should use it for all your Fortran programs, even while learning.

3-1 NOTATION

In describing the organization method in the next two sections of this chapter, I use some Fortran keyterms and special characters that require a brief explanation. The notation is not complicated but you need to learn it.

First, each asterisk used denotes a comment line in a Fortran program and, therefore, each one is located in column 1 of a Fortran line. Second, terms containing capitals only are to be entered into Fortran lines exactly as shown. Finally, lowercase words are to be replaced in Fortran program lines with the information described by the words.

3-2 PROGRAM FRAMEWORK

In Chapter 2 I indicated to you that a Fortran executable program consists of one or more program units. If only one program unit is present, it is referred to as a main program. If there is more than one program unit, the first one is the main program and all others are subprograms. Consistency in the organization of program units can be attained by the use of the two program unit skeletons given below and the program unit arrangement of the next section.

Main Program Skeleton

*I.   Main Program Identification: a brief, descriptive title
       PROGRAM name
*   PROGRAMMER: name of original programmer or reviser
*   DATE: date completed or revised
       Program Unit Sections (see Section 3-3)

Subprogram Skeleton

*n.   Subprogram Identification: a brief, descriptive title
       Subprogram Statement (FUNCTION, SUBROUTINE, or BLOCK DATA)
*   PROGRAMMER: name of original programmer or reviser
*   DATE: date completed or revised
       Program Unit Sections (see Section 3-3)

In the first line of the subprogram skeleton above, n represents the sequence number of the program unit—any Roman numeral greater than I.

3-3 PROGRAM UNIT ARRANGEMENT

There are 50 distinguishable statements, in addition to comments, in FORTRAN 77. Do not let that large number bother you because you will first be learning only the ones that are the most useful. Later you can learn the others as you need them.

The statements are easier to learn and use if they are first grouped according to the major functions they perform. Four main groups can be identified. I refer to them as Commentary, Declaration, I/O Layout, and Action. Other authors and authorities recommend or use similar groupings, although they usually do not name the groups. I name them to help beginners learn and to help practitioners attain consistent design and complete documentation.

Each program unit, accordingly, is made up of four unique sections. Each section begins with a heading that has a comment indicator in column 1, a letter used as a section label, and the section title. A program unit outline, which identifies and explains the contents of each of the four sections, is given below. It should be used as a guide in program unit coding.

```
*       A. COMMENTARY
*
*       The purpose of this section is to introduce and provide documenting
*       information about the problem and the program unit. It is included for
*       the benefit of people who write and read the program—the computer
*       does not use it. It should contain, first, a narrative description of the
*       problem and the program unit. Following the description should be a
*       dictionary that consists of an alphabetical list of program symbolic
*       names and uses, with value ranges when appropriate. Other document-
*       ing information that will aid people in the use and revision of the pro-
*       gram unit can also be included.
*
*       B. DECLARATION
*
        This program unit section is for specifying characteristics of the pro-
        gram and its data so that the computer will process them properly. The
        statements that appear in this section are discussed at suitable points in
        the text beginning in Chapter 4.
*
*       C. I/O LAYOUT
*
        Section C is used for describing the layout and appearance of data on
        the input and output media. Accordingly, only FORMAT statements,
```

as described in Chapter 6, are placed here, in ascending numerical sequence by statement number.

```
*
*    D. ACTION
*
```

The Action section contains the executable processes of the program unit. Therefore, all the executable statements required to specify the solution procedure are placed here in algorithmic sequence. These statements are covered at appropriate locations in the text beginning in Chapter 4.

Also in this program unit section, indentation of repetitive and dependent code sequences should be used to further improve readability and understanding; statement numbers should be in ascending numerical sequence to provide order and decrease the potential of confusion; and comments should be used responsibly to increase understanding but avoid clutter in executable code sequences. Each of these items is discussed later in the text.

For completeness, each of the four sections should always be present in every program unit. If there are no program statements to be entered in a section, the line

```
*    NONE
```

should be entered below that particular section heading.

3-4   AN EXAMPLE PROGRAM: AVERAGING

In Chapter 2 I went through the kilometer conversion program, explaining in detail the function of each program line. Here, in Figure 3-1, I give you a second Fortran program to examine. It solves another familiar problem: finding the arithmetic average of a set of numbers (called "EXPERIMENTAL OBSERVATIONS" in the program). It can be used as a solution to Exercise 5 of Section 2-5, although it is more general in nature. A detailed description of this program will enable you to begin to learn how the program organization method of this chapter is used; it will also increase your understanding of Fortran programming prior to the time you begin to study the language.

First, observe that the organization of the kilometer conversion program presented in Figure 2-12(a) corresponds to the specification of this chapter. Similarly, the arithmetic averaging program of Figure 3-1 consists of only a main program with a title line, program information, and the four program unit sections. My explanation of this program, in a manner like that of the kilometer conversion program explanation, is given below.

```
*I, ARITHMETIC AVERAGE
*
        PROGRAM AVRAGE
*       PROGRAMMER:  JARRELL C, GROUT
*       DATE:  9/8/80
*
*  A, COMMENTARY
*
*          FIND THE ARITHMETIC AVERAGE OF A SET OF
*       EXPERIMENTAL OBSERVATIONS WHICH MAY VARY IN
*       VALUE FROM -999,99 THROUGH +999,99, INCLUSIVE,
*       VALUES ARE ENTERED ONE PER INPUT RECORD,
*
*          DICTIONARY,
*       AVE:  OBSERVATION ACCUMULATOR AND AVERAGE
*       CI:  INPUT DEVICE IDENTIFIER
*       COUNT:  THE COUNT OF OBSERVATIONS
*       HIOBS:  THE HIGHEST ALLOWABLE OBSERVATION (+999,99)
*       LOWOBS:  THE LOWEST ALLOWABLE OBSERVATION (-999,99)
*       OBS:  AN OBSERVATION (-999,99 THRU +999,99)
*       PO:  OUTPUT DEVICE IDENTIFIER
*
*  B, DECLARATION
*
        INTEGER  CI, COUNT, PO
        REAL  AVE, HIOBS, LOWOBS, OBS
        PARAMETER  (CI=5, PO=6,  HIOBS=+999,99, LOWOBS=-999,99)
*
*  C, I/O LAYOUT
*
  900 FORMAT ('1', 'EXPERIMENTAL OBSERVATIONS', /)
  910 FORMAT ('0', 'INVALID INPUT VALUE, UNUSED: ',
      :          E14,7, /)
  920 FORMAT ('  ', 9X, F7,2)
  930 FORMAT ('0', 'AVERAGE: ', F7,2, /,
      :        '  ', 'ON ', I10, ' VALUES', /, '1')
*
*  D, ACTION
*
        WRITE (PO, 900)
        AVE = 0,0
        COUNT = 0
  200     READ (CI, *, END=300) OBS
          IF (OBS ,LT, LOWOBS
      :       ,OR, OBS ,GT, HIOBS) THEN
            WRITE (PO, 910) OBS
          ELSE
            WRITE (PO, 920) OBS
            AVE = AVE + OBS
            COUNT = COUNT + 1
          ENDIF
          GO TO 200
  300 IF (COUNT ,GT, 0) AVE = AVE / COUNT
      WRITE (PO, 930) AVE, COUNT
      STOP
      END
```

Figure 3-1. Arithmetic Averaging Program

    The first line gives the program a title and the third line gives it a name. The second line, as with all blank lines, serves as spacing to make the program easier to read. You can pick out the four program unit sections because the section headings are present, so I will relate the remainder of my explanation to those sections. (Notice that if the section headings were not present, it would not be possible to discuss the statements in groups. Inclusion of the section headings provides conveniences for this discussion as well as for the understanding, debugging, maintaining, and comparing of programs.)

    The content of the Commentary section is self-explanatory. The only points about it that I want to emphasize are that the description is brief, yet complete, and the symbolic names in the dictionary are in alphabetical order so that they can be easily located.

In the Declaration section, the INTEGER statement indicates that the symbolic names CI, COUNT, and PO are to have whole-number values; the REAL statement declares that the symbolic names AVE, HIOBS, LOWOBS, and OBS are to have real number values; and the PARAMETER statement specifies that CI and PO are symbolic constants with the respective values 5 and 6, and that HIOBS and LOWOBS are also symbolic constants with the respective values +999.99 and −999.99. The statements in the I/O Layout section—all FORMAT and all numbered—tell the computer where the output values are to be printed on each print line. Furthermore, some actual output information, such as "EXPERIMEN-TAL OBSERVATIONS," is specified. Take note that, as explained below, each FORMAT statement is referenced by number in the Action section.

The Action section contains the executable statements that cause the computer to find the average. Statement by statement, the action is as follows.

WRITE (PO, 900): Print a title for the output table at the top of a page. Use FORMAT statement 900 to determine what is to be printed.

AVE = 0.0: Assign the variable AVE an initial value of 0.0.

COUNT = 0: Assign the variable COUNT an initial value of 0.

200 READ (CI, *, END=300) OBS: From an input record, read in a value for the variable OBS. The 200 on this statement gives it a number by which it can be referenced. The * indicates that a FORMAT statement will not be used. The END=300 is used to cause the computer to transfer to statement 300 when there are no more values of OBS to be read in. It serves to cause the computer to exit from the read and summation loop.

IF (OBS .LT. LOWOBS

: .OR. OBS .GT. HIOBS) THEN: Perform a check on the input value just read to determine if it is outside the allowed range. If so, print it using the WRITE statement below and ignore it in calculating the average. The statement is purposely written on two lines for readability.

WRITE (PO, 910) OBS: Print an invalid value of OBS with an appropriate message using FORMAT statement 910.

ELSE: Allows execution of the following (indented) statements when the previous IF test yields a "false" result, indicating that the value of OBS just read in is in the allowed range.

WRITE (PO, 920) OBS: Print a valid input value of OBS using FORMAT statement 920. The printout of an input value is known as an *input echo*—a device used to verify the actual correctness of the input data.

AVE = AVE + OBS: Add the value of OBS to the current value of AVE and assign that sum to the variable AVE as its new current value.

COUNT = COUNT + 1: Add 1 to the current value of COUNT and assign that sum to the variable COUNT as its new value.

ENDIF: Designates the end point of the IF-THEN-ELSE sequence of statements.

GO TO 200: Causes the computer to transfer to statement 200, establishing a loop for the read and summation process.

300 IF (COUNT .GT. 0) AVE = AVE / COUNT: Test to see if the value of COUNT is greater than zero and, if so, divide AVE by COUNT to obtain the new value of AVE, the average. The test is performed before the division to make sure that a division by zero does not occur—a situation that could happen if there were no input values processed.

WRITE (PO, 930) AVE, COUNT: Print the value of AVE, the average, and COUNT, the number of observations used in calculating the average, using FORMAT statement 930.

STOP: Terminate execution of the program unit; return control to the operating system of the computer.

END: Designates the physical end of the program unit, indicating that there are no more statements in the program unit.

Without further explanation, but for your study and use should you decide to run this program, an example set of input and corresponding output is given in Figure 3-2.

```
75
80
65
83
72
60
100
91
75
63
88
```

(a) Input Data (Each value begins in column 1 of an input record)

```
EXPERIMENTAL OBSERVATIONS
         75.00
         80.00
         65.00
         83.00
         72.00
         60.00
        100.00
         91.00
         75.00
         63.00
         88.00

AVERAGE:  77.45
ON        11 VALUES
```

(b) Output

Figure 3-2. Example I/O for the Arithmetic Averaging Program

3-5 A FINAL NOTE ABOUT PROGRAM ORGANIZATION

Clearly, for Fortran programs, I recommend the use of the organization method described in this chapter. It was derived from practice and experience, and represents a synthesis of ideas. Other authorities organize their Fortran programs in similar ways but they usually do not specify program unit sections. Personally, I believe that it is helpful for students, and beneficial for practitioners and teachers, to do so.

As mentioned earlier, the program organization requirements of FORTRAN 77 are not as rigid as those I have prescribed in this chapter. FORTRAN 77 does have some definite requirements, though, and so that you may know them, they are depicted in Figure 3-3. In this figure, vertical lines separate varieties of statements that can be intermixed; horizontal lines separate varieties of statements that cannot be intermixed. For example, FORMAT statements can be mixed in anywhere after a PROGRAM, FUNCTION, SUBROUTINE, or BLOCK DATA statement, and before an END statement. For another example, the END statement must be the final statement; it cannot be mixed in with other statements.

As you look at Figure 3-3, don't be concerned that you do not yet know all the statements and their functions. You will know them soon enough, and you will want to refer to the figure as you learn to use them.

Beginning of Program Unit

Comment Lines	PROGRAM, FUNCTION, SUBROUTINE, or BLOCK DATA Statement		
	FORMAT and ENTRY Statements	PARAMETER Statements	IMPLICIT Statements
			Other Specification Statements
		DATA Statements	Statement Function Statements
			Executable Statements
END Statement			

End of Program Unit

Figure 3-3. FORTRAN 77 Required Statement Order. (This figure is reproduced with permission from American National Standard Programming Language FORTRAN, ANSI X3.9-1978, Copyright 1978 by the American National Standards Institute. Copies of this standard may be purchased from the American National Standards Institute at 1430 Broadway, New York, N.Y. 10018.)

3-6 EXERCISES

1. Explain these three Fortran statements, individually, as well as possible.

   (a) READ (CI, *) COST

   (b) SUMCST = SUMCST + COST

   (c) WRITE (PO, 950) SUMCST

2. Give the name of the final statement in every Fortran program unit.

3. Explain these two Fortran statements, individually, as well as possible.

   (a) PROGRAM PAYROLL

   (b) SUBROUTINE DEDUCT

4. Prepare the arithmetic averaging program of this chapter and run it on the computer. Use the input data given in Figure 3-2 to test the program. Then make a run with some data of your own, one value per input record.

REFERENCES

1. ASA Sectional Committee X3. USA Standard Fortran X3.9-1966. American National Standards Institute (formerly USASI), New York, 1966.

2. ANSI Subcommittee X3J3. American National Standard Programming Language FORTRAN, X3.9-1978. American National Standards Institute, New York, 1978.

Fundamental
Fortran Elements

In Chapter 2 I stated that a computer language consists of a character set and clearly stated rules for organizing the characters into meaningful statements that human beings can use to communicate with computers. The primary purpose of this chapter is to introduce you to the Fortran computer language by acquainting you with the Fortran character set and other elementary components of the language, including the simplest forms of a few statements that you can quickly learn to use well.

4-1 CHARACTER SET

The Fortran character set consists of 26 letters, 10 digits, and 13 special characters. They are all depicted in Figure 4-1. As you can see, you are familiar with all of them.

Fortran statements are written with uppercase letters and, therefore, the figure contains no letters that are not capitalized. The digits are all decimal, base 10, the number system with which you and I are most familiar. Together as one group, the letters and digits are referred to as the *alphanumeric characters*.

The special characters are well known to you. One of them that tends to confuse some learners at first, however, is the blank. In a given position of a Fortran statement, the presence of a blank character is indicated by the absence of any of the other characters in that position. Blanks are often used in Fortran statements to make the statements easy for human beings to read. When this is the case, the blanks are ignored by the compiler and are not stored in the computer as part of the

1. Letters

     A B C D E F G H I J K L M N O P Q R S T U V W X Y Z

2. Digits

                 0 1 2 3 4 5 6 7 8 9

3. Special Characters

Character	Name
	Blank
=	Equals
+	Plus
−	Minus
*	Asterisk
/	Slash
(	Left parenthesis
)	Right parenthesis
,	Comma
.	Decimal point
$	Currency symbol
'	Apostrophe
:	Colon

Figure 4-1. The Fortran Character Set

program. Sometimes, however, blanks are critical to the program. In these cases, each blank is stored internally in the computer's memory by means of a particular bit configuration (e.g., the EBCDIC configuration for a blank character is 01000000.) As you study Fortran in this book I will tell you when blanks are critical and must be included in the program. I will also suggest to you when and where you can use them to make your programs easy to read.

4-2 RECORD FORMAT

A line in a Fortran program is a sequence of 72 characters or less. The positions in a line, into which the characters are placed, are called *columns*. The columns are numbered, left to right, from 1 through 72. There are three types of lines that can appear in a Fortran program unit: comment, initial, and continuation.

A *comment line* is any line in a program unit that contains an asterisk or a C in column 1, or contains only blank characters in columns 1 through 72. Comment lines, or comments, are used for program documentation and spacing. The compiler, and thus the computer, ignores comments except to read them in and print them out as part of the program listing.

An *initial line* is any line that is not a comment and that contains a blank character or the digit 0 in column 6. A *continuation line* is any line that contains blank characters in columns 1 through 5 and a nonblank, nonzero character in column 6. Each Fortran statement can be written anywhere in columns 7 through 72 of one initial line and as many as 19 continuation lines following the initial line.

In general, a *record* is a collection of related items of information. The information consists of input data values for input records, or instruction contents for program records. A Fortran program record consists of an initial line and its corresponding continuation lines. The items contained in a Fortran record are depicted in Figure 4-2. The columns reserved for an item of information are known collectively as the *field* for that item, and thus we speak of columns 1 through 5 as the statement label field, column 6 as the continuation field, and columns 7 through 72 as the Fortran statement field. As applied generally to data and programs, whether in Fortran or any other programming language, a field is a specified area of a record that is used for a particular category of information.

Statement labels allow statements to be referenced elsewhere in a program unit. Therefore, only the statements that are referenced should be labeled. Each statement label, also called *statement number*, must be a whole number; each must be unique within a program unit. When used, a statement number can be placed anywhere in columns 1 through 5; blanks and leading zeros in the field are treated as being insignificant. A statement number must not have a plus or minus sign.

Coding forms, like the one shown in Figure 4-3, are useful for writing Fortran lines. One coding form line can contain one Fortran line. For entry of a program into the computer, one coding form line corresponds to one punched card—such as the one pictured in Figure 4-4—if a card reader is used, or to one computer terminal line if a computer terminal is used.

The punched card is the traditional medium for entry of both programs and data. Its use is decreasing rapidly as computer terminals, which allow more direct communication with the computer, are becoming more readily available. Even though punched card use is giving way to terminal use, some of the punched card characteristics have been carried over into terminal usage.

The most notable carryover characteristic is the 80-column punched card length. Thus many computer terminals allow entry of 80 characters per line. Since Fortran lines require 72 columns at the most, both punched cards and computer ter-

Columns (Field)	Item Name (Field Name)	Contents
1–5	Statement label	When used, an unsigned whole number (1–99999) in an initial line only; otherwise, blank
6	Continuation	Blank character or 0 (zero) in an initial line; nonblank, nonzero character in a continuation line
7–72	Statement	As described later

Figure 4-2. Fortran Record Description

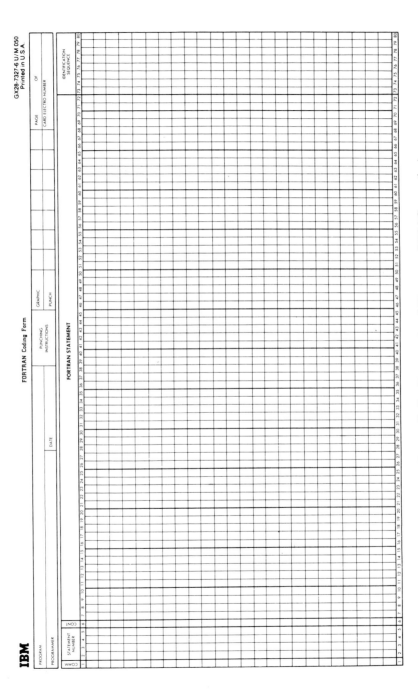

Figure 4-3. A Fortran Coding Form—reduced (Courtesy of IBM Corporation)

65

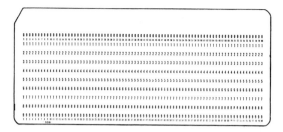

Figure 4-4. A Punched Card-reduced

minal lines can easily hold a Fortran line with eight columns to spare. FORTRAN 77 does not say what should be done with the extra eight columns.

4-3 STATEMENT CONTENTS

As indicated in Figure 4-2 and stated in the previous section, each Fortran statement is written in columns 7 through 72 of an initial line and as many as 19 continuation lines. Usually, only an initial line is required. For examples of the use of continuation lines, refer back to the kilometer conversion program of Figure 2-11, which has two continuation lines in FORMAT statement 900. Because it is a rather inconspicuous but connective character, I choose to use a colon as the nonblank, nonzero character in column 6 to designate each continuation line.

Each Fortran statement is either executable or nonexecutable. Executable statements specify actions—operations that the computer is to carry out. Program execution always begins with the first executable statement in the main program and proceeds sequentially from there. Nonexecutable statements classify program units; describe the characteristics, arrangement, and initial values of data; contain editing information; specify statement functions; and specify entry points within subprograms.

The compiler recognizes a statement by its keywords and structure or by its structure alone. For example, the statement

```
WRITE (PO, 920) OBS
```

is recognized as an output statement by the keyword WRITE combined with the arrangement of the other items. For another example, the statement

```
AVE = AVE + OBS
```

has no keywords, but is recognized as an assignment statement by the arrangement of the items it contains.

Each statement is made up of specific items from the set of possible syntactic items available in Fortran. This set consists of constants, symbolic names, keywords, operators, and special characters.

A *constant* is an item that always has the same value; its value never changes within a program unit. For instance, the number −999.99 used in PROGRAM AVRAGE of Figure 3-1 is a constant. In addition to numeric constants, Fortran also has logical (true, false) and character (groups of symbols) constants.

A *symbolic name* is a sequence of one to six letters or digits, the first of which must be a letter. In Chapter 2 the symbolic name KILMIL was used to name the kilometer-to-miles conversion program. In Chapter 3 the symbolic name AVRAGE was used to name the averaging program.

Many Fortran statements contain special symbolic names known as variable names. A *variable name* is the symbolic name of a datum that can be defined (given a value), redefined as desired, and referenced. Each variable name used in a program refers symbolically to a location in the computer's memory (e.g., a word or a byte) that contains a desired value in binary form. The importance of variables is that during execution they can be assigned different values from a given set of values, although only one value at a time. As an example, the statement used in program KILMIL,

```
MILES = KILOS * 0.6214
```

contains the variable KILOS, already having a defined value, and the variable MILES, being assigned a value. It also contains the constant 0.6214 and the two special characters = and *, representing assignment and multiplication, respectively.

Another kind of special symbolic name is known as an *array name* or, for simplicity, an array. Arrays allow several different values stored in memory at the same time to be referenced by one name in the program unit. For instance, if you knew the age of every one of your fellow students, you could write a Fortran program to store all of their ages in memory at one time and then refer to them in the program by using the array name AGES. This would let you do much more with them (such as finding the highest, lowest, median, and average age) than you could if you were only able to store one age at a time in memory. Even so, in this text you will be working with arrays only in Chapter 8 and beyond. You need to become adept at the use of less complicated structures before you attempt to use arrays.

4-4 NOTATION FOR STATEMENT DESCRIPTIONS

In the next section I begin describing the form of each of the statements you can use in a Fortran program. The notation used there and throughout the remainder of this text is not complicated but you must know it in order to understand the structure of each statement and learn how to write each one properly. Here are the conventions and symbols I use in describing the form of each Fortran statement and its parts.

1. All Fortran statement structures depicted are intended to appear only in columns 7 through 72 of a Fortran line. Unless otherwise indicated, the line shown is an initial line.

2. Fortran special characters, uppercase letters, and uppercase words are to be written as shown except where otherwise noted. For example, the special character = is to be entered into your program at the same place and in the same way as it appears in my description.

3. Lowercase letters and words are to be replaced by specifically defined Fortran items. For instance, in the statement

   ```
   PROGRAM name
   ```

   the lowercase word "name" is to be replaced by the symbolic name that you choose as the name of the main program.

4. An ellipsis (. . .) indicates that additional items, like the ones preceding the ellipsis, can be included as desired.

5. Blank characters (spaces in lines) are used to make statements easier for human beings to read, but have no significance to the computer unless otherwise indicated. For example, in program AVRAGE of Chapter 3, the statement

   ```
   READ (CI, *, END=300) OBS
   ```

   could be written in the form

   ```
   READ (CI, *, END=300) OBS
   ```

   and still mean the same thing. In either form the computer will have no trouble interpreting it. But you and I might have some difficulty with the second form because we are not used to interpreting terms that are crammed together.

6. As each statement is described, it will be identified as being executable or nonexecutable. It may then be given a program unit location in accordance with the Fortran program organization specified in Chapter 3.

7. As a reminder, comment lines are not included in the Fortran statement descriptions because they are not considered to be Fortran statements; they are lines of documentation and spacing. Comment lines can appear anywhere in a program unit, as long as the last one comes before the END statement of that program unit. Any comment line occurring after an END statement is considered, by the compiler, to be contained in another program unit.

4-5   THREE FUNDAMENTAL STATEMENTS: PROGRAM, STOP, AND END

The three statements described here are the ones that appear first in an executable program and last in a program unit. From what you have already read, you probably know and understand them. However, it will be beneficial for you to have a formal description of them.

The PROGRAM statement is a nonexecutable statement that gives a name to the main program of an executable program. The form of the statement is

```
PROGRAM name
```

where name is the symbolic name of the main program as selected by the programmer.

A PROGRAM statement is not required to appear in an executable program. If one does appear, however, it must be the first statement (noncomment line) in the main program and the only PROGRAM statement in the executable program. Even though it is not a required statement, I recommend that you always include a PROGRAM statement in your main program because it provides you with a convenient means of referring to the program. It also makes it easy to find the beginning point of a main program and allows it to have an organization similar to the one required for subprograms.

The STOP statement is executable. Its purpose is to terminate the execution of the program. Its basic form is

```
STOP
```

Optionally, a number containing five digits or less, or a group of characters having an apostrophe at each end can be added after the P.

A STOP statement should be placed anywhere in a program unit that logic dictates. The logic of the algorithm you use determines its location. When it is encountered during execution, the STOP will cause program termination to occur and, usually, execution control to be restored to the operating system of the computer. A solution procedure may have more than one logical termination point, and therefore a program unit may have more than one STOP statement.

A program unit can have only one END statement, and every program unit—main program or subprogram—must have exactly one END statement. It must be the last line of each program unit. Its primary purpose is to indicate the end of the sequence of statements and comment lines in a program unit. Secondarily, it will terminate execution if encountered during execution of a main program or, if encountered during execution of a subprogram, will return execution control to the program unit that called for the subprogram to be executed.

Because of its secondary purpose, the END statement is an executable statement. Its form, the simplest of these three fundamental statements, is

```
END
```

From the above, you can see that an END statement could be used in the place of a STOP statement if the termination point of the program occurs right before the END statement in the main program. It is better practice to go ahead and use the STOP statement in this situation, and thus avoid the inconsistency created by the use of two different statements for program termination.

4-6 ELEMENTARY INPUT/OUTPUT

As you have learned from Chapters 2 and 3, the input of problem data values into the computer's memory is accomplished by the use of the READ statement. You have also learned that the output of solution data values from the computer's memory can be accomplished by the use of the WRITE statement. Further, you have observed in the programs of Chapters 2 and 3 that I made use of FORMAT statements in conjunction with the WRITE statements to establish a strictly defined arrangement of the printed output values.

The capability of using FORMAT statements for describing printed output is advantageous to have because it gives a programmer control over the appearance of results. To acquire the ability to code FORMAT statements, however, requires a good deal of concentrated study and practice which can be facilitated by a more in-depth knowledge of a number of other programming features that you have not yet studied in this book. Therefore, the presentation of FORMAT statements is held until Chapter 6, after these facilitating features have been covered. Here, we will consider two types of input/output statements that allow you to have an input/output programming capability, but to be free of any concern about the appearance of the printed results or, for that matter, the specific location of input data values in an input record. The statements are executable and are referred to as "list-directed input/output" statements.

4-6-1 List-Directed Input

The list-directed input statement can be written in the form

```
READ *, iolist
```

where the * indicates that the input operation is list-directed, and iolist is a group of variables for which values are to be read into memory from the next input record. The variables in the list must be separated by commas. The values contained in the input record must be separated by blanks, commas, or slashes. They will be assigned one by one, in sequence, to the variables in the list. For example, if the circumference of a circle is to be read into memory from an input record, use the statement

```
READ *, CIRCUM
```

in which the variable name CIRCUM has been chosen to represent the circumference. Then, the first value on the input record will be established in memory as the value of CIRCUM.

As another example, if the principal (PRIN), the interest rate (RATE), and the number of years (NYEARS) for an investment are to be read into memory from an input record, use the statement

```
READ *, PRIN, RATE, NYEARS
```

to accomplish the input operation. The values to be read in for PRIN, RATE, and NYEARS can be entered anywhere in the input record as long as they are in sequence and are separated by blanks or commas or slashes.

Notice that the foregoing form of the READ statement does not include an identification of the input device being used. In such a case, the computer system default device for the type of processing you are doing will be assumed, by the computer, to be the input device for data. If you are doing interactive execution through a terminal, the computer will look for your input values to be entered through the terminal. If your program is being compiled from punched cards, the computer will expect your input data to be in punched cards. There are more comprehensive forms of the list-directed READ statement that allow you to specify a particular input device and other useful items. They are covered in Chapter 6.

4-6-2   List-Directed Output

List-directed input can be referred to as ''free-format'' because input values can be entered anywhere in an input record as long as they appear in the ''iolist'' sequence and are separated. List-directed output, however, should be referred to as ''fixed-format'' because the Fortran processor, rather than the programmer, determines where and how the output values will be printed.

The simplest form of a list-directed output statement uses the keyword PRINT, rather than WRITE, and is coded as follows:

```
PRINT *, iolist
```

All other forms of output statements—covered in Chapters 6 and 12—use the keyword WRITE. As in the READ statement, the * indicates that the operation is list-directed and iolist is the group of variables whose values are to be printed. Additionally, though, this iolist can also contain numbers and messages to be printed. The output created by the PRINT statement will be displayed on your terminal if you are doing interactive work and, otherwise, will be sent to the printer for printing on paper.

List-directed output examples for the input examples above can be written as

```
PRINT *, CIRCUM
```

for the first one and

```
PRINT *, PRIN, RATE, NYEARS
```

for the second one. Alternatively, it is desirable to print a descriptive message so that the person who reads the output will know what the numbers are for. In algorithms, recall, messages are enclosed in single quotes (apostrophes). The same is true in the iolist of a PRINT statement.

For example, assume that the values of PRIN, RATE, and NYEARS read into memory by the list-directed READ are 1000, 0.10, and 2. Then the statements

```
READ *, PRIN, RATE, NYEARS
PRINT *, 'INVESTMENT DATA'
PRINT *, ' '
PRINT *, 'PRINCIPAL:   ', PRIN
PRINT *, 'INTEREST RATE:   ', RATE
PRINT *, 'NUMBER OF YEARS:   ', NYEARS
```

will yield the following printed output:

```
INVESTMENT DATA

PRINCIPAL:    1000.00
INTEREST RATE:    .100000
NUMBER OF YEARS:    2
```

The extra digits in the values of PRIN and RATE, and the extra space between the identifiers and their values are caused by the "fixed format" of the Fortran output processor. The blank line after the heading INVESTMENT DATA is caused by the third statement in the program segment: PRINT *, ' '.

For further study, a complete example program that uses list-directed input and output, as well as the other features of this chapter, is given in Section 4-9 after the following discussions about assignment and program control.

4-7 ELEMENTARY ASSIGNMENT

Reading external input data values into memory is one means of giving values to variables. Another method is to use the assignment statement to define values internally. The assignment statement corresponds to the "variable ← expression" algorithmic primitive described in Table 2-2. It is executable.

The simplest form of the Fortran assignment statement is

```
var = val
```

where var is a variable and val is a constant or variable or simple expression involving one arithmetic operation such as multiplication (*), division (/), addition (+), or subtraction (−). For examples, the statement

```
COUNT = 0
```

assigns the value 0 to the variable COUNT; the sequence of statements

```
HOLD  = ALPHA
ALPHA = BETA
BETA  = HOLD
```

interchanges the values of the variables ALPHA and BETA; the statement

```
COUNT = COUNT + 1
```

first adds 1 to the current value of the variable COUNT and then assigns the result as the new value of COUNT; and the statement

```
GRSPAY = HRSWKD * PARATE
```

multiplies the values of the variables HRSWKD and PARATE, assigning the resulting product to the variable GRSPAY. The more comprehensive form of the assignment statement, in which several arithmetic operations are specified, is discussed in Chapter 5.

4-8   ELEMENTARY PROGRAM CONTROL

Unless instructed otherwise by a program statement, the computer executes the action statements of a program in sequential order, one by one, from beginning to end. This sequential order of execution is a control logic structure called *simple sequence*.

One useful feature of the computer, however, is its ability to compare one value with another and then, based on the result of the comparison, to select one of two alternative statements or sequences of statements to execute. The comparison usually involves determining the truth or falsity of two values being equal, or one being less than or equal to another, or one being greater than another, and so on. This process involves a control structure known as *selection*.

A third control structure, *repetition* or *looping*, describes one of the most powerful attributes of the computer—its capability of being able to perform one or more instructions over and over again, as many times as necessary, doing them correctly every time.

These three control logic structures—simple sequence, selection, and repetition—are the fundamental building blocks of the action in a program. They are illustrated in general form in Figure 4-5 and have already been specifically applied in the algorithms and programs of Chapters 2 and 3 (see, for example, how

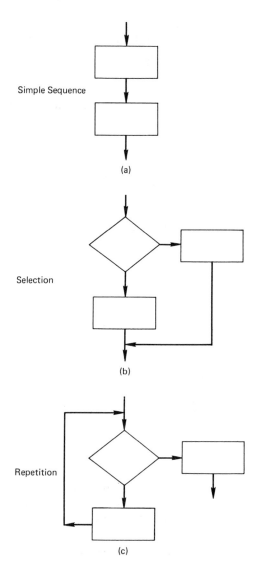

Figure 4-5. Fundamental Control Logic Structures: General Forms

the flowcharts given in Chapter 2 compare to the forms in Figure 4-5). When used properly, they lead to the development of a well-structured program. In the remainder of this major section, we examine elementary forms of Fortran statements that can be used to establish the selection and repetition structures. Advanced forms are described in Chapter 7.

4-8-1   Simple Selection

The block IF (or IF-THEN) statement is used with the ENDIF statement and, optionally, the ELSE statement to produce the simple selection structure. Taken together, the statements are usually coded in the form

```
IF (re) THEN
   .  {Statements to be
   .  executed whenever
   .  re is true}
ELSE
   .  {Statements to be
   .  executed whenever
   .  re is false}
ENDIF
```

where re is a relational expression. A relational expression involves the comparison of one value with another in an equality, inequality, greater than, greater than or equal to, less than, or less than or equal to context. The relational operators are shown in Figure 4-6.

For example, the following statement sequence compares an insurance premium (PRMIUM) with an allowable insurance deduction (ALLOWD) in order to determine the basic insurance deduction (BASDED) and the insurance premium balance (PREBAL) for the "Medical and Dental Expense" portion of an itemized Federal income tax return.

```
IF (PRMIUM .LT. ALLOWD) THEN
   BASDED = PRMIUM * 0.5
   PREBAL = BASDED
ELSE
   BASDED = ALLOWD
   PREBAL = PRMIUM − ALLOWD
ENDIF
```

The relational expression, PRMIUM .LT. ALLOWD, will be true if the value of PRMIUM is less than the value of ALLOWD. In such a case, the statements between THEN and ELSE will be executed and those between ELSE and ENDIF

Operator	Meaning (Mathematical)
.EQ.	Equality (=)
.NE.	Inequality (≠ or <>)
.GT.	Greater than (>)
.GE.	Greater than or equal to (>=)
.LT.	Less than (<)
.LE.	Less than or equal to (<=)

Figure 4-6. The Relational Operators

will be bypassed. Alternatively, the relational expression will be false if the value of PRMIUM is not less than the value of ALLOWD. In this case, the statements between THEN and ELSE will be bypassed and those between ELSE and ENDIF will be executed. Therefore, when PRMIUM=50.00 and ALLOWD=150.00, the computed values of BASDED and PREBAL will both be 25.00. In contrast, when PRMIUM=500.00 and ALLOWD=150.00, the computed values of BASDED and PREBAL will be 150.00 and 350.00 respectively.

There must always be exactly one ENDIF statement for each block IF statement; however, the ELSE and its block of statements are optional. For instance, the sequence

```
GRSPAY = HRSWKD * PARATE
IF (HRSWKD .GT. 40.0) THEN
    OTHRS = HRSWKD - 40.0
    OTDIF = PARATE * 0.5
    OTPAY = OTHRS * OTDIF
    GRSPAY = GRSPAY + OTPAY
ENDIF
```

can be used to compute a week's gross pay (GRSPAY) for an employee. First, the hours worked (HRSWKD) and pay rate (PARATE) are multiplied to obtain an initial value of the gross pay. Then the initial value is adjusted only if the hours worked exceed 40. When, for instance HRSWKD=40.0 and PARATE=10.50, the initial gross pay will not be adjusted because the relational expression, HRSWKD .GT. 40.0, will be false and, therefore, the statements between THEN and ENDIF will be bypassed. However, when HRSWKD=60.0 and PARATE=10.50 the relational expression will be true; the statements between THEN and ENDIF will therefore be executed, and the computed value of GRSPAY will be 735.00.

Notice, in the above general form and examples, that the statements between the block IF and ELSE statements are indented. The identation has no effect upon the execution; it is used for readability.

A special case of selection, in which only one statement is executed whenever the relational expression is true and is bypassed otherwise, can be conveniently performed by the use of a simpler IF statement known as the logical IF. The form of this statement is

```
IF (re) es
```

where es is the one executable statement to be executed only when re is true. An ENDIF is not used with the logical IF. Its associated algorithmic primitive is "If condition action."

The logical IF statement in this sequence from the arithmetic averaging program of Figure 3-1,

```
300 IF (COUNT .GT. 0) AVE = AVE / COUNT
    WRITE (PO, 930) AVE, COUNT
```

is used to make sure that a division by zero does not occur. The assignment statement

```
AVE = AVE / COUNT
```

is executed only if the value of COUNT is greater than zero. Then the WRITE statement is executed regardless of the value of COUNT. An equivalent segment, using the block IF, can be written like this:

```
300 IF (COUNT .GT. 0) THEN
        AVE = AVE / COUNT
    ENDIF
    WRITE (PO, 930) AVE, COUNT
```

4-8-2   Simple Repetition

Repetition of a sequence of statements, or looping, can be accomplished through the use of statements that alter the process of sequential execution by directing the computer to transfer execution control to an executable statement other than the next one in sequence. These transfers are termed *branching*. Branching can be programmed to take place conditionally or unconditionally.

Conditional branching is the action of transferring control to a statement, other than the next sequential one, based on the outcome of a test. Several different Fortran statements can be used for this purpose. They are described in Chapter 7.

Unconditional branching is the action of immediately transferring to a statement, other than the next sequential one, without first performing any kind of test. It is accomplished by the use of the GO TO statement, which has the form

```
GO TO stn
```

where stn is the statement number of the executable statement to which execution control is to be transferred. The GO TO statement corresponds to the "Go To label(direction)" algorithmic primitive. The statement labeled stn can be located backward or forward in the program unit; a direction indication is not included. The direction will be clear, however, if program unit statement numbers are always ordered in ascending sequence.

GO TO statements are to be used with care and caution—only when absolutely essential. A program unit with more than a very few GO TOs is suspect. Their indiscriminate and abundant use reflects a lack of proper planning. They create additional paths in a program, causing it to be more difficult to debug, understand, and maintain. In Fortran, however, the use of some GO TOs cannot be avoided. One valid and acceptable usage is explained below.

The IF-THEN and GO TO statements can be carefully combined to create a control logic structure that allows the repeated execution of a series of statements to occur for as long as a defined condition exists. The general form of this structure is depicted in flowchart form in Figure 4-5(c).

As an illustration, consider this problem: An unknown number of input records are available. Each record contains a pair of cost values in dollars. The last record has a negative cost value for the second cost of the pair to denote end-of-data. The higher cost of each pair of costs is to be determined. A small typical set of input records appears as follows.

```
1.55  1.75
0.38  0.35
2.79  2.78
0.98  1.03
-999  -999
```

The part of the program code that is of primary interest can then be written. For example:

```
200     READ *, FRCOST, SECOST
        IF (SECOST .GE. 0.0) THEN
            HICOST = FRCOST
            IF (SECOST .GT. HICOST) HICOST = SECOST
            PRINT *, 'OF THE COSTS  $', FRCOST,
     :                 ' AND  $', SECOST
            PRINT *, 'THE HIGHER IS  $', HICOST, '.'
            PRINT *, ' '
            GO TO 200
        ENDIF
        PRINT *, 'END OF COST COMPARISON.'
```

The repetition sequence, or loop, is established by the unconditional branching statement GO TO 200. The loop consists of all statements except the last PRINT statement. Statements in the loop are indented to make the loop easy to locate in a complete program. The IF−THEN statement is used to establish a test for determining whether the statements following it in the loop are to be executed or, alternatively, whether an exit from the loop is to occur. This exit test statement causes the loop to become finite—to have a termination point. All statements following it in the loop are further indented so that they are easy to recognize as being dependent on the test statement result for execution. The interpretation of this loop is that as long as SECOST is greater than or equal to zero, execute the statements in the loop following the exit test. Since the exit test is executed essentially at the beginning of the loop, this structure is sometimes called a *pretest loop*. It is also referred to as a *Do-while loop*—"Do the statements in the loop while SECOST is greater than or equal to zero." For the given input data, the printed output will, in part, look like this:

```
OF THE COSTS   $ 1.55000   AND   $ 1.75000
THE HIGHER IS   $ 1.75000   .

OF THE COSTS   $ .380000   AND   $ .350000
THE HIGHER IS   $ .380000   .
   .
   .
   .
OF THE COSTS $ .980000 AND $ 1.03000
THE HIGHER IS $ 1.03000   .

END OF COST COMPARISON.
```

4-9   AN EXAMPLE PROGRAM: SEARCH

A fairly common problem is that of locating the maximum and minimum value in a given set of numbers. Given that a group of input records each contain one number (a grade, an age, a temperature, a cost, etc.), the problem is to write a program to find and print the largest and smallest of the numbers.

To solve this problem with the programming tools we have considered thus far, assume first that a negative input number, invalid as an input value according to the problem statement, is used as an end-of-data indicator. A small typical set of input records might appear as shown below.

```
    100
    107
     92
    105
    105
     89
   -999
```

The output for these values may be expected to look something like this:

```
            INPUT NUMBERS

                100
                107
                 92
                105
                105
                 89

MAXIMUM:        107
MINIMUM:         89
```

Algorithm development, beginning from a broad view of the problem, can be accomplished in a few refinement stages. The first stage should take the form of a list of English sentences similar to the ones following.

As long as an input number is valid,
   print it,
   hold the maximum number so far, and
   hold the minimum number so far.
Then print the maximum number and
   the minimum number.
Then stop.

Indentation has been used in these sentences to provide a clear indication of some of the individual operations that are to be performed. Each sentence of the first stage can then be broken down into a group of more concise statements which describe the operations more precisely. For instance:

```
Read a number.
If the number is negative,
    print an error message and stop.
Else, let the number be the maximum and
    the minimum so far.
    While the numbers are not negative,
        read and print the next number;
        hold the number as maximum if it is
        larger than the current maximum; or
        hold the number as minimum if it is
        smaller than the current minimum.
    Print the maximum.
    Print the minimum.
Stop.
```

ALGORITHM Maxmin
```
{   Find and print the maximum and minimum value in a
given set of nonnegative input numbers.}

Write heading:    'INPUT NUMBERS'
Read number
Write number
If number < 0 Then
    Write message:   'FIRST VALUE SIGNALS END OF DATA',
                     'NO DATA'
Else
        max -- number                    {initialize max}
        min -- number                    {initialize min}
NEXT.       Read number
            If number >= 0 Then
                Write number
                If number > max Then
                    max ← number
                Else
                    If number < min Then
                        min ← number
                Go To NEXT. (Back)
        Write 'MAXIMUM: ', max
        Write 'MINIMUM: ', min
    Stop
    END
```

Figure 4-7. Algorithm for Finding the Maximum and Minimum

Further refinement, which includes adding rules for printing headings and messages, leads to a final formal algorithm such as the one in Figure 4-7. Then the flowchart, Figure 4-8, can be drawn. Finally, the program can be written. Figure

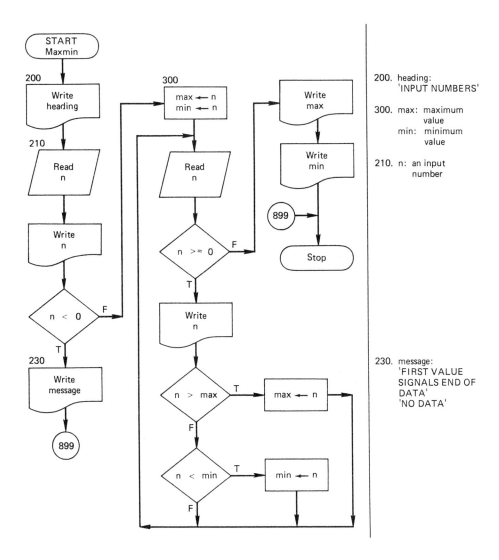

Figure 4-8. Flowchart for Finding the Maximum and Minimum (Find and print the maximum and minimum value in a given set of non-negative input numbers.)

```
*I.    MAXIMUM AND MINIMUM
*
       PROGRAM MAXMIN
*      PROGRAMMER:  JARRELL C. GROUT
*      DATE:  11/6/80
*
*  A. COMMENTARY
*
*          FIND AND PRINT THE MAXIMUM AND MINIMUM VALUE
*      IN A GIVEN SET OF NON-NEGATIVE INPUT NUMBERS.
*      NUMBERS ARE ENTERED ONE PER INPUT RECORD.  A
*      NEGATIVE INPUT NUMBER IS USED TO SIGNAL
*      END-OF-DATA-FILE.
*
*          DICTIONARY.
*      MAX:  THE MAXIMUM VALUE
*      MIN: THE MINIMUM VALUE
*      NUMBER:  AN INPUT VALUE
*
*  B. DECLARATION
*
       REAL  MAX, MIN, NUMBER
*
*  C. I/O LAYOUT
*
*      NONE:  LIST-DIRECTED I/O IS USED.
*
*  D. ACTION
*
       PRINT *, 'INPUT NUMBERS'
       PRINT *, ' '
       READ *, NUMBER
       PRINT *, NUMBER
       IF (NUMBER .LT. 0.0) THEN
          PRINT *, 'FIRST VALUE SIGNALS END OF DATA',
        :          'NO DATA'
       ELSE
          MAX = NUMBER
          MIN = NUMBER
   310    READ *, NUMBER
          IF (NUMBER .GE. 0.0) THEN
             PRINT *, NUMBER
             IF (NUMBER .GT. MAX) THEN
                MAX = NUMBER
             ELSE
                IF (NUMBER .LT. MIN) THEN
                   MIN = NUMBER
                ENDIF
             ENDIF
             GO TO 310
          ENDIF
          PRINT *, ' '
          PRINT *, 'MAXIMUM: ', MAX
          PRINT *, 'MINIMUM: ', MIN
       ENDIF
       STOP
       END
```

Figure 4-9. Program for Finding the Maximum and Minimum

4-9 contains the complete program, which consists of not only the Action statements corresponding to the algorithm and flowchart, but also the Commentary, Declaration, and I/O Layout information. Print statements for line spacing have also been included in the Action.

In the Action section of the program, observe the indentation (loop and dependent statements are indented so that they can be easily located), and study the use of the selection and repetition control structures as discussed in this chapter. In the Declaration section, observe that the program variables MAX, MIN, and

```
INPUT NUMBERS
100.000
107.000
92.0000
105.000
105.000
89.0000

MAXIMUM:  107.000
MINIMUM:  89.0000
```

Figure 4-10. Results of a Computer Run on Program Maxmin

NUMBER are identified as having REAL numeric values. These are the kind of numbers you are most used to. The REAL data type is covered in detail, with others, in Chapter 5.

For your further understanding of this program, the actual printed results— using the input data given earlier—are shown in Figure 4-10. Observe that the output contains the headings, identifiers, and values that were expected, but the numbers are not centered. They also contain more digit positions than are necessary. This is due to the use of list-directed output—the Fortran processor controls the formatting. As an exercise, you might find it worthwhile to prepare and run the program on your computer.

4-10 EXERCISES

1. Interpret each of the following statements by discussing exactly what happens when the computer executes each one individually.

   (a) READ *, LENGTH, BREDTH, HEIGHT

   (b) IF (OUTGO .GT. INCOME) LOSS = GREAT

   (c) PRINT *, GROSS, TAXES, INSUR, NET

   (d) IF (RADIUS .GT. 0.0) THEN

   (e) STOP

2. Below you are given a program segment (part of a program Action section) and several input records. Write down exactly what will be printed by the computer when it executes the program with the input data.

   Program segment:

```
      PRINT *, 'SALES LIST'
280      READ *, PARTNO
         IF (PARTNO .GT. 0) THEN
            SALE = 0
            READ *, UPRICE, ONHAND
            READ *, REQEST
            IF (REQEST .LE. ONHAND) SALE = REQEST
            PRINT *, PARTNO, REQEST, SALE, UPRICE
            GO TO 280
         ENDIF
      PRINT *, 'END OF SALES LIST'
```

Input records:

```
4200
10.5    2000
100
4210
15.00    600
3000
4220
9.00    50
50
-9999
```

3. Below you are given a program segment. Discuss the control structure used to establish the loop. What, if anything, is good about it? What is bad about it? Rewrite it to improve it. (*Hint:* Look closely at the GO TOs, especially the one with the logical IF.)

```
        READ *, LIMIT
280     READ *, PRICE, DISC
        IF (PRICE .GT. LIMIT) GO TO 300
            PRINT *, PRICE, DISC
            GO TO 280
300 PRINT *, 'END OF DISCOUNT LIST'
```

4. Plan and write a complete Fortran program to print information about yourself: your full name, date of birth, place of birth, current address (street or box, city, state, zip), and any other descriptive information items. Then print a brief paragraph in which you tell why you are learning programming. Make it all look nice and make it easy to understand. Use descriptive identifiers for the individual items, such as

```
NAME: JEREMIAH CARLTON FITZHUGH
DATE OF BIRTH: FEBRUARY 29, 1964
```

5. Write a complete Fortran program for the flowchart in Figure 2-8. The problem, to write out two input numbers in order of larger and then smaller, is also solved in algorithmic form in Chapter 2. Rather than using a, b, and h for the variable names—as used in the algorithm and flowchart—use ALPHA, BETA, and HOLD. Assume that the numbers are real numbers. Print the output with some descriptive identifying information (title, and designation of larger and smaller).

6. Change Exercise 5 above to say that the numbers are to be written out from smaller to larger. Consider carefully the program changes that are necessary. Plan and write the complete program.

7. Make the modifications necessary to turn the Maxmin program of this chapter into one that also finds and prints the range (algebraic difference between the smallest and largest) of the input numbers. Modify algorithm, flowchart, and program completely.

8. Write a complete program to read, find, and print the sum of each of several pairs of nonnegative numbers, each pair of which is entered into one input record.

9. An assignment statement of the form

    ```
    var  = var  + 1
    ```

    can be conveniently used for instructing the computer to count the number of items in a set of items. In the form, the use of var indicates that the same variable name appears on both sides of the = sign, as in

    ```
    COUNT  = COUNT  + 1
    ```

    In order to perform a counting operation, the variable must first be given an initial value, usually zero, as in

    ```
    COUNT  = 0
    ```

    The counting operation is then performed by placing the initialization statement above a loop and the counting statement within the loop. Given this information, write a program to read, print, and count the exam grades in a set. Use the name NGRADE, rather than COUNT, for the counting variable. The grades are entered one per input record. Be sure and print the number of grades.

10. Below you are given a program segment and an input record. Write down exactly what will be printed by the computer when it executes the program with the data value. Use the information given in Exercise 9 to help you understand the code. Explain in English what the program segment does. Flowchart the segment and discuss the control structure used for looping.

    Program segment:

    ```
        POSSUM = 0
        LOOKER = 1
        READ *, LIMIT
    380 IF (LOOKER .LE. LIMIT) THEN
            POSSUM = POSSUM + LOOKER
            LOOKER = LOOKER + 1
            GO TO 380
        ENDIF
        PRINT *, 'FOR ', LIMIT, ' THE ANSWER IS ', POSSUM
    ```

    Input record:

    ```
    9
    ```

11. Plan and write a complete Fortran program to compute the medical and dental (m&d) expense deduction of a Federal income tax return. Concisely stated, the m&d expense deduction is equal to a basic insurance deduction plus a deduction for allowed m&d expenses that exceed three percent of a

person's adjusted gross income. The allowed m&d expenses include insurance premiums paid in excess of the basic insurance deduction, drug and medicine costs that exceed one percent of a person's gross income, and other m&d costs such as those for doctors, dentists, hospitals, eyeglasses, and so on.

The input to your program consists of an adjusted gross income, an insurance premium, an incurred cost for drugs, and an incurred cost for other m&d expenses. The basic insurance deduction is equal to one-half of the insurance premium if the insurance premium is less than $150; otherwise, it is equal to $150. Use these variable names:

AGRINC: Adjusted Gross Income

BASDED: Basic insurance deduction

BASEMD: Base for computing allowable m&d expenses (3% of AGRINC)

DEDMDE: Deduction for m&d expenses

DGBASE: Base for computing allowable drug expense (1% of AGRINC)

DGCOST: Incurred cost for drugs

DRUGDN: Drug deduction (drug cost above 1% of AGRINC)

OTHMED: Incurred cost for other m&d expenses

PREBAL: Premium balance above basic deduction

PRMIUM: Insurance premium

Then use this statement in your declaration section:

```
REAL AGRINC, BASDED, BASEMD, DEDMDE, DGBASE, DGCOST,
:     DRUGDN, OTHMED, PREBAL, PRMIUM
```

Chapter

5

Numbers

The Fortran language was originally designed to be used primarily for performing arithmetic operations—numeric processing. After more than two decades of use and improvement, and now as FORTRAN 77, it is capable of much more than just numeric processing. At that, even its numeric-processing capabilities have been vastly improved, and it is extremely useful and usable in that respect.

The purpose of this chapter is to explore Fortran's capabilities for operating on numbers after they have been stored in memory. In Chapter 6, additional means for getting the numbers into and out of memory will be considered.

5-1 TYPES OF NUMBERS

In a Fortran program, numbers are used mainly as constants, values of variables, values of array elements, or values of functions. Only base 10 numbers are used. However, just as you and I think of numbers in different forms, such as whole numbers and fractions, Fortran operates on numbers of different types. The different types exist principally to take advantage of the way the computer is designed to store numbers internally—using words, bytes, and bits.

There are four types, or modes, of numbers in Fortran: integer, real, double precision, and complex. These are referred to as numeric *data types*. Every number of each data type can be written with a plus or minus sign to indicate whether it is positive or negative, but none of the numbers can contain any commas. The first three of these types are discussed below.

5-1-1 Integer Numbers

An *integer* is a whole number that must be written without a decimal point or fractional part. Another common designation for integer number is *fixed-point number*.

Each integer is normally stored in pure binary form and usually occupies one word of memory. Then the number of bits in the word determines the range of decimal integers that can be represented. For example, if the word size is 32 bits and one of the bits is used to denote the plus or minus sign, the remaining 31 bits can represent all the whole numbers in the range 0 through $2^{31} - 1$, or 2147483647, inclusive. Remember though, different computers have different word sizes. They may, therefore, represent different ranges of integers.

5-1-2 Real Numbers

A *real number* is one that is written with a decimal point and, if necessary, a real exponent. Real numbers are sometimes called *floating-point numbers*. The form of a real number, left to right, is as follows: an optional plus or minus sign, an integer part, a decimal point, a fractional part, and an optional real exponent. Either the integer part or the fractional part, but not both, may be omitted. The real exponent denotes a power of 10.

The form of a real exponent is the letter E followed by an optionally signed integer constant. Ordinarily, most real numbers that are used in programs and data can be written without exponents. The value of a real number that contains a real exponent is the product of the number that precedes the E and the power of 10 indicated by the integer following the E. Figure 5-1 contains several examples of real numbers written in mathematical form and Fortran real form. It also has the double-precision equivalents, which are discussed in Section 5-1-3.

The numbers in Figure 5-1 are arranged in ascending numerical sequence only for purposes of this illustration—to help you see the Fortran equivalents in relation to each other. Notice that numbers which may be written as fractions or whole numbers in mathematical form (such as ⅛, 0, and −1), are written with a decimal point in Fortran real form. Also observe that the exponent portion of a number in mathematical form consists of an ×, to indicate multiplication, followed by the number 10 and then a positive or negative integral power of 10. The Fortran real-form equivalent is the letter E followed by the positive or negative integral power of 10. Thus the E effectively takes the place of ×10 in this form. It

Mathematical	Fortran Real	Fortran Double Precision
−272.2	−272.2	−272.2D0
−1	−1.0	−1.0D0
-0.1×10^{-10}	−0.1E−10	−1p'1D−10
0	0.0	0.0D0
1.6021×10^{-19}	1.6021E−19	1.6021D−19
1/8	0.125	0.125D0
2.71828	2.71828	2.71828D0
2.9979×10^{8}	2.9979E8	2.9979D8

Figure 5-1. Numbers in Mathematical and Fortran Forms

is ordinarily beneficial to include a real exponent only when the number is very small or very large, as in the case of several scientific constants. So for readability, real numbers should usually be written without the real exponent.

In similarity with integers, real numbers are usually stored in one computer word, and one bit in the word is used to denote the sign of the number. In contrast to integers, however, the remaining bits must not only represent the integer portion of the real number; they must also represent the fractional portion and the real exponent portion (whether or not a real exponent is initially written into the number).

The maximum number of significant digits in a real number is limited by the number of bits available to represent the integer and fractional digits. For a 32-bit word computer, real numbers can contain up to about seven significant digits and have real exponents that vary from about −78 to +75. Larger word sizes allow more significant digits and smaller word sizes usually further restrict the maximum number of significant digits. It all depends on the computer you use and the way the real numbers are handled in that computer; it does not depend on Fortran.

5-1-3   Double-Precision Numbers

Seven significant digits are sufficient for solving many problems that involve the use of real numbers, but there are problems that require more digits. For the solution of these problems, double-precision numbers can be used.

A *double-precision number* is similar to a real number, but it is ordinarily stored in two consecutive words in memory; thus it contains at least twice as many bits and, therefore, it can have at least twice as many decimal digits as a real number.

Double-precision numbers are written in a form similar to that of real numbers having real exponents except that a D is used in place of an E to precede the exponent. If you will look back at Figure 5-1, you can see how double-precision numbers are written in Fortran and how they compare with the mathematical and Fortran real forms. Although none of the double-precision numbers in the figure contain more decimal digits than their corresponding mathematical and Fortran real numbers, they will contain more bits in memory. For example, in a 32-bit-word computer, a double-precision number is ordinarily stored in two consecutive words, for a total of 64 bits. When 8 bits are used for the sign and exponent, 56 bits are available for the significant digits. This is equivalent to about 17 decimal digits. Therefore, it is possible to have 17-digit precision if the computer has a 32-bit word length, and more or less precision with more or fewer bits per word.

You should not, however, use double-precision numbers in a program indiscriminately. Since they take up double the amount of memory compared to real numbers, you are wasting memory by using them when you do not need more digits than real numbers have. You are also wasting computer time because, ordinarily, the more bits involved in an operation, the more computer time required.

5-2 DECLARING NUMERIC DATA TYPES

Each numeric variable and constant in a Fortran program can only have a value that is one of the four data types discussed in Section 5-1. In order to compile a program unit so that it will execute properly, the compiler must be told the data type of each variable and constant that appears in the program unit. This is usually accomplished by means of explicit declaration or default recognition.

5-2-1 *Explicit Declaration*

As described in Section 5-1, numbers written as constants in a program are known, by the compiler, to be of the appropriate type due to the way in which they are written. In contrast, numeric variable and symbolic constant types can be explicitly declared through the use of the type statements: INTEGER, REAL, and DOUBLE PRECISION. These statements are also used to specify the data types of array names and functions (discussed later). They are placed in the Declaration section of a program unit.

The INTEGER statement identifies the variables and symbolic constants that are to have integer values in the program unit. Its form is

    INTEGER list

where the list contains the symbolic names of the variables and constants whose values are integer numbers. As many names as necessary can appear in the list, and commas are used to separate them. As an example, the kilometer conversion program of Figure 2-12(a) contains the statement

    INTEGER KILOS, PO

which specifies that KILOS and PO have integer values in the program unit. Actually, PO is a symbolic constant that has the value 6 throughout the program unit, whereas KILOS is a variable that has integer values varying from 1 through 10.

The REAL statement is used to designate the variables and symbolic constants that are to have real number values in the program unit. The form of this statement is

    REAL list

where the list consists of symbolic names of the variables and constants whose values are real numbers. In similarity to the INTEGER statement, as many names as necessary can appear in the list.

With reference again back to the kilometer conversion program of Figure 2-12(a), the statement

    REAL MILES

declares that the variable MILES is to have real number values. Then, Figure 2-12(b) shows that the printed values of MILES are real numbers, varying from 0.62 through 6.21.

Figure 3-1 has the statement

```
REAL  AVE, HIOBS, LOWOBS, OBS
```

which specifies that the variables AVE, HIOBS, LOWOBS, and OBS have real number values. HIOBS and LOWOBS are defined with the real values +999.99 and −999.99 in the PARAMETER statement of the program. A glance at Figure 3-2 will verify the specification for AVE and OBS.

The DOUBLE PRECISION statement declares that the symbolic names in its list have double precision values. Its form is

```
DOUBLE PRECISION  list
```

As an arbitrary example, say that the variables DELTA, GAMMA, NU, and IOTA require more digits than are provided by real numbers, and that the symbolic constant PI is to be equal to the 11-digit number 3.1415926536. The statement specifying the needed digits of precision is easily written as

```
DOUBLE PRECISION  DELTA, GAMMA, NU, IOTA, PI
```

5-2-2 *Default Recognition*

It is possible to avoid explicit declarations for integer and real symbolic names, and to let the compiler recognize the numeric data type of a symbolic name by default. Although it is possible, and frequently done, the use of the default recognition is not necessarily good practice. Let me explain what I mean.

If a variable or symbolic constant is used in a program unit but does not appear in a type statement of that program unit, the compiler assumes its data type to be integer or real based on its first character. In the absence of an explicit declaration, a first character of I, J, K, L, M, or N implies integer type, and any other first character (letter) implies real type. Thus the symbolic names KILOS, MILES, LOWOBS, NU, and IOTA would be treated as being integers, and PO, AVE, HIOBS, OBS, DELTA, GAMMA, and PI would be treated as being real unless explicit declarations dictated otherwise.

The default recognition has been available in Fortran longer than the explicit declaration, and many Fortran programs have been written containing symbolic names for which no explicit declarations have been made. As one result, real variable names such as RMILES, XNET, and ZMAX have been created and used where MILES, NETPAY, and MAX might have been more descriptive. Similarly, integer variable names such as IWT, JTIME, and KOUNT have been devised and used where WEIGHT, TIME, and COUNT might have been more descriptive.

The use of descriptive symbolic names is important because it helps to make programs readable and understandable. Furthermore, by explicitly declaring data types, you can use descriptive names without having to impose a confusing first letter on the names in order to fit the default. You can then simply glance at your declarations and quickly identify the data type of every symbolic constant and variable in a program unit. It is worthwhile, therefore, to use descriptive symbolic names and explicitly declare data types. Specifically, you should use descriptive, meaningful names for all symbolic constants and variables; then include, in appropriate type statements, the names of all symbolic constants and every variable associated with input or output.

5-2-3 Exercises on Numbers and Data Types

1. Designate each of the following as integer, real, double-precision, or invalid Fortran numbers.
   - (a) 1/4
   - (b) 1990
   - (c) 0.17320508E+1
   - (d) 3.1623
   - (e) $\sqrt{4}$
   - (f) 1234567.E50
   - (g) 1.414213562D0
   - (h) −2.71828
   - (i) −2147483650
   - (j) $1.125 \times 10-4$
   - (k) −360
   - (l) π

2. Identify the data type, based on the defaults, of each of the valid symbolic names in the list below. For those that are invalid, state why.
   - (a) RATE
   - (b) DISTANCE
   - (c) B12VIT
   - (d) 1TIME
   - (e) MONTH
   - (f) $MONEY
   - (g) NX-ONE
   - (h) NUMBR9

3. Interpret the three statements below.

```
INTEGER  DAY, INCDAY, MONTH, WEEK, YEAR
REAL  HOUR, INCSEC, MINUTE, SECOND
DOUBLE PRECISION  INTIME, OUTIME
```

5-3 SPECIFYING SYMBOLIC NUMERIC CONSTANTS

Numbers can be used freely as constants. Also, as implied earlier, symbolic names can be given to numeric constants. This is accomplished by the use of the PARAMETER statement.

The form of the PARAMETER statement is

```
PARAMETER  (sn=ce, ...)
```

where sn is a symbolic name, ce is an arithmetic constant expression, and the ellipses indicate that other symbolic names and constant expressions can also be included within the parentheses. The PARAMETER statement is placed in the Declaration section of a program unit.

The effect of this nonexecutable statement is to cause each symbolic name in the list to be defined, prior to execution, with the value of its corresponding constant expression. The name can then be used, elsewhere in the program unit, in place of the actual number.

An arithmetic constant expression (the "ce" part of the statement) is made up of numbers, previously defined symbolic numeric constants, and arithmetic operators, and its value is determined in accordance with the rules for arithmetic assignment statements discussed later in the chapter. The simplest form of arithmetic constant expression consists of one number.

Once a symbolic constant has been defined in the PARAMETER statement of a program unit, it cannot be redefined in that program unit. It is particularly useful to define a constant by this means whenever the constant is repeated several times in a program unit. As you may have noticed, I used symbolic constants as input and output device identifiers in the kilometer conversion program (Figure 2-12) and the arithmetic averaging program (Figure 3-1). Other uses are depicted in programs of later chapters.

If, for instance, I chose the symbolic name PI for the well-known constant which is the ratio of the circumference to the diameter of a circle, I could define it by including the lines

```
REAL  PI
PARAMETER  (PI= 3.14159)
```

in the Declaration section of my program unit. In another situation, I might need to have a more precise value of PI, such as the one mentioned in the section on double precision. If so, I would use the following two statements:

```
DOUBLE PRECISION  PI
PARAMETER  (PI= 3.1415926536D0)
```

5-4   INITIALIZING NUMERIC VARIABLES

Variables can also be given values prior to execution by means of another nonexecutable statement: the DATA statement. The basic form of the DATA statement is

```
DATA  nlist/vlist/, ...
```

where nlist contains variable names, vlist contains numeric values for the variables, and the ellipses indicate that other sets of nlist and vlist, as needed, can also be present. The items within nlist and vlist are separated by commas. The DATA statement is placed in the Declaration section of a program unit; it must not, however, appear before any type statement or PARAMETER statement. The value list (vlist) can contain numeric constants and previously defined symbolic names of numeric constants.

The basic purpose of this statement is to provide initial values for the corresponding variables—values that are defined prior to execution but which may be changed during execution. The first value in a vlist corresponds to the first variable name in the nlist preceding that vlist, the second value corresponds to the second variable name, and so on. Thus each nlist and its vlist must have the same number of entries and each set of corresponding entries must be of the same numeric data type. More comprehensive applications of the DATA statement allow initial values to be assigned to variables and array elements having non-numeric, as well as numeric, data types. These applications are described at appropriate points in the text.

I could have used a DATA statement, rather than a PARAMETER statement, to define values for CI and PO in the example program of Figure 3-1 by writing

```
DATA  CI, PO /5, 6/
```

CI would thus have had an initial value of 5, PO an initial value of 6, and the program would then have worked just as well as before. I did not do this because CI and PO actually have unchanging values in the program—I want them to remain constant and never change during the execution of the program unit in which they are defined. This is, however, one of the ways that many Fortran programmers used the DATA statement before FORTRAN 77 became available with its PARAMETER statement.

Another way of writing the DATA statement above is

```
DATA  CI, PO /
:        5,  6 /
```

By writing it this way, with the variables on one line and the values on a continuation line, variables can be placed above their corresponding values for readability.

As another example of the use of the DATA statement, say that the real variables BOTTOM and TOP are to have values of 0.0 and 100.0, the integer variable LOWER is to have a value of 0, and the double-precision variable DIFF is to have a value of 0.00000001. This can all be accomplished by the following sequence of declaration statements:

```
INTEGER  LOWER
REAL  BOTTOM, TOP
DOUBLE PRECISION  DIFF
DATA  LOWER, BOTTOM,    TOP,    DIFF /
:             0,     0.0, 100.0, 1.0D-8 /
```

If the values of the variables above do not change during execution, this method of assigning values is satisfactory. Otherwise, however, it would be wiser to initialize with assignment statements—discussed later in this chapter. Perhaps the most useful feature of the DATA statement, explained in Chapter 8, is the capability it provides for initializing values of array elements.

5-5 AN EXERCISE ON THE PARAMETER AND DATA STATEMENTS

Interpret the following statements:

```
INTEGER  INCDAY, YEAR
REAL  INCSEC, SECOND
PARAMETER  (INCDAY=1, INCSEC=0.001)
DATA  SECOND, YEAR /
:          0.0, 1900 /
```

5-6 THE ARITHMETIC ASSIGNMENT STATEMENT

The arithmetic assignment statement is one of four assignment statements available in Fortran. The other three, covered in later chapters, are for use with other data types (logical and character) and assignment of statement labels.

The purpose of the arithmetic assignment statement is to define the numeric value of a variable or array element through the evaluation of an arithmetic expression. The statement is executable, and its form is

var = ae

where var represents the name of the variable or array element whose value is to be defined, and ae represents an arithmetic expression. The execution of an arithmetic assignment statement causes the arithmetic expression (ae) to be evaluated by the rules described in the next section, then conversion—if necessary—of that value to the data type of the variable var, and finally, assignment of the converted value to var.

It is important for you to know that the value of ae and the value of var are usually of the same data type (INTEGER, REAL, or DOUBLE PRECISION), but they can be of different types. For example, the value of ae may be real while the value of var is integer. The data type of ae depends on the data types of its contents, whereas the data type of var depends upon its own type declaration.

Examples of assignment statements, taken from the programs of Chapters 2, 3, and 4, are listed and explained below.

KILOS = 1: Here, var is KILOS and ae is 1, a constant. Both are of integer type. The result is the assignment of the value 1 to KILOS.

MIN = NUMBER: MIN, an integer variable, is var and NUMBER, also an integer variable, is ae. The current value of NUMBER is assigned to MIN. NUMBER retains its value.

KILOS = KILOS + 1: KILOS, to the left of =, is var; KILOS + 1 is ae. Again, both are of integer type. The arithmetic expression value is the current value of KILOS plus 1. Thus, when the current value of KILOS is 8, the new value of KILOS becomes 9. (After the assignment of 9, the 8 is lost.)

AVE = AVE / COUNT: (As part of a logical IF statement.) The leftmost real variable, AVE, is to be assigned the current value of AVE divided by COUNT. If, for example, the current value of AVE is 720.0 and the value of COUNT is 10, the newly assigned value of AVE will be 72.0.

5-7 ARITHMETIC EXPRESSIONS

An arithmetic expression is used to express a numeric computation. Thus the evaluation of an arithmetic expression produces a numeric value—a number of type integer, real, or double precision.

Writing an arithmetic expression in Fortran is a lot like writing an arithmetic expression in mathematics. In each case, an expression is formed by using operands, operators, and parentheses. Operands are quantities upon which operations are performed. Operators are symbols that specify operations such as addition, subtraction, and multiplication. Parentheses are always used in pairs, the same way they are used in mathematics, to cause the operations in an expression to be performed in a desired order. Wherever parentheses are not present, the order in which the operands are combined is determined by the evaluation rules discussed shortly in this section. You should feel free to use parentheses as much as you wish, to force the evaluation order to be in a certain sequence; or as little as you wish, to let the compiler use the rules to determine the sequence of evaluation.

The simplest form of an arithmetic expression consists of one operand—an unsigned constant, the symbolic name of a constant, a variable name, an array element reference, or a function reference (discussed in Section 5-8)—and no operators or parentheses. The value of such an expression is simply the value of the operand. For example, in the assignment statement

```
KILOS = 1
```

the arithmetic expression is the constant operand 1.

More complicated arithmetic expressions involve the use of one or more of the following operators:

**	for exponentiation
*	for multiplication
/	for division
+	for addition or identity
−	for subtraction or negation

One of the operators above must always be present to specify an arithmetic operation; no arithmetic operation is ever just "understood" as is sometimes the case in mathematics (e.g., *AB* in a mathematical expression may mean *A* times *B*; which, in Fortran, must be written A*B.)

The first three of the operators above, **, *, and /, always operate on two operands. In use, each is written between the two operands upon which the operation is to be performed. Thus in the expression

```
PI * RADIUS ** 2
```

the operand RADIUS is to be exponentiated by (raised to the power of) the operand 2, and the resulting operand is to be multiplied by the operand PI.

The operators + and − either operate on two operands, for addition and subtraction, or each operates on a single operand and is written preceding that operand. In the latter case, the operations are "identity" for + and "negation" for −. For example, the fairly complicated quadratic root expression,

```
(−B − SQRT(B**2 − 4.0 * A * C)) / (2.0 * A)
```

contains one negation (− B) and two subtraction operations.

Two or more operators appearing in an arithmetic expression can never be written next to each other. Therefore,

```
ALPHA * − BETA
```

is invalid. However, it is sometimes convenient to use negation or identity in conjunction with one of the other operators. When so, the negation or identity operation is enclosed in parentheses. Thus the expression

```
ALPHA * (− BETA)
```

is acceptable.

The rules for evaluating arithmetic expressions are based on a precedence among the arithmetic operators that determines the order in which operations are to be performed unless the order is changed by the use of parentheses. The precedence of the arithmetic operators is shown in Figure 5-2. The meaning of the precedence relationships is that, where parentheses are not used to establish the operation evaluation sequence, all ** operations are first evaluated right to left, then * and / operations are evaluated one by one in a left-to-right fashion, and finally + and − operations are evaluated one by one in a left-to-right order.

Operator	Precedence Level
**	Highest
*, /	Mid
+, −	Lowest

Figure 5-2. Arithmetic Operator Precedence

1. Substitute the appropriate values for all variables and symbolic constants in the expression.
2. If the expression contains no parentheses, go on to rule 4.
3. Select a part of the expression that is bounded by one left and one right parenthesis and contains no other parentheses. (This part can be called a "subexpression.") Perform rules 4 through 9, on this part, in sequence.
4. Determine the value of each ** operation in right-to-left order.
5. Determine the value of each * and / operation, as it occurs, in left-to-right order.
6. Determine the value of each + and − operation, as it occurs, in left-to-right order.
7. Remove the bounding left and right parentheses, if any.
8. If this evaluation is for an array element reference (Chapter 8) or function reference (Section 5-8), substitute the appropriate value.
9. Repeat rules 2 through 8 until a numeric value (real, integer, or double precision) is obtained for the expression.

Figure 5-3. Evaluating Arithmetic Expressions

A more comprehensive explanation of the evaluation rules is given in Figure 5-3. To illustrate how the rules work, several evaluation examples are included in Figure 5-4. In the examples, the evaluation rules are applied step by step to show you how to apply them. You should study the explanation and the examples, and then practice using the rules—first with simple expressions and then with fairly complex expressions—until you understand them well.

1. Given that MOST=25 and LEAST=10, evaluate

   (a) MOST − MOST / LEAST * LEAST

       25 − 25   / 10 * 10   {substitution of values}

       25 −   2   * 10

       25 −   20

               5

   (b) (MOST − MOST) / (LEAST * LEAST)

       (25 − 25) / (10 * 10)   {substitution}

           0   /   100

              0

   (c) (MOST − LEAST) / (LEAST * MOST)

       (25 − 10) / (10 * 25)   {substitution}

         15   /   250

             0

Figure 5-4. Examples of Expression Evaluation (In these examples, data types for variables are governed by first letters unless otherwise specified.)

2. Given that ALPHA = 5.0 and BETA = 2.5, evaluate
    (a) ALPHA − (BETA + (ALPHA − ALPHA / BETA))
        5.0 − (2.5 + (5.0 − 5.0 / 2.5))   {substitution}

        5.0 − (2.5 + (5.0 −   2.0   ))

        5.0 − (2.5 +   3.0   )

        5.0 −   5.5

               − 0.5
    (b) ALPHA − BETA + ALPHA − ALPHA / BETA
        5.0 −   2.5 + 5.0 −   5.0 / 2.5   {substitution}

        5.0 −   2.5 + 5.0 −   2.0

          2.5   + 5.0 −   2.0

                 7.5   −   2.0

                        5.5

3. Given that HEIGHT = 5.0, LENGTH = 3, and WIDTH = 4.0, evaluate

        HEIGHT * LENGTH * WIDTH
         5.0 *   3   * 4.0 {substitution}
                   ↓
         5.0 *   3.0 * 4.0

             15.0   * 4.0

                    60.0

4. Given that PI is double precision and equal to 3.1415926536, and
    RADIUS = 2.0, evaluate

        PI * RADIUS ** 2
        3.1415926536D0 * 2.0 ** 2 {substitution}

        3.1415926536D0 *   4.0
                              ↓
        3.1415926536D0 *   4.0D0

             12.5663706144D0

5. Given that HIGH = 15.5, LOW = 2, and ANGLE = 2.0, evaluate

        7.0 * ANGLE / (LOW ** 4 − HIGH) / ANGLE
        7.0 * 2.0 / (2 ** 4 − 15.5) / 2.0 {substitution}
        7.0 * 2.0 / (16   − 15.5) / 2.0
                          ↓
        7.0 * 2.0 / (16.0 − 15.5) / 2.0

        7.0 * 2.0 /   0.5   / 2.0

           14.0   /   0.5   / 2.0

                 28.0   / 2.0

                            14.0

Figure 5-4. (Continued)

6. This expression contains the function SQRT, which computes a square root value. Given that X = 3.0 and Y = 4.0, evaluate

```
(-X + SQRT (X ** 2 + Y * Y)) / Y
(-3.0 + SQRT(3.0 ** 2 + 4.0 * 4.0)) / 4.0   {substitution}

(-3.0 + SQRT(    9.0    + 4.0 * 4.0)) / 4.0

(-3.0 + SQRT(    9.0    +    16.0  )) / 4.0

(-3.0 + SQRT            25.0          ) / 4.0

(-3.0 +   5.0                         ) / 4.0

        2.0                            / 4.0

                                       0.5
```

Figure 5-4. (Continued)

As you examine the arithmetic expressions of Figure 5-4, you may be surprised to find that some of them contain mixtures of integer, real, and double-precision operands. You might have expected that all the operands in an expression would have to be of the same data type. The 1966 Fortran standard does inherently have some restrictions on the mixing of data types (often called *mixed mode*), and you should look into them if you use a compiler based on that standard. But FORTRAN 77 has no such restrictions on integer, real, or double-precision data. It is, therefore, more representative of actual computation situations, and is more convenient to use.

Of course, the numeric value resulting from an arithmetic operation between two operands has only one data type. It should be clear to you that if the two operands have the same data type, the result will also have that data type. But when the two operands have different data types, the determination of the type of the result is based on rules that are paraphrased and illustrated in Figure 5-5. Examine closely the way in which the rules of Figure 5-5 are applied in examples 3 through 6 of Figure 5-4. Be sure that you understand the rules. The mixing of these data types, although unrestricted in Fortran, should not be done arbitrarily. Unexpected results can occur. You should know, at all times, what type of result to expect from your arithmetic expressions.

Particular attention needs to be given, at this point, to what occurs when a division operation takes place between two integer operands. The resulting data type should be no mystery to you—it will be integer. Think about what that means. Integers are whole numbers; they do not have decimal points or fractional parts. Therefore, when the integer 8 is divided by the integer 3, the result is the integer 2, not 2.6666... or 3! This is an important point; don't overlook it or treat it lightly. In Figure 5-4, example 1 contains some integer divisions that illustrate the point.

The following paraphrased rules apply to any part of an arithmetic expression that has the form

    opd1 opr opd2

where opd1 and opd2 are operands of two different numeric data types (integer, real, double precision) and opr is an arithmetic operator.

1. When opr is +, −, *, or /.
    (a) If either opd1 or opd2 is double precision, find the double-precision equivalent of the other operand and then perform the operation. The result is of double-precision type.
    (b) If neither opd1 or opd2 is double precision but one is real, find the real equivalent of the other operand and then perform the operation. The result is of real type.
2. When opr is **.
    (a) If opd2 is double precision, find the double-precision equivalent of opd1 and then perform the operation. The result is of double-precision type.
    (b) If opd2 is real and opd1 is double precision, find the double-precision equivalent of opd2 and perform the operation. The result is of double-precision type.
    (c) If opd2 is real and opd1 is integer, find the real equivalent of opd1 and perform the operation. The result is of real type.
    (d) If opd2 is integer, an equivalent value need not be found. The exponentiation is simply a series of multiplications, and the result has the data type of opd1. *Suggestion:* When possible, make the second operand, opd2, an integer.
3. Illustration: symbolic evaluation.
        Let i stand for any integer operand, r stand for any real operand, and d stand for any double-precision operand.

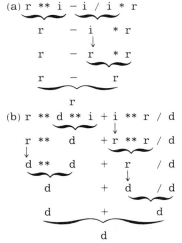

Figure 5-5. Evaluating Arithmetic Operations between Two Operands Having Different Data Types

5-7-1   *Exercises on Arithmetic Expressions and Assignment Statements*

1. Each of the following represents an attempt to write an arithmetic expression. State what is wrong with each one.
    (a)   DIVDND / −2 + ROUND
    (b)   (1.0 + RATE) PRIN
    (c)   XOBS * (XOBS * (XOBS * (XOBS + 1.0) + YOBS + YOBS ** 2)
    (d)   (NXES − 1) ** − 1
    (e)   (HOURS) (PAY) − TAXES & INS

2. Given that ALPHA= 6.0, BETA= 4.8, MU= 16, IT= 3, K= −1, IOTA= 11, RIT= 3.0, and that the data type declarations are

    ```
    INTEGER  IOTA, IT, K, MU
    REAL  ALPHA, BETA, RIT
    ```

    state the value of each of the following arithmetic expressions.
    (a)   ALPHA + (BETA − (ALPHA / 2 − BETA))
    (b)   (MU * (IT + MU * K / IOTA)) / IOTA
    (c)   IOTA * MU ** 4 ** K / 10
    (d)   IOTA * MU ** 4.0 ** K / 10
    (e)   (−1.0) ** (IT − 1) * (4.0 / (2.0 * RIT − 1.0))
    (f)   MU * 0.5E−5 * ALPHA

3. For each of the expressions in Exercise 2, give the name of a variable that can be assigned the computed value. Use default data types only.

4. Given that the variables below are assigned, in sequence, to the expressions in Exercise 2, what will be the assigned value of each variable? Assume the additional declarations

    ```
    INTEGER  KAPPA
    REAL  RHO, ZETA
    DOUBLE PRECISION  DELTA, GAMMA
    ```

    and remember that a variable can only have a value that has the data type of the variable.
    (a)   KAPPA [i.e., KAPPA = ALPHA + (BETA − (ALPHA / 2 − BETA)) as in Exercise 2(a)]
    (b)   RHO
    (c)   DELTA
    (d)   ZETA
    (e)   GAMMA
    (f)   ALPHA [i.e., ALPHA = MU * 0.5E−5 * ALPHA, as in Exercise 2(f)]

5-8 FUNCTIONS

A function is a program unit or procedure that can be referenced by name in an expression. When referenced, a function supplies a value to the expression. The value supplied is the value of the function. The program unit containing the expression in which the reference occurs is known as the *referencing program*.

There are three kinds of functions in Fortran: statement functions, external functions, and intrinsic functions. A *statement function* is a procedure specified within a referencing program by a single statement similar in form to an assignment statement. An *external function* is a procedure specified in a program unit that is external to the referencing program. The data type of the value supplied by a statement function or external function is the same as the data type of the name of the function. Statement functions and external functions are fully described in Chapter 11.

An *intrinsic function* is a subprogram that is furnished with the Fortran processor. Any main program or subprogram can reference an intrinsic function. Some of the more generally useful intrinsic functions are described in Figure 5-6. The complete set is described in the Appendix at the end of this book. The data type of the value supplied by an intrinsic function is the same as the function type for that intrinsic function, as given in the descriptions.

Each of the functions in the table below has only one argument. Function and argument types are designated symbolically by I for integer, R for real, and D for double precision.

Function Name	Function Type	Argument Type	Value Supplied to the Expression
FLOAT or REAL	R	I	Real equivalent of I
IFIX or INT	I	R	Integer equivalent of R (truncated)
NINT	I	R	Integer equivalent of R (rounded to nearest integer)
DBLE	D	I or R	Double-precision equivalent of I or R
IABS	I	I	Absolute value of the argument
ABS	R	R	Absolute value of the argument
DABS	D	D	Absolute value of the argument
SQRT	R	R	Positive square root of the (nonnegative) argument
EXP	R	R	Exponential of the argument (e**arg)
DEXP	D	D	Exponential of the argument (e**arg)
ALOG	R	R	Natural logarithm of the argument
ALOG10	R	R	Common logarithm of the argument
SIN	R	R	Sine of the argument
COS	R	R	Cosine of the argument
TAN	R	R	Tangent of the argument

Figure 5-6. Some Generally-Useful Intrinsic Functions for Arithmetic Operations

Regardless of kind, all functions are referenced in the same way. The reference always appears as an operand in an expression. Its form is

    fname(args)

where fname, a symbolic name, is the name of the function and args is a list of arguments separated by commas. The arguments provide the values that a function uses to perform its operations. An argument in an intrinsic function reference may be a constant, the symbolic name of a constant, a variable, a function reference, or an arithmetic expression; but each argument must agree in order, number, and type with the requirements of the intrinsic function.

In the expression

    KILOS * 0.6214

from the kilometer conversion program of Figure 2-12(a), a mixing of data types—an integer variable with a real constant—occurs. This poses no problem for the FORTRAN 77 processor because it will simply convert the value of KILOS to a real value and then perform the multiplication between two real values. The earlier version of Fortran, however, did not allow such data type mixing to occur. Therefore, it was usually necessary to use a different variable to represent the kilometers, say RKILOS, or to use a type conversion function such as FLOAT. If the function was used, the expression could be written

    FLOAT(KILOS) * 0.6214

Then, when KILOS was equal to 5 during execution, the expression evaluation could be depicted as follows:

    FLOAT(5) * 0.6214   {substitution}
    ‾‾‾‾‾‾‾‾‾‾‾
      5.0   * 0.6214
    ‾‾‾‾‾‾‾‾‾‾‾‾‾‾‾‾‾‾‾‾
          3.1070

Thus FLOAT is the name of an intrinsic function subprogram that finds the real (or floating-point) equivalent of an integer value.

A presently more useful intrinsic function is the one with the name SQRT. This function, for finding a square root, was used in Figure 5-4, example 6. The example has a more complicated expression than the one above containing the FLOAT function. Furthermore, the SQRT function itself is more complicated than the FLOAT function. Take time now to study the example. Make certain that you understand it.

Now consider why the SQRT function is more complicated than the FLOAT function. In the example, the expression needed the value of the square root of 25.0. It does not take much effort to say that the value needed is 5.0. But what if the value of the SQRT argument had been 25.5555? The square root of that number can be guessed at, but can be determined accurately only with considerable effort. Can you write a program to find the square root of any positive number? That is what it takes, but you need not take the time to write it; it is already available; its name is SQRT.

Let us take another example in which the square root function is referenced. Earlier in this chapter I used the quadratic root expression

```
(−B − SQRT(B ** 2 − 4.0 * A * C)) / (2.0 * A)
```

Undaunted by such a complicated-looking expression, let us evaluate it for B= 6.5, A= 4.5, and C= 2.5. Substituting first, then evaluating, we obtain

```
(− 6.5 − SQRT(6.5 ** 2 − 4.0 * 4.5 * 2.5)) / (2.0 * 4.5)

(− 6.5 − SQRT(   42.25   −   18.0   * 2.5)) / (2.0 * 4.5)

(− 6.5 − SQRT(   42.25   −        45.0   )) / (2.0 * 4.5)

(− 6.5 − SQRT        − 2.75              ) / (2.0 * 4.5)
```

and we have encountered a difficulty. The square root of a negative number is an imaginary number—a complex number. The SQRT function, however, is a real function; it is not designed to compute imaginary numbers. Therefore, an error has occurred: the SQRT function has been used incorrectly or the values of the variables are incorrect. The computer should print an error indication in this situation. You may want to try this on your computer to see what error message it gives you. I have included this illustration here to emphasize that intrinsic functions must be used properly to yield correct results.

Before moving on to another subject, it will be worthwhile for us to examine one function that requires two arguments. The remaindering function, which has the integer name MOD and the real name AMOD, performs the operation of finding the remainder of the division of one number by another. Written in one of the forms

```
MOD(ia1, ia2)
```

or

```
AMOD(ra1, ra2)
```

where ia1 and ia2 are integer arguments, and ra1 and ra2 are real arguments, the respective functions compute values based on the two formulas

```
ia1 − (ia1 / ia2) * ia2
```

and

```
ra1 − INT(ra1 / ra2) * ra2
```

both of which yield the remainder of the division of the first argument by the second argument.

So, for example, if the integer variables MORE and LESS have values of 20 and 6, the variable LEFT in the assignment statement

```
LEFT  =  MOD (MORE,  LESS)
```

will be assigned the value 2 [i.e., 20−(20/6)∗6]. Similarly, if the real variables OVER and UNDER are equal to 10.5 and 10.0, respectively, the assignment statement

```
REMAIN  =  AMOD (OVER,  UNDER)
```

will cause REMAIN to be given a value of 0.5 [i.e., 10.5−INT(10.5/10.0)∗10.0]. When both argument values are greater than zero, the value of the remaindering function is always equal to or greater than zero, but less than the value of the second argument—the divisor.

5-8-1 *Exercises on Functions*

1. If possible, state the value of each of the following functions. If not possible, state why. You are given that DIFF=−0.001, GRADE=89.9, MONE=1, and MTWO=2.

   (a) ABS(DIFF)

   (b) IFIX(GRADE)

   (c) ABS(MONE − MTWO)

   (d) NINT(GRADE)

   (e) ALOG10(FLOAT(MONE ∗ 10))

   (f) ABS(1 − DIFF)

   (g) DBLE(DIFF)

   (h) FLOAT(NINT(GRADE))

   (i) MOD(100, MTWO)

   (j) AMOD(GRADE, FLOAT(IFIX(GRADE)))

2. Given that MU=16, IT=3, LOWEND=5, LOC=12, SIZE=6, and that all are declared integer variables, state the values of ROOTCB, NEWLOC, and INDIF in the assignment statements below. Assume that ROOTCB is declared real and that NEWLOC and INDIF are declared integer.

   (a) ROOTCB = SQRT(FLOAT(MU)) ∗∗ IT

   (b) NEWLOC = LOWEND + MOD(LOC − 1, SIZE)

   (c) INDIF = IABS(LOWEND − LOC)

3. Devise an algorithm that could be used to develop the function for finding the absolute value of a real variable. The algorithm should be devised in the usual way—as if the function is to be a main program. The absolute value of a variable, VAR, is defined very simply to be −VAR if the value of VAR is negative, and VAR otherwise.

4. Devise an algorithm that could be used to develop the NINT function. As described in Figure 5-6, the NINT function takes the value of a real argu-

ment and finds the nearest integer. Some example input/output values are as follows:

Real Value	NINT Value
98.6	99
1.4	1
−0.1	0
−459.67	−460

5-9   THE ARITHMETIC ASSIGNMENT STATEMENT REVISITED

Let ivar represent any integer variable, rvar stand for any real variable, iae denote any integer-valued arithmetic expression, and rae indicate any real-valued arithmetic expression. The four following arithmetic assignment statements, then, are valid:

```
ivar = iae
rvar = rae
ivar = rae
rvar = iae
```

You should have no difficulty with the first two forms; but direct your attention to the last two forms.

You know that an integer variable can only have an integer value and that a real variable can only have a real value. So what must take place when a real-valued expression is assigned to an integer variable or an integer-valued expression is assigned to a real variable? The answer is conversion—conversion of the arithmetic expression value to the data type of the variable to which it is assigned. Consider the statement

```
RATIO = MAX / MIN
```

where RATIO is real and MAX and MIN are integer. Now when MAX=100 and MIN=2, the evaluation and assignment proceed as follows:

```
RATIO = MAX / MIN
        100 /  2   {substitute}

              50     {evaluate integer division}
              ↓
RATIO =      50.0   {convert and assign}
```

That's not too surprising, but when MAX=100 and MIN=51, we have

```
RATIO = MAX / MIN
        100 / 51   {substitute}

               1     {evaluate integer division}
               ↓
RATIO =       1.0   {convert and assign}
```

and that may make you think again: Are the data types correctly declared? They may or may not be; it depends on the problem.

In like manner, consider the statement

NETPAY = GRSPAY – DEDUCT

where NETPAY is integer and GRSPAY and DEDUCT are real. When GRSPAY=500.0 and DEDUCT=100.0, evaluation and assignment take place as follows:

```
NETPAY = GRSPAY – DEDUCT
          500.0 – 100.0   {substitute}

             400.0        {evaluate real subtraction}
               ↓
NETPAY =       400         {convert and assign}
```

and that seems all right. But when GRSPAY=499.99 and DEDUCT=100.0, we have

```
NETPAY = GRSPAY – DEDUCT
          499.99 – 100.0   {substitute}

             399.99        {evaluate real subtraction}
               ↓
NETPAY =       399         {convert and assign}
```

which may or may not be what was intended. (If your gross pay is $499.99 and your deductions are $100.00, you, no doubt, want to be paid the full $399.99 net. I know I do.) The point I am trying to make is that you must make sure that all of your data types are correct. By explicitly declaring the data types of all variables (such as RATIO, MAX, MIN, NETPAY, GRSPAY, and DEDUCT) in appropriate type statements, you force yourself to consider data types more carefully than if you just depend on the defaults. Use explicit declarations.

5-10 ANOTHER CONVERSION EXAMPLE

Exercise 2 of Section 2-5 poses this problem:

> Develop and print a table of Fahrenheit and corresponding Celsius temperatures (to the nearest tenth) for the integral Fahrenheit temperatures lowf through highf inclusive. Use the relationship
>
> $$Celsius = (5/9)(Fahrenheit - 32)$$
>
> The variables lowf and highf must be given values by input; a limitation, that must be checked, is that lowf $<=$ highf.

This problem is similar to the kilometer conversion problem, except that the lower bound (lowf) and higher bound (highf) on the Fahrenheit temperatures are variables rather than constants as were the bounds on kilometers. A typical set of values for lowf and highf might be 32 and 80. The desired output for this set of values, then, is depicted by the following table.

FAHRENHEIT AND CELSIUS TEMPERATURES

FAHRENHEIT	CELSIUS
32	0.0
33	0.6
34	1.1
.	.
.	.
.	.
78	25.6
79	26.1
80	26.7

It should be noted that, for this particular set of lowf and highf values, 49 lines of temperatures will be printed. Since a common page size for computer paper is 66 lines, these temperatures should all fit onto one page.

In developing the algorithm to solve this problem, a first consideration should be given to the mathematical conversion relationship,

$$\text{Celsius} = (5/9)(\text{Fahrenheit} - 32)$$

Although the relationship is perfectly valid mathematically, and could be directly written in the algorithmic form

$$\text{Celsius} \leftarrow (5/9) * (\text{Fahrenheit} - 32)$$

this is not necessarily desirable from a computational standpoint. It is definitely not desirable from the Fortran program standpoint. First, consider the difficulty that will be encountered if the relationship is translated directly into the Fortran assignment statement

$$\text{CEL} = (5 / 9) * (\text{FAHREN} - 32)$$

What will happen when 5, an integer, is divided by 9, also an integer? The result will be zero and then, regardless of the value of FAHREN, CEL will always be assigned a zero value. Not good. Second, it is usually a good practice to simplify a mathematical relationship before using it in computing many values. At the least, one operation between two constants can always be simplified. Thus 5/9 could be divided out. But this will produce the repeating fractional number 0.555555..., which is also undesirable. However, if the division is reversed—that is, 9 is divided by 5—an exact value of 1.8 is obtained. The simplified relationship can then be written as

$$\text{Celsius} = (\text{Fahrenheit} - 32)/1.8$$

which, in turn, can be written algorithmically as

$$\text{Celsius} \leftarrow (\text{Fahrenheit} - 32) / 1.8$$

and then as the Fortran assignment statement

$$\text{CEL} = (\text{FAHREN} - 32) / 1.8$$

Algorithm development now proceeds in a stepwise fashion similar to the following.

First try:

```
Read lowf and highf.
As long as lowf is less than or equal to highf,
take the following actions for Fahrenheit temperatures
from lowf to highf:
  Find Celsius = (Fahrenheit - 32) / 1.8
  Write Fahrenheit and Celsius
Stop.
```

Second try:

```
      Read lowf, highf
      If lowf > highf Then
        Write error message
      Else
        Assign lowf as the initial value of Fahrenheit
EOD.  While Fahrenheit is less than or equal to highf,
        Celsius ← (Fahrenheit - 32) / 1.8
        Write Fahrenheit, Celsius
        Assign next value of Fahrenheit
        Go To EOD. (Back)
      Stop
```

More refinement, including the addition of printing rules, results eventually in a final algorithm such as the one in Figure 5-7. A corresponding flowchart is given in Figure 5-8 and the program in Figure 5-9.

Observe in the program the way in which the statements discussed in this chapter have been written. In the Declaration section, the symbolic names FAHREN, HIGHF, LOWF, and PO are designated as integer data types; the data type of CEL is specified to be real; and PO is declared to be a symbolic constant with a value of 6. In the action section, there are three assignment statements: FAHREN = LOWF initializes FAHREN with the already defined value of LOWF; CEL = (FAHREN − 32) / 1.8 allows a Celsius temperature, corresponding to the current Fahrenheit temperature, to be computed; and FAHREN = FAHREN + 1 causes the integral incrementation of FAHREN to

ALGORITHM Farcel
{ Celsius temperatures, corresponding to integral
Fahrenheit temperatures from lowf to highf inclusive,
are computed and printed.}

Write title: 'FAHRENHEIT AND CELSIUS TEMPERATURES',
     and headings: 'FAHRENHEIT', 'CELSIUS'
Read lowf, highf
If lowf > highf Then
  Write error message
Else
  Assign lowf as the initial value of Fahrenheit
EOD.   While Fahrenheit is less than or equal to highf,
     Celsius ← (Fahrenheit − 32) / 1.8
     Write Fahrenheit, Celsius
     Assign next value of Fahrenheit
     Go To EOD. (Back)
Stop

Figure 5-7. Algorithm for Conversion of Fahrenheit to Celsius

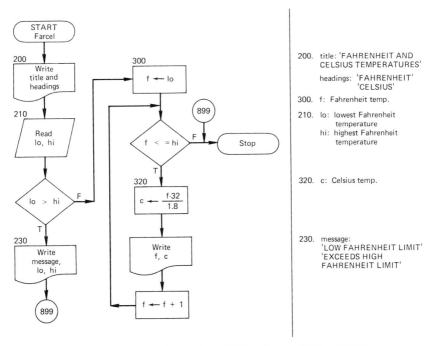

Figure 5-8. Flowchart for Conversion of Fahrenheit to Celsius (Celsius temperatures, corresponding to integral Fahrenheit temperatures from lowf (lo) to highf (hi), inclusive, are computed and printed.)

```
*I,   CONVERSION OF FAHRENHEIT TO CELSIUS
      PROGRAM FARCEL
*     PROGRAMMER:   JARRELL C, GROUT
*     DATE:  12/2/80
*
*  A, COMMENTARY
*
*         CELSIUS TEMPERATURES, CORRESPONDING TO INTEGRAL
*     FAHRENHEIT TEMPERATURES FROM LOWF TO HIGHF INCLUSIVE,
*     ARE COMPUTED AND PRINTED TO THE NEAREST TENTH,
*
*         DICTIONARY,
*     CEL:  CELSIUS TEMPERATURE
*     FAHREN:   FAHRENHEIT TEMPERATURE
*     HIGHF:  HIGHEST FAHRENHEIT TEMPERATURE
*     LOWF:  LOWEST FAHRENHEIT TEMPERATURE
*     PO:  PRINT-OUT DEVICE IDENTIFIER
*
*  B, DECLARATION
*
      INTEGER  FAHREN, HIGHF, LOWF, PO
      REAL  CEL
      PARAMETER  (PO=6)
*
*  C, I/O LAYOUT
*
  920 FORMAT (' ', 2X, I11, 3X, F12,1)
*
*  D, ACTION
*
      PRINT *, 'FAHRENHEIT AND CELSIUS TEMPERATURES'
      PRINT *, ' '
      PRINT *, '    FAHRENHEIT       CELSIUS'
      PRINT *, ' '
      READ *, LOWF, HIGHF
      IF (LOWF ,GT, HIGHF) THEN
         PRINT *, 'LOW FAHRENHEIT LIMIT:  ', LOWF
         PRINT *, 'EXCEEDS HIGH FAHRENHEIT LIMIT:  ', HIGHF
      ELSE
         FAHREN = LOWF
  310    IF (FAHREN ,LE, HIGHF) THEN
            CEL = (FAHREN - 32) / 1,8
            WRITE (PO, 920) FAHREN, CEL
            FAHREN = FAHREN + 1
            GO TO 310
         ENDIF
      ENDIF
      STOP
      END
```

Figure 5-9. Program for Conversion of Fahrenheit to Celsius

occur. When, for example, the value of FAHREN gets to be 50, the value of CEL will be evaluated as follows:

$$
\begin{array}{rl}
\text{CEL} = & (\text{FAHREN} - 32) / 1.8 \\
& (\underbrace{\quad 50 \quad - 32)}_{} / 1.8 \\
& \underbrace{18 \qquad / 1.8}_{} \\
& \downarrow \\
& 18.0 \quad / 1.8 \\
& 10.0
\end{array}
$$

List-directed i/o is used except in one instance: formatted output is used to print the columnar values of FAHREN and CEL so that they will be reasonably well centered and so that the Celsius temperatures will be printed to the nearest 0.1 as desired. The two statements

```
920 FORMAT (' ', 2X, I11, 3X, F12.1)
```

and

```
WRITE (PO, 920) FAHREN, CEL
```

work together to serve this purpose. Formatted input/output is covered in the next chapter.

I purposely have not included a printout of results from this program, leaving it as an exercise for you. You may wish to run the program for further study, then, on your computer. If so, the input record for the suggested values of lowf and highf should look something like this:

```
32 80
```

You may use these or other values—including negative values. Notice, however, that the program only prints the title and column headings one time during one execution. If you print more than about 60 lines of output, the computer will automatically begin printing on a new page but will not reprint the title or column headings.

5-11 EXERCISES

1. Write a complete Fortran program to solve the problem posed in Exercise 1 of Section 2-5. It involves developing a table of ounces and corresponding grams—a conversion problem similar to the Fahrenheit−Celsius problem. Notice, however, that both the ounces and the grams have real number values; furthermore, the increment on ounces is 0.1 rather than 1 as with Fahrenheit.

2. Write a complete Fortran program for the square inches to square centimeters conversion problem of Exercise 3 of Section 2-5. Both square inches and square centimeters have real number values, and the increment on square inches is 0.5. For your test runs, choose values of lowin and highin that are realistic and will not cause an excessive number of pages to be printed.

3. Make up your own conversion problem—English to metric or some other type of conversion you are interested in. Define the problem well, then plan and devise a complete Fortran program to solve it.

4. Write a complete Fortran program to solve the problem of Exercise 5 of Section 2-5. This is an arithmetic averaging problem similar to the one solved in Chapter 3. The primary differences are that the input data values—grades— are integers and the end of the input data is to be designated by an invalid grade (a negative input value).

5. Devise an algorithm that might be used to develop the function for finding the square root of an arithmetic expression that has a nonnegative real value. Use any valid square root finding method you know about or can find. Be sure and check the given number, rejecting it with an appropriate error message if it is negative.

6. The factorial of a positive integer n is written as $n!$ and is defined to be the product of the integers from 1 to n. Thus

$$n! = 1 \times 2 \times 3 \times \cdots \times (n - 1) \times n \qquad \text{(and also, 0! = 1)}$$

Below, you are given a factorial algorithm. Use the algorithm as a starting point from which to plan and develop a complete Fortran program that will compute the number of combinations, c, of n things taken k at a time from the formula

$$c = \frac{n!}{k!\,(n - k)!}$$

ALGORITHM Factorial
```
{ Compute the factorial of a nonnegative integer n.}
Read n
fact ← 1
If n > 1 Then
     i ← 2
NCOMP.   If i <= n Then
             fact ← i * fact
             i ← i + 1
             Go To NCOMP. (Back)
Print 'THE FACTORIAL OF ', n, ' IS ', fact
Stop
END
```

7. Plan and write a complete Fortran program for one or more of the following mathematically oriented problems. Use Fortran intrinsic functions where possible. Echo all input values and make your output easy to understand.

(a) The argument of each of the trigonometric intrinsic functions SIN, COS, and TAN, must be an angle given in radians. Given the relationship

$$2\pi \text{ radians} = 360 \text{ degrees}$$

develop a table containing the sine, cosine, and tangent for angles from 0 through 360 degrees in increments of 10 degrees. Do not use the TAN intrinsic function; rather, use the relationship

$$\tan a = \frac{\sin a}{\cos a}$$

to find the tangent. Do not, however, reference any intrinsic function more than once per angle. The printed table is to contain five columns of numbers: degrees, radians, sine, cosine, and tangent.

(b) The kth root of a positive-valued real variable, VAR, may be found by using the relationship

$$\sqrt[k]{\text{VAR}} = e^{\ln(\text{VAR})/k}$$

where e is the base of the natural logarithms. Given positive values of n and VAR, find and print each of the kth roots of VAR as k varies from 1 through n. Design your program to continue processing pairs of n and VAR until a negative value of VAR is encountered; then stop.

(c) The two roots of the quadratic equation

$$ax^2 + bx + c = 0$$

can be found from the formula

$$x = \frac{-b \pm \sqrt{b^2 - 4ac}}{2a}$$

The roots are complex if the term $b^2 - 4ac$ is negative; they are real and equal if the term is zero; otherwise, they are real and unequal. Given input values of a, b, and c, find only the real roots if they exist. Print the real roots with an appropriate message. Print only an appropriate message if the roots are complex. Design your program to continue processing sets of a, b, and c, until a zero value of a is encountered (the equation is not quadratic); then stop.

8. Plan and write a complete Fortran program for one or more of the following business-oriented problems. Echo all input values and make your output easy to understand.

(a) An amount of money p is borrowed at a monthly interest rate r to be paid back in equal amounts a each month over a period of m months. Given, as input, values of p, r, and m, develop an amortization schedule for repayment of the loan. The equal payment amount can be calculated from

$$a = p\frac{r(1 + r)^m}{(1 + r)^m - 1}$$

The schedule should be in tabular form, one line per month, with these six columns per line: month, beginning debt, interest payment, principal payment, total payment, and ending debt. Round each monthly interest payment to the nearest cent and pay any excess necessary in the final month so that the ending debt of that month is zero. For example, if $p = 1000.00$, $r = 0.01$, and $m = 3$, the following results should be printed:

LOAN AMORTIZATION SCHEDULE

AMOUNT BORROWED: 1000.00   INTEREST RATE: 0.01

MONTH	BEGINNING DEBT	INTEREST PAYMENT	PRINCIPAL PAYMENT	TOTAL PAYMENT	ENDING DEBT
1	1000.00	10.00	330.02	340.02	669.98
2	669.98	6.70	333.32	340.02	336.66
3	336.66	3.37	336.66	340.03	0.00

(b) Develop a depreciation schedule using the sum-of-the-years'-digits method. In this method, the depreciation factor for a particular year is determined by dividing the number of years of life remaining at the beginning of that year by the sum of the digits corresponding to the number of each year of life. For example, for a physical asset having a life of 4 years, the factors are

Year	Depreciation Factor
1	4/10
2	3/10
3	2/10
4	1/10
(10 = sum of digits)	

The depreciation, then, for a particular year is found by multiplying the depreciable value (original cost less residual value) of the asset by the depreciation factor for that year. Given as input the original cost, the residual value, and the number of years of useful life of an asset, your program should print a depreciation schedule containing three numbers—year, depreciation for the year, and accumulated depreciation—for each year of the useful life of the asset.

EXERCISE REFERENCE

The following book is one excellent reference and resource for many more valuable algorithmic and programming exercises. You can use parts of it now and more of it later.

Maurer, H. A., and Williams, M. R. *A Collection of Programming Problems and Techniques*. Prentice-Hall, Inc., Englewood Cliffs, N.J., 1972.

APPENDIX: ADDITIONAL NUMERIC CAPABILITIES

As mentioned in Section 5-1, Fortran can also process complex data. A complex number is written as an ordered pair of real numbers enclosed in parentheses. For example, $4 + 3i$ is written as (4.0,3.0). Each complex number pair occupies two computer words in memory. Complex variables are declared by means of the COMPLEX data type statement, which has essentially the same form as the other data type statements.

Data types can also be declared implicitly by the use of the declaration statement of the form

```
IMPLICIT type (list)
```

where type is one of the valid data types and list consists of one or more single letters or letter ranges. The effect is to give the specified types to all symbolic names that begin with one of the indicated letters, except those explicitly declared otherwise. For example,

```
IMPLICIT INTEGER (A-Z)
REAL   GRSPAY, DEDUCT, NETPAY
```

declares that all symbolic names in the program unit are of integer type except GRSPAY, DEDUCT, and NETPAY.

Chapter

6

Input and Output
of Data

At this point in your study, we begin to examine language facilities and programming techniques that will broaden your programming foundation by adding depth and flexibility. The first portion of these facilities and techniques, which I would term as being at an intermediate level compared to previous material, includes thorough consideration of data input and output, program control, arrays, and character processing—the coverage of this and the next four chapters.

6-1 AN I/O PERSPECTIVE

Regardless of the simplicity or complexity of a problem, thoughtful consideration should be given to the form that the input and output data can and should have, to ensure that the computer is used effectively, and what is more important, to make certain that people have a useful and beneficial interaction with the computer. People who use the input data, program, or output data in any way should be able to do so easily. They should—because of good input design—readily understand what input data are required and how they are to be entered. They should—because of good output design—be able to interpret printed output easily.

To create good i/o designs, the programmer should be familiar with the characteristics and expectations of the people who will interact with the input or output. The programmer should also be familiar with i/o design concepts. Some of the latter are discussed in the next few sections.

6-1-1 Files, Records, and Fields

Data are usually kept in collections called *files*. You are, no doubt, familiar with one or more of these kinds of data files: student information files, personnel files, library catalog files, grade files, customer files, and so on. Formally, a file is a collection of related records. The records are related because they all pertain to the type of information the file contains, as described by its name.

A *record* consists of items of information that together describe an individual member of the file. For example, a record in a student information file contains information about one student. The items of information, then, are placed in appropriate fields of the record. Some possible names of fields in a student record include student name, street address, city, state, zip code, classification, major, hours passed, grade points, and so on. The values in the fields (e.g., Dan D. Donn, 1111 Anystreet, Bigtown, Texas, 79999, Sophomore, Physical Education, 40, 130) are the data items that describe a particular member of the file.

In Fortran, an input operation is usually designed to read into memory the information contained in the fields of one input record; an output operation is usually designed to write out the information to be contained in the fields of one output record. The variable names in the iolist of a READ statement are the Fortran names of the fields in the input record. The variable names, and perhaps constants, in the iolist of a PRINT or WRITE statement are the Fortran names or values of the fields in the output record. For example, the statement

```
READ *, PRIN, RATE, NYEARS
```

identifies three fields—PRIN, RATE, and NYEARS—that can be present in one input record. These particular variables may represent such actual field names as "principal," "interest rate," and "number of years." The values in the three sequential fields of the input record become the values of the variables whenever the READ statement is executed. Each time the statement is executed, a new record from the input file—and thus a new set of values—must be read in.

Similarly, the statements

```
PRINT *, 'PRINCIPAL: ', PRIN
PRINT *, 'INTEREST RATE: ', RATE
PRINT *, 'NUMBER OF YEARS: ', NYEARS
```

each identify two fields that are to be present in an output record (a print line). The first statement identifies a field that contains the literal value "PRINCIPAL: ", and a field that contains the numeric value of the variable PRIN. Therefore, if the value of PRIN in computer memory is 5283.24, the corresponding output record will appear as

```
PRINCIPAL:  5283.24
```

The interpretations of the other print operations are similar; as an exercise you should interpret them.

We would probably prefer to look upon the printout example above as if it took three print lines to make up one record in the output file. This is logical since the six items printed, including literals, are directly related to each other. In a case like this, we say that the six items together make up one *logical record*, and that the one logical record requires three *physical records* (print lines in this case) to contain all its fields.

6-1-2 Input Design

Simplicity and clarity are two good words to think about when designing for input; efficiency is another. These thoughts may often lead to the use of a list-directed READ, either in the simplest form already covered or a more comprehensive form to be covered shortly, because then the program user need only enter the values—separated by blanks, commas, or slashes—in the proper sequence, without any concern for where they are physically located in an input record.

However, there are situations in which the data are not readily adaptable for list-directed entry, and situations in which it is necessary or desirable to have programmed control over the appearance of the data in the input medium. In such cases, input formats may be specified and referenced in the program.

It is not difficult to develop a FORMAT statement that explicitly describes how data are arranged in an input medium. One needs only to know what the input record description is and how to use the format field descriptors discussed shortly. The record description can be depicted by a simple specification of field names with corresponding data descriptions and locations.

To illustrate, Figure 6-1 contains two example input record descriptions. The first—an investment record—contains only numeric data. In the data descriptions, capital Xs are used to represent digit positions. The term "right-justified" means that the value must end in the rightmost column of the field. The second example—a student information record—contains both character and numeric data. Character data consists of alphabetic letters or numeric digits or combinations of both; it is often referred to as alphanumeric data. The term "left-justified" means that the value begins in the leftmost position of the field.

1.　An Investment Record

Field Name	Data Description	Location (columns)
Principal	Real, XXXX.XX	1–7
Rate	Real, 0.XX	8–11
Number of years	Integer, XX, right-justified	12–13

2.　A Student Information Record

Field Name	Data Description	Location (positions)
Student name	Character, left-justified	1–30
Street address	Character, left-justified	31–45
City	Character, left-justified	46–57
State	Character, left-justified	58–59
Zip code	Character, left-justified	60–68
Classification	Two-character code	69–70
Major	Three-character code	71–73
Hours passed	Integer, XXX, right-justified	74–76
Grade points	Integer, XXX, right-justified	77–79

Figure 6-1. Example Input Record Descriptions

The field locations are given in terms of "columns" in the first example and "positions" in the section example. Location refers to relative positions in the record and, therefore, either term is appropriate for any input (or output) medium.

Notice that the field locations in both examples are contiguous; there are no unused positions between fields. When formatted input is used, the computer does not "care" whether there are any separators (blanks, commas, or slashes) between fields or not. Thus fields can be contiguous or separated for the convenience of the programmer and other people.

6-1-3   Printed Output Design

Simplicity, clarity, and efficiency are also important terms to keep in mind when designing for printed output. Clearly stated, accurate titles are essential on printed output. Concise, lucid, and well-arranged column headings and messages are also important. When it is necessary to abbreviate, only standard abbreviations should be used, or an explanation of each abbreviation should be printed on the output page that contains the abbreviation.

The reading directions for printed output should be the normal top to bottom, left to right that we use for most reading. For continuity, pages should be numbered when more than one output page is required.

In tabular output, data values should be centered under column headings. Tables and all other printed results should be person-oriented rather than computer-oriented; they are being produced for people—not computers—to read. List-directed output, which depends on processor-established formatting, is more computer-oriented than person-oriented. It is, therefore, less often appropriate than output created by formats that are explicitly specified and referenced in a program.

Devising specific FORMAT statements for output is no more difficult than doing so for input. First the design is established and represented on an appropriate layout form; then the format descriptors—discussed shortly—are used in coding the FORMAT statements directly from the layout.

A sample output layout form is shown in Figure 6-2. As an output layout is developed using such a form, several things should be kept in mind about printers and printed pages: most printers print 10 characters per inch horizontally and six lines per inch vertically; printer width varies, but a common size allows up to 132 printed characters on a line; standard vertical page length is 11 inches; it is fairly common for printers to provide half-inch margins automatically at the top and bottom of a page (usually leaving 60 lines per page for printing); and standard page widths are 8.5 and 14 inches.

Exercise 8(a) of Section 5-11 suggested that you plan and write a program to develop a schedule for repayment of a loan. The desired printed results were depicted by an example. If a layout form and explicit formats had been used, it would have been possible to code the table more directly, and then programmatically reproduce it more exactly. Figure 6-3 contains a representation of the schedule on a layout form. If you will take the time to compare it with the output originally suggested in Chapter 5, you should begin to see the benefits of using the

OUTPUT LAYOUT FORM

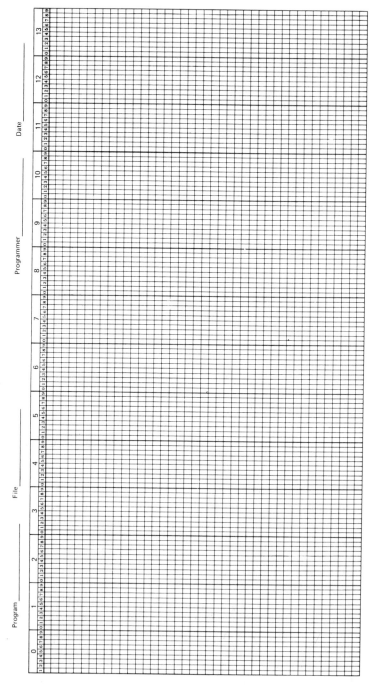

Figure 6-2. An Output Layout Form (Reduced)

122

layout form. Observe that capital Xs are used to represent digit positions for numbers that are to be printed; an entire group of Xs, together with a decimal point and a leading position for a sign (usually blank when the number is positive), represent the field for a number that will be printed; also, the curving lines are used to indicate that more values than are depicted may appear in each column.

So the layout shows a picture of the output. You should be able to see that any type of printed output—lengthy narrative, simple message, tabular, printer-graphical, or other—can be depicted on a layout form. Then the coding of the FORMAT statements required for producing the actual printout is relatively straightforward. Formatted input or output is accomplished by the use of a READ or a WRITE statement in conjunction with a FORMAT statement, as explained in Sections 6-2 and 6-3.

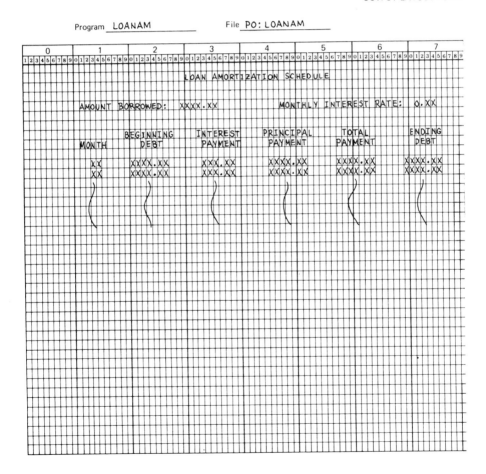

Figure 6-3. Loan Amortization Schedule Layout

6-1-4   *Exercises*

1. Find out some things about the different kinds of files maintained by your computer center. Try to learn some of the file names, record contents in terms of field names, and storage media. Ask why some data files are stored on magnetic disk, others on magnetic tape, and very few—if any—on punched cards. Also ask how the data in the files are used.

2. Most large computer manufacturers and business form companies have forms, similar to the one in Figure 6-2, for the layout of printed output. Other names used for such forms are "print chart," "printer spacing chart," and "spacing chart," among others. They are often kept for sale in college bookstores or office supply companies. Obtain one or two pads of such forms for your own use.

3. Using the forms you obtain as instructed in Exercise 2, depict the output design layout for the following programs that I completed for you in earlier chapters.

   (a)   The kilometer-to-miles conversion program of Figure 2-12(a).

   (b)   The averaging program of Figure 3-1.

   (c)   The maximum and minimum program of Figure 4-9.

   (d)   The Fahrenheit-to-Celsius conversion program of Figure 5-9.

4. Devise an input layout for the problems below. None of these problems has just one specific answer, so use your imagination.

   (a)   Each of the programs mentioned in Exercise 3(b) through (d).

   (b)   The number of combinations of n things taken k at a time problem of Exercise 6 of Section 5-11, in which there are two integer input variables: n and k.

   (c)   The quadratic equation roots problem of Exercise 7(c) of Section 5-11, in which there are three real input variables: the quadratic equation coefficients a, b, and c.

5. Show what will be printed when the computer executes the following statements. Assume that the values of CUSTMR, ITEM, NUMORD, and PRICE in memory are 12345, 4424, 111, and 1.11. You are playing the part of the computer here, so write down the results just the way the printer would print them.

```
INTEGER  CUSTMR, ITEM, NUMORD
REAL   OWED, PRICE
   .
   .
   .
OWED = NUMORD * PRICE
PRINT *,  'CUSTOMER NUMBER: ',  CUSTMR
PRINT *,  'ITEM NUMBER : ',  ITEM
PRINT *,  'UNIT PRICE:   $',  PRICE
PRINT *,  'NUMBER ORDERED: ',  NUMORD
PRINT *,  'TOTAL BILL:   $',  OWED
```

6-2   THE READ, PRINT, AND WRITE
FOR FORMATTED I/O

The READ, PRINT, and WRITE are the data transfer input/output statements. Their execution causes data values to be brought into memory or taken out of memory. As an aid in describing their use, as well as the use of the FORMAT statement of Section 6-3, the arithmetic averaging program of Figure 3-1 is reproduced here as Figure 6-4. I refer to it frequently throughout this and the next section.

The READ statement can be written in either of the two forms

```
READ f, iolist
```

```
*I, ARITHMETIC AVERAGE
*
*      PROGRAM AVRAGE
*      PROGRAMMER:   JARRELL C, GROUT
*      DATE:  9/8/80
*
*   A, COMMENTARY
*
*          FIND THE ARITHMETIC AVERAGE OF A SET OF
*      EXPERIMENTAL OBSERVATIONS WHICH MAY VARY IN
*      VALUE FROM -999.99 THROUGH +999.99, INCLUSIVE,
*      VALUES ARE ENTERED ONE PER INPUT RECORD,
*
*          DICTIONARY,
*      AVE:  OBSERVATION ACCUMULATOR AND AVERAGE
*      CI:   INPUT DEVICE IDENTIFIER
*      COUNT:  THE COUNT OF OBSERVATIONS
*      HIOBS:  THE HIGHEST ALLOWABLE OBSERVATION (+999.99)
*      LOWOBS:  THE LOWEST ALLOWABLE OBSERVATION (-999.99)
*      OBS:  AN OBSERVATION (-999.99 THRU +999.99)
*      PO:  OUTPUT DEVICE IDENTIFIER
*
*   B, DECLARATION
*
*      INTEGER  CI, COUNT, PO
*      REAL  AVE, HIOBS, LOWOBS, OBS
*      PARAMETER  (CI=5, PO=6,  HIOBS=+999.99, LOWOBS=-999.99)
*
*   C, I/O LAYOUT
*
  900 FORMAT ('1', 'EXPERIMENTAL OBSERVATIONS', /)
  910 FORMAT ('0', 'INVALID INPUT VALUE, UNUSED: ',
    :         E14.7, /)
  920 FORMAT (' ', 9X, F7.2)
  930 FORMAT ('0', 'AVERAGE: ', F7.2, /,
    :         ' ', 'ON ', I10, ' VALUES', /, '1')
*
*   D, ACTION
*
      WRITE (PO, 900)
      AVE = 0.0
      COUNT = 0
  200    READ (CI, *, END=300) OBS
         IF (OBS .LT. LOWOBS
    :        .OR. OBS .GT. HIOBS) THEN
            WRITE (PO, 910) OBS
         ELSE
            WRITE (PO, 920) OBS
            AVE = AVE + OBS
            COUNT = COUNT + 1
         ENDIF
         GO TO 200
  300 IF (COUNT .GT. 0) AVE = AVE / COUNT
      WRITE (PO, 930) AVE, COUNT
      STOP
      END
```

Figure 6-4. Arithmetic Averaging Program Reproduced from Figure 3-1

or

        READ (u, f, END=s) iolist

where f is a format identifier, u is an input unit identifier, END=s is an end-of-file specifier in which s is a statement number, and iolist is the group of variables for which values are to be read into memory from the next input record. Similarly, the PRINT and WRITE statements can be written in the forms

        PRINT f, iolist

and

        WRITE (u, f) iolist

where f is again a format identifier, u is an output unit identifier, and iolist designates the defined values to be written to the appropriate output unit.

   Notice that the simplest forms for list-directed i/o occur whenever an asterisk is used for f, the format identifier, in the first form of the READ statement and the PRINT statement. The use of an asterisk for f in the second form of the READ statement and in the WRITE statement, results in more comprehensive and flexible forms for list-directed i/o. For instance, the statement

        READ (CI, *, END=300) OBS

which is used in the arithmetic averaging program, is a list-directed input statement for reading values of OBS that also includes a particular input unit reference and an end-of-file specifier. Neither the input unit reference nor end-of-file specifier is allowed in the simplest forms.

   Still, the asterisk as a format identifier allows only list-directed i/o, and thus causes dependence on field separators in input records, and processor-established formats to produce output records. To avoid this dependence and, instead, to use explicit formatting in the program, f must be one of the following: the statement number of a FORMAT statement, an integer variable or symbolic constant that has been assigned a FORMAT statement number, or one of two other forms—involving character data—that are described in a later chapter. In the averaging program, for example, the execution of the output statement

        WRITE (PO, 930) AVE, COUNT

causes the values of AVE and COUNT to be written on the output unit specified by the value of PO, in the form described by the FORMAT statement numbered 930.

   There are three other WRITE statements in the averaging program; each identifies the same output unit through the value of PO, and each explicitly specifies a FORMAT statement. Consider, for a moment, the first of the three:

        WRITE (PO, 900)

This statement contains no iolist. Its purpose is not to print values of variables, but to direct the computer to use the contents of FORMAT statement 900 as output. A part of the contents of statement 900 is the character string "EXPERIMENTAL OBSERVATIONS," which is also the title of the output table. Therefore, the purpose of this first WRITE statement is to cause the table title to be printed. The io-list, then, is not required—neither in the WRITE statement nor in the READ statement. If one is not present in a READ statement, an input record will be processed but nothing will be read into memory.

Turn your attention toward the other two items in the READ statement: the input unit identifier and the end-of-file specifier. An *input unit identifier* provides a means of referring to a particular input file; an *end-of-file specifier* designates the next statement to be executed after all the records of an input file have been processed by a READ statement.

An input unit identifier may be an asterisk, or an integer expression with a zero or positive value. When an asterisk is used, the input unit is the same as the one used for the simple form of the list-directed READ statement. When an integer expression is used, the identifier refers to an input device that contains a file that has been associated for input with the value of the identifier by means of a system default or a Job Control Language (JCL) statement external to the program. In the READ statement

```
READ (CI, *, END=300) OBS
```

of the averaging program, CI is the input unit identifier or, as indicated in the program dictionary, an "INPUT DEVICE IDENTIFIER."

The end-of-file specifier, END=300 in this case, is an optional item which identifies the statement that is to be executed after an attempt to read from the file has resulted in an indication that all the input data have been read in. The end-of-file specifier is a conditional branching operation combined with the reading operation. Do not let the use of the word "END" confuse you; what is meant is "end-of-file," not "end-of-program."

The interpretation of this particular portion of the averaging program is depicted in flowchart form in Figure 6-5, at the point where two paths lead from the READ symbol, indicating that a decision is made in conjunction with the reading operation. I use the more accurately descriptive EOF, rather than END, as the indicator of the path to be taken when the end-of-file occurs. Clearly, the end-of-file specifier provides the exit from the loop.

Algorithmically, a primitive that can be used to designate a reading operation with an end-of-file test is the following:

```
Read values, at EOF Go To label(direction)
```

Specifically, for this example, you might use

```
Read obs, at EOF Go To 300. (Ahead)
```

Now consider the WRITE statement and its output unit identifier. An *output unit identifier* is much like an input unit identifier except that it refers to an output file rather than an input file. When an asterisk is used, the output unit is the same

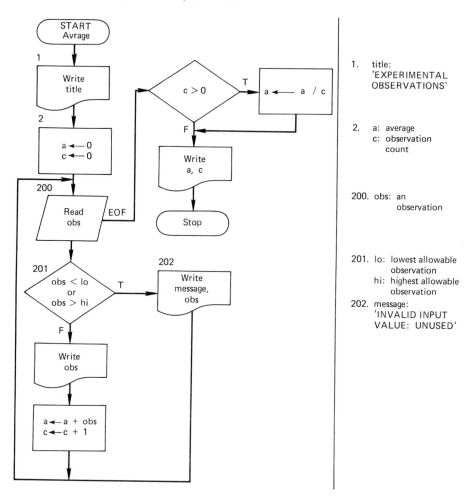

Figure 6-5. Flowchart for Arithmetic Averaging (Find the arithmetic average of a set of experimental observations which may vary in value from "lo" to "hi," inclusive. Values are entered one per input record.)

as the one used for the PRINT statement. When an integer expression is used, the identifier refers to an output device that contains, or is to contain, a file which has been associated for output with the value of the identifier by means of a system default or a JCL statement external to the program.

In all of the WRITE statements of the averaging program, I used PO—having a value of 6 defined in the PARAMETER statement—as the output unit identifier. My reference is, by system default, to the printer of my computer system.

6-3   THE FORMAT STATEMENT

A FORMAT statement used in conjunction with a READ, PRINT, or WRITE statement provides information that describes the layout of data in an input or output record, or record sequence, in a file. The computer does not execute FORMAT statements, but it uses them to determine how data in input records are to be converted and edited for internal representation and how data in memory are to be converted and edited for external presentation.

The form of a FORMAT statement is

```
FORMAT (flist)
```

where flist consists of one or more *edit descriptors* separated by commas and, when appropriate, groups of edit descriptors enclosed in parentheses. The edit descriptors are also called *format specifications* or *codes*. Because FORMAT statements are used only when referenced by READ, PRINT, or WRITE statements, they each must always be given a unique statement number.

When the computer executes a READ, PRINT, or WRITE statement that references a FORMAT statement, it examines the edit descriptors in the flist of the FORMAT statement, one by one, left to right, to determine how the i/o data are arranged externally. As it scans through the edit descriptors it matches those that describe numeric fields with the numeric variables in the READ, PRINT, or WRITE iolist, and then locates and edits the variable values appropriately. Other edit descriptors are used to create titles, column headings, and messages; and still others are used for horizontal and vertical spacing.

As an aid in illustrating FORMAT edit descriptors and developing FORMAT statements in the following sections, an output layout for the averaging program is given in Figure 6-6. Further, some example i/o for the program is given in Figure 6-7.

6-3-1   *Printer Carriage Control: Printed Output Only*

If you have ever used a typewriter, you know that you can control the vertical spacing on each page by first setting the machine for single or double spacing. Then, when you hit the return key after typing a line, the typewriter will automatically move the paper so that the next typed line will be appropriately spaced from the previous one. Similarly, when a line printer is used for computer output, the printer's vertical spacing must be controlled; and the control must be present for every line that is to be printed. It is accomplished by the use of the first character of the output record.

Notice then that in the layouts of Figures 6-3 and 6-6, I left column 1 open on all lines to implicitly indicate that a carriage control character would be generated—but not printed— in that column. Therefore, when a formatted record

Program AVRAGE   File PO: AVRAGE

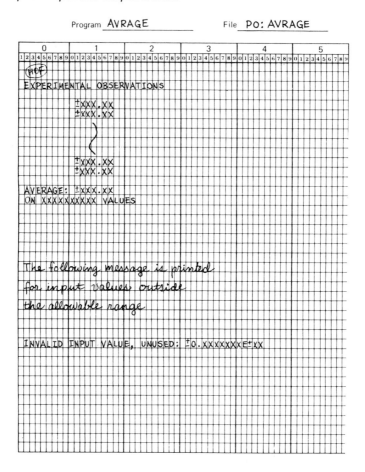

Figure 6-6. Layout of Averaging Program Output

is printed, the first character of the record is not printed; it is used to determine vertical spacing as follows:

Carriage Control Character	Vertical Spacing before Printing
Blank	Single
0	Double
1	New page (head-of-form)
+	None (suppressed spacing)

The "new page" spacing means that the paper is ejected by the printer so that it is positioned at the first line of the next page. This is commonly called *head-of-form* (HOF). The "none" spacing means that no vertical spacing occurs prior to printing when the + is the carriage control character.

```
43.25
 4.25
48.62
15.38
15.25
40.12
68.0
18.75
12.25
42.62
28.75
16.88
46.38
 4.62
 4.88
```

(a.) Input Data (one value per input record)

```
EXPERIMENTAL OBSERVATIONS

     43.25
      4.25
     48.62
     15.38
     15.25
     40.12
     68.00
     18.75
     12.25
     42.62
     28.75
     16.88
     46.38
      4.62
      4.88

AVERAGE:   27.33
ON         15 VALUES
```

(b.) Output

Figure 6-7. Some Example I/O for the Averaging Program (a) Input Data (one value per input record) (b) Output

The carriage control character for a print line is generated by a format edit descriptor, but there is no one particular descriptor that has to be used. I prefer to use the one that is designated for printing literal information—discussed in the next section—and to specify the carriage control as the first individual item of each print line that is described by the flist in a FORMAT statement. The particular specifications I use, then, are these:

Carriage Control Specification	Vertical Spacing Action
' '	Single
'0'	Double
'1'	HOF
'+'	None

All of the above except '+' are illustrated in the FORMAT statements of the averaging program of Figure 6-4. The '1' in the first flist position of statement 900 results in HOF spacing before the title is printed; thus the title is printed at the top of a new page. The '0' in statement 910 causes double spacing before the error message "INVALID INPUT VALUE, UNUSED: " and the invalid value are printed. The ' ' in statement 920 causes single spacing prior to the printing of each line that contains an observation value. And the '0' in the first flist position of statement 930 results in double spacing. FORMAT statement 930 also contains two other carriage control specifications: a ' ', for single spacing before printing the word ON, and a '1', for HOF after all printing is complete. Each of these last two carriage control specifications immediately follow a slash (/) in the flist of statement 930. A slash in an flist denotes the end of a physical record. Any output, then, that occurs after a slash in an flist must begin with a carriage control specification.

6-3-2 Printing Literal Information: Output Only

Another name for literal is *character constant*. When a character constant appears in the flist of a FORMAT statement, the editing performed upon it for output is referred to as *apostrophe editing*. Thus apostrophe editing causes a group of characters enclosed within a pair of apostrophes to be written to an output file.

Any characters allowed by the computer and output device you are using can appear in a character constant. Furthermore, blanks are not ignored in character constants; each blank actually occupies one character position. However, to include an apostrophe within a character constant, it is necessary to place two apostrophes together with no blanks or other characters in between. For example,

```
'MARY''S LITTLE LAMB'
```

As discussed in Section 6-3-1, each of the FORMAT statements in the averaging program has a character constant for carriage control. Each of the FORMAT statements 900, 910, and 930 has at least one other character constant. These, you should realize by now, are used for printing the title and other descriptive information as identified on the output layout.

6-3-3 Horizontal Spacing and Tabbing: Input and Output

For output, horizontal spacing can be accomplished with apostrophe editing whenever only a few columns are involved. After all, a blank in a character constant is a space when printed. However, for spacing in input data or to space over several columns on an output line, either the nX edit descriptor, for horizontal spacing between values, or the T edit descriptor, for tabbing directly to a particular columnar location, should be used.

The form of the descriptor that provides spaces between values on an input or output record is

nX

where n is the number of spaces occurring at that point in the record. Statement 920 of the averaging program,

```
920 FORMAT (' ',  9X,  F7.2)
```

contains one spacing example: the 9X. The flist of this statement contains three edit descriptors: the first, ' ', for carriage control—single spacing; the second, 9X, for spacing over 9 columns on the line; the third, F7.2, for printing a real number—to be explained shortly. This FORMAT statement corresponds to each of the lines, on the output layout form, that contain ±XXX.XX in columns 11 through 17. Thus column 1 is set aside to implicitly designate carriage control, and columns 2 through 10 are left blank because they are to be spaced-over due to the 9X edit descriptor.

To exemplify the use of the nX descriptor for input and a more involved output, consider the problem of Exercise 7(c) of Section 5-11, in which the real values of the coefficients A, B, and C were to be read in, two quadratic roots calculated if they existed, and then the results printed. Assume that the input layout is as follows.

Field Name	Data Description	Columns
A coefficient	Real, XXXX.X	1–6
B coefficient	Real, XXXX.X	11–16
C coefficient	Real, XXXX.X	21–26

Also assume that the output layout for the lines containing the values of the coefficients A, B, and C, and the two roots—in sequence and with columnar alignment—is as follows.

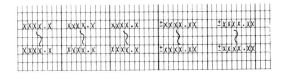

Then the FORMAT statements, describing the input and output records, and the READ and WRITE statements, for execution of data transfer, can be coded directly from the layouts as shown below.

```
140 FORMAT (F6.1,  4X,  F6.1,  4X,  F6.1)
940 FORMAT (' ',  F6.1,  3X,  F6.1,  3X,  F6.1,  4X,  F8.2,
     :           4X,  F8.2)
     .
     .
     .
READ (CI,  140,  END=899) ACOEF,  BCOEF,  CCOEF
     .
     .
     .
WRITE (PO,  940) ACOEF,  BCOEF,  CCOEF,  ROOT1,  ROOT2
```

Upon an execution of the READ statement, the computer will read in three values sequentially—the values of ACOEF, BCOEF, and CCOEF—from an input record, using the sequence of edit descriptors in FORMAT statement 140. The first edit descriptor, F6.1, indicates that a real value is in columns 1 through 6—the value of ACOEF. The second edit descriptor, 4X, is for spacing-over (skipping-over or ignoring) the next four columns. The third one, F6.1, is for a real value in the next six columns—the value of BCOEF. The fourth, 4X, is for ignoring columns 17 through 20. And the fifth, F6.1, is for placement of a real value in the last six columns of the record—the value of CCOEF. The record length for input in this example is 26 characters.

Upon an execution of the WRITE statement, the computer will write out five values from memory: first the value of ACOEF, then those of BCOEF, CCOEF, ROOT1, and ROOT2—in sequence. FORMAT statement 940 will be used, in conjunction with the WRITE, for accomplishing the following in sequence: single space, write a real value (ACOEF) in a six-column field, space-over three columns, write a real value (BCOEF) in a six-column field, space-over three columns, write a real value (CCOEF) in a six-column field, space-over four columns, write a real value (ROOT1) in an eight-column field, space-over four columns, and write a real value (ROOT2) in an eight-column field. Ten edit descriptors are used, including one for carriage control, four for horizontal spacing, and five for printing values. The output record length is 49 characters.

The T edit descriptor, commonly called the *tab code*, can also be used for horizontal spacing. It is used to designate the location, in an i/o record, at which the next value is to begin. It has three forms:

```
Tc
TLc
TRc
```

In the Tc form, c is the column number at which the next value in the record begins. The use of this form, then, requires that the exact column numbers be specified. In the example FORMAT statement above, the nX edit descriptors could be replaced by Tc form edit descriptors, to yield identical results, in this way:

```
140 FORMAT (F6.1, T11, F6.1, T21, F6.1)
940 FORMAT (' ', F6.1, T11, F6.1, T20, F6.1, T30, F8.2,
    :        T42, F8.2)
```

In the TLc and TRc forms, c is the number of columns to the left or right, respectively, that the next value is, or is to be, from the current position in the i/o record. For example, the FORMAT statements above can be rewritten as follows, yet still yield the same results:

```
140 FORMAT (F6.1, TR5, F6.1, TR5, F6.1)
940 FORMAT (' ', F6.1, TR4, F6.1, TR4, F6.1, TR5, F8.2,
    :        TR5, F8.2)
```

6-3-4 Numeric Field Specifications:
Input and Output

Each numeric variable in the iolist of a formatted READ, PRINT, or WRITE statement must have an associated numeric field edit descriptor in the FORMAT statement that is referenced by the READ, PRINT, or WRITE statement. Integer variables require the Iw or Iw.m descriptor, real variables normally use the Fw.d or Ew.d descriptor, and double-precision variables ordinarily use the Dw.d descriptor. In each of these descriptors, w represents the width of the numeric field in terms of the number of character positions occupied by the value in the i/o record. Where used, m specifies a minimum number of digits for the output of an integer value, and d identifies the number of fractional digits for either the input or output of a real or double-precision number. In each actual use, w, m, and d must be unsigned integer constants and, furthermore, w must be nonzero.

The simplest uses of the Iw, Fw.d, and Ew.d descriptors for output are illustrated in the averaging program. The last WRITE statement in the program

```
WRITE (PO, 930) AVE, COUNT
```

specifies that the values of the real variable AVE and the integer variable COUNT are to be printed using FORMAT statement 930, which looks like this:

```
930 FORMAT ('0', 'AVERAGE: ', F7.2, /,
    :          ' ', 'ON', I10, ' VALUES', /, '1')
```

Upon the execution of the WRITE statement, the computer will scan through the WRITE iolist and the FORMAT flist left to right, performing editing into the output record as indicated in the flist, and matching numeric variables with numeric field descriptors as they occur in sequence. AVE, then, will be associated with the F7.2 descriptor, resulting in its value being printed right-justified in the seven-column field following the characters 'AVERAGE: '. (Output values are always right-justified in a specified field.) Further, the value of AVE will contain two digits to the right of the decimal point and, because real output values are always rounded, it will be rounded to the nearest hundredth. COUNT will be associated with the next numeric field descriptor, I10, which, because of its position in the flist, will cause the value of count to be printed right-justified in the 10-column field following the characters 'ON'.

The third WRITE statement, which references FORMAT statement 920, calls for a real value—the value of the variable OBS—to be printed. For OBS, the only numeric field descriptor, F7.2, in the FORMAT statement will be used. This is an example of a WRITE statement that is executed several times—to print all the values of OBS—and, therefore, a FORMAT statement that is referenced several times. Thus the FORMAT statement describes each of several lines of output—those that contain the input echo.

The second WRITE statement,

```
WRITE (PO, 910) OBS
```

and its referenced FORMAT statement,

```
910 FORMAT ('0', 'INVALID INPUT VALUE, UNUSED: ',
    :         E14.7, /)
```

produce output that is depicted at the bottom of Figure 6-6. These statements do not come into play in Figure 6-7. Since they illustrate the use of the Ew.d descriptor, however, it is worthwhile to consider another set of input data that will cause them to be used. Refer to Figure 6-8 for the input and its corresponding output.

The third value in the input list, 19473, causes the WRITE statement that references FORMAT statement 910 to be executed, resulting in the printout of the line that contains

```
INVALID INPUT VALUE, UNUSED:    .1947300E+05
```

in which the value of OBS at that point is printed as a real value with a real exponent due to the use of the E14.7 descriptor. Interpreted, the E14.7 identifies a real numeric field of width 14 in which seven significant digits are printed to the right of the decimal point.

An output number associated with an Ew.d field descriptor will always have the form

```
+0.XXX...XE+exp
```

where the leading + sign and zero may or may not be printed (they are not by my processor), the Xs represent exactly "d" significant digits, and the E+exp is the

```
3.216
2.146
19473
2.625
3.996
3.011
2.615
```

(a.) Input Data (one value per input record)

```
EXPERIMENTAL OBSERVATIONS
        3.22
        2.15
INVALID INPUT VALUE, UNUSED:    .1947300E+05
        2.63
        4.00
        3.01
        2.61
AVERAGE:    2.93
ON          6 VALUES
```

(b.) Output

Figure 6-8. More Example I/O for the Averaging Program (a) Input Data (one value per input record) (b) Output

real exponent as described in Chapter 5. The number 19473 is invalid and unused because it is outside the range of input observations allowed by the program. The Ew.d descriptor can be used to print the unknown and unexpected invalid numbers in such cases, even if the numbers are very large or very small, because the exponent allows the decimal point to "float" through the number so that as many significant digits as possible can be printed. If the F7.2 descriptor had been used to print the invalid number there would not have been enough positions for the number in the output field; the computer would then have printed ******* to indicate that the field was too small for the number.

The Dw.d descriptor, for i/o of double-precision numbers, is essentially the same as the Ew.d descriptor except that the exponents of the numbers contain a D rather than an E. Although the Dw.d descriptor should ordinarily be used for i/o of double-precision values, it is permissible to use either the Fw.d or the Ew.d codes for them; the variable name, not the format code, determines the data type of an i/o value.

Input with the I and F Descriptors

In the numeric field of an input record, blanks may be ignored or treated as zeros; a completely blank field is considered to be a zero value. The FORTRAN 77 standard indicates that ignoring blanks is the default option. This provides the advantage of not having to be concerned about where in the field the number is placed.

Under the earlier Fortran standard, all blanks in numeric input fields were treated as zeros; that was the only option available. It is reasonable to expect, therefore, that many FORTRAN 77 processors will treat the zero option as the default. It becomes necessary, then, to give some consideration to the placement of values in numeric input fields.

In an integer numeric field, trailing blanks are significant whenever they are treated as zeros. Therefore, integer values must always be right-justified in such input fields. For example, if an input code of I5 is used to describe the first five-column field of an input record in which blanks are handled as zeros, and the record contains

```
Columns:    1 2 3 4 5
Contents:     2 1 2
```

then the value read into memory will be 02120 or, simply, 2120. If 212 is the intended input value, it must be entered into columns 3, 4, and 5 of the record, that is, right-justified.

In real numeric fields trailing blanks may also be significant. This is the case only when the number in the field does not contain an explicit decimal point. For instance, if an input specification of F8.2 is used to describe the first eight-column field of an input record in which blanks are handled as zeros, and the record contains

```
Columns:    1 2 3 4 5 6 7 8
Contents:   — 4 5 9
```

then the value read into memory will be −45900.00; that is, the decimal point is placed by the computer—due to the ''d'' part of the field specification—in such a way that the rightmost two digits of the field are to the right of the decimal point and the others are to the left. The decimal point is therefore implied, by the format code, to be between columns six and seven of the input record. This is fine, but if −459 was the intended value, the number should have been entered in the record this way:

Columns:	1 2 3 4 5 6 7 8
Contents:	− 4 5 9

or with a decimal point something like this:

Columns:	1 2 3 4 5 6 7 8
Contents:	− 4 5 9 . 0

where columns 7 and 8 are going to be assumed, by the computer, to contain zeros. By including the decimal point with the number in the input field, as in the last example above, you do not have to be concerned with the ''d'' part of the F code; it must be present but it is overridden by the decimal point itself. You also need not be concerned about how blanks are handled.

Establishing input with the I and F specifications is not difficult if you develop an input layout first. As one more illustration, refer back in Figure 6-1 to the layout for the investment record. The data type, FORMAT, and READ statements for that record can be written as follows.

```
      INTEGER  CI, NYEARS
      REAL   PRIN, RATE
      .
      .
      .
150  FORMAT (F7.2, F4.2, I2)
      .
      .
      .
      READ (CI, 150) PRIN, RATE, NYEARS
```

Then, if an actual input record has these contents

Columns:	1 2 3 4 5 6 7 8 9 10 11 12 13
Contents:	5 0 0 0 . 0 0 0 . 1 6

the values read into memory for PRIN, RATE, and NYEARS, will be 5000.00, 0.1, and 6. Think about it.

Output with the I and F Descriptors

Developing appropriate formats and output statements when using these descriptors is straightforward if the output layouts are developed first. To illustrate the coding of a fairly comprehensive output layout, consider the Loan Amortization Schedule of Figure 6-3. Letting you figure out the variable usage simply by the names used for the variables, I offer the following program code to represent the output.

```
REAL   AMBORR, BGDEBT, ENDEBT, MIRATE, INTPAY,
:         PRIPAY, TOTPAY
INTEGER  MONTH, PO
.
.
.
960 FORMAT ('1', T30, 'LOAN AMORTIZATION SCHEDULE', /)
962 FORMAT ('0', 9X, 'AMOUNT BORROWED: ', F8.2, 11X,
:             'MONTHLY INTEREST RATE: ', F5.2, /)
964 FORMAT ('0', 17X, 'BEGINNING', 4X, 'INTEREST', 4X,
:             'PRINCIPAL', 5X, 'TOTAL', 7X, 'ENDING')
966 FORMAT (' ', 9X, 'MONTH', 6X, 'DEBT', 7X, 'PAYMENT',
:             5X, 'PAYMENT', 5X, 'PAYMENT', 7X, 'DEBT', /)
967 FORMAT (' ', 10X, I3, 4X, F8.2, 5X, F7.2, 5X,
:             F8.2, 4X, F8.2, 4X, F8.2)
.
.
.
WRITE (PO, 960)
WRITE (PO, 962) AMBORR, MIRATE
WRITE (PO, 964)
WRITE (PO, 966)
WRITE (PO, 967) MONTH, BGDEBT, INTPAY, PRIPAY,
:                TOTPAY, ENDEBT
```

Frankly, you should be able to interpret this code almost completely without my help. There is only one item I want to mention right now. It has to do with the use of the slash (/) in an flist.

Earlier, I said that a slash in an flist denotes the end of a physical record; for output, the end of a print line. (Of course, if a slash appears as part of a character constant inside apostrophes, it is just another character to be printed and does not, in that case, designate the end of a record.) FORMAT statements 960, 962, and 966 each contain a slash as the last item in the flist. What the slash does in this position is to provide an extra blank line before the printing of the next line takes place. Thus, an ending slash combined with a beginning '0' carriage control speci-fication effectively yields a triple space; a slash—' ' combination yields a double space. Additional ending slashes would yield more blank lines. At any point in an flist, a group of slashes can be used to provide blank lines. Furthermore, within an flist, the sequence

```
..., 11(/), ...
```

which specifies 11 repetitions of the slash, will provide 10 blank lines at that point. You can, of course, vary the number of repetitions as desired.

6-3-5   *Repetition of Edit Descriptors:*
Input and Output

A general form for the slash repetition is

```
n(/)
```

where n, a constant, is the number of times that the slash is to be repeated at that point in the flist. Actually, any group of edit descriptors in an flist can be repeated by surrounding the group with parentheses and preceding it by the number of repetitions. For example, FORMAT statement 967 of the preceding section can be rewritten in the following shortened form that involves repetition of the last few codes.

```
967 FORMAT (' ', 10X, I3, 4X, F8.2, 5X, F7.2, 1X,
    :          3(4X, F8.2) )
```

Similarly, FORMAT statements 140 and 940, which were written earlier like this

```
140 FORMAT (F6.1, 4X, F6.1, 4X, F6.1)
940 FORMAT (' ', F6.1, 3X, F6.1, 3X, F6.1, 4X, F8.2,
    :          4X, F8.2)
```

can be rewritten in the shorter, but identical, forms

```
140 FORMAT (F6.1, 2(4X, F6.1) )
940 FORMAT (' ', F6.1, 2(3X, F6.1), 2(4X, F8.2) )
```

The numeric field descriptors—I, F, E, and D—can even be repeated individually, without using parentheses. The individual forms for repetition of these codes are

```
nIw
nIw.m
nFw.d
nEw.d
nDw.d
```

where, in each case, n is the number of repetitions of that format code at that point. For example, the FORMAT statement for an input record that has five consecutive eight-column fields of real data items could be written as

```
170 FORMAT (F8.0, F8.0, F8.0, F8.0, F8.0)
```

or, more simply, as

```
170 FORMAT (5F8.0)
```

and the READ statement in either case could be

```
READ (CI, 170) TMPTUR, PRESUR, SPGRAV, DNSITY, HUMITY
```

Similarly, the FORMAT statement for an output record that has six consecutive 10-column fields of integer data items could be written as

```
970 FORMAT (' ', I10, I10, I10, I10, I10, I10)
```

or, more simply, as

```
970 FORMAT (' ', 6I10)
```

and the WRITE statement, in either case, could be

```
WRITE (PO, 970) IN, KADINC, IDIN, KID, INK, IDO
```

6-3-6   Exhausting the iolist and the flist

In all of the examples of this chapter so far, the READ or WRITE iolist has contained exactly the same number of variables as there were numeric field edit descriptors (I, E, F, or D) in the corresponding FORMAT flist. The input implication has been that the execution of a READ statement causes exactly one input record, described precisely by a FORMAT statement, to be transmitted to memory. The output implication is similar: the execution of a WRITE statement causes exactly one output record, also described precisely by a FORMAT statement, to be transmitted to an output file. These implications are usually true, but not always.

It is possible for an iolist to have more or fewer variables than its corresponding flist has numeric field descriptors. For instance, in the combination

```
175 FORMAT (F6.0)
    .
    .
    .
    READ (CI, 175) AMTONE, AMTTWO, AMTTHR
```

the flist contains only one field specification, whereas the iolist contains three variables. This is a case in which the flist gets used up or exhausted before the iolist does. You should have little difficulty understanding what happens in this situation if you will remember that the READ statement is the one being executed, and therefore the iolist is in control; the computer must read values for all three variables before it can go on any further in the program.

You know that the value of AMTONE will be in the first six columns of the first record, so where will the value of AMTTWO be? The answer is: in the first six columns of the second record. Following through, then, the value of AMTTHR had better be in the first six columns of the third record. The rule, when an flist is exhausted first, is that the computer scans back from the right to the first open parenthesis in the flist, moves to the right from there, and looks to the next input record for the next value.

In a contrasting situation such as

```
180 FORMAT (2I3, 4X, F8.0)
    .
    .
    .
    READ (CI, 180) INITAL, LIMIT
```

the reading will be complete after only two format codes, 2I3, have been used and only two values have been read in. Here, as above, the READ statement is being executed and the iolist controls. Since the iolist has no need for the remaining specifications in the flist, they will be ignored and execution will proceed with the next executable statement after the READ.

6-4   AN EXAMPLE PROGRAM FOR I/O STUDY: REPORT CREATION

Early in this chapter I mentioned that a student record might contain some character data fields, such as student name and address, and some numeric data fields, such as hours passed and grade points. Information like this can be used to produce a variety of useful reports, one of which is a report of student grade point averages (GPA).

Only a small part of the information contained in each record is needed in the creation of a grade point average report. The grade point average itself depends on the hours attempted and the grade points received, in the relationship

$$\text{grade point average} = \frac{\text{grade points received}}{\text{hours attempted}}$$

The other input information needed is dictated by the format of the overall report.

One item that might be desirable in the report is the name of each student. In this chapter I showed you how character data, such as student names, are produced as output from a program. However, I did not show you how character data are read into memory from input records—that comes in Chapter 9. So you are not yet prepared to deal with character input data. For this report, then, individual student identification can be by number—perhaps Social Security Number—rather than by name.

The report layout to be produced is shown in Figure 6-9. It is to be a rather simple, straightforward report that may consist of a number of pages. Each page should be numbered, as shown, and contain the title and column headings. The top line, containing "YOUR OWN COLLEGE OR UNIVERSITY," has been included to indicate that the specific college or university should usually be identified in reports like this. The input data items dictated by the report include—for each student—an identification number, hours tried, hours passed, and grade points. Also the report date, in terms of month (MM), day (DD), and year (YY), can be supplied as input data. The page number can be generated internally in the logic of the program. All of the other printed information can be produced as constant data in FORMAT statements.

The first input record should contain the month, day, and year, and have this layout:

Field Name	*Data Description*	*Columns*
Month	Integer, MM	1−2
Day	Integer, DD	3−4
Year	Integer, YY	5−6

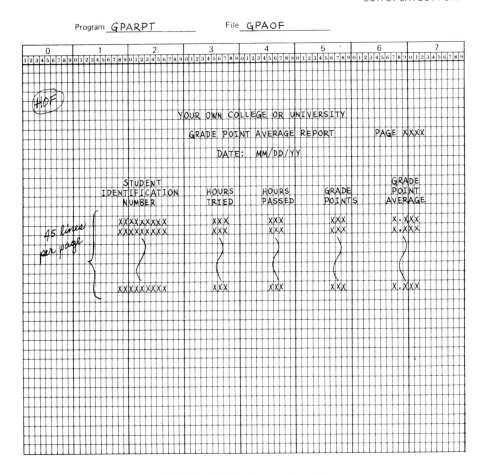

Figure 6-9. Grade Point Average Report Layout

The other input records—call them "grade point records"—have this layout:

Field Name	Data Description	Columns
Student I.D. number	Integer, XXXXXXXXX	1–9
Hours tried	Integer, XXX	10–12
Hours passed	Integer, XXX	13–15
Grade points received	Integer, XXX	16–18

The algorithm is fairly straightforward, but requires consideration of two factors that we have not encountered in previous algorithms: output line counting and paging. The number of pages in the report depends on the number of student records processed and the number of lines printed on each page. As you can see in Figure 6-9, I decided to print all the header information—11 lines, counting blanks—plus 45 lines of detail information (one per student record) on each page. This leaves 10 lines unused on each page—room enough for $\frac{5}{6}$-inch margins at the top and bottom. With these additional considerations, the algorithm can be developed top-down, in a stepwise fashion, as usual.

First try:

```
Read the month, day, and year.
As long as there are pages to print, do the following:
    Print heading information;
    As long as there are not more than 45 lines printed,
    do the following:
        As long as there are more input records,
        do the following:
            Read an input record,
            Compute a grade point average (gpa),
            Print an output record.
Stop.
```

Second try:

```
        Read month, day, year
        Initialize page counter to 1
HEAD.   Write heading: (see layout), page counter, month,
            day, year
        Initialize line counter to 1
            While line counter is not greater than maximum line
                count, do the following:
            Read student identification number, hours tried,
                hours passed, grade points received,
                at EOF Go To FIN. (Ahead)
            gpa ← 0
            If hours tried > 0,
                gpa ← grade points / hours tried
            Write student identification number, hours tried,
                hours passed, grade points received,
                grade point average
            Increment line counter by 1
        Increment page counter by 1
        Go To HEAD. (Back)
    FIN. New Page
        Stop
```

In the second try above, notice that the maximum line count has been changed from the fixed constant 45 to a symbolic constant. This will provide generality in the program. Also observe that the grade point average is computed from the hours tried only if the latter is greater than zero. It is possible that one or more students have been admitted but not yet taken any courses, in which case the hours taken would all be zero. Division by zero, however, would be disastrous.

After going through another try, or two if necessary, a final algorithm, something like the following one, can be written.

ALGORITHM GPA:report
{   A report of student grade point averages (gpa) is
created from input records containing student
identification number, hours tried, hours passed, and
grade points received.}
Read month, day, year
page ← 1
HEAD.   Write heading (see layout), page, month, day, year
         line ← 1
NXLN.   If line <= maxline Then
             Read student id, hours tried, hours passed,
                 grade points, at EOF Go To FIN. (Ahead)
             gpa ← 0
             If hours tried > 0,
                 gpa ← grade points / hours tried
             Write student id, hours tried, hours passed,
                 grade points, gpa
             line ← line + 1
             Go To NXLN. (Back)
         page ← page + 1
         Go To HEAD. (Back)
FIN. Write HOF
     Stop
     END

Leaving the drawing of the flowchart for you to do as an exercise, I proceed directly to the complete program shown in Figure 6-10. The program should be easy for you to read and understand. Rather than using CI and PO to identify input and output devices as I did in earlier programs, I used the more specific file identifiers DATEIF (for input of the record containing the date), GPRIF (for input of the grade point records), and GPAOF (for output of the grade point average report). DATEIF and GPRIF were given the same value, 5, because they refer to the same input device.

A sample set of i/o for the program is given in Figure 6-11. The input values are totally arbitrary but cover fairly well the grade point record information that might occur. Some values are realistic; others are not. A complete test of the program would require more data.

```
*I.   GRADE POINT AVERAGE REPORT
      PROGRAM GPARPT
*     PROGRAMMER:  JARRELL C. GROUT
*     DATE:  1/24/81
*
*  A. COMMENTARY
*
*        A REPORT OF STUDENT GRADE POINT AVERAGES IS CREATED
*     FROM INPUT RECORDS CONTAINING STUDENT IDENTIFICATION
*     NUMBER (SIDNUM), HOURS TRIED (HRSTRI), HOURS PASSED
*     (HRSPAS), AND GRADE POINTS RECEIVED (GPRCVD).
*
*        DICTIONARY.
*     DATEIF:  DATE INPUT FILE IDENTIFIER
*     DAY:  DAY OF THE MONTH REPORT IS PRODUCED (01 THRU 31)
*     GPA:  GRADE POINT AVERAGE
*     GPAOF:  GPA OUTPUT FILE IDENTIFIER
*     GPRCVD:  GRADE POINTS RECEIVED
*     GPRIF:  GRADE POINT RECORD INPUT FILE IDENTIFIER
*     HRSPAS:  HOURS PASSED (0 THRU 999)
*     HRSTRI:  HOURS TRIED (0 THRU 999)
```

Figure 6-10. Program for Producing a Grade Point Average Report

```
*      LINE:   LINE COUNTER FOR OUTPUT PAGES
*      MAXLIN:   MAXIMUM LINES OF DETAIL PER PAGE
*      MONTH:   MONTH THE REPORT IS PRODUCED (01 THRU 12)
*      PAGE:   PAGE COUNTER FOR OUTPUT PAGES
*      SIDNUM:   STUDENT IDENTIFICATION NUMBER (ALWAYS 9 DIGITS)
*      YEAR:   YEAR THE REPORT IS PRODUCED (0 THRU 99)
*
*  B. DECLARATION
*
       INTEGER  DATEIF, DAY, GPAOF, GPRCVD, GPRIF, HRSPAS,
      :         HRSTRI, LINE, MAXLIN, MONTH, PAGE, SIDNUM,
      :         YEAR
       REAL   GPA
       PARAMETER  (DATEIF=5, GPRIF=5,  GPAOF=6,  MAXLIN=45)
*
*  C. I/O LAYOUT
*
  100 FORMAT (3I2)
  110 FORMAT (I9, 3I3)
  900 FORMAT ('1', //, ' ', T29, 'YOUR OWN COLLEGE OR UNIVERSITY', /
      :         '0', T31, 'GRADE POINT AVERAGE REPORT', 7X, 'PAGE', I5, /
      :         '0', T36, 'DATE:   ', I2, 2('/', I2), //
      :         '0', T19, 'STUDENT', 41X, 'GRADE', /
      :         ' ', T15, 'IDENTIFICATION', 5X, 'HOURS', 5X,
      :         'HOURS', 6X, 'GRADE', 7X, 'POINT', /
      :         ' ', T19, 'NUMBER', 9X, 'TRIED', 5X, 'PASSED',
      :         5X, 'POINTS', 5X, 'AVERAGE', /)
  910 FORMAT (' ', T18, I9.9, 8X, I3, 7X, I3, 8X, I3, 8X, F5.3)
  999 FORMAT ('1')
*
*  D. ACTION
*
       READ (DATEIF, 100) MONTH, DAY, YEAR
       PAGE = 1
  200    WRITE (GPAOF, 900) PAGE, MONTH, DAY, YEAR
         LINE = 1
  210    IF (LINE .LE. MAXLIN) THEN
           READ (GPRIF, 110, END=230) SIDNUM, HRSTRI, HRSPAS, GPRCVD
           GPA = 0.0
           IF (HRSTRI .GT. 0) GPA = FLOAT(GPRCVD) / HRSTRI
           WRITE (GPAOF, 910) SIDNUM, HRSTRI, HRSPAS, GPRCVD, GPA
           LINE = LINE + 1
           GO TO 210
         ENDIF
         PAGE = PAGE + 1
         GO TO 200
  230  WRITE (GPAOF, 999)
       STOP
       END
```

Figure 6-10. (continued)

(a.) Input (one record per line; each begins in column 1)

```
012481
111111111 30 30 90
222222222130120259
444444444  0  0  0
555555555 15 11 13
777777777 99 99300
888888888999999999
999999999 85 85340
```

(b.) Output

```
              YOUR OWN COLLEGE OR UNIVERSITY

           GRADE POINT AVERAGE REPORT        PAGE     1

           DATE:   1/24/81


                                                     GRADE
        STUDENT                                       POINT
     IDENTIFICATION    HOURS      HOURS      GRADE    AVERAGE
        NUMBER         TRIED      PASSED     POINTS

       111111111        30         30         90      3.000
       222222222       130        120        259      1.992
       444444444         0          0          0       .000
       555555555        15         11         13       .867
       777777777        99         99        300      3.030
       888888888       999        999        999      1.000
       999999999        85         85        340      4.000
```

Figure 6-11. Sample I/O for the Grade Point Average Report Program (a) Input (one record per line; each begins in column 1) (b) Output

6-5 EXERCISES

1. Discuss why, in the ''grade point average report'' program of Figure 6-10, the GPA computation was written

   ```
   GPAVE = FLOAT(GPRCVD) / HRSTRI
   ```

   rather than

   ```
   GPAVE = GPRCVD / HRSTRI
   ```

2. Below, you are given several sets of FORMAT and READ statements together with some input records. In each case, state what values will be placed in memory for each of the input variables when the computer executes the READ statements. Assume default data types and make sure that your values are of the correct types. Also assume that the input unit identifiers are properly defined, and that input values begin in column 1.

   (a) Program statements:

   ```
   100 FORMAT (I1, I2, I3)
       READ (CI, 100) IOTA, KAPPA, LAMBDA
   ```

   Input record:

   ```
   56 7
   ```

   (b) Statements:

   ```
   105 FORMAT (F5.4, I4, 1X, F8.0)
       READ (CI, 105) DELTA, MU, RHO
   ```

   Record:

   ```
   123456789 1.0
   ```

   (c) Statements:

   ```
   110 FORMAT (4I3)
       READ (CI, 110) NU
   ```

   Record:

   ```
   1
   ```

   (d) Statements:

   ```
   115 FORMAT (F10.2)
       READ (CI, 115) ZETA, ETA, THETA
   ```

   Records:

   ```
   1
      5.55555555
            -1
   -232.0    -459.0
   ```

3. Below you are given a program segment containing WRITE statements and their associated FORMAT statements. Given that, in memory, ALPHA=10.0, BETA=−20.0, IOTA=9999, KAPPA=−5, LAMBDA =100, GAMMA=99.995, DELTA=−0.874, and EPSILN=0.5, show exactly what will be printed when the WRITE statements are executed. Clearly indicate the carriage control action for each print line. Assume default data types and proper assignment of the output unit identifier.

```
900 FORMAT ('1', T5, 'HERE ARE THE PRINTED RESULTS', /)
905 FORMAT ('0', 2(F8.2, 4X), I8)
910 FORMAT (' ', T6, I4)
920 FORMAT (' ', T4, 2F6.2)
930 FORMAT (' ', T2, F8.2, 4X, E8.1, F12.1, /
    :         '0', T20, 'AND THAT''S ALL.')

    .
    .
    .

    WRITE (PO, 900)
    WRITE (PO, 905) ALPHA, BETA, IOTA
    WRITE (PO, 910) KAPPA, LAMBDA
    WRITE (PO, 920) GAMMA
    WRITE (PO, 930) DELTA, EPSILN, EPSILN
```

4. Below you are given a WRITE statement and its associated FORMAT statement. Given that AMTINV=1000.0, RATEIN=0.055, GAIN=56.1447, and FINBAL=1056.1447 in memory, exactly what will be printed when the WRITE statement is executed?

```
920 FORMAT ('0', 'WHEN THE AMOUNT INVESTED IS $ ', F7.2, /
    :         ' ', 'AND THE INTEREST RATE IS ', F5.3, /
    :         ' ', 'THEN, IF COMPOUNDING IS QUARTERLY,', /
    :         ' ', 'THE AMOUNT OF INTEREST GAINED WILL BE $ ',
    :         F6.2, /
    :         ' ', 'AND THE FINAL BALANCE WILL BE $ ',
    :         F8.2, '.')

    .
    .
    .

    WRITE (PO, 920) AMTINV, RATEIN, GAIN, FINBAL
```

5. Below you are given two program segments and their associated input records. In each case, write down exactly what will be printed by the computer when it executes the program with the input data. Clearly indicate the carriage control action for each print line. Additionally, explain as best you can what is accomplished by each program: what problem is solved.

(a) Program segment:

```
*   B. DECLARATION
*
        INTEGER CI, I, NINV, PERIDS, PO
        REAL FWORTH, INRATE, PRIN
        PARAMETER (CI=5, PO=6)
*
```

```
*  C. I/O LAYOUT
*
   100 FORMAT (I3)
   110 FORMAT (F7.2, F4.2, I1)
   900 FORMAT ('1', 'ANALYSIS PROGRAM ANSWERS')
   910 FORMAT ('0', I3, 4X, F8.2, 4X, F5.2, 6X, I2, 4X,
     :            F9.2)
   999 FORMAT ('1')
*
*  D. ACTION
*
        WRITE (PO, 900)
        READ (CI, 100) NINV
        I = 1
   200 IF (I .LE. NINV) THEN
            READ (CI, 110) PRIN, INRATE, PERIDS
            FWORTH = PRIN * (1.0 + INRATE) ** PERIDS
            WRITE (PO, 910) I, PRIN, INRATE, PERIDS, FWORTH
            I = I + 1
            GO TO 200
        ENDIF
        WRITE (PO, 999)
        STOP
        END
```

Input records:

```
    2
1000.  0.10102
 100000001010
10000000000102
```

(b) Program segment:

```
*  B. DECLARATION
*
        INTEGER  EMPID, WHIF, WPOF
        REAL  HOURS, OTFACT, OTHRS, PAY, RATEPA
        PARAMETER  (WHIF=5, WPOF=6, OTHRS=40.0, OTFACT=0.5)
*
*  C. I/O LAYOUT
*
   100 FORMAT (I9, F5.2, F4.1)
   900 FORMAT ('1', T20, 'XYZ COMPANY', /
     :          '0', T17, 'WEEKLY PAY REPORT', //
     :          '0', T2, 'EMPLOYEE NUMBER', 3X, 'PAY RATE',
     :          3X, 'HOURS WORKED', 4X, 'PAY', /)
   910 FORMAT (' ', 3X, I9.9, 8X, F5.2, 8X, F4.1, 7X, F6.2)
   999 FORMAT ('1')
*
*  D. ACTION
*
        WRITE (WPOF, 900)
   200    READ (WHIF, 100, END=210) EMPID, RATEPA, HOURS
         PAY = HOURS * RATEPA
         IF (HOURS .GT. OTHRS)
     :       PAY = PAY + (HOURS - OTHRS) * OTFACT * RATEPA
         WRITE (WPOF, 910) EMPID, RATEPA, HOURS, PAY
         GO TO 200
   210 WRITE (WPOF, 999)
        STOP
        END
```

149

Input records:

```
123456789 8.5040.0
23456789010.1040.0
345678901 9.2550.5
45678901215.0035.0
567890123 4.5020.0
67890123410.00 0.0
78901234512.5540.0
```

6. The "Your Own College or University" Department of Computer Science professors want to use the computer to help them figure the final grades for students in their courses. They developed an idea of what the output report should contain—something like this:

```
          YOCU DEPARTMENT OF COMPUTER SCIENCE

        REPORT OF STUDENT GRADES AND COURSE AVERAGE      PAGE XX

    COURSE:   XXX         SECTION:   XX         DATE:   MM/DD/YY

                EXAM A   EXAM B   EXAM C   HOMEWORK   FINAL     COURSE
STUDENT I.D.    (XX %)   (XX %)   (XX %)   (XX %)     (XX %)    AVERAGE

XXXXXXXXX        XXX      XXX      XXX      XXX        XXX       XXX.X
   .              .        .        .        .          .         .
   .              .        .        .        .          .         .
   .              .        .        .        .          .         .
XXXXXXXXX        XXX      XXX      XXX      XXX        XXX       XXX.X

CLASS, OVERALL:  XXX.X    XXX.X    XXX.X    XXX.X      XXX.X     XXX.X
```

They also developed input layouts, as follows.

Date record:

Field Name	Data Description	Columns
Month	Integer, XX	1−2
Day	Integer, XX	3−4
Year	Integer, XX	5−6

Course and percent record:

Field Name	Data Description	Columns
Course number	Integer, XXX	List-directed;
Section number	Integer, XX	one space between
Exam A percent	Integer, 1−2 digits	each number pair
Exam B percent	Integer, 1−2 digits	A zero percent
Exam C percent	Integer, 1−2 digits	must be
Homework percent	Integer, 1−2 digits	entered if
Final exam percent	Integer, 1−2 digits	appropriate

Student grade records:

Field Name	Data Description	Columns
Student I.D. number	Integer, XXXXXXXXX	List-directed;
Exam A grade	Integer, 1–3 digits	one space between
Exam B grade	Integer, 1–3 digits	each number pair
Exam C grade	Integer, 1–3 digits	A zero must be
Homework grade	Integer, 1–3 digits	entered for
Final exam grade	Integer, 1–3 digits	no grade

Your task is to plan and write a complete Fortran program for the professors.

7. Plan and write a complete Fortran program to produce an interplanetary weight chart indicating how much an object might weigh on various planets, based on these factors:

Planet	Percent of Earth Weight
Mercury	38
Venus	91
Earth	100
Mars	38
Jupiter	264
Saturn	113

Each page of the chart should look something like this:

```
            INTERPLANETARY WEIGHT CHART        PAGE XX

EARTH      MERCURY      VENUS      MARS      JUPITER      SATURN

XXX        XXX.XX      XXX.XX    XXX.XX     XXXX.XX      XXXX.XX
  .           .           .         .          .            .
  .           .           .         .          .            .
  .           .           .         .          .            .
```

where the complete range of Earth weights are integral values from, say, LOWEWT to HIEWT, inclusive, in increments of INCEWT. Thus LOWEWT, HIEWT, and INCEWT are the input data variables. Some representative values for these variables might be 1, 100, and 1, which would result in a chart for all integer Earth weights from 1 to 100 inclusive.

8. A person borrows an amount of money to be repaid with interest in equal monthly payments over a period of several months. Letting r be the monthly interest rate and n the total number of payments to be made, a useful factor, f, can be computed from the relationship

$$f = \frac{r(1 + r)^n}{(1 + r)^n - 1}$$

This factor can be multiplied by the amount borrowed to yield the monthly payment required to amortize (pay off) the loan in *n* months. With interest rates changing frequently and borrowing being one of the nation's most popular activities, some tables of these factors might prove to be handy. In addition to the number of months to repay, the monthly interest rate, and the factors, it will also be useful to include the annual interest rate (the one usually stated with a loan) and the annual effective interest rate (the one actually charged). Letting *a* be the annual interest rate and *e* be the effective annual interest rate, the following relationships apply:

$$a = 12 \times r \quad \text{or} \quad r = \frac{a}{12}$$

and

$$e = (1 + r)^{12} - 1$$

Plan and write a complete Fortran program to print an amortization factor table. The layout for the table is indicated below.

```
                  AMORTIZATION FACTORS BY MONTHS                PAGE XX

    MULTIPLY A FACTOR BY THE AMOUNT BORROWED TO OBTAIN THE MONTHLY
PAYMENT FOR REPAYING A LOAN.   USE THE FACTOR THAT CORRESPONDS TO
THE INTEREST RATE BEING CHARGED AND THE NUMBER OF MONTHS ALLOWED
FOR REPAYMENT. THE INTEREST RATES ARE IDENTIFIED BELOW AS "AIR,"
THE ANNUAL INTEREST RATE; "AEIR," THE ANNUAL EFFECTIVE INTEREST
RATE; AND "MIR," THE MONTHLY INTEREST RATE.

                  AIR:  XX.XX     XX.XX     XX.XX     XX.XX     XX.XX
MONTHS FOR        AEIR: XX.XX     XX.XX     XX.XX     XX.XX     XX.XX
REPAYMENT         MIR:  X.XXX     X.XXX     X.XXX     X.XXX     X.XXX

    XX                 X.XXXXXX  X.XXXXXX  X.XXXXXX  X.XXXXXX  X.XXXXXX
     .            .         .         .          .          .
     .            .         .         .          .          .
     .            .         .         .          .          .
```

Notice that each line requires the computation of five values, using the factor formula, before the line is printed. The input data for the program should consist of the lower and upper limits, and the increments, of the annual interest rate and number of months for repayment. Suggested values are 11-20-1 and 1-60-1, which will produce four output pages—two for months from 1 through 40 and two for months from 41 through 60. The use of this table, as well as some specific i/o values, is reflected in this statement: when the annual interest rate is 18 percent and the number of months to pay is 36, the annual effective interest rate will be 19.56 percent, the monthly interest rate will be 1.5 percent, and the factor will be 0.036152. If you financed $8000 of a new car purchase under these conditions, your monthly payment would be $289.22.

9.   Plan and write a complete Fortran program for one of the following mathematically oriented problems. Use Fortran intrinsic functions where possible. Early in the process, design complete layouts for input and output.

(a) Develop a table of exponential functions for numbers ranging from 0 through 10, inclusive, in increments of 0.1. For a number n, the exponential functions in the table should be the values of

$$e^n$$

and

$$e^{-n}$$

where e is the base of the natural logarithms. Each page of the table should contain three columns: one for the numbers, one for the positive exponential function values, and one for the negative exponential function values. The function values should be printed to the nearest ten-thousandth.

(b) Develop a table of natural logarithms, to the nearest ten-thousandth, for numbers ranging from 0 through 100, inclusive, in increments of 0.1. Each page of the table should contain six columns, as depicted below.

NUMBER	LOG	NUMBER	LOG	NUMBER	LOG
XXX. X	X. XXXX	XXX. X	X. XXXX	XXX. X	X. XXXX

Structures for Program Control

The subject of program control was first approached in Section 4-8, where you were introduced to the fundamental building blocks of the action in a program: the sequence, selection, and repetition control logic structures. To this point you have been using the simplest form of the IF—THEN statement in combination with the ELSE, ENDIF, and GO TO statements to establish the selection and repetition structures. Selection may be performed more comprehensively by taking advantage of the logical data processing features of FORTRAN 77, as described in Section 7-1. Repetition can often be specified more conveniently by using FORTRAN 77's DO-loop processing capabilities, which are presented and explained subsequently in this chapter.

7-1 LOGICAL DATA OPERATIONS AND SELECTION

Numeric data—with which you have been primarily concerned to this point in your study of this book—consist of numbers. There are many numbers and therefore many different possible numeric data values. In contrast, there are only two possible values for logical data: true and false. Thus the only two possible logical constants are true and false, the only two possible logical variable values are true and false, and the only two possible logical expression values are true and false. Since Chapter 4 you have studied and worked with one kind of logical expression—the relational expression—in its simplest form.

7-1-1 Relational Expressions

A relational expression specifies a comparative relationship between two arithmetic expressions. The general form of a relational expression is

    ae1 ro ae2

where ae1 and ae2 are arithmetic expressions, and ro is one of the following relational operators:

Operator	Meaning (Mathematical)
.EQ.	Equality (=)
.NE.	Inequality (≠ or <>)
.GT.	Greater than (>)
.GE.	Greater than or equal to (>=)
.LT.	Less than (<)
.LE.	Less than or equal to (<=)

When a relational expression is evaluated during execution, the values of the arithmetic expressions are found and then compared on the basis of the relational operator. The value of the relational expression is either true or false, depending on whether the relational comparison holds or does not hold between the arithmetic expression values.

Examples of relational expressions in the simplest form abound in the previous programs of this book. For example:

Expression	Value
KILOS .LE. 10	True if KILOS is less than or equal to 10; otherwise, false
OBS .LT. LOWOBS	True if OBS is less than LOWOBS; otherwise, false
COUNT .GT. 0	True if COUNT is greater than 0; otherwise, false.

Relational expressions can appear to be more complicated than the simple ones shown above, but only because they may contain more complicated arithmetic expressions. Once the arithmetic expressions have been evaluated, regardless of how complicated, the relational expression evaluation only involves a simple comparison between the two arithmetic values. For example, in order to solve Exercise 7(c) of Section 5-11, the quadratic term

$$b^2 - 4ac$$

must be compared to zero. You were purposely not told exactly at that point how to write the relational expression to accomplish the comparison because I wanted you to do some investigating on your own to figure it out.

There are a couple of ways to write the relational expression. Letting ACOEF represent a, BCOEF represent b, and CCOEF represent c, the expression can be written in either of the two equivalent forms

```
BCOEF ** 2 - 4.0 * ACOEF * CCOEF .LT. 0.0
```

or

```
BCOEF ** 2 .LT. 4.0 * ACOEF * CCOEF
```

If, at a point during execution, ACOEF=2.0, BCOEF=3.0, and CCOEF=4.0, the first of the two expressions above is evaluated as follows.

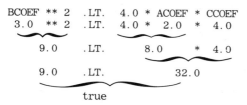

```
BCOEF ** 2 - 4.0 * ACOEF * CCOEF   .LT.   0.0
  3.0  ** 2 - 4.0 *  2.0  *  4.0    .LT.   0.0

       9.0   - 4.0 *  2.0  *  4.0

       9.0   -    8.0       *  4.0

       9.0   -          32.0

          -23.0                     .LT.   0.0

                    true
```

And the second one, similarly:

```
BCOEF ** 2  .LT.  4.0 * ACOEF * CCOEF
  3.0  ** 2  .LT.  4.0 *  2.0  *  4.0

       9.0   .LT.     8.0     *  4.0

       9.0   .LT.        32.0

              true
```

Thus in both expressions the evaluation involving the relational operator took place only after the arithmetic expression values had been determined, and was concerned with comparing only two simple numeric values.

As another illustration, the following expression might appear in a program designed to find the square root of a given number, RLNUM.

```
ABS((RLNUM / (SQROOT ** 2)) - 1.0) .GE. EPSLON
```

ABS, of course, refers to the intrinsic function for finding the absolute value, so the expression is a little more complicated than the ones in the previous examples. During execution with EPSLON set at 0.00001, if RLNUM=20.0 and SQROOT=4.47222 in memory, the value of the arithmetic expression to the left of the relational operator will be about 0.0000376; thus the relational expression will be true. Again, the relational operation is easy to evaluate after the arithmetic expression values have been found.

It is possible, and often appropriate, to devise logical expressions that are more complicated than the relational expressions just described. To do so may involve the combining of one or more relational expressions with one or more operators that specify operations upon the relational expressions. These operators are called *logical operators*.

7-1-2   *Logical Expressions with Logical Operators*

A logical expression is used to express a logical computation—one whose value is either true or false. In similarity with arithmetic computation, a logical computation is written in terms of operands, operators, and parentheses. Operands can be logical constants, logical variable names, logical array references, logical function references, relational expressions, or more complicated logical expressions. In this section we are concerned primarily with relational expressions and more complicated logical expressions; the other logical operand types are covered later.

The logical operators are written in a form similar to that of relational operators—a point followed by a keyword followed by a point. The operators and their meanings are described below.

Operator	*Meaning*
.NOT.	Negation of the following operand: .NOT. true has the value "false"; .NOT. false has the value "true"
.AND.	Conjunction of two operands: true .AND. true has the value "true"; all other "AND" combinations have the value "false"
.OR.	Inclusive disjunction of two operands: false .OR. false has the value "false"; all other "OR" combinations have the value "true"
.EQV.	Equivalence of two operands: true .EQV. true and false .EQV. false have the value "true"; the other combinations have the value "false"
.NEQV.	Nonequivalence of two operands: true .NEQV. false and false .NEQV. true have the value "true"; the other combinations have the value "false"

Take particular notice that the .NOT. operator operates on only one operand, whereas each of the others always operates on two operands. Furthermore, a .NOT. operator may be placed immediately to the right of any of the other operators, but none of the other operators may appear next to each other—an operand must separate them.

As with the arithmetic and relational operators, a precedence exists among the logical operators. First in a logical expression, before any logical operation is evaluated, all the arithmetic and then all the relational operations are evaluated. Then the order of evaluation for the logical operators is the following:

Operator	*Precedence*
.NOT.	Highest
.AND.	Next
.OR.	Next
.EQV. or .NEQV.	Lowest

At each precedence level, the operators at that level are evaluated left to right. However, as in arithmetic expressions, parentheses can be used to force the operations to be evaluated in any desired order.

For a first example of a logical expression containing a logical operator, recall the arithmetic averaging program of Figure 6-4. The first IF statement in that program, one used to check the validity of the input data, contains the logical expression

```
OBS .LT. LOWOBS .OR. OBS .GT. HIOBS
```

Given that OBS=50, LOWOBS=0, HIOBS=100, and letting T and F mean true and false, the expression will be evaluated as follows.

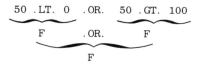

Similarly, given that OBS=110 and with LOWOBS and HIOBS as above, the evaluation will be

```
110 .LT. 0  .OR.   110 .GT. 100
```

```
      F      .OR.         T
```

```
              T
```

Consider also, these descriptive examples:

1. To determine if an employee is eligible for retirement, an expression such as

    ```
    AGE .GE. HIAGE   .OR.
    (AGE .GE. LOAGE   .AND.   SRVICE .GT. 20)
    ```

    might be used. Then, if HIAGE=70, and LOAGE=60, an AGE value of 70 or more will cause the expression to be true. Further, an AGE value greater than or equal to 60 combined with a SERVICE value of more than 20 will also cause the expression to be true.

2. Leap years occur every 4 years except for the years ending in 00 that are not divisible by 400. To determine, then, whether a given YEAR value is a leap year, the following expression can be used.

    ```
    (MOD(YEAR, 4) .EQ. 0  .AND. .NOT.  MOD(YEAR, 100) .EQ. 0)
     .OR.  (MOD(YEAR, 400)  .EQ. 0)
    ```

    Before illustrating the evaluation of this expression, let me point out that it can be written a little more efficiently and simply. I will show you how in a later section, but here I purposely want it to appear as is. Assume that YEAR values of 2000 and 3000 are given. For 2000, after the MOD function values have been computed, we obtain

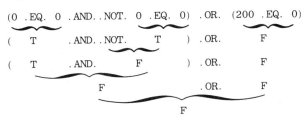

Or, in other words, the year 2000 is a leap year. Then, for 3000, we have

(0 .EQ. 0 .AND. .NOT. 0 .EQ. 0) .OR. (200 .EQ. 0)

(T   .AND. .NOT.   T   ) .OR.   F

(T   .AND.   F   ) .OR.   F

F   .OR.   F

F

Or, in other words, even though 3000 is evenly divisible by 4, the year 3000 will not be a leap year (or was not a leap year, depending on when I finish this book). To verify the expression further, and understand it better, you may want to evaluate it with leap years such as 1776, 1984, and 3004, and non-leap years such as 1494, 1969, and 2002.

Logical expressions, like the ones presented in this and the preceding section, can appear in IF−THEN and logical IF statements, thus yielding the most comprehensive forms of these statements. For instance, the following program segment determines whether a given year is or is not a leap year, and then prints an appropriate message.

```
INTEGER YEAR
.
.
.
IF ((MOD(YEAR, 4) .EQ. 0
:     .AND. .NOT.  MOD(YEAR, 100) .EQ. 0)
:    .OR.  (MOD(YEAR, 400) .EQ. 0)  THEN
    PRINT *, YEAR, ' IS A LEAP YEAR. '
ELSE
    PRINT *, YEAR, ' IS NOT A LEAP YEAR. '
ENDIF
```

As an illustration of the logical If, the statement below specifies that the variable ELGIBL is to be assigned the value of the variable YES whenever the logical expression is true.

```
IF (AGE .GE. HIAGE
:    .OR. (AGE .GE. LOAGE  .AND. SRVICE .GT. 20))
:    ELGIBL = YES
```

7-1-3 Logical Constants, Variables, and Assignment

The very simplest form of a logical expression is one logical constant or one logical variable. The logical constants are

    . TRUE.

and

    . FALSE.

A logical constant can be written explicitly, as above, or symbolically. A symbolic logical constant is identified by a symbolic name that has been given a value in a PARAMETER statement. A logical variable is identified by a variable name that has been specified in a LOGICAL data type statement. Logical constants and variables can then be used as logical expressions or operands in any Fortran statement that can contain logical expressions and operands.

The form of a LOGICAL type statement is similar to the form of the numeric data type statements (INTEGER, REAL, etc.). Specifically,

    LOGICAL list

where the list contains the symbolic names of variables and constants whose values can only be true or false. As many names as necessary can appear in the list, and commas are used to separate them.

Once declared, logical variables and constants can appear in assignment statements of the form

    lvar = le

where lvar is a logical variable and le is any valid logical expression including an explicit logical constant (.TRUE. or .FALSE.), symbolic logical constant, logical variable, logical array element, logical function reference, relational expression, or one of the more complicated logical expressions covered earlier in Section 7-1-2. Logical assignment statements are evaluated in a manner analogous to arithmetic assignment statement evaluation; that is, the expression value is determined and then assigned to the variable. The difference is that the value of the expression and the variable is either true or false; it is not a number.

As an example, consider the "leap year" program segment of the preceding section. By introducing two temporary logical variables, it becomes possible to write the block IF statement in a simpler form. This may make the program easier to read because it eliminates the need for a continuation line and breaks the logical expression into two easier-to-understand parts. Here is the new code.

```
INTEGER  YEAR
LOGICAL  CENLYR, ORDLYR
   .
   .
   .
```

```
ORDLYR = MOD(YEAR, 4) .EQ. 0 .AND. MOD(YEAR, 100) .NE. 0
CENLYR = MOD(YEAR, 400) .EQ. 0
IF (ORDLYR .OR. CENLYR) THEN
    PRINT *, YEAR, ' IS A LEAP YEAR.'
ELSE
    PRINT *, YEAR, ' IS NOT A LEAP YEAR.'
ENDIF
```

The logical variable ORDLYR refers to an "ordinary" leap year. As indicated by the first assignment statement, it will be true whenever the year is divisible by 4 and, concurrently, is not a year ending in 00. (Notice, too, that the .NOT.-.EQ. combination has been replaced by the simpler .NE. relational operator.) The logical variable CENLYR, referring to "century" leap year, will be true whenever the year is divisible by 400 as indicated by the second assignment statement. Then the decision process beginning with the block IF statement can be readily interpreted to mean: "If the year is an ordinary leap year or a century leap year, then the year is a leap year; otherwise, it is not a leap year."

7-1-4 A Multiple-Alternative Selection Structure

As introduced in Chapter 4 and exemplified above, the block IF and ELSE statements work together to produce a simple selection structure that contains two alternatives. Some selection situations, however, have more than two alternatives. Consider, for instance, this problem:

A retail chain assigns a one-digit "credit-status" code to each customer. The code is associated with a credit limit, and is used to determine the amount of any additional charges that the customer is allowed to make. The codes and credit limits are as follows.

Code	Credit Limit ($)
0	0
1	100
2	500
3	1000

Given the credit code (CREDIT) and the current account balance (CURBAL) for a particular customer, determine the allowable additional charge (ALLOW) for the customer.

The following program segment provides a solution to the problem.

```
INTEGER CREDIT
REAL ALLOW, CURBAL
 .
 .
 .
IF (CREDIT .EQ. 0) THEN
    ALLOW = 0.0
ELSE IF (CREDIT .EQ. 1) THEN
    ALLOW = 100.0 - CURBAL
```

```
ELSE IF (CREDIT .EQ. 2) THEN
    ALLOW = 500.0 - CURBAL
ELSE IF (CREDIT .EQ. 3) THEN
    ALLOW = 1000.0 - CURBAL
ELSE
    PRINT *, 'ERROR.  CREDIT CODE IS ', CREDIT, '.'
    PRINT *, 'IT MUST, HOWEVER, BE 0, 1, 2, OR 3.'
ENDIF
```

The interpretation of this multiple-alternative selection structure is that only one of the assignment statements will be executed, or the two PRINT statements will be executed, for a given CREDIT value because only one, or none, of the relational expressions is true for a given CREDIT value.

The ELSE IF statement has been introduced in the above example to provide additional mutually exclusive alternatives between the block IF and ELSE statements. It has the general form

```
ELSE IF (le) THEN
```

where le is a logical expression. Letting lej represent the jth logical expression in a mutually exclusive set, the multiple-alternative selection structure is usually coded in the form

```
IF (le1) THEN
    .    {Statements to be
    .     executed whenever
    .     le1 is true}
ELSE IF (le2) THEN
    .    {Statements to be
    .     executed whenever
    .     le2 is true}
{Additional ELSE IF blocks as needed}
    .
    .
    .
ELSE
    .    {Statements to be executed
    .     whenever none of the previous
    .     logical expressions is true}
ENDIF
```

The ELSE statement and its following block of statements are optional; but no more than one ELSE is allowed in the structure. The ELSE IF statements (when present) must always appear after the block IF and before the ELSE (if present) and ENDIF. Indentation is used for readability; it does not affect the execution in any way.

7-1-5 Exercises

1. The quadratic relational expressions of Section 7-1-1 were written so that a true value would indicate that the roots were complex rather that real. Rewrite the expressions to indicate real roots when true. Place the expressions in IF statements to show how the test would be performed.

2. Again, rewrite one of the quadratic expressions so that it is not necessary to have the quadratic term

$$b^2 - 4ac$$

itself in the IF statement. Instead, assign the term to an appropriate variable and then test only the variable so that real roots are indicated when the relational expression is true.

3. Once more, rewrite the quadratic test so that only a single logical variable, rather than a relational expression, is tested. A true test value should indicate real roots. Declare the data types of all variables. Including the data type statements, four Fortran statements will be required.

4. Compare my "square root completion test expression," given in Section 7-1-1, with the one you devised in algorithmic form as a solution to Exercise 5 of Section 5-11. Using your algorithm, write a complete Fortran main program. If you have not done Exercise 5 of Section 5-11, do it, and then this one, now.

5. Rewrite this expression from Section 7-1-2,

```
OBS .LT. LOWOBS   .OR.   OBS .GT. HIOBS
```

so that the .OR. is replaced by .AND. but the resulting logical expression value will still be the same for the same values of OBS, LOWOBS, and HIOBS. Use any one other logical operator that is necessary and replace the relational operators if necessary.

6. Given that SALARY=399.75, LIMIT4=400.00, and DPNDTS=5, what is the value of the following expression?

```
SALARY .LE. LIMIT4   .OR.   DPNDTS .GT. 10
```

7. Given that the real variables ALPHA, BETA, DELTA, and GAMMA have the respective values 2.0, 1.5, 3.0, and 4.0, and that the integer variables IOTA and NU have the respective values 4 and 2, what is the value of each of the expressions below?

(a) ALPHA .GE. BETA*2   .OR.   IOTA .EQ. NU**2
   .AND.   GAMMA .GT. DELTA

(b) ALPHA .GT. DELTA   .AND..NOT.   IOTA .GE. NU

(c) NU .GT. IOTA   .AND.   BETA .LE. DELTA
   .OR..NOT.   GAMMA .LT. ALPHA

(d) .NOT.   ALPHA + BETA .GE. GAMMA   .AND.   IOTA / 2 .LE. NU
   .OR..NOT.   IOTA / 2 * 2 .GE. NU

8. Rewrite the leap year problem code, given in Section 7-1-3, with the following changes. Introduce another logical variable, POSLYR (Possible Leap Year), as MOD(YEAR,4).EQ.0. Use it first to determine whether to go ahead with further testing for a leap year or not. If so, compute a modified value of ORDLYR—it need not contain the MOD(YEAR,4) term—and then use it and CENLYR to determine whether the year is or is not a leap year. A significant code modification is involved; consider it carefully.

9. Write a program segment to read in four numbers from one input record, then find and print only the smallest of the four. Use logical operations, as needed, and the selection statements.

10. A company offers quantity discounts (percent off purchase price) on certain items based on the following table.

Quantity Ordered	Discount Percent
1 – 20	0
21 – 50	1
51 – 100	3
101 – up	5

The quantity discounts apply in full only if the bill is paid by the customer within 10 days after the end of the month during which the item was purchased. Otherwise, the discount percent is reduced by one-half if the bill is paid within 30 days; it is reduced to zero if not paid within 30 days. Write a program segment that reads for one customer and one item purchased, the quantity ordered, the unit price, and the number of days that elapsed between the end of the month and the time that the full payment was received. The program segment should then compute and print the amount that should have been paid.

7-2 REPETITION

Most modern widely used programming languages have a DO statement for invoking a repetitive sequence or loop. The loop so invoked is called a *DO-loop*. DO-loops in different programming languages have similar purposes—to allow a sequence of statements to be conditionally executed repeatedly—but they do not always accomplish the task in the same way. Some are designed to perform the task by testing the condition at the beginning of each execution of the sequence of statements; this is called *Do-while looping*. Others are designed to test the condition at the end of each execution of the sequence; this is called *Do-until looping*. These are depicted, by means of flowchart segments, in Figure 7-1.

The FORTRAN 77 DO-loop is a Do-while mechanism. It is the one that we are concerned with in this section. The Do-until mechanism, which was used in the older Fortran, is discussed in Section 7-3.

7-2-1 The Do-while Concept

Some learners have difficulty understanding how DO-loops are applied, invoked, and executed. You will not have this difficulty if you will carefully compare,

A. The Do-while mechanism

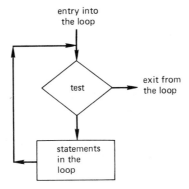

B. The Do-until mechanism

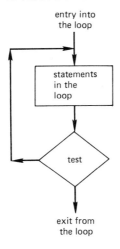

Figure 7-1. DO-loop Mechanisms

analyze, and practice the coding of pairs of loops that accomplish the repetitive tasks identically—with one of the pair having no DO statement and the other having a DO statement.

The Fahrenheit-to-Celsius temperature conversion program of Figure 5-9, for example, contains the following sequence of statements.

```
        FAHREN = LOWF
310     IF (FAHREN .LE. HIGHF) THEN
        CEL = (FAHREN - 32) / 1.8
        WRITE (PO, 920) FAHREN, CEL
        FAHREN = FAHREN + 1
        GO TO 310
        ENDIF
```

Clearly, a loop exists between the first assignment statement and the ENDIF. In fact, it is a DO-while loop since the loop exit condition, FAHREN .LE. HIGHF, is tested at the beginning point of the repetitive sequence. By applying the DO-loop facilities of Fortran, the code can be written in a simpler, more readable fashion that accomplishes exactly the same task:

```
       DO 320 FAHREN = LOWF, HIGHF, 1
          CEL = (FAHREN - 32) / 1.8
          WRITE (PO, 920) FAHREN, CEL
   320    CONTINUE
```

Let it be clear in your mind: The above two sequences of Fortran statements accomplish exactly the same task; they should be interpreted as being identical in performance.

Here is a verbal interpretation of the sequence containing the DO-loop, beginning with the DO statement:

> Assign FAHREN an initial value of LOWF. Then, while FAHREN is less than or equal to HIGHF, perform the statements following the DO statement up to and including the statement numbered 320, incrementing FAHREN by 1 as the final action each time. Finally, when FAHREN is greater than HIGHF, exit from the loop to the next statement following the loop in sequence.

The interpretation of the first sequence of statements is virtually the same.

So even though you haven't yet studied the DO statement or the CONTINUE statement specifically, you should have a pretty good idea of how they are used in DO-loops, and how a DO-loop works. Now consider these two statements in detail.

7-2-2   The DO and CONTINUE Statements

The general form of the DO statement is

```
DO stn var = ae1, ae2, ae3
```

where stn is the statement number of an executable statement called the terminal statement of the DO-loop or, in other words, the DO-terminal; var is the name of an integer, real, or double-precision variable called the DO-variable or control variable of the DO-loop; ae1, ae2, and ae3 are integer, real, or double-precision expressions that are used, respectively, to establish the initial, test, and increment values of the DO-variable prior to the first execution of the repetitive statements. Often, as in the example of the preceding section, simple integer variables or constants are used for var, ae1, ae2, and ae3. The third expression, ae3, can be omitted, in which case the increment value will be 1 by default.

The DO-terminal must, naturally, appear somewhere after the DO statement, not before it; then, during each execution of the repetitive statements, it is always the last statement executed in the loop. In the example of the last section, I used a CONTINUE statement as the DO-terminal—a common practice among the experts. But actually, the DO-terminal can be any executable statement except one of the selection statements or one that causes a transfer of control to occur. In particular, it cannot be a GO TO, arithmetic IF, block IF, ELSE IF, ELSE, ENDIF, RETURN, STOP, END, DO or a logical IF that contains any of the others mentioned. Given that long list, you can see why a CONTINUE statement is a safe and simple choice for a DO-terminal.

The form of a CONTINUE statement is

```
CONTINUE
```

It is an executable statement, but its execution has no effect. When used as the terminal of a DO-loop, it can serve, with the DO statement, to ''bracket'' the loop and thus make the loop easy to locate. This is accomplished by beginning the DO statement and its corresponding CONTINUE statement in the same column of their respective lines, and indenting the statements in between. If this method is used, the general appearance of any DO-loop will be like the following, in which the indentation is indicated by the ellipses.

```
DO stn var = ae1, ae2, ae3
   .
   .
   .
stn CONTINUE
```

The range of a DO-loop consists of all executable statements following the DO statement up to and including its terminal statement. The statements in the range of a DO-loop can be executed only if execution control enters into the range through the DO statement. That is, a transfer of control into the range of a DO-loop from outside is not permitted.

Here is what happens whenever a DO-statement is executed:

The arithmetic expressions ae1, ae2, and ae3 are evaluated to establish, respectively, the initial value, test value, and increment value of the DO-variable. These three values are called the *DO-parameters*; they have the same data type as the DO-variable regardless of the data types of the arithmetic expressions. If ae3 is omitted, the increment value is 1 by default. The DO-variable is then assigned the initial value. An iteration (repetition) count is established as the value of the expression

```
MAX(INT((test - init + incr) / incr), 0)
```

where init, test, and incr represent the initial, test, and increment DO-parameters. The iteration count, and thus the number of executions of the DO-range, is zero whenever

```
init > test, and incr is positive-valued
```

or

```
init < test, and incr is negative-valued.
```

Thus it is possible—as indicated by the conditions above—to bypass a DO-range completely during execution; in such a case, execution proceeds with the first executable statement immediately following the DO-terminal. It is also possible—depending upon the relationship of the DO-parameters—to vary the DO-variable from large to small or positive to negative as well as from small to large or negative to positive.

Ordinarily, after the execution of a DO-statement, the DO-range will be executed a number of times, equal to the established iteration count. This repetitive execution process takes place like this:

The iteration count is tested. If it is zero, an exit from the loop occurs to the first executable statement following the DO-terminal. If it is not zero, the DO-range is executed beginning with the first statement in the range and proceeding through the DO-terminal. The value of the DO-variable is incremented by the value of the incrementation parameter, which may be positive or negative. The iteration count is decremented by one. The process is repeated.

The repetition process, or iteration process as it is also called, can be interpreted by the statement: "Do the range while the iteration count is not zero." It is clear, therefore, that the FORTRAN 77 DO-loop is a Do-while structure.

7-2-3 DO-Loop Application Examples

Exercise 10 of Section 4-10 contains this program segment:

```
        POSSUM = 0
        LOOKER = 1
        READ *, LIMIT
    380 IF (LOOKER .LE. LIMIT) THEN
            POSSUM = POSSUM + LOOKER
            LOOKER = LOOKER + 1
            GO TO 380
        ENDIF
        PRINT *, 'FOR ', LIMIT, ' THE ANSWER IS ', POSSUM
```

By determining that a portion of this segment contains a looping process in which a variable (LOOKER) is initialized (to 1), tested (against LIMIT), and incremented (by 1), we can begin to decide whether or not a DO-loop could be used. The added information that the exit test on the variable occurs prior to the execution of the statements in the loop allows us to be able to interpret the loop with the statement: "Do the range of the loop while the variable LOOKER is less than or equal to the variable LIMIT." Therefore, we have a Do-while loop, and the code can be rewritten in an improved way like this:

```
        READ *, LIMIT
        POSSUM = 0
        DO 390 LOOKER = 1, LIMIT
            POSSUM = POSSUM + LOOKER
    390 CONTINUE
        PRINT *, 'FOR ', LIMIT, ' THE ANSWER IS ', POSSUM
```

Nine statements have been replaced by six, yet the segment accomplishes exactly the same task. Clearly, a DO-loop cannot only be used but it is highly desirable.

Notice something else. I made no mention of what the program segment accomplishes. It was not necessary to do so; we were only interested in the looping features of the code. We wanted to know whether or not the Fortran DO-loop—a special case of the general Do-while mechanism—would fit the looping structure that had already been established by the solution procedure logic. By systematically searching for and finding a looping process controlled by a variable that was initialized, tested prior to execution of the loop range, and then incremented, we were able to say that the DO-loop could be applied.

The following segment accomplishes the same task as the two above.

```
      READ *, LIMIT
      POSSUM = 0
      DO 390 LOOKER = LIMIT, 1, -1
         POSSUM = POSSUM + LOOKER
390 CONTINUE
      PRINT *, 'FOR ', LIMIT, ' THE ANSWER IS ', POSSUM
```

Here, LOOKER is first initialized to the value of LIMIT, then compared to the test value 1 and incremented by −1 after each iteration. An exit from the loop occurs only when LOOKER becomes less than 1 prior to a repetition of the statements in the DO-range.

The Fortran DO-loop cannot always be used for every Do-while loop. Exercise 2 of Section 4-10, for example, contains this segment:

```
      PRINT *, 'SALES LIST'
280   READ *, PARTNO
      IF (PARTNO .GT. 0) THEN
         SALE = 0
         READ *, UPRICE, ONHAND
         READ *, REQEST
         IF (REQEST .LE. ONHAND) SALE = REQEST
         PRINT *, PARTNO, REQEST, SALE, UPRICE
         GO TO 280
      ENDIF
      PRINT *, 'END OF SALES LIST'
```

Although the segment can be interpreted by "Do the range of the loop while PARTNO is greater than zero," the loop control variable PARTNO undergoes no incrementation process; furthermore, it is initialized by reading rather than by assignment.

Consider another example. The following program segment finds and prints the sine, cosine, and tangent for all the odd-numbered angles from 1 degree to 45 degrees inclusive.

```
      REAL   ANGLE, COSINE, DEGREE, HIDEG, INCDEG, LOWDEG,
    :         PI, RADIAN, SINE, TANGNT
      PARAMETER  (LOWDEG=1.0, HIDEG=45.0, INCDEG=2.0,
    :             PI=3.14159, RADIAN=PI/180.0)
```

```
       .
       .
       .
      DO 300 DEGREE = LOWDEG, HIDEG, INCDEG
         ANGLE = RADIAN * DEGREE
         SINE = SIN(ANGLE)
         COSINE = COS(ANGLE)
         TANGNT = SINE / COSINE
         PRINT *, DEGREE, SINE, COSINE, TANGNT
  300 CONTINUE
      STOP
      END
```

Notice that all variables and symbolic constants in this segment are real. Thus the DO-variable and DO-parameters are real. The DO-parameter expressions themselves are declared as symbolic constants, having their specified values assigned in a PARAMETER statement. This provides more program generality than does the explicit use of numbers in the DO statement like this:

```
DO 300 DEGREE = 1.0, 45.0, 2.0
```

Also observe that the DO-loop is clearly evident because the DO and CONTINUE statements bracket the group of indented statements that are repetitively executed based on the conditions established by the DO statement. The indentation does not affect the execution; it enhances the readability of the program.

I mentioned earlier that branching into the range of a DO-loop from outside the range is not allowed; but branching from the inside to the outside of a DO-loop range is acceptable—often necessary. Consider the following example, in which branching from inside is necessary.

The problem is to read in up to N positive whole numbers until a negative number is encountered; then compute the average of the positive numbers. The value of N is to be read in first, and a negative number may or may not be present in the input data. Here are four of the many possible sets of input data.

Set 1	Set 2	Set 3	Set 4
5	5	4	4
130	130	130	130
100	100	100	100
124	124	124	124
115	115	115	
112	−999		
−999			

The calculator-computed averages of these sets are 116.2, 117.25, 117.25, and 118.0. Here is a major portion of a program to solve the problem.

```
      INTEGER AVEOF, COUNT, I, INTIF, N, NUMBER, SUM
      REAL AVE
      PARAMETER (AVEOF=6, INTIF=5)
```

```
      .
      .
      .
      READ (INTIF, *) N
      IF (N .LE. 0) THEN
         WRITE (AVEOF, 910) N
      ELSE
         SUM = 0
         COUNT = 0
         DO 300 I = 1, N
            READ (INTIF, *, END=350) NUMBER
            IF (NUMBER .LT. 0) GO TO 350
               WRITE (AVEOF, 915) NUMBER
               SUM = SUM + NUMBER
               COUNT = I
 300     CONTINUE
 350     IF (COUNT .GT. 0) THEN
            AVE = FLOAT (SUM) / COUNT
            WRITE (AVEOF, 920) AVE, COUNT
         ELSE
            WRITE (AVEOF, 925)
         ENDIF
      ENDIF
```

In the action statements above, there are actually these three possible exits from the DO-loop: an exit because the iteration count is equal to zero, called a *normal exit*; an exit by a conditional branch at the READ statement in the loop; and an exit by a conditional branch at the IF statement in the loop. I call these last two *prenormal exits* to distinguish them from the normal exit, because if they occur, they will do so prior to the time when the normal exit would occur. For this particular program segment, the statement numbered 350 will be the one executed after any one of the three possible exits has occurred. Take note, however, that the statement number is required only because the prenormal exits are present, not because of the normal exit.

If you will perform traces on the program segment using the four sets of input data I listed for you, you will find that the first set results in a normal exit, and its last value, −999, is not even read in; the second set results in a prenormal exit from the IF statement right after its −999 is read in; the third set results in a normal exit after all its values have been read in; and the fourth set results in a prenormal exit at the READ when an attempt is made to read in a fourth value. In all cases, the average is computed correctly for the input data supplied; if there are no input vaues, the average is not computed but an appropriate message is printed.

Two other points to observe are these: all input values are monitored (checked) by the program, and the DO-variable is used to establish the count of input numbers during each iteration of the loop. Study these points in the program. Figure out for yourself why the DO-variable, I, cannot be used in place of the variable COUNT, thereby eliminating the need for COUNT. As a point of interest— one often overlooked or misunderstood by learners—I mention that any particular variable name can be used as the DO-variable for more than one DO-loop. Thus, if there was another DO-loop between DO-terminal statement 300 and the STOP statement, the variable I could be used as its DO-variable.

DO-loops can be contained within other DO-loops; that is, they can be *nested*. This facility is particularly useful for array processing; therefore it is described in full in a later chapter. At this point I will simply say that for nested DO-loops, complete nesting is necessary; that is, when a DO statement appears after another DO statement but before the terminal of the first DO statement, the terminal of the second DO statement must appear before the terminal of the first DO statement. This situation is represented by the following skeleton in which the ellipses also show indentation.

```
      DO s1
         .
         .
         .
         DO s2
            .
            .
            .
            DO s3
               .
               .
               .
    s3         CONTINUE
               .
               .
               .
    s2      CONTINUE
            .
            .
            .
   s1  CONTINUE
```

7-2-4   *Algorithm and Flowchart Representations*

The DO-loop can be represented in the following algorithmic primitive sequence.

```
Do var ← init to test by incr
   .
   .     range
   .
End Do
```

Labels are not necessarily required if indentation is used carefully and the Do is always matched with an End Do. You may prefer to use Continue, rather than End Do, since the algorithmic sequence would then look more like the corresponding Fortran program segment. I prefer End Do because of its precise "Do" reference and its actual use in some of the other modern programming languages.

For the first program segment with a DO-loop presented in Section 7-2-3, the algorithmic sequence is

```
Read Limit
positivesum ← 0
Do looker ← 1 to limit by 1
    positivesum ← postivesum + looker
End Do
Write 'FOR ', limit, 'THE ANSWER IS ', positivesum
```

For the segment involving trigonometric functions, the algorithmic sequence is

```
Do degree ← lowdegree to highdegree by incdegree
    angle ← radian * degree
    sine ← SIN(angle)
    cosine ← COS(angle)
    tangent ← sine / cosine
    Write degree, sine, cosine, tangent
End Do
Stop
END
```

The flowcharting of DO-loops can be handled by using the preparation symbol for depicting the entry into a Do-loop, as well as the initialization, testing, and incrementation of the DO-variable, and the exiting from the loop. Figure 7-2 illustrates the flowcharting technique.

For particular examples, the trigonometric algorithm sequence is flowcharted in Figure 7-3; the final program segment of the preceding section, involving the average of up to N numbers, is depicted in Figure 7-4; and the third program segment of the preceding section—the one having negative incrementation—is represented in Figure 7-5.

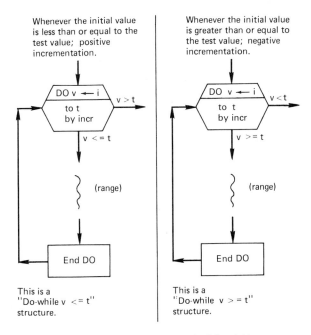

Figure 7-2. Flowcharting the DO-loop

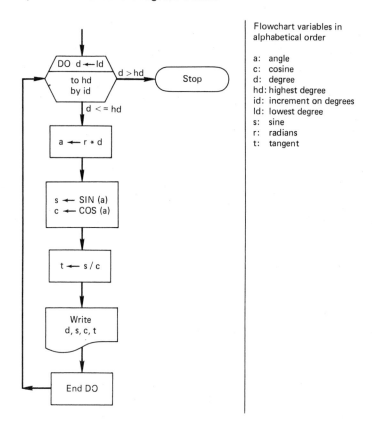

Flowchart variables in
alphabetical order

a: angle
c: cosine
d: degree
hd: highest degree
id: increment on degrees
ld: lowest degree
s: sine
r: radians
t: tangent

Figure 7-3. Flowchart Segment for the Trigonometric Sequence

7-3   Two More Control Logic Structures

Complete programs can always be written using only the three fundamental control logic structures—simple sequence, selection, and repetition—in the forms already presented. There are, however, a few other control structures that are useful; they are actually extensions of the fundamental structures. Two of these others, the Do-until and the Case, are discussed here.

7-3-1   *The Do-Until Control Structure*

In contrast to the pretest looping of the Do-while, the Do-until structure is one that involves posttest looping. That is, the loop exit test is performed after each execution of the other statements in the loop. This means that that the Do-until loop is always executed at least once. Figure 7-6(a), depicts the process.

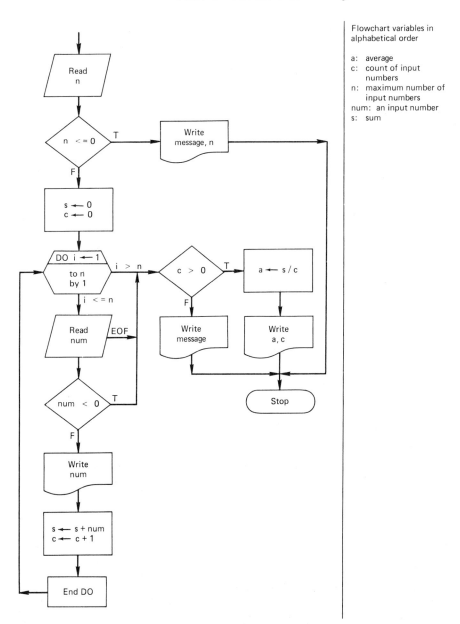

Flowchart variables in
alphabetical order

a: average
c: count of input
      numbers
n: maximum number of
      input numbers
num: an input number
s: sum

Figure 7-4. Flowchart for Averaging up to N Positive Numbers

The FORTRAN 77 DO statement is not used to accomplish Do-until looping. Rather, the Do-until loop with positive incrementation can be created in a FORTRAN 77 program by a combination of the IF-GO TO statements in a manner like the following, in which lcvar is the loop control variable.

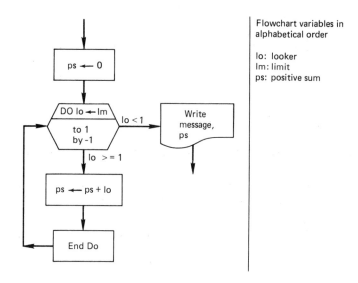

Flowchart variables in alphabetical order

lo: looker
lm: limit
ps: positive sum

Figure 7-5. Flowchart Segment for Positive Summation

```
        lcvar = initial value
stn     first statement in the loop
              .
              .   other statements in the loop range
              .
        lcvar = lcvar + increment value
        If lcvar <= test value, Go To stn(Back)
       .{normal exit when the condition is false}
              .
              .
```

The action sequence in the program of Section 7-2-3 that involved finding the sine, cosine, and tangent can be rewritten in a Do-until form as follows:

```
        DEGREE = LOWDEG
290     ANGLE  = RADIAN * DEGREE
        SINE   = SIN(ANGLE)
        COSINE = COS(ANGLE)
        TANGNT = SINE / COSINE
        PRINT *, DEGREE, SINE, COSINE, TANGNT
        DEGREE = DEGREE + INCDEG
        IF (DEGREE .LE. HIDEG) GO TO 290
```

Let me make you aware of a potential problem with the Fortran DO statement. I have said that in FORTRAN 77, the DO statement creates a Do-while loop—and it does. But in compilers that are based on the 1966 Fortran standard, the DO statement will be handled as if it created a Do-until loop. Thus, when such a compiler is used, all DO-loops will be executed at least once. Furthermore, the 1966 standard does not allow negative incrementation to occur in DO-loops, the DO-variable and DO-parameter expressions must all be integers, and the value of

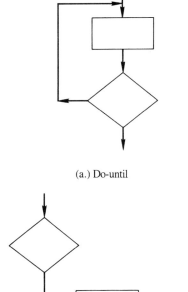

(a.) Do-until

(b.) Case

Figure 7-6. Do-Until and Case Control Structures

the DO-variable is lost when a normal exit from a DO-loop occurs. Therefore, if you use a compiler based on the 1966 Fortran standard, make sure that you design your DO-loops so that they will be processed properly by that compiler; read the Fortran manual for that compiler.

7-3-2   *The Case Control Structure*

The Case mechanism depicted in Figure 7-6(b) is a special instance of the selection structure which involves selecting one of several possible alternatives. In Fortran, this structure can be created by using the IF-THEN-ELSEIF(one or more)-ELSE-ENDIF sequence of statements, as described in Section 7-1-4, or the computed GO TO statement.

The form of the computed GO TO statement is

```
GO TO (stn1, stn2, ..., stnN), iae
```

where stn1, stn2, ..., stnN is a list of statement labels of executable statements, and iae is an integer-valued arithmetic expression. The purpose of this statement is to allow one of several possible groups of statements—beginning with a statement labeled with one of the stns—to be executed, depending on the value of iae.

The execution of a computed GO TO results first in an evaluation of the expression iae. The value so obtained must be a whole number in the range 1 through N inclusive, where N is the number of statement labels in the list. The value corresponds to the position of a statement label in the list. Execution control is then transferred to the statement which has that label. This computed GO TO processing is depicted in Figure 7-7. Notice that the Case structure (Figure 7-6) is fully implemented only if the final statement in each of the groups of statements transfers control to the same statement as the final statement in all of the other groups. Also, carefully read the caution at the bottom of the figure; the value of iae should always be a whole number in the range 1 through N inclusive.

An illustration is in order. Say that a high school has administered an exam to all its students, at all levels—freshman, sophomore, junior, and senior—and the

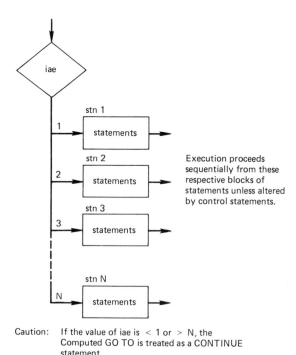

Figure 7-7. Computed GO TO Processing

high school administration wants to be able to compare all students to each other. An input record has been created for each student, containing the student's identification number, classification code (1, 2, 3, 4 for freshman, sophomore, junior, senior), and exam score. Further, an adjustment method, involving applying a particular weighting factor to each test, has been devised. A program is needed to read each student record, apply the appropriate weighting factor to the exam, and then print the input data plus the weighted exam score. The following is a program segment to partially accomplish the task.

```
200     READ (EXAMIF, *, END=499) SIDNUM, CLASS, RAWSCR
        IF (CLASS .LT. 1 .OR. CLASS .GT. 4) THEN
            PRINT *, SIDNUM, CLASS, RAWSCR,
  :                      ' ERROR, INCORRECT CLASSIFICATION CODE'
        ELSE
            GO TO (310, 320, 330, 340), CLASS
310             WTDSCR = RAWSCR * FRSFAC
                GO TO 400
320             WTDSCR = RAWSCR * SPHFAC
                GO TO 400
330             WTDSCR = RAWSCR * JNRFAC
                GO TO 400
340             WTDSCR = RAWSCR * SNRFAC
400         PRINT *, SIDNUM, CLASS, RAWSCR, WTDSCR
        ENDIF
        GO TO 200
499 STOP
    END
```

One of the primary difficulties with this segment is the number of explicit paths it contains, as indicated by the number of GO TOs and statement labels. The segment containing the computed GO TO can be written in a more readable fashion if the computed GO TO is replaced by the block IF statement—something like the following.

```
IF (CLASS .EQ. 1) THEN
    WTDSCR = RAWSCR * FRSFAC
ELSE IF (CLASS .EQ. 2) THEN
    WTDSCR = RAWSCR * SPHFAC
ELSE IF (CLASS .EQ. 3) THEN
    WTDSCR = RAWSCR * JNRFAC
ELSE
    WTDSCR = RAWSCR * SNRFAC
ENDIF
```

An even better program segment can be produced by replacing all the statements between 200 and GO TO 200 with one multiple-alternative selection structure as described in Section 7-1-4.

7-4   EXAMPLE PROGRAM: CONTROL STRUCTURE AND PROGRAM MODIFICATION STUDY

One of the primary tasks facing professional programmers, or even people who do a reasonable amount of personal or job-related programming, is program maintenance. Maintenance involves modifying and changing a completed and certified program so that it will meet new needs or requirements, run more efficiently, compile on a different compiler, or run on a different computer. The example program presented here is a revision of the one developed in Section 6-4—the GPA report program (Figure 6-10).

What I want to illustrate primarily in this section is the use of the program control structures discussed in this chapter. Secondarily, I want to illustrate program maintenance. The GPA report program is a good one to choose for both of these purposes because it contains a fair amount of looping and some selection structures, and it can be improved by the use of the more advanced program control features described in this chapter.

In revising a program, here are two guidelines you should always follow: (1) apply the "Steps of Good Programming Practice" (Section 2-1) just as you do when you are developing a program from scratch, to guarantee that the new program will meet all requirements, old and new; and (2) work with a copy of the old program—not the original. The first guideline implies that not only the program listing but also the problem definition, documentation, solution procedure, program test, and certification must be brought up to date. The second guideline protects the old program; after all, it is a certified program that may have been used as a production program for some time. Do not get rid of it until its replacement has been certified and has taken its place as the production program for the purpose it serves.

For the GPA report program, the problem definition will be altered slightly. Say that experience with the original program indicates that occasionally input errors have been made in the date record. Manual checking of this input record is performed but is not considered to be sufficient; some checking must be built into the program. We prefer never to produce a lengthy report with an incorrect date on it, but this may not be completely possible. It is possible, however, to make sure that the month and day can actually occur. So it is decided to build into the solution procedure and program a test that will allow the report generation to take place only if the month and day values are valid; if not, a message will be printed, and the program terminated. An addition to the output layout, shown in Figure 7-8, is required. The original layout is still good for error-free processing, and the original test data can be used for testing this part of the revised program.

It has also been observed that whenever the number of students is divisible by the number of detail lines per page, the original program prints an extra page containing only a title. A minor modification will be made so that the extra page will not be printed.

Now we want to apply some of the control structures of this chapter to the program so that it will be a better program. Before changing the program statements, however, we should revise the algorithm.

I have already taken the liberty of going ahead with the revision, expecting you to learn how I did it by studying it in final form and comparing it to the original in Section 6-4. The revised algorithm is shown in Figure 7-9. Observe that the

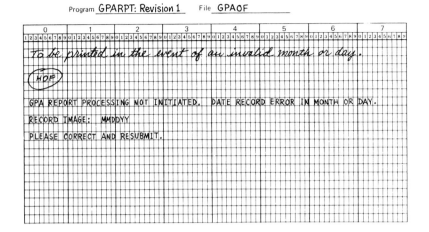

Figure 7-8. GPA Input Error Report Layout

ALGORITHM GPA:report.rev1
{ A report of student grade point averages (gpa) is created
from input records containing student identification number,
hours tried, hours passed, and grade points received.}

```
Read month, day, year
If month > 0 and month < 13 and day > 0 and day < 32, Then
    Do page ← 1 to maxpage by 1
        Do line ← 1 to maxline by 1
            Read student id, hours tried, hours passed,
                grade points, at EOF Go To FIN. (Ahead)
            If line = 1, Write heading, page, month, day, year
            If hours tried > 0, Then
                gpa ← grade points / hours tried
            Else
                gpa ← 0
            Write student id, hours tried, hours passed,
                grade points, gpa
        End Do
    End Do
Else
    Write 'GPA REPORT PROCESSING NOT INITIATED.
            DATE RECORD ERROR IN MONTH OR DAY.
            RECORD IMAGE:   ', month, day, year,
            'PLEASE CORRECT AND RESUBMIT. '
FIN. Stop
    END
```

Figure 7-9. GPA Report Algorithm: Revision 1

input data test occurs at the first If rule. When an input error occurs in month or day, the Else clause is executed and execution is terminated. Then, notice that the Do-End Do construct is used to step through the pages as well as the lines on each page. The Do-loops are actually "nested," with the line-counting Do-loop being totally contained (completely nested) within the page-counting Do-loop. In order to set up the page-counting Do-loop, I established a new parameter, "maxpage," that must be given the value of the maximum number of pages the report might contain. Another item to give attention to is the use of the If-Then-Else selection mechanism for computing the value of gpa. Given the revised algorithm, tested and accepted, the revised Fortran program, given in Figure 7-10, is a cinch.

```
*I.   GRADE POINT AVERAGE REPORT:  REVISION 1
*
      PROGRAM GPARPT
*     PROGRAMMER:   JARRELL C. GROUT
*     DATE OF ORIGINAL:   1/24/81
*     DATE OF REVISION 1:   3/26/81
*
*  A. COMMENTARY
*
*         A REPORT OF STUDENT GRADE POINT AVERAGES IS CREATED
*     FROM INPUT RECORDS CONTAINING STUDENT IDENTIFICATION
*     NUMBER (SIDNUM), HOURS TRIED (HRSTRI), HOURS PASSED
*     (HRSPAS), AND GRADE POINTS RECEIVED (GPRCVD).
*         REVISION 1 INCORPORATES ADVANCED PROGRAM CONTROL
*     STRUCTURES FOR PROGRAM IMPROVEMENT.
*
*         DICTIONARY.
*     DATEIF:  DATE INPUT FILE IDENTIFIER
*     DAY:  DAY OF THE MONTH REPORT IS PRODUCED (01 THRU 31)
*     GPA:  GRADE POINT AVERAGE
*     GPAOF:  GPA OUTPUT FILE IDENTIFIER
*     GPRCVD:  GRADE POINTS RECEIVED
*     GPRIF:  GRADE POINT RECORD INPUT FILE IDENTIFIER
*     HRSPAS:  HOURS PASSED (0 THRU 999)
*     HRSTRI:  HOURS TRIED (0 THRU 999)
*     LINE:  LINE COUNTER FOR OUTPUT PAGES
*     MAXLIN:  MAXIMUM LINES OF DETAIL PER PAGE
*     MAXPAG:  MAXIMUM NUMBER OF OUTPUT PAGES
*     MONTH:  MONTH THE REPORT IS PRODUCED (01 THRU 12)
*     PAGE:  PAGE COUNTER FOR OUTPUT PAGES
*     SIDNUM:  STUDENT IDENTIFICATION NUMBER (ALWAYS 9 DIGITS)
*     YEAR:  YEAR THE REPORT IS PRODUCED (0 THRU 99)
*
*  B. DECLARATION
*
      INTEGER  DATEIF, DAY, GPAOF, GPRCVD, GPRIF, HRSPAS,
     :         HRSTRI, LINE, MAXLIN, MAXPAG, MONTH, PAGE,
     :         SIDNUM, YEAR
      REAL  GPA
      PARAMETER  (DATEIF=5, GPRIF=5, GPAOF=6, MAXLIN=45, MAXPAG=1000)
*
*  C. I/O LAYOUT
*
  100 FORMAT (3I2)
  110 FORMAT (I9, 3I3)
  900 FORMAT ('1', //, ' ', T29, 'YOUR OWN COLLEGE OR UNIVERSITY', /
     :        '0', T31, 'GRADE POINT AVERAGE REPORT', 7X, 'PAGE', I5, /
     :        '0', T36, 'DATE:  ', I2, 2('/', I2), //
     :        '0', T19, 'STUDENT', 41X, 'GRADE', /
     :        ' ', T15, 'IDENTIFICATION', 5X, 'HOURS', 5X,
     :        'HOURS', 6X, 'GRADE', 7X, 'POINT', /
     :        ' ', T19, 'NUMBER', 9X, 'TRIED', 5X, 'PASSED',
     :        5X, 'POINTS', 5X, 'AVERAGE', /)
  910 FORMAT (' ', T18, I9.9, 8X, I3, 7X, I3, 8X, I3, 8X, F5.3)
  920 FORMAT ('1', 'GPA REPORT PROCESSING NOT INITIATED.  ',
     :        'DATE RECORD ERROR IN MONTH OR DAY.', /
     :        '0', 'RECORD IMAGE:  ', 3I2, /
     :        '0', 'PLEASE CORRECT AND RESUBMIT.')
  999 FORMAT ('1')
*
```

Figure 7-10. Grade Point Average Report Program: Revision 1

```
*   D. ACTION
*
      READ (DATEIF, 100) MONTH, DAY, YEAR
      IF (MONTH .GT. 0  .AND. MONTH .LT. 13
    :      .AND.  DAY .GT. 0  .AND.  DAY .LT. 32) THEN
          DO 220 PAGE = 1, MAXPAG
             DO 210 LINE = 1, MAXLIN
                READ (GPRIF, 110, END=230) SIDNUM, HRSTRI, HRSPAS, GPRCVD
                IF (LINE .EQ. 1) WRITE (GPAOF, 900) PAGE, MONTH,
    :                                               DAY, YEAR
                IF (HRSTRI .GT. 0) THEN
                   GPA = FLOAT(GPRCVD) / HRSTRI
                ELSE
                   GPA = 0
                ENDIF
                WRITE (GPAOF, 910) SIDNUM, HRSTRI, HRSPAS, GPRCVD, GPA
  210        CONTINUE
  220     CONTINUE
      ELSE
          WRITE (GPAOF, 920) MONTH, DAY, YEAR
      ENDIF
  230 WRITE (GPAOF, 999)
      STOP
      END
```

Figure 7-10. (Continued)

7-5 EXERCISES

1. Revise the kilometer-to-miles conversion program, KILMIL, given in Chapter 2, to take advantage of the program control structures of this chapter. Specifically, use the DO-loop mechanism.

2. Revise the program segment of Exercise 5(a) of Section 6-5 so that it uses a DO-loop.

3. Explain, for each of the following (individually), exactly why it is not possible to directly rewrite their looping mechanisms as Fortran DO-loops.

   (a) The program segment of Exercise 5(b) of Section 6-5

   (b) Program AVRAGE, Figure 6-4

   (c) Program MAXMIN, Figure 4-9

   (d) The program segment given in Section 4-8-2

4. There are a couple of program segments in Section 7-2-3 that contain DO-loops for which I did not furnish the equivalent segments not containing DO-loops (i.e., with explicit DO statements). You furnish the equivalent segments.

5. Write or revise (if you wrote them previously) complete Fortran programs for one or more of the following. Use the program control structures of this chapter.

   (a) Exercise 6 of Section 6-5

   (b) Exercise 7 of Section 6-5

    (c)   Exercise 8 of Section 6-5

    (d)   Exercise 9(a) of Section 6-5

    (e)   Exercise 9(b) of Section 6-5

    (f)   Exercise 6 of Section 5-11

    (g)   Exercise 7(b) of Section 5-11

    (h)   Exercise 7(c) of Section 5-11

    (i)   Exercise 8(a) of Section 5-11

    (j)   Exercise 8(b) of Section 5-11

6.   Draw a flowchart for the program segment in Section 7-3 that uses the computed GO TO in determining the weighted exam scores of high school students at different levels.

7.   Draw a flowchart for the program segment following the one mentioned in Exercise 6. Rather than the computed GO TO, the IF-THEN-ELSEIF-ELSE-ENDIF statements are used in this segment.

8.   Rewrite the program segment mentioned in Exercise 7 so that the input error test is performed last rather than first. Use only one IF-THEN statement. Check out both segments with a computer run.

9.   Rewrite the program segment you wrote for Exercise 10 of Section 7-1-5 so that the computed GO TO statement (case structure) is used in finding the discount amount based upon the quantity ordered. You will have to convert the quantity intervals to single-digit integers. For example, the relationship INT(Quantity_ordered/50.5)+1 will convert the intervals $21-50$, $51-100$, and $100-$up to 1, 2, 3, respectively.

10.   Rewrite the program segment given in Section 7-1-4 so that the computed GO TO is used in determining whether or not the charge will be allowed.

11.   You may have to brief yourself about bowling for this one; but not so if you know how to keep score. You are given, below, a partial algorithm for computing the score of a bowling game. It assumes that the pin count for each ball actually rolled is entered into one input record, and that the records are in the same sequence as the rolls. The algorithm contains no input data checks or i/o. It is documented very lightly. Your task is to write a complete Fortran program to compute and print (nicely) the complete results of a bowling game—individual and cumulative frame scores for each frame through the last one.

partial ALGORITHM Bowling:scoring
```
{   Count1, count2, and count3 are used to store the values of
successive pin counts from the first ball rolled through the
last ball rolled.  Frame indicates the bowling frame number,
and score is used to keep track of the bowling score as it
accumulates during the game.}
score ← 0
Read count1, count2
```

```
Do frame ← 1 to 10 by 1
    If count1 + count2 < 10 Then              {open frame}
        score ← score + count1 + count2
        Read count1, count2
    Else
        Read count3
        If count1 = 10 Then                   {strike frame}
            score ← score + 10 + count2 + count3
            count1 ← count2
            count2 ← count3
        Else                                  {spare frame}
            score ← score + 10 + count3
            count1 ← count3
            Read count2
End Do
END
```

12. Plan and write a complete Fortran program to produce a monthly statement for your own bank checking account. The first input record contains the previous statement balance. The other input records each contain a check/debit or deposit/credit transaction amount, that is always positive, and a transaction code: 0 for check/debit, 1 for deposit/credit. The printed statement should look something like this:

```
                    YOUR BANK'S NAME
                    YOUR BANK'S ADDRESS
               YOUR BANK'S CITY, STATE & ZIP


STATEMENT FOR:                  STATEMENT DATE:   MM/DD/YY
    YOUR NAME                   ACCOUNT NUMBER:  XXXXXXXXX
    YOUR STREET                 PAGE NUMBER:             X
    YOUR CITY, STATE & ZIP

CHECKS/OTHER DEBITS     DEPOSITS/OTHER CREDITS      BALANCE

    XXXX.XX                     XXXX.XX            XXXXX.XX

     (Only a debit or a credit is entered on each line)

    XXXX.XX                     XXXX.XX            XXXXX.XX

PREVIOUS STATEMENT BALANCE:                        XXXXX.XX
TOTAL CHECKS AND OTHER DEBITS:                     XXXXX.XX
TOTAL DEPOSITS AND OTHER CREDITS:                  XXXXX.XX
CURRENT STATEMENT BALANCE:                         XXXXX.XX
```

13. A positive integer greater than 1 is said to be a prime number if it is divisible only by itself and 1. The integers 2, 3, 5, and 7, for example, are prime numbers, but 4, 6, 8, and 9 are not. Plan and write a complete Fortran program to read in integers and determine if they are prime numbers. Use this additional information: The integer 2 is the only even prime number; if an integer is not divisible by another integer less than or equal to its square root, it is a prime number.

14. Using the formula below, plan and write a complete Fortran program to determine the approximate value of e, the base of the natural logarithms, to a given degree of accuracy.

$$e^x \approx 1 + x + \frac{x^2}{2!} + \frac{x^3}{3!} + \cdots + \frac{x^n}{n!}$$

By letting $x = 1$, the formula can be used directly to approximate the value of e. Your program should read in a degree of accuracy value and, by an iterative process, compute approximations to the value of e until the last term added in is less than or equal to the required degree of accuracy. Use double precision, if necessary, and be careful to establish an appropriate upper limit for the number of iterations (n). Finally, print the computed value of e, the value of n, and the degree of accuracy. As an example: for an accuracy value of 0.0005, n will turn out to be 7.

15. Plan and write a complete Fortran program to reverse the digits of a given positive integer that contains no more than 10 digits. Read the given integer; then print it and its reverse. For example, the reverse of 12345 is 54321.

APPENDIX: THREE LESS IMPORTANT FORTRAN CONTROL STATEMENTS

Briefly, I want to tell you about the three remaining Fortran control statements. One of the three might have some benefits of use in some situations; the other two I do not recommend for use.

The one that might be of use is the PAUSE statement. Its general form is

```
PAUSE string
```

where string is a character constant or a number of up to five digits. When used, and when the system allows its use, the PAUSE will cause program execution to cease. The string value may also be printed. Execution may be initiated again, beginning with the first executable statement following the PAUSE, only by a command from outside the program—perhaps from the computer operator or from you at your terminal. The PAUSE statement might be used, for example, during the program debugging process to allow the programmer time to review accumulated results before resuming execution.

The assigned GO TO statement has the form

```
GO TO iae (stn1, stn2, ..., stnN)
```

and, although it looks similar to the computed GO TO, it is not the same at all. The iae is an integer arithmetic expression and the stns are statement numbers. The list of statement numbers is not required. Upon execution of the statement, the value of iae must be one of the given statement numbers (not a statement number index as with the computed GO TO), or another statement number in the program unit if the list is not present. Execution causes a branch, then, to the statement that is labeled with the value of iae. The value of iae must have been previously established in an ASSIGN statement of the form

```
ASSIGN stn to iae
```

The use of the ASSIGN and assigned GO TO can cause significant program maintenance problems because of the dependence upon statement numbers. It is never necessary to use these statements.

The arithmetic IF statement has the form

```
IF (ae) stn1, stn2, stn3
```

in which ae is an arithmetic expression and the stns are statement numbers of executable statements in the program unit. The execution of this statement causes a branch to the statement labeled stn1 if ae is less than zero, the statement labeled stn2 if ae is equal to zero, or the statement labeled stn3 if ae is greater than zero.

The arithmetic IF is an old Fortran statement, having been a part of Fortran prior to the other types of IF statement. Its use detracts from the readability of the program. Situations in which it might be used are better described by the use of other Fortran statements such as the logical IF and the block IF.

Chapter

8

One-Dimensional Arrays

In earlier chapters, whenever we used a variable name in a program, we were referring to one location in the computer's memory that could have different values during execution, but only one value at any one time. Thus a variable name refers to one value at a time. In contrast, an array name refers to any given number of values of the same data item at one time. Therefore, an array can be looked upon as a set of item values identified by one name; or, more precisely, as a set of memory locations identified by one name. The purpose of this chapter is to acquaint you with the array data structure and provide you with a thorough exposition of one-dimensional arrays—from why they are essential in programming to how they are used in Fortran programs.

8-1 ARRAY RATIONALE

To help you see the reasons for having the array data structure, and realize the benefits of knowing how to use it, I offer the following comparative illustration.

The set of data given below consists of mid-1970s per capita income of each of 16 Texas counties.

```
$3747
 3258
 2877
 3838
 3668
 3787
 3629
 2915
 3267
 3576
 3839
 3803
 4616
 4519
 3281
 3161
```

If I asked you to use the computer to find the average per capita income of the 16 counties, you could do so by either writing a program now, or using a program that you have already written, or using a slightly modified version of the averaging program given in Chapter 6.

However, if I asked you to use the computer to find the median per capita income, you would find it extremely difficult to do with only the programming knowledge and ability you have acquired in your study of the chapters prior to this one. Consider what is involved. The median of a set of numbers is the "middle value"; that is, half of the numbers in the set are larger and half are smaller than the median. The first step in finding the median is to arrange the numbers into ascending or descending order. Then, the median is the middle number (for an odd-size set) or the arithmetic average of the two middle numbers (for an even-size set). To arrange the numbers into ascending or descending order, you would have to write instructions to compare them with each other and move them around in memory—just as you would have to move them around on paper if you were sequencing them manually. Thus the numbers would all have to be in memory at the same time. Keep in mind that the program you might use for finding the average would not have all of the numbers in memory at the same time—only one at a time; only the last value would be in memory when the average was computed. By the techniques we have covered so far, the only way that the numbers could all be in memory at the same time would be to give each one a unique variable name. The logic of the comparison and moving instructions would then be unnecessarily complicated. Furthermore, the program could not have much generality because it would be directly dependent on the number of values in the input data set; therefore, it would not be a very useful program.

To get an idea of the complexity involved, consider the following algorithmic segment, in which the interchange technique mentioned in Section 2-2-2 is used to find the median of four arbitrary input values.

```
Read a, b, c, d
Do i ← 1 to 3 by 1
   If a < b, Then
        h ← a                    {interchange a and b}
        a ← b
        b ← h
   If b < c, Then
        h ← b                    {interchange b and c}
        b ← c
        c ← h
   If c < d, Then
        h ← c                    {interchange c and d}
        c ← d
        d ← h
End Do
median ← (b + c) / 2
```

You should verify, by trace, that the segment does solve the stated problem. Then you should consider this question: What changes, if any, could be made so that the segment would generally solve the problem for an input data set that contains any number of input values?

My answer to the question is, simply, "none." Without the availability of a more flexible data structure than the scalar variable, we might as well devise a specific median algorithm for every size of data set—or, better yet, solve the problem manually! With the array data structure, however, the solution approach above modifies into a nice general solution procedure. The same holds true for many other problems and solution procedures. This one and others are examined in detail later in this chapter.

8-2 ARRAY NAMES AND ELEMENT REFERENCES

If the per capita income data were given the general name PCINC, then the individual 16 values could be referred to by the group of individual variable names PCINC1, PCINC2, PCINC3, . . . , PCINC15, and PCINC16, where the appended numbers 1, 2, 3, . . . , 15, and 16 serve to designate the relative positions of the values and to make the variable names unique. The primary trouble with these variable names is that they are data dependent and are therefore inflexible and nongeneral. A secondary trouble is that each of the last seven variable names contain more characters than FORTRAN 77 allows. The idea behind the formulation of these variable names, however, extends directly to the use of arrays.

By declaring PCINC to be an array name rather than a variable name, the individual values can be referenced by PCINC qualified with an index—called a *subscript expression*—that is used in identifying the locations of the values in the array. The individual array element references, then, can be PCINC(1), PCINC(2), PCINC(3), . . . , PCINC(15), and PCINC(16), where the numbers in parentheses are the subscript expressions, and the subscript expressions together with the parentheses are termed *subscripts*. PCINC(1) is read as "PCINC sub 1," and the others likewise. On the surface, these references may appear to be no more flexible than the individual variable name references; but they are, because the subscript expressions can vary in value during execution. For instance, if we let the variable "COUNTY" be the subscript expression, then the array element reference PCINC(COUNTY) can refer to any individual per capita income, depending on the currently defined value of COUNTY.

An array such as PCINC in which the individual elements are referenced via one subscript expression, is a one-dimensional array. One-dimensional arrays are the simplest kind of arrays. Other kinds are covered in a later chapter. The individual elements of one-dimensional arrays can be read-in, assigned, compared, and written-out; that is, they can be computer-processed just like scalar variables. The arrays must first be known to the compiler as arrays rather than scalar variables. This is accomplished by means of array declarations.

8-3 DECLARATIONS

You already know that every scalar variable must have a data type. Similarly, each array must have a data type; and array type declarations are made in the same manner as variable type declarations. Furthermore, every element of an array has the same data type.

Each array also has another property that must be known to the compiler and therefore must be declared; that is, the number of elements in the array. This declaration enables the compiler to establish a storage area for the array. It is accomplished by attaching a dimension declarator, enclosed in parentheses, to the array name in either a data type statement or a DIMENSION statement. For example, either the type declaration

```
INTEGER  PCINC(16)
```

or the type and DIMENSION declaration sequence

```
INTEGER  PCINC
DIMENSION  PCINC(16)
```

but not both, can be used to establish PCINC of the previous section as a one-dimensional array containing 16 elements.

The purpose of a DIMENSION statement is to identify arrays by name and specify their sizes so that their number of elements can be determined by the compiler. Although it is never necessary to use a DIMENSION statement, because the type statements can serve the purpose, you should remember its purpose and know its form:

```
DIMENSION  alist
```

where alist is a group of array names and declarations separated by commas.

The form of a dimension declarator may be either

```
udb
```

or

```
ldb:udb
```

where udb is the upper dimension bound and ldb is the lower dimension bound. Thus the array declaration for PCINC could be written in the form

```
INTEGER  PCINC(1:16)
```

In a main program, both bounds are arithmetic expressions consisting only of integer constants or symbolic names of integer constants. Any symbolic names used for this purpose must have had their values previously defined in a PARAME-TER statement. Often, the bounds are simple integer numbers. Either or both bounds may be negative, zero, or positive in value, but the upper bound must be numerically larger than the lower bound. If the lower bound is omitted, it is assumed to be 1.

As a wrap-up to this section, consider the following one-dimensional array declaration examples.

1. The local weather service has accumulated data for the previous month, consisting of each day's low and high temperature and precipitation. The

declarations that would establish arrays so that this information can be read into memory for processing might be written as follows.

```
INTEGER  HITEMP(31), LOTEMP(31)
REAL  PRECIP(31)
```

Alternatively, the lower bounds could also be specified, and the statements written like this:

```
INTEGER  HITEMP(1:31), LOTEMP(1:31)
REAL  PRECIP(1:31)
```

As another alternative, a DIMENSION statement could be used, in which case the declarations (omitting lower bounds) could be

```
INTEGER  HITEMP, LOTEMP
REAL  PRECIP
DIMENSION  HITEMP(31), LOTEMP(31), PRECIP(31)
```

2.   Each year, more than 50 but fewer than 100 institutions of higher learning submit grant applications to a particular foundation. The applications, consisting of completed forms and a written proposal concerning the need for and the proposed use of the grant funds, are committee-evaluated by a quantifying process that produces a value known as "proposal worth." A computer is then used to weight each proposal worth by one of four factors that reflects the highest degree-granting level of the institution—Associate, Bachelor, Master, Doctorate—and then produce a ranking of the weighted proposals. The statements below could be used to declare some of the appropriate arrays in the computer program.

```
INTEGER  PROPID(100)
REAL  DEGFAC(4), PROWTH(100)
```

Alternatively, with lower bounds specified and the DIMENSION statement used, the declaration statements could be:

```
INTEGER  PROPID
REAL  DEGFAC, PROWTH
DIMENSION  DEGFAC(1:4), PROPID(1:100), PROWTH(1:100)
```

3.   It is desired to compute once and store in memory, certain values of the exponential function,

$$e^n$$

so that they do not have to be computed each time they are needed. By using the declaration

```
DOUBLE PRECISION  EXPFUN(-10:10)
```

the exponential function for integral values of n from -10 to $+10$, inclusive, can be calculated and stored. The assignment relationship is

$$expfun_n \leftarrow e^n$$

In the Fortran program, this relationship can be written in the interesting form

EXPFUN (N) = DEXP (DBLE (N))

where the right-side consists of references to the DBLE and DEXP intrinsic functions (see Chapter 5 and the Appendix at the end of the book) and the left-side consists of an array element name. The interpretation of this statement is "Compute, using the DEXP intrinsic function, the value of e raised to the (double precision) power N; then assign that value to the array element EXPFUN(N)." Subsequently in the program, all that is required to obtain the value of e raised to the power N is to reference the array element EXPFUN(N). Some values that will be obtained by referencing elements of the EXPFUN array are approximately the following.

Reference	Approximate Value
EXPFUN(−2)	0.135335
EXPFUN(0)	1.0
EXPFUN(2)	7.389056

Observe in each of the examples above that the array sizes are specified in terms of the maximum number of values that the array will or might contain. The compiler reserves storage on a maximum size basis. During execution, however, either all or only a portion of the array element positions may be referenced. In example 1, for instance, 31 was specified as the size of the arrays because it is the most number of days a month can have. During execution, when the month in question is January, all elements in each array will be used; when the month is June, only 30 of the elements in each array will be used; when the month is February, either 28 or 29 of the elements in each array will be used, depending on whether the year is a leap year or not. It is normal to use fewer array elements during execution than are declared; it is always abnormal, and therefore an error, to try to use more array elements than are declared.

Consider this modification to example 2, which provides some generality and flexibility in specifying dimension sizes:

```
INTEGER   MAXPRO
PARAMETER   (MAXPRO= 100)
INTEGER   PROPID (MAXPRO)
REAL   DEGFAC (4) ,  PROWTH (MAXPRO)
```

This sequence takes advantage of allowing symbolic constants to be dimension bounds. Clearly, it requires the PARAMETER statement to appear before the array declarations, and another INTEGER statement to appear before the PARAMETER statement. Care should be taken with this type of sequence. Observe thoughtfully that the dimension bound, MAXPRO, of PROPID and PROWTH, is a symbolic constant, not a variable. As is, this sequence accomplishes exactly the same thing as the sequences in example 2. However, it allows a minor program modification—a change in only the PARAMETER statement—to cause useful changes in several array bounds. For instance, an increase in the number of accepted proposals to 200 requires only the simple change

```
PARAMETER   (MAXPRO=200)
```

8-4 INPUT AND OUTPUT

Array element values are read into or written out of memory one at a time, just like scalar variable values. Rather than being able to specify the reading or writing of only one array element in an iolist, however, the reading or writing of all or any part of an array may be specified in one iolist. Let arn represent an array name, and loce denote a "location expression"—the subscript expression used to identify the location of a particular element in the array. Then the reference with subscript,

```
arn(loce)
```

in an iolist, identifies one array element to be read in or written out. In stark contrast, the reference without subscript,

```
arn
```

in an iolist, indicates that as many elements as the array might possibly have—as identified in the array dimension declaration—are to be read in or written out.

With reference to the per capita income problem posed in Section 8-1, for example, the program segment

```
INTEGER   COUNTY, PCINC(16)
         .
         .
         .
DO 300 COUNTY = 1, 16
    READ *, PCINC(COUNTY)
    PRINT *, PCINC(COUNTY)
300 CONTINUE
```

establishes an array, PCINC, of size 16, and then reads and prints the individual array element values one by one. The array element references here are of the first form explained above. Because the READ statement is executed exactly 16 times and references only one array element each time, the per capita income values must appear individually on sixteen sequential input records.

In contrast, in the alternative segment,

```
INTEGER   PCINC(16)
         .
         .
         .
READ *, PCINC
PRINT *, PCINC
```

the entire PCINC array is referenced by one execution of the READ statement and then one execution of the PRINT statement. Here, the array references are of the second form explained above. Thus, exactly sixteen values, no more and no less, will be read sequentially into the array; then they will all be printed in sequence. The income values can be entered one or more—up to all 16—per input record. Although this segment provides for some input efficiency and is simpler to code than the previous one, it lacks generality, or the potential for generality, because the number of elements to be processed is fixed by the dimension declaration. Remember this.

In between the two extremes noted above is the implied-DO reference form,

```
(arn(locv), locv = ae1, ae2, ae3)
```

that can be used in an iolist to specify the reading or writing of any number of array elements from none up to as many as are specified in the array dimension declaration. For an input operation, the implied-DO form can be interpreted like this: "Read arn sub locv as locv varies from ae1 to ae2 in increments of ae3." The output interpretation is identical except that the word "Write" or "Print" replaces the word "Read." Observe that the form of the implied-DO is similar to the form of a DO statement. Thus locv is the implied-DO control variable; ae1, ae2, and ae3 are the implied-DO parameter expressions that are used to establish the initial, test, and increment values of the implied-DO control variable; and ae3 is optional. The range of the implied-DO is delimited by the outside parentheses.

As a first example of the use of the implied-DO, consider the following program segment.

```
INTEGER COUNTY, PCINC(16)
    .
    .
    .
READ *, (PCINC(COUNTY), COUNTY = 1, 16)
PRINT *, (PCINC(COUNTY), COUNTY = 1, 16)
```

The variable COUNTY is used as the subscript variable for the array PCINC as well as the control variable in both implied-DOs. The read and print operations can be interpreted as, "Read PCINC sub COUNTY as COUNTY varies from 1 to 16 in increments of 1; then print PCINC sub COUNTY as COUNTY varies from 1 to 16 in increments of 1." An important feature of the implied-DO used in this way is that as many or as few of the input values as desired can be in one physical input record. In the case of the 16 per capita income values, all of them could be entered into one input record if desired; or they could be entered one per input record, two per record, three per record, and so on. Also, by this method, as many values as possible will be printed on one output line. Since it may not be desirable to have so many values on one output line, other ways of printing are given in examples later.

An alternative to the implied-DO READ/PRINT statement sequence above is:

```
READ *, PCINC(1), PCINC(2), PCINC(3), PCINC(4),
  :         PCINC(5), PCINC(6), PCINC(7), PCINC(8),
  :         PCINC(9), PCINC(10), PCINC(11), PCINC(12),
  :         PCINC(13), PCINC(14), PCINC(15), PCINC(16)
 PRINT *, PCINC(1), PCINC(2), PCINC(3), PCINC(4),
  :         PCINC(5), PCINC(6), PCINC(7), PCINC(8),
  :         PCINC(9), PCINC(10), PCINC(11), PCINC(12)
  :         PCINC(13), PCINC(14), PCINC(15), PCINC(16)
```

In fact, you could say that this sequence is an "interpretation" of the implied-DO sequence; it should help you understand the implied-DO. Which statement sequence would you want to code and key-in? The one with the implied-DO, no doubt.

Besides being longer and more tedious, the sequence immediately above is not as potentially general as the implied-DO sequence. Consider a modification of the implied-DO sequence that provides it with considerable generality.

```
INTEGER  MAXCTY
PARAMETER  (MAXCTY= 16)
INTEGER  COUNTY, NOCTYS, PCINC(MAXCTY)

  .

  .

READ *, NOCTYS
IF (NOCTYS .GT. 0 .AND. NOCTYS .LE. MAXCTY) THEN
    READ *, (PCINC(COUNTY), COUNTY = 1, NOCTYS)
    PRINT *, (PCINC(COUNTY), COUNTY = 1, NOCTYS)

  .

  .

ELSE
```

Here the constant MAXCTY is the maximum number of counties, and the variable NOCTYS is the number of counties for which input data are available. MAXCTY provides some generality, as previously discussed, because a change in its value in the PARAMETER statement allows the array size of PCINC to change. The important generality here, however, is in the use of the variable NOCTYS. Its value can vary without a program change, therefore allowing data sets to be of different sizes—as long as they contain no more than MAXCTY per capita income values. The interpretation of the second READ statement is: "Read PCINC sub COUNTY as COUNTY varies from 1 to the value of NOCTYS in increments of 1"; the PRINT statement, similarly. The IF-THEN-ELSE statements are included in the segment to make sure that the array bounds, lower and upper, are not violated—a catastrophic error.

All three of the iolist forms for reading and writing arrays—single element reference, entire array reference, or the more flexible implied-DO reference—are valid and useful. The one to use in a given instance depends on the program logic and either the input or the output design. For illustration, consider in the following paragraphs the input/output possibilities for the examples initiated in the preceding section.

The weather data on low temperatures, high temperatures, and precipitation are collected daily and recorded in the following way for a given 30-day month.

Day	Low Temperature	High Temperature	Precipitation
1	52	74	0.10
2	48	69	1.12
3	57	73	—
.	.	.	.
.	.	.	.
.	.	.	.
29	60	79	—
30	57	75	0.45
31			

The data are then entered into input records, day by day, so that the input file looks like this by the end of the month:

```
52 74 0.10
48 69 1.12
57 73 0
  .    .    .
  .    .    .
  .    .    .
60 79 0
57 75 0.45
```

A printed report, similar in part to the following, is to be produced.

```
                    LOCAL WEATHER REPORT
                 MONTH OF XXXXXXXXX,  19XX

   DAY    LOW TEMPERATURE    HIGH TEMPERATURE    PRECIPITATION

    1          XXX                 XXX              XX.XX
    2          XXX                 XXX              XX.XX
    .           .                   .                .
    .           .                   .                .
    .           .                   .                .
   30          XXX                 XXX              XX.XX

 EXTREMES      XXX                 XXX
 AVERAGES      XXX                 XXX              XX.XX
```

Thus each input record contains one element value for each of three array items. Furthermore, the detailed output records each contain four values, three of which are the element values of three different array items (the DAY values are really indexes that can be generated internally and therefore need not be stored in an array). Given this information, the following segment, representing a portion of the full program, may be written.

```
      INTEGER   DAY, HITEMP(31), LOTEMP(31), NUMDAY,
    :             WEDAIF, WERPOF
      REAL   PRECIP(31)
      PARAMETER   (WEDAIF=5, WERPOF=6)
        .
        .
        .
  920 FORMAT (' ', I3, 9X, I3, 16X, I3, 13X, F5.2)
        .
        .
        .
      DO 300 DAY = 1, 31
          READ (WEDAIF, *, END=310) LOTEMP(DAY), HITEMP(DAY),
    :                              PRECIP(DAY)
          NUMDAY = DAY
  300 CONTINUE
  310 . {Statements for the calculation of extremes
      .    and averages can appear here.}
      DO 500 DAY = 1, NUMDAY
          WRITE (WERPOF, 920) DAY, LOTEMP(DAY), HITEMP(DAY),
    :                              PRECIP(DAY)
  500 CONTINUE
```

The declarations are similar to the ones given in the earlier section, with the addition of integer variables to designate the day of the month (DAY) and the number of days in the month (NUMDAY), and integer symbolic constants for the weather data input file name (WEDAIF) and weather report output file name (WERPOF). The FORMAT statement goes with the write operation and corresponds to the detail output lines. The first DO-loop reads temperature and precipitation values from the input file into the appropriate positions of the respective arrays; it also keeps track of the number of records read in. The second DO-loop simply prints the detail lines. Single array elements of each array are referenced by the READ iolist during one execution of the statement; the same is true of the WRITE statement. Additionally, the WRITE iolist causes the value of the DO-loop control variable, DAY, to be printed, designating the appropriate day of the month on each detail line of the report. An explicit DO-loop is used, for both the reading and the writing operation, to "step through" the array elements sequentially. The read operation uses the input file to define array element values in memory; the write operation writes-out array element values, previously defined in memory, into the report file.

To save some coding effort, the implied-DO can be used in the WRITE statement; the FORMAT will then control the number of values written on each output line. In particular, the entire writing operation can be accomplished by the single statement

```
      WRITE (WERPOF, 920) (DAY, LOTEMP(DAY), HITEMP(DAY),
    :                      PRECIP(DAY), DAY = 1, NUMDAY)
```

If used, this one statement replaces all three statements of the DO-500 loop; it is not, then, indented. This should indicate to you that the implied-DO has more flexibility than I have shown you so far. In fact, the implied-DO list is extremely flexible, having the general form

```
(idlist, locv = ae1, ae2, ae3)
```

where idlist is an input/output list [like DAY, LOTEMP(DAY), HITEMP(DAY), PRECIP(DAY)], and the other items are as described previously. Tremendous added flexibility is available because idlist can, itself, contain implied-DO lists. Ponder that for a moment.

Let us move on to the second example of the preceding section, in which grant proposals submitted to a particular foundation by institutions of higher learning are quantified by committee, then weighted and ranked by computer. Proposal identifiers are to be read into elements of array PROPID; the quantified proposal worth values are to be read into corresponding elements of array PROWTH; one of four factors stored in array DEGFAC are to be applied; and then the proposal identifiers, together with the unweighted and weighted proposal worth values, are to be printed in ranked order, most worthy to least worthy.

The degree weighting factors are stored in input file DGWFIF, all on one record, like this:

```
1.20 1.10 1.05 1.0
```

The proposal identifiers and worth values are stored in input file PRPSIF, with each record containing an identifier followed by the corresponding worth, like this:

```
101 78.5
102 98.0
  .    .
  .    .
  .    .
215 80.4
  .    .
  .    .
  .    .
309 97.6
  .    .
  .    .
  .    .
422 71.2
423 99.2
```

The first digit of each identifier designates the highest degree-granting level of the institution and is therefore used to select the weight factor to be applied. The other two digits of the identifier are proposal numbers, in sequential order within that degree-granting level. The output, for a portion of the given data, is to look something like this:

```
                 PROPOSAL EVALUATION:   RANK BY WEIGHTED WORTH
```

PROPOSAL I.D.	RAW WORTH	WEIGHTED WORTH	RANK
102	98.0	117.60	1
.	.	.	.
.	.	.	.
.	.	.	.
309	97.6	102.48	20
.	.	.	.
.	.	.	.
423	99.2	99.2	25
.	.	.	.
.	.	.	.
.	.	.	.

Finally, the declarations, and the statements for reading and writing, are as follows:

```
      INTEGER  MAXPRO
      PARAMETER   (MAXPRO=100)
      INTEGER  DGWFIF, EVRPOF, NEXT, NUMPRO, PROPID(MAXPRO),
     :          PRPSAL, PRPSIF, RANK(MAXPRO)
      REAL   DEGFAC(4), PROWTH(MAXPRO), WTDWTH(MAXPRO)
      PARAMETER   (DGWFIF=5, PRPSIF=4, EVRPOF=6)
       .
       .
       .
      READ (DGWFIF, *) DEGFAC
      DO 300 PRPSAL = 1, MAXPRO
         READ (PRPSIF, *, END=310) PROPID(PRPSAL), PROWTH(PRPSAL)
         NUMPRO = PRPSAL
  300 CONTINUE
  310 .   {The weighting and
       .    ranking statements
       .    appear here}
      DO 600 PRPSAL = 1, NUMPRO
         NEXT = RANK(PRPSAL)
         WRITE (EVRPOF, 930) PROPID(NEXT), PROWTH(NEXT),
     :                        WTDWTH(NEXT), PRPSAL
  600 CONTINUE
```

The first reading operation addresses array DEGFAC as a unit, causing exactly four values to be read into it as specified in its dimension declaration. If four values are not available in the file, an error has occurred and processing cannot continue. Following the reading of DEGFAC, the read loop is similar to the one in the last example program segment except that the DO test parameter expression, MAXPRO, is a symbolic constant. The write loop is also similar to the one in the last example except that the subscript expression value for the arrays is obtained from elements of the array named RANK, which contains the subscript values of the proposals in ranked order. The entire write loop could be replaced by this one statement:

```
      WRITE (EVRPOF, 930)  (PROPID(RANK(PRPSAL)),
     :                       PROWTH(RANK(PRPSAL)),
     :                       WTDWTH(RANK(PRPSAL)),
     :                       PRPSAL, PRPSAL = 1, NUMPRO)
```

Judge for yourself whether this is more, or less, understandable. It is definitely less efficient, even though it eliminates the temporary variable NEXT, because it references the same element of RANK three times each time the implied loop is executed, thus requiring the computer to search for and fetch the same value many times unnecessarily. The introduction of the temporary variable NEXT and the use of the explicit DO are the better practices in this program segment—both for readability and for execution efficiency.

In the third example of Section 8-3, where certain values of the exponential function are computed and stored in memory, there are no input values for the exponential function array elements; they are computed internally. Actually, there is not meant to be any direct output of these elements either; they are to be used later during execution for simple lookup so that the intrinsic exponential function will not have to be referenced each time one of the function values is needed. However, it is worthwhile to create some output so that you can see how an array having a lower bound not equal to 1 is handled. Consider this program segment:

```
      INTEGER  EXPOF, N
      DOUBLE PRECISION  EXPFUN(-10:10)
      PARAMETER  (EXPOF= 6)
      .
      .
      .
  910 FORMAT (' ', I3, 3X, F13.7)
      .
      .
      .
      DO 300 N = -10, 10
          EXPFUN(N)  = DEXP(DBLE(N))
          WRITE  (EXPOF, 910) N, EXPFUN(N)
  300 CONTINUE
```

A portion of the printed output from this segment will be

```
  -10        0.0000454
   -9        0.0001234
    .            .
    .            .
    .            .
   -1        0.3678794
    0        1.0000000
    1        2.7182818
    .            .
    .            .
    .            .
    9     8103.0839276
   10    22026.4657948
```

where the numbers in the first column are not only the DO-variable values but also the subscript expression values for the array EXPFUN. Thus EXPFUN(1)=2.7182818, EXPFUN(0)=1.0, EXPFUN(-1)=0.3678794, and so on. This simply points out that negative and zero, as well as positive values, are valid subscripts in FORTRAN 77. (Negative and zero are invalid as subscripts in the earlier version of standard Fortran.)

Observe in the program segment above that array element values can also be defined via assignment statements as well as input statements. In fact, array elements can be used just like variables in assignment statements and IF statements. This observation and fact are the subjects of the next section.

8-5   ASSIGNMENT AND COMPARISON

An array element reference of the previously given form

```
arn(loce)
```

where arn is the array name and loce is the location expression for the array element, can be used anywhere in a program that a scalar variable reference can be used. The array element reference form above is actually an array element name form. It refers to one value just as a variable name refers to one value. Therefore, the array element names

```
PCINC(10)
PCINC(COUNTY)
HITEMP(DAY)
RANK(PRPSAL)
```

as well as any other array element names—each of which refer to one value in memory at a time—can appear in arithmetic expressions of assignment statements and IF statements. They can also appear to the left of the = sign in assignment statements.

It was pointed out at the end of the last section that the assignment statement

```
EXPFUN(N)  = DEXP(DBLE(N))
```

contains an array element reference that appears to the left of the = sign. The result of one execution of the statement is to cause one element, the Nth, of the array EXPFUN to be assigned a value. For further illustration, reconsider the other two continuing examples.

Since the weather report output is to contain the extremes and averages of the temperature lows and highs, it can be expected that the program will contain statements similar to the following.

```
INTEGER  AVHITP, AVLOTP, DAY, HITEMP(31), LOTEMP(31),
:             MAXTMP, MINTMP, NUMDAY, WEDAIF, WERPOF
REAL   AVPRCP, PRECIP(31)
PARAMETER   (WEDAIF=5, WERPOF=6)
  .
  .
  .

   IF (LOTEMP(DAY) .LT. MINTMP) MINTMP = LOTEMP(DAY)
   IF (HITEMP(DAY) .GT. MAXTMP) MAXTMP = HITEMP(DAY)
   AVLOTP = AVLOTP + LOTEMP(DAY)
   AVHITP = AVHITP + HITEMP(DAY)
   AVPRCP = AVPRCP + PRECIP(DAY)
```

```
.
.
.
AVLOTP  = FLOAT(AVLOTP)  /  NUMDAY  +  0.5
AVHITP  = FLOAT(AVHITP)  /  NUMDAY  +  0.5
AVPRCP  = AVPRCP  /  NUMDAY
```

Here, the INTEGER and REAL statements have been extended to include additional variables for summations and averages (AVHITP, AVLOTP, and AVPRCP) and extremes (MAXTMP and MINTMP). The primary items of interest right now are the array element references LOTEMP(DAY), HITEMP(DAY), and PRECIP(DAY). In each appearance, these array element names refer to one value at a time, during execution, depending upon the value of the subscript variable DAY (which must be defined when referenced, even though its defining statement is not shown in the code here). Thus, they are used just like variable names.   .

In the grant application ranking program, statements like the following can be used to apply the weighting factors to the raw proposal worth values.

```
      INTEGER  MAXPRO
      PARAMETER  (MAXPRO=100)
      INTEGER  DEGLEV, DGWFIF, EVRPOS, NEXT, NUMPRO,
     :            PROPID(MAXPRO), PRPSAL, PRPSIF, RANK(MAXPRO)
      REAL  DEGFAC(4), PROWTH(MAXPRO), WTDWTH(MAXPRO)
      PARAMETER  (DGWFIF=5, PRPSIF=4, EVRPOF=6)
      .  {Input statements, given previously,
      .    appear here.}
      DO 430 PRPSAL = 1, NUMPRO
         DEGLEV = PROPID(PRPSAL) / 100
         IF (DEGLEV .LT.1  .OR.  DEGLEV .GE. 5) THEN
*            ERROR IN PROPOSAL I.D.; PRINT ERROR NOTATION.
             WRITE (EVRPOF, 930) PROPID(PRPSAL)
         ELSE
*            PROPOSAL I.D. IS O.K.; WEIGHT THE PROPOSAL WORTH.
             WTDWTH(PRPSAL) = PROWTH(PRPSAL) * DEGFAC(DEGLEV)
         ENDIF
  430 CONTINUE
```

I point out that DEGLEV—the degree level—has been added to the list of integers, but here again, our primary interest is in array element references. They occur in the first assignment statement, in which the scalar variable DEGLEV is assigned the value of the array element PROPID(PRPSAL) divided by 100, and in the last assignment statement, in which two array element values are multiplied and the resulting value is assigned to WTDWTH(PRPSAL), the corresponding element of the "weighted worth" array. Thus these array element references, or names, are also used just like variable names.

The entire sequence in the DO-loop above could conceivably be replaced by one Fortran statement. This would be possible only if we were sure that all the proposal identifier input values were always entered correctly and that the input data check in the segment above was, therefore, unnecessary. Here is the replacement statement:

```
      WTDWTH(PRPSAL) = PROWTH(PRPSAL) *
     :                  DEGFAC(PROPID(PRPSAL) / 100)
```

Of course, we cannot always be sure of the input data; so the error check should be left in. The statement above, however, gives me an opportunity to point out to you that subscript expressions can be very complicated—as complicated as you need for them to be, as long as they produce integer values. Let us go ahead, for illustrative purposes, and evaluate the statement above for the values, given earlier, of the second proposal in the input file. Thus PRPSAL=2, PROPID(2)=102, and PROWTH(2)=98.0. The degree-level weighting factors, read in from a different file, were also previously given as DEGFAC(1)=1.20, DEGFAC(2)=1.10, DEG-FAC(3)=1.05, and DEGFAC(4)=1.0. Beginning with the substitution of subscript variable values, then, the evaluation proceeds as follows.

```
WTDWTH(2)  = PROWTH(2)  * DEGFAC(PROPID(2)  / 100)
                 98.0   * DEGFAC(    102     / 100)

                 98.0   * DEGFAC(           1      )

                 98.0   *              1.20
WTDWTH(2)  =                    117.6
```

And that is correct, as shown earlier in the representative output. The conclusion that you should draw from this section is that array element names can be used anywhere that variable names can be used; both types of names refer to one value at a time in each use.

8-6   INITIALIZATION

The four degree-level weighting factors were defined earlier via the input statement

```
READ (DGWFIF, *) DEGFAC
```

which references the four-element array as a unit. The factors are probably fairly constant and do not vary in value each time the program is executed as do the proposal worths. Therefore, it may be more appropriate to treat the factors as internal data rather than storing them in an external file that requires a separate secondary storage area. The DATA statement can be used for this purpose.

Given that DEGFAC was declared earlier as a one-dimensional real array of size four by the statement

```
REAL  DEGFAC(4), PROWTH(MAXPRO), WTDWTH(MAXPRO)
```

the following DATA statement can be used in place of the execution-time initialization with the READ statement.

```
DATA  DEGFAC/1.20, 1.10, 1.05, 1.0/
```

Alternatively, an implied-DO form can be used to show more clearly, perhaps, that four elements of DEGFAC are being initialized; like this:

```
DATA  (DEGFAC(LEVEL), LEVEL = 1, 4)/
:             1.20, 1.10, 1.05, 1.00/
```

For an array this small, the elements can even be named individually, in the following way.

```
DATA  DEGFAC(1), DEGFAC(2), DEGFAC(3), DEGFAC(4)/
:           1.20,     1.10,     1.05,     1.00/
```

All three of the DATA statements above accomplish exactly the same thing since DEGFAC is declared to have exactly four elements. They also eliminate the need for the data file DGWFIF, and the associated READ statement.

The implied-DO in a DATA statement is identical in form and interpretation to the implied-DO in a READ, PRINT, or WRITE statement. Furthermore, the implied-DO can be used only in these four statements; it cannot be used in an assignment, IF, or any other statement except DATA, READ, PRINT, and WRITE.

Occasionally, it may be desirable to initialize all, or many, of the elements of an array to the same value. For this purpose, the value list in a DATA statement can contain a repetition factor attached to the value to be repeated. The form to use is

```
rf * val
```

where rf is the repetition factor, an unsigned integer constant or the symbolic name of an integer constant, and val is the value to be assigned to each of the rf elements. For example, the statements

```
INTEGER  ABLE(50)
DATA  ABLE/50*0/
```

not only establish an array of size 50 named ABLE, but also initialize all 50 elements of the array to zero. For another example, the statements

```
INTEGER  BSIZE, CSIZE
PARAMETER  (BSIZE=5, CSIZE=25)
REAL  BAKER(BSIZE), CHARLY(CSIZE)
DATA  BAKER,        CHARLY(CSIZE) /
:         BSIZE*(-1),           -1/
```

not only establish arrays BAKER and CHARLY of size BSIZE and CSIZE, respectively, but also initialize all elements of BAKER to -1 and the last element (only) of CHARLY to -1.

Although this initialization capability is handy to have, you should use it only if the array element values are not changed by the executable statements in the program action; if they are, do the initialization with executable statements.

For instance, if the elements of array ABLE above change in value during program execution, it would be better to perform the initialization in an executable loop similar to the following.

```
    DO 220 INDEX = 1, 50
        ABLE(INDEX) = 0
220 CONTINUE
```

8-7 EXAMPLE PROGRAM: MEDIAN WITH SORTING

We can use the median per capita income problem to examine thoroughly the proper handling of a one-dimensional array in a program. We will first modify the problem so that the resulting program will be more flexible and useful. We will also use the problem to study a technique for programming a particular process that commonly occurs in computer applications—the sorting of data.

The modified problem is stated as follows.

Given per capita income data for a certain number of counties in any particular state in the United States, compute and print the median and average per capita income values.

As stated, the problem requires the program to be capable of accepting and processing per capita income data for any state, regardless of the number of counties in the state. By examining appropriate references, you will find that the largest number of counties in any one state is 254. We will, therefore, use this value to specify the number of elements in our per capita income array. The average is included in the problem statement because it allows me to show you how the average is obtained for a set of array elements, so that you can compare the method with the one used to find the average for a set of scalar variable values. An additional benefit of this problem is that it allows us to consider the solution procedure not only from the standpoint of a top-down design, but also with a view toward the development of individual program modules or subprograms. Before we proceed to the solution procedure, however, consider the input and output designs.

An input data set consists of one "Identification Record" followed by as many physical "Per Capita Income Records" as necessary. A physical per capita income record can contain as many or as few income values as desired; each income value, however, constitutes a logical per capita income record. List-directed input will be used; therefore, the values in the physical input records should be separated by blanks. The input layouts are described in the following way.

Identification Record:

Field Name	Data Description	Location
State identifier	Integer, XX (2 digits)	Free form,
Number of counties	Integer, 1–3 digits	separated
Output option selector	Integer, a 1 or a 0	by blanks

Per Capita Income Records:

Income values are entered free form, separated by blanks. There must be exactly as many income values as there are counties—as specified in the Identification Record.

In the identification record, the state identifier is a user-selected two-digit code number. The code for each state should be unique. With judicious selection you could use the first two digits of a zip code assigned to a state by the United States Postal Service. The number of counties, an integer greater than or equal to 1 and less than or equal to 254, must be equal to the number of per capita income values. The output option selector, 1 (or any nonzero integer) to print the sorted per capita income values or 0 to suppress the printing, is included to show you another feature that you may sometimes want to include in a program. Its specific use is reflected in the output layout discussed below.

The output layout is depicted in Figure 8-1. Notice that the median and average are to be "nearest-integer" values, the sorted per capita incomes are to be

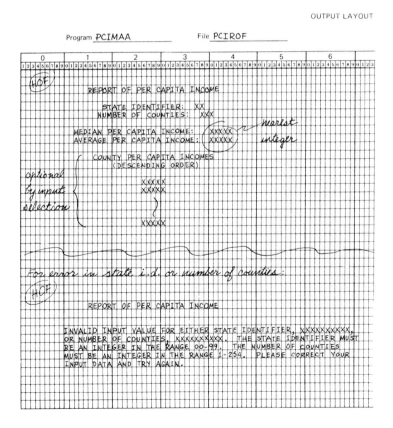

Figure 8-1. Per Capita Income Report Layout

optionally printed as mentioned above, and if either the state identifier or the number of counties is outside the allowable value range, only an error message is to be printed.

The first attempt at devising an algorithm can now be made.

```
Print the title.
Read the state identifier, number of counties,
    and output option selector.
If either the state identifier
    or the number of counties is invalid, then
    write an error message.
Otherwise, do the following:
    print the state identifier and number of counties;
    read the per capita incomes;
    sort the per capita incomes;
    compute the median;
    compute the average;
    print the median and average;
    if the output option selector is not zero,
        print the per capita incomes.
Stop.
```

This "first try" algorithm contains three subproblems that are worthy of individual consideration: sort the per capita incomes, compute the median, and compute the average. In Section 11-5 you will learn that these three subproblems might best be solved by means of subprograms that are physically separate from each other and the main program. Here we will develop their solution procedures as individual algorithms (subalgorithms, if you will) and then incorporate them into the main algorithm and the main program.

Sorting—that is, arranging logical data records into an ascending or descending order based on a particular item in the records called a *sort key*—can be performed by any of a number of different methods. One of the easier to learn but least-efficient methods is known by the names *bubble sort*, *exchange sort*, and *interchange sort*. We use this method here, and other methods in exercises and later chapters.

The records we want to sort each consist of one data item—the per capita income. This item, then, is our sort key. In memory, the per capita income values will be stored in an array. Therefore, what we want to do is to reorder the per capita income values in the array so that they are in descending sequence. For example, if the input data consisted of only the first five per capita income values listed near the beginning of this chapter, our array would initially contain the values

```
3747
3258
2877
3838
3668
```

in sequential positions one through five. After sorting, the values would be in the following order in array positions one through five.

```
3838
3747
3668
3258
2877
```

The bubble sort method for an array involves making several scans or passes through the array elements, comparing adjacent element values in pairs and interchanging the element values, of each pair, that are not ordered properly with respect to each other. For example, by letting c mean "compare," n mean "no interchange," and i mean "interchange," the first pass involving the five unordered elements above can be depicted as follows.

Array (Initially)		*Array (End of Pass 1)*
3747		3747
	c, n	
3258		3258
	c, n	
2877	3838	3838
	c, i	
3838	2877	3668
	c, i	
3668	3668	2877
		2877

At the end of one pass, the array is partially ordered; that is, at least the last value is in the proper position. The others are "bubbling up." At most, N − 1 passes are required to complete the sorting task, where N is the number of elements being sorted. Here are the results of additional passes on the data above:

Array (End of Pass 2)	*Array (End of Pass 3)*
3747	3838
3838	3747
3668	3668
3258	3258
2877	2877

For these data, sorting is complete after only three passes, compared to the four passes required in the worst case. But let me encourage you to remember this: Even though only three passes were required to put the values into the desired order, the computer will have to make one additional partial pass to verify that sorting is complete. In fact, if the values had been in the desired order to begin with, one pass would still have been required to verify the ordering (after all, you and I would have to make a "sight" verification if we were going to sort the numbers manually). The ordering can be verified by the use of an interchange indicator that is initialized to zero just before a pass begins, and is set to one anytime an interchange occurs. At the end of a pass, then, if the interchange indicator is still equal to zero, the ordering is verified and sorting is complete; otherwise, another pass is required.

Here, then, is a first try at the bubble sort algorithm.

```
As long as sorting is incomplete, do the following:
    make a pass through the array elements,
    performing the following:
        compare adjacent element values in pairs
        and interchange the element values, of each pair,
        that are not properly ordered with respect to each other.
```

A second try is as follows.

```
Set the number of compares equal to the number of elements.
Set the interchange indicator to 1.
While the interchange indicator is 1,
    pass through the array elements performing the following:
        set the interchange indicator to 0;
        decrement the number of compares by 1;
        while there are compares to be made, do the following:
            if the value of the first element of the pair is the
                smaller of the two,
                interchange the element values
                and set the interchange indicator to 1.
```

Finally, a general bubble sort algorithm, like the one below, is developed. It assumes that the array element values and the number of elements to be sorted are already defined. For generality and simplicity, the assumed array name is "a" and the number of elements being sorted is "n."

```
        ALGORITHM Bubblesort.descending
        { Values stored in the n elements of array a are sorted
        into descending order in the array by the bubble sort
        method.}
        number of compares ← n
        interchange indicator ← 1
PASS.  If interchange indicator = 1 Then
            interchange indicator ← 0
            number of compares ← number of compares − 1
            Do element ← 1 to number of compares by 1
                If a(element) < a(element+1), Then
                    h ← a(element)              {interchange}
                    a(element) ← a(element+1)
                    a(element+1) ← h
                    interchange indicator ← 1
            End Do
            Go To PASS. (Back)
        {sorting is complete}
        END
```

The array is identified in the algorithm as an array by its appended subscript expression in parentheses.

The median computation subproblem is simpler than the sort subproblem. It can be performed only after the sorting process has been completed. A first-try solution procedure for this computation can be described generally as follows.

```
If the number of values is an even number, then
    the median is the average of the two middle values.
Otherwise, the median is the middle value.
```

By using the notation of the sorting algorithm above and letting m represent the approximate midpoint of the array elements being sorted, the median computation procedure can be specified more precisely, something like this:

```
m ← INT[n/2]
If MOD[n, 2] = 0 Then
    median ← NINT[(a(m) + a(m + 1)) / 2]
Else
    median ← a(m+1)
```

Here INT is a function reference meaning "truncated integer value," MOD is a function reference meaning "remainder of the division of the first argument by the second," and NINT is a function reference meaning "nearest integer." Square brackets are used in the algorithm to enclose function arguments, thus distinguishing them from array subscripts.

The average computation subproblem is also simpler than the sort subproblem. The solution procedure can be stated, in overview, like this:

```
Initialize an accumulator variable to zero.
While there are array element values,
    add them to the accumulator variable value.
Find the average by dividing the number of array element
    values into the accumulator variable value.
```

Using previous notation, the solution procedure is stated in algorithmic form as follows.

```
ave ← 0
Do element ← 1 to n by 1
    ave ← ave + a(element)
End Do
ave ← ave / n
```

The adaptation (from general to specific) and incorporation of these three algorithmic sequences into the main algorithm, yields the final algorithm given in Figure 8-2. Observe, in the algorithm, the following items.

1. In the first IF rule, the maximum number of counties is implied to be a predefined symbolic constant rather than the fixed number 254.

2. All references to per capita income have an appended set of parentheses containing an expression. This notation identifies per capita income as an array; the expression in parentheses, then, is the subscript expression. The term "per capita income(county)" can also be read as "per capita income of county."

ALGORITHM PCI:median&average
{ A report of per capita income for a particular state
based on given per capita incomes of counties in the state
is created and printed. Primary items in the report are the
median and average per capita income. Optionally, the per
capita incomes are printed in descending order.}

```
Write title (see layout)
Read state identifier, number of counties,
       output option selector
If state identifier < 00 or state identifier > 99
    or number of counties < 1
    or number of counties > maximum number of counties, Then
    Write invalid-input error message (see layout)
Else
    Write state identifier, number of counties
    Do county ← 1 to number of counties by 1
       Read per cap income(county)
    End Do
    {Begin sort procedure on per cap income}
    number of compares ← number of counties
    interchange indicator ← 1
```

PAS.
```
    If interchange indicator = 1 Then
        interchange indicator ← 0
        number of compares ← number of compares − 1
        Do county ← 1 to number of compares by 1
            If per cap income(county) <
               per cap income(county+1), Then
               {interchange}
               temp ← per cap income(county)
               per cap income(county) ← per cap income(county+1)
               per cap income(county+1) ← temp
               interchange indicator ← 1
        End Do
        Go To PAS. (Back)
    {End sort procedure; begin median procedure.}
```

MED.
```
    m ← INT[number of counties / 2]
    If MOD[number of counties, 2] = 0 Then
        median ← NINT[(per cap income(m) +
                      per cap income(m+1)) / 2]
    Else
        median ← per cap income(m+1)
    {End median procedure; begin average procedure}
    ave ← 0
    Do county ← 1 to number of counties by 1
       ave ← ave + per cap income(county)
    End Do
    ave ← NINT[ave / number of counties]
    {End average procedure}
    Write median, average
    If output option selector <> 0, Then
        Do county ← 1 to number of counties by 1
           Write per cap income(county)
        End Do
Stop
END
```

Figure 8-2. Algorithm for Finding the Median and Average Per Capita Income

3. Comments, in brackets, are used to identify the beginning and end of the sort, median, and average procedures.

4. The NINT function reference in the average computation is included to indicate that the average is to be found to the nearest integer.

As the data structures used in a solution procedure become more complex, detailed program flowcharting increases in difficulty. Even with only one array in this solution procedure, the difficulty is significant. However, the primary benefit of detailed flowcharting—that is, giving additional insight into the solution procedure for purposes of improving the chances of the program being correct sooner—can still be realized, and it may therefore be worthwhile to go ahead and draw the flowchart before writing the program. For your study purposes, I have done so for this algorithm. It is given in Figure 8-3.

The corresponding Fortran program is given in Figure 8-4. Notice that MAXCTY, representing the maximum number of counties, is defined in a PARAMETER statement as implied above. It is then used to establish the size of the per capita income array, PCINC. In light of the information already given, the remainder of the program should be self-explanatory. Take the time to study it thoroughly. The per capita incomes, given toward the beginning of this chapter, were used with the program to provide the example i/o shown in Figure 8-5.

8-8   EXERCISES

1. Interpret the following statements collectively; that is, explain precisely what is accomplished by the statements if they appear together in the same program unit.

   ```
   INTEGER  NU
   PARAMETER   (NU=75)
   INTEGER   ALPHA(NU), BETA(2*NU), LAM
   REAL   DELTA, GAMMA(5)
   DATA   ALPHA, BETA(1) /
   :        NU*0,        1/,
   :        DELTA,  (GAMMA(LAM), LAM = 1, 5) /
   :        0.001,  1.0, 1.1, 1.2, 1.3, 1.5/
   ```

2. Revise the sequence of statements above so that the initialization of all array elements and variables requiring initial values is accomplished only with executable statements. Show all necessary declaration statements and add whatever executable statements are needed.

3. Given the declaration

   ```
   INTEGER  HEIGHT(3), LENGTH(3), WEIGHT(3)
   ```

   rewrite each of the page 219 i/o statements (individually) using implied-DOs wherever possible.

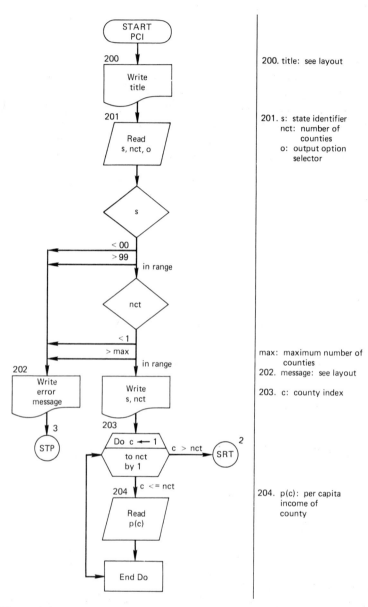

Figure 8-3. Flowchart for Finding the Median and Average Per Capita Income (Page 1 of 3)

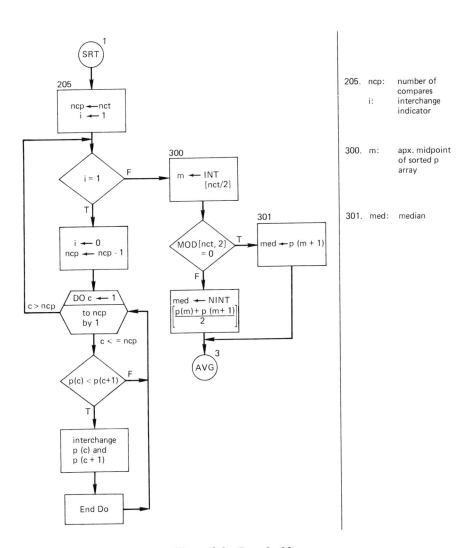

Figure 8-3. (Page 2 of 3)

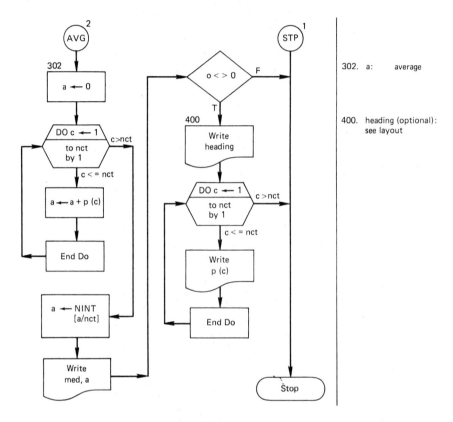

Figure 8-3. (Page 3 of 3)

```
*I.   PER CAPITA INCOME MEDIAN AND AVERAGE
*
      PROGRAM PCIMAA
*     PROGRAMMER:  JARRELL C. GROUT
*     DATE:  5/8/81
*
*  A. COMMENTARY
*
*          A REPORT OF PER CAPITA INCOME FOR A PARTICULAR
*     STATE, BASED ON GIVEN PER CAPITA INCOMES OF COUNTIES
*     IN THE STATE, IS CREATED AND PRINTED.  PRIMARY ITEMS
*     IN THE REPORT ARE THE MEDIAN AND AVERAGE PER CAPITA
*     INCOME.  OPTIONALLY, THE INDIVIDUAL COUNTY PER CAPITA
*     INCOMES ARE PRINTED IN DESCENDING ORDER.
*
*          THE INPUT TO THE PROGRAM CONSISTS OF AN
*     IDENTIFICATION RECORD FOLLOWED BY ONE OR MORE PER
*     CAPITA INCOME RECORDS.  INPUT ENTRY INTO EACH RECORD
*     IS FREE-FORM; VALUES MUST BE SEPARATED BY BLANKS.  THEY
*     ARE READ IN LIST-DIRECTED.
*
*          THE IDENTIFICATION RECORD CONTENTS ARE AS FOLLOWS.
*     STATE IDENTIFIER (STATID):  A TWO DIGIT INTEGER.
*     NUMBER OF COUNTIES (NOCTYS):  A ONE-THREE DIGIT INTEGER.
*     OUTPUT OPTION SELECTOR (OPTION):  A ONE DIGIT INTEGER;
*          1 (OR ANY NON-ZERO INTEGER) TO PRINT ALL PER
*          CAPITA INCOMES; 0 TO SUPPRESS THE PRINTING OF THEM.
*
*          THE PER CAPITA INCOME RECORDS SHOULD EACH CONTAIN AS
*     MANY PER CAPITA INCOME VALUES AS DESIRED, SEPARATED BY
*     BLANKS.
*
*          DICTIONARY.
*     AVRAGE:  THE PER CAPITA INCOME AVERAGE (NEAREST INTEGER)
*     COUNTY:  THE COUNTY INDEX FOR PER CAPITA INCOME VALUES
*     INTCHG:  INTERCHANGE INDICATOR; 1 WHEN INTERCHANGE OCCURS
*              DURING SORT; 0 WHEN SORTING IS COMPLETE
*     MAXCTY:  MAXIMUM NUMBER OF COUNTIES (PARAMETER)
*     MEDIAN:  THE MEDIAN PER CAPITA INCOME (NEAREST INTEGER)
*     MIDPCI:  APPROXIMATE MIDPOINT OF SORTED PCINC
*     NCOMPS:  NUMBER OF COMPARES REQUIRED IN ONE SORT PASS
*     NOCTYS:  NUMBER OF COUNTIES (1-254)
*     OPTION:  OUTPUT OPTION SELECTOR (1 OR 0)
*     PCIDIF:  PER CAPITA INCOME DATA INPUT FILE
*     PCINC:   PER CAPITA INCOME (ARRAY)
*     PCIROF:  PER CAPITA INCOME REPORT OUTPUT FILE
*     STATID:  STATE IDENTIFIER (00-99)
*     TEMPIV:  TEMPORARY INCOME VARIABLE TO FACILITATE THE
*              INTERCHANGE OF PER CAPITA INCOME VALUES
*
*  B. DECLARATION
*
*     ESTABLISH MAXIMUM NUMBER OF COUNTIES:  PCINC ARRAY SIZE
      INTEGER  MAXCTY
      PARAMETER  (MAXCTY=254)
*
      INTEGER  AVRAGE, COUNTY, INTCHG, MEDIAN, MIDPCI,
     :         NCOMPS, NOCTYS, OPTION, PCIDIF, PCINC(MAXCTY),
     :         PCIROF, STATID, TEMPIV
      PARAMETER  (PCIDIF=5, PCIROF=6)
*
*  C. I/O LAYOUT
*
  900 FORMAT ('1', T15, 'REPORT OF PER CAPITA INCOME')
  905 FORMAT ('0', T10, 'INVALID INPUT VALUE FOR EITHER ',
     :        'STATE IDENTIFIER, ', I10, ',', /
     :        ' ', T10, 'OR NUMBER OF COUNTIES, ', I10, '. ',
     :        'THE STATE IDENTIFIER MUST', /
     :        ' ', T10, 'BE AN INTEGER IN THE RANGE 00-99. ',
     :        'THE NUMBER OF COUNTIES', /
     :        ' ', T10, 'MUST BE AN INTEGER IN THE RANGE 1-254, ',
     :        'PLEASE CORRECT YOUR', /
     :        ' ', T10, 'INPUT DATA AND TRY AGAIN.')
  910 FORMAT ('0', T18, 'STATE IDENTIFIER: ', I2, /
     :        ' ', T17, 'NUMBER OF COUNTIES: ', I3)
  920 FORMAT ('0', T12, 'MEDIAN PER CAPITA INCOME:   ', I5, /
     :        ' ', T12, 'AVERAGE PER CAPITA INCOME: ', I5)
  930 FORMAT ('0', T16, 'COUNTY PER CAPITA INCOMES', /
     :        ' ', T20, '(DESCENDING ORDER)', /)
  940 FORMAT (' ', T26, I5)
*
*  D. ACTION
```

Figure 8-4. Program for Finding the Median and Average Per Capita Income

```
*            WRITE (PCIROF, 900)
             READ (PCIDIF, *) STATID, NOCTYS, OPTION
             IF (STATID .LT. 00 .OR. STATID .GT. 99
          :     .OR. NOCTYS .LT. 1 .OR. NOCTYS .GT. MAXCTY) THEN
                WRITE (PCIROF, 905) STATID, NOCTYS
             ELSE
                WRITE (PCIROF, 910) STATID, NOCTYS
                READ (PCIDIF, *) (PCINC(COUNTY), COUNTY = 1, NOCTYS)
*
*               BEGIN SORT PROCEDURE ON PCINC.
                NCOMPS = NOCTYS
                INTCHG = 1
      210       IF (INTCHG .EQ. 1) THEN
                   INTCHG = 0
                   NCOMPS = NCOMPS - 1
                   DO 220 COUNTY = 1, NCOMPS
                      IF (PCINC(COUNTY) .LT. PCINC(COUNTY + 1)) THEN
                         TEMPIV = PCINC(COUNTY)
                         PCINC(COUNTY) = PCINC(COUNTY + 1)
                         PCINC(COUNTY + 1) = TEMPIV
                         INTCHG = 1
                      ENDIF
      220          CONTINUE
                   GO TO 210
                ENDIF
*               END SORT PROCEDURE ON PCINC.
*
*               BEGIN MEDIAN PROCEDURE.
                MIDPCI = NOCTYS / 2
                IF (MOD(NOCTYS, 2) .EQ. 0) THEN
                   MEDIAN = NINT((PCINC(MIDPCI) + PCINC(MIDPCI + 1)) / 2.0)
                ELSE
                   MEDIAN = PCINC(MIDPCI + 1)
                ENDIF
*               END MEDIAN PROCEDURE.
*
*               BEGIN AVERAGE PROCEDURE.
                AVRAGE = 0
                DO 310 COUNTY = 1, NOCTYS
                   AVRAGE = AVRAGE + PCINC(COUNTY)
      310       CONTINUE
                AVRAGE = NINT(FLOAT(AVRAGE) / NOCTYS)
*               END AVRAGE PROCEDURE.
*
                WRITE (PCIROF, 920) MEDIAN, AVRAGE
                IF (OPTION .NE. 0) THEN
                   WRITE (PCIROF, 930)
                   DO 410 COUNTY = 1, NOCTYS
                      WRITE (PCIROF, 940) PCINC(COUNTY)
      410          CONTINUE
                ENDIF
             ENDIF
             STOP
             END
```

Figure 8-4. (Continued)

```
                              REPORT OF PER CAPITA INCOME

                                STATE IDENTIFIER:   75
                                NUMBER OF COUNTIES:   16

                              MEDIAN PER CAPITA INCOME:    3649
                              AVERAGE PER CAPITA INCOME:   3611

                                 COUNTY PER CAPITA INCOMES
                                    (DESCENDING ORDER)
       75 16 1
       3747                                   4616
       3258                                   4519
       2877                                   3839
       3838                                   3838
       3668                                   3803
       3787                                   3787
       3629                                   3747
       2915                                   3668
       3267                                   3629
       3576                                   3576
       3839                                   3281
       3803                                   3267
       4616                                   3258
       4519                                   3161
       3281                                   2915
(a.) Input  3161          (b.) Output          2877
```

Figure 8-5. Example I/O for the Per Capita Income Median and Average Program

```
(a)   READ *, HEIGHT
(b)   READ *, LENGTH(1), WEIGHT(1), LENGTH(2), WEIGHT(2),
      :        LENGTH(3), WEIGHT(3)
(c)   PRINT *, HEIGHT, LENGTH, WEIGHT
(d)   PRINT *, WEIGHT(3), HEIGHT(3), LENGTH(3),
      :         WEIGHT(2), HEIGHT(2), LENGTH(2),
      :         WEIGHT(1), HEIGHT(1), LENGTH(1)
```

4. Rewrite each of the following segments as one statement using an implied-DO. Assume that the declarations have been properly made.

   (a)
   ```
          DO 600 NEXT = 1, NIR
              PRINT *, ALPHA(NEXT), BETA(NEXT)
      600 CONTINUE
   ```
   (b)
   ```
          DO 300 MEAS = 1, NRACES
              READ *, DIST(MEAS), RATE(MEAS), TIME(MEAS)
      300 CONTINUE
   ```

5. Given this program segment:

   ```
       INTEGER OBSIF
       REAL XOBS(4), YOBS(4)
       PARAMETER (OBSIF=5)
          .
          .
          .
   110 FORMAT (F3.1)
          .
          .
          .
       DO 220 IN = 1, 4, 2
           READ (OBSIF, 110) XOBS(IN), YOBS(IN)
   220 CONTINUE
   ```

   and this set of input data where each value begins in column 1:

   ```
   003
   2.5
   .16
   223
   100
   004
   62.
   115
   ```

   state the values of each element of the XOBS and YOBS arrays, and the value of IN, following the complete execution of the DO-loop.

6. Below you are given a partial algorithm designed to print the change due on a dollar for a purchase price of a dollar or less. Complete the algorithm and write the corresponding Fortran program. Use the DATA statement to establish the cent values of the coins, with the first being equal to 50 (half-dollar) and the last being equal to 1 (penny). There are, of course, only five different cent values. As example i/o: if the purchase price is 33 cents, the change should be

   ```
   50
   10
    5
    1
    1
   ```

The partial algorithm:

partial ALGORITHM Changemaker
```
Read price                        {in cents}
change ← 100 - price
If change <= 0, Then
    Write price, change
Else
    Write price
    Do coin ← 1 to 5 by 1
CNT.        If change / centvalue(coin) >= 1 Then
            Write centvalue(coin)
            change ← change - centvalue(coin)
            Go To CNT. (Back)
    End Do
Stop
END
```

7. The bubble sort algorithm given in Section 8-7 is designed to perform a descending sort. Devise a corresponding algorithm to perform an ascending sort.

8. Another method for sorting values in a one-dimensional array is the "selection sort." To perform a descending sort by this method, the largest value in the array is located first and then is either interchanged with the value in the first position of the array or is placed in the first position of another array that corresponds in data type and size with the one containing the unsorted data. After the first element is properly placed, the second largest element is located and then interchanged with the value in the second position or placed in the second position of the other array. The process continues until all values have been placed in the proper array positions. The process is depicted by the following example, in which it is assumed that only one array is used.

Array Contents Initially	End of Pass 1	End of Pass 2	End of Pass 3	...	End of Last Pass
82	100	100	100		100
97	97	100	100		100
100	82	82	97		97
78	78	78	78		95
100	100	97	82		82
95	95	95	95		78

Notice that one element value is selected and placed in the proper position during each pass. Also during each pass, another element is placed in a different improper position.

Devise an algorithm for an ascending sort by the selection sort method. Use only one array. Write the complete Fortran program.

9. In Exercise 11 of Section 7-5, you are given a partial algorithm for scoring a bowling game. Using an array to hold the pin counts made on every ball rolled, devise a better algorithm for scoring the game. First read all pin counts into the array, then perform the scoring computations. In addition, design the algorithm so that any number of games can be processed during one computer run. Write the complete Fortran program.

10. Plan and write a complete Fortran program that for any exam given to any college class on your campus will find the number of students making above average. In overview, your program should read and store all the exam grades, then compute the average, then count the number of grades (students) above average, and finally print all input data and answers.

11. In addition to requiring you to use arrays, this exercise is also designed to get you to consider the significant digit capability of your computer and the accuracy of the computed results.

    Plan and write a complete Fortran program that will find not only the average but also the standard deviation of a set of numerical data. Allow any input number to be processed that can be represented by your computer as a real value. Limit the maximum size of input data sets that can be processed so that you use your computer's main storage efficiently, and yet handle data sets from a variety of sources.

    Whereas the average is a measure of central tendency, the standard deviation is a measure of dispersion or variation, the tendency for values to vary from the average. It is as commonly used as the average, is of the same order of magnitude as the input values and the average, and is commonly calculated from either of the two mathematically equivalent formulas,

$$s_1 = \sqrt{\frac{\sum_{i=1}^{n} [v(i) - \text{ave}]^2}{n - 1}}$$

and

$$s_2 = \sqrt{\frac{\sum_{i=1}^{n} v(i)^2 - \frac{\left[\sum_{i=1}^{n} v(i)\right]^2}{n}}{n - 1}}$$

where s_1 and s_2 represent the standard deviation by formula 1 and formula 2, respectively, n is the number of values in the data set, $v(i)$ represents one value (the ith) in the set, ave is the average, and the symbol $\sum$ means "the sum of." Thus the first term under the first square root symbol above is interpreted as the sum of the squares of the differences of the individual values from the average. Your program is to compute the standard deviation by both formulas, for comparison purposes, and print the results to the nearest hundredth.

First, declare the data type of v, ave, s_1, and s_2 to be REAL. Make a debugged computer run with at least 10 values, each of which have the maximum number of significant digits that your computer allows for real data. You should notice a small difference in the printed values of s_1 and s_2. Then, declare the data types of the items above to be DOUBLE PRECISION, and make a computer run with the same data set. There should be no difference between the printed values of s_1 and s_2.

The conclusion you should draw is that, even though two formulas are mathematically identical, they may not be computationally identical, particularly if the limit on significant digits is being pushed. Computers are finite machines, capable of representing real values approximately; mathematics usually assumes exact representation capability.

12. This is a business-oriented problem that involves file searching, file updating, and transaction processing.

A company maintains an inventory master file consisting of one record for each item the company sells. Each record contains three fields: item number, units on hand, and price per unit. The file is kept in ascending order by item number. As orders are received from customers, they are put together to form a daily order transaction file. Each record of this file contains three fields: customer number, item number (of the item ordered), and number of units ordered. Each customer may have several records in sequence, depending on the number of different items ordered at one time. The transaction records are not kept in any definite order. An example master file looks like this:

Item No.	Units on Hand	Price/Unit
0010	500	5.00
0015	1000	7.50
0020	0	2.50
0025	150	10.00
0030	100	9.50

An example transaction file looks like this:

Customer No.	Item No.	Units Ordered
825	0030	50
317	0025	15
317	0020	10
317	0030	75
548	0015	50
548	0025	50

Plan and write a complete Fortran program to read the complete master file into memory (treat each field as a one-dimensional array and limit the number of records to an appropriate amount, say 100 for test purposes), print it for checking purposes, then read and process the daily order transaction records to bring the master file up to date and produce a daily transaction report that looks like the one below for the example input data given above. Then print the updated master file for checking purposes.

SOME LOCAL COMPANY

DAILY TRANSACTION REPORT
MM/DD/YY

CUSTOMER NUMBER	ITEM ORDERED	UNITS ORDERED	UNITS SOLD	UNITS BACKORDERED	UNIT PRICE	TOTAL PRICE	
825	0030	50	50	0	5.00	250.00	
						250.00	CHG
317	0025	15	15	0	10.00	150.00	
	0020	10	0	10	2.50	0.00	
	0030	75	50	25	9.50	475.00	
						675.00	CHG
548	0015	50	50	0	7.50	375.00	
	0025	50	50	0	10.00	500.00	
						875.00	CHG
TOTAL CHARGES						1800.00	

13. Plan and write a complete Fortran program to convert binary (base 2) integers to decimal (base 10) integers. Your program should read each digit of a binary integer into memory as an array element and then convert the integer bit by bit into the decimal equivalent. Further, it should process any number of binary integers varying in length from one to the word size, in bits, of your computer. Of course, it should also print each binary integer and its decimal equivalent. If possible, the program should be interactive; that is, the input and output should take place through an online terminal, allowing the program user to enter binary integers directly—when prompted by the program—and should be conversational in nature, something like the following.

HELLO,
I AM HERE TO CONVERT BINARY INTEGERS   ⎫
TO DECIMAL EQUIVALENTS. WHICH BINARY   ⎬ Program output
INTEGER WOULD YOU LIKE TO SEE CONVERTED ⎪ to terminal
FIRST?   ⎭

110000111   ⎫ User input
                                         ⎬ from terminal
                                         ⎭

ALL RIGHT.   THE DECIMAL EQUIVALENT
OF 110000111 IS 391.

WOULD YOU LIKE TO SEE ANOTHER
(PLEASE ANSWER YES OR NO)?

Output

YES

Input

WHICH ONE?

Output

110110110110110

Input

ALL RIGHT.   THE DECIMAL EQUIVALENT
OF 110110110110110 IS 28086.

WOULD YOU LIKE TO SEE ANOTHER
(PLEASE ANSWER YES OR NO)?

Output

NO

Input

THANK YOU.   SO LONG FOR NOW.

Output

Chapter

9

Character Data

With the exception of printed titles and column headings, to this point we have been concerned primarily with numeric data. We are only now beginning to consider how such commonly occurring items as names, addresses, cities, states, individual alphabetic letters, and such—that is, character data—are read-in, stored, manipulated, and printed-out.

FORTRAN 77 has character data processing features that are flexible, capable, and easy to use. In a FORTRAN 77 program, character data occurs as character constants, values of symbolic character constants, values of character variables, and values in character arrays.

In the first part of Chapter 6 I described a "Student Information Record" that contains character as well as numeric data. A slightly modified version of that record description, in which the student name field has been divided into first, middle, and last name, is given in Figure 9-1. It indicates that there are nine fields—first name, middle name, last name, street address, city, state, zip code, classification, and major—that should each be treated as a character variable or character array in the program. A very small sample set of student information records is also given in Figure 9-1, to show the kinds of values that each field can contain. Each value in the first nine fields of each record is referred to generally as a character datum.

A character datum—known more commonly as a *character string* or, simply, string—is a sequence of characters. A string may contain any of the characters that can be represented by the computer; it is not just limited to the Fortran character set. Furthermore, the blank character, represented hereafter by Ƅ when necessary, is valid and significant in a string. You can see in Figure 9-1 that several of the fields in each record contain blank positions. The contents of these positions are actually blank characters that are valid and significant.

1. Student information record description:

Field name	Data Description	Location
First name	Character, left-justified	1–9
Middle name	Character, left-justified	10–18
Last name	Character, left-justified	19–30
Street address	Character, left-justified	31–45
City	Character, left-justified	46–57
State	Character, left-justified	58–59
Zip code	Character, left-justified	60–68
Classification	Two-character code	69–70
Major	Three-character code	71–73
Hours passed	Integer, XXX, right-justified	74–76
Grade points	Integer, XXX, right-justified	77–79

2. Sample set of student information records:

Record No.	Contents
1	Wendy Water Windmill Rt. W, Box CW Countryside TX759999999FRCSC017051
2	Thomas All Terrific 9999 Skyline Dr Megalopolis NY123459999SRACC115460
3	Susan Quin Prettyface 1 Dream Place Beach City CA922229999JRHPA090090
4	Johnny Cool Skilift 14000 Mountop SnowmountainCO808889999JRMUS095285
5	Judy J Judy 1940 Cary Rd Grantstown CA902999999SOTHE062178

Figure 9-1. Record Description and Sample Set of Records Containing Character Data

The character positions in a string are numbered consecutively, left to right, from 1 to the number of characters in the string. The length of the character datum is equal to the number of characters in the string. Therefore, in the records of Figure 9-1, the length of First Name is 9, the length of Last Name is 12, the length of City is 12, and so on.

Through FORTRAN 77 you can have the computer perform such character processing operations as input, comparison, assignment, and output. Also, character variables and arrays can be initialized, and the values of character symbolic constants can be specified. It all begins, in the program, with the appropriate type declarations.

9-1 DECLARING CHARACTER DATA TYPES

Symbolic constants, variables, and array elements that are to take on character values are explicitly typed by means of the CHARACTER type statement. With one item of exception besides the keyword, the form of a CHARACTER statement is identical to the form of the other type statements: INTEGER, REAL, DOUBLE PRECISION, and LOGICAL. The item of exception is that each character entity must be assigned a length that is equal to its number of character positions.

The CHARACTER statement, therefore, can be written in the preferred simple form,

```
CHARACTER  clist
```

where clist contains the symbolic names of constants, variables, and arrays with or without array declarations, plus a length specifier for each one. Items in clist are separated by commas. If we let "citem" represent the symbolic name of a constant, variable, or array with or without an array declaration, and "len" represent the corresponding length, then an item in clist can be written in the form

```
citem*len
```

For example, assuming that 100 records are to be in memory at one time, the statement

```
CHARACTER  CITY(100)*12, CLASS(100)*2, MAJOR(100)*3,
  :        SFNAME(100)*9, SLNAME(100)*12, SMNAME(100)*9,
  :        STADRS(100)*15, STATE(100)*2, ZIPCDE(100)*9
```

can be used to declare the character types described in Figure 9-1.

In a main program, "len" must be either an unsigned nonzero integer number—as in the CHARACTER statement above—or an integer constant expression enclosed in parentheses and having a positive value. It can also be omitted, in which case its value is either 1 or is defined by the following slightly different form of the CHARACTER statement:

```
CHARACTER*len  clist
```

In this form, len applies to all items in clist that do not have a length specification. For instance, three items in the CHARACTER statement above have a length of nine. Thus, the statement could be written

```
CHARACTER*9  CITY(100)*12, CLASS(100)*2, MAJOR(100)*3,
  :          SFNAME(100), SLNAME(100)*12, SMNAME(100),
  :          STADRS(100)*15, STATE(100)*2, ZIPCDE(100)
```

where SFNAME, SMNAME, and ZIPCDE depend on the length specification appearing beside the keyword. For consistency and better program reliability, I recommend only the form in which the length specification is explicitly made for each item in clist.

Since collections of student information records can be expected to be subjected to such processing operations as input, searching, sorting, updating, and output, they provide us with one basis for exemplifying not only character data declarations but also the other topics of this chapter. To provide additional illustrations of character data declarations, as well as the other topics, two more examples are introduced in the remaining paragraphs of this section.

The first of the other two examples will be of interest to you if you like to keep track of money; it has to do with producing bank statements for your local bank. With just a few changes to make the situation more realistic, Exercise 12 of Section 7-5 describes the problem. You should take a few minutes now to refamiliarize yourself with it.

Having done that, consider the problem in light of these four changes:

1. Rather than producing just one monthly statement for your own checking account, the program should produce monthly statements for all customer checking accounts. This requires that customer names and addresses, and other such character data be read in and printed out.

2. Rather than including the bank name and address data in the form of character constants in FORMAT statements, they are to be stored as values of symbolic character constants.

3. Rather than printing the date in the form MM/DD/YY, it is to be printed so that the month is identified by a common three-character abbreviated name—JAN for January, FEB for February, and so on. Thus an input date in the form 062182 would be printed as JUN 21, 1982.

4. Rather than treating customer account numbers as numeric values, they will be treated as character strings.

If you now have the problem in mind, you should begin to understand how the following character data type declarations apply.

```
CHARACTER   BKADRS*15, BKCITY*12, BKNAME*30, BKSTAT*2,
    :       BKZIPC*9, CRACCT*9, CRCITY*12, CRNAME*30,
    :       CRSTAT*2, CRSTRT*15, CRZIPC*9, MTHNAM(12)*3
```

For your complete understanding, the symbolic name usage in the statement above is explained as follows.

Name	*Usage*	*Contents*
BKADRS	Bank's address	15 characters
BKCITY	Bank's city	12 characters
BKNAME	Bank's name	30 characters
BKSTAT	Bank's state	2 characters
BKZIPC	Bank's zip code	9 characters
CRACCT	Customer's account number	9 characters
CRCITY	Customer's city	12 characters
CRNAME	Customer's name	30 characters
CRSTAT	Customer's state	2 characters
CRSTRT	Customer's street	15 characters
CRZIPC	Customer's zip code	9 characters
MTHNAM	Month name abbreviations	3 characters for each of 12 values

Thus the CHARACTER statement types five symbolic constants relating to the bank, six variables associated with customers, and one array that contains 12 elements of three characters each for the month name abbreviations.

The second of the other two examples will be of particular interest to you if you enjoy sports. The example has to do with major league baseball, but the concepts can be readily extended to many other sports such as football, basketball, soccer, tennis, bowling, and so on.

Virtually every daily newspaper has a sports section and, in that section, a report of the latest team standings and game scores. A sample report for major league baseball is shown in Figure 9-2.

You can see that a program can be written to produce each day's report for the two leagues. This we will do in part, in order to exemplify the topics of this chapter, using the following first-try algorithm as a guide.

```
Read the day of the games.
For the two leagues, do the following:
   read and print the league name;
   for the two divisions in the league, do the following:
      read the division name;
      read the standings of the division—that is, the team
      names and won-lost records individually;
   for the games of the league, do the following:
      read the winner's name and score,
      and the loser's name and score;
      search for the winner's name in the standings
      and add one to the ''won'' column;
      search for the loser's name in the standings
      and add one to the ''lost'' column;
   for the two divisions in the league, do the following:
      for the teams in the division, do the following:
         compute the percent and the games behind;
      as necessary, reorder the teams to produce the
      new standings of the division;
   print the day and the games of the league.
```

Subsequent refinement of the first-try algorithm leads to the development of a character data type statement like the following.

```
CHARACTER  BLANK*1, DAY*9, DVNAME(2)*4, LGNAME*8,
:          LOSER(14)*13, TMNAME(14)*13, WINNER(14)*13
```

To clarify, let me explain the use of each item in clist, saving the symbolic constant BLANK until last. DAY is the variable name used for the day of the games; it is given a length of nine because the longest day name—Wednesday—contains nine letters. DVNAME represents the Division name; it is a two-element array because there are two divisions in each league, and the information on both divisions needs to be in memory at the same time. In contrast, LGNAME, representing the league name, has either the value AMERICAN or the value NATIONAL, but not both, at once; it, therefore, is a scalar variable. LOSER is an array used to hold the names of the losing teams in the games; WINNER holds the names of the corresponding winning teams. Fourteen was chosen as the number of

AMERICAN LEAGUE

EAST

	WON	LOST	PCT	GB
Baltimore	28	16	.636	
Milwaukee	27	19	.587	2
Cleveland	23	17	.575	3
New York	25	20	.556	3.5
Boston	25	21	.543	4
Detroit	23	24	.489	6.5
Toronto	16	32	.333	14

WEST

	WON	LOST	PCT	GB
Oakland	31	20	.608	
Chicago	26	17	.605	1
Texas	26	19	.578	2
California	23	27	.460	7.5
Kansas City	15	25	.375	10.5
Seattle	17	30	.362	12
Minnesota	14	32	.304	14.5

Games Played Sunday:

California 7, Chicago 4
Oakland 6, Toronto 5
Detroit 5, Baltimore 4
Milwaukee 5, Boston 2
Cleveland 7, New York 2
Minnesota 5, Kansas City 4
Seattle 5, Texas 3

Figure 9-2. A Sample Report of Baseball Standings and Scores

elements in each because it is the number of teams in the largest league and is therefore the maximum number of games that could possibly be played in one day (if all teams played double headers). Their elements, like the elements of TMNAME (team name), each have a length of 13 because the longest team name—San Francisco—contains 13 characters counting the blank between the two words. TMNAME has 14 elements in order to hold all the team names of the largest league.

BLANK is a special symbolic constant that will actually be given a blank character as a value. It will be used to detect the end of the input data for a league, much as an invalid number can be used to detect the end of a set of numeric data.

Keep these example problems in mind as you read the rest of this chapter. I refer to them freely as I continue to describe the character processing features of FORTRAN 77.

NATIONAL LEAGUE

EAST

	WON	LOST	PCT	GB
Philadelphia	27	19	.587	
Montreal	26	19	.578	0.5
St Louis	23	17	.575	1
Pittsburgh	20	20	.500	4
New York	15	27	.357	10
Chicago	10	33	.233	15.5

WEST

	WON	LOST	PCT	GB
Los Angeles	33	15	.688	
Cincinnati	27	20	.574	5.5
San Francisco	25	25	.500	9
Houston	24	24	.500	9
Atlanta	22	23	.489	9.5
San Diego	19	29	.396	14

Games Played Sunday:

Montreal 5, Pittsburgh 1
Philadelphia 6, St Louis 1
New York 3, Chicago 2
Los Angeles 16, Cincinnati 4
San Diego 5, Atlanta 1
San Francisco 6, Houston 1

Figure 9-2. (Continued)

9-2 SPECIFYING SYMBOLIC CHARACTER CONSTANTS

The values of symbolic character constants, like those of other symbolic constant types, are specified by means of the PARAMETER statement. As identified in the preceding section, the symbolic names of the constants for the bank statement problem are BKADRS (bank's address), BKCITY (bank's city), BKNAME (bank's name), BKSTAT (bank's state), and BKZIPC (bank's zip code). For this example we use a fictitious Texas bank which has the name "Fictitious State Bank." Its address is P.O. Box 0; city: Countryside; state: Texas; zip code: 75999-9999. The symbolic constants, therefore, are defined by the following statement.

```
PARAMETER  (BKADRS='P. O. Box 0',
  :         BKCITY='Countryside'
  :         BKNAME='FICTITIOUS STATE BANK'
  :         BKSTAT='TX', BKZIPC='759999999')
```

Notice that only BKSTAT and BKZIPC are defined with the exact number of characters designated by the length specifiers in the CHARACTER statement of the preceding section; BKADRS, BKCITY, and BKNAME are defined with fewer characters than are allowed for them. In memory, the strings will all be exactly the specified length. When there are fewer characters in the definition than the length specifier indicates for the string, the compiler stores the characters as far left in the string as possible and fills the string, to the right, with blanks. On the other hand, if a character symbolic name is assigned too many characters in a PARAMETER statement, some of the characters will be lost. For instance, the statements

```
CHARACTER  BKCITY*12
PARAMETER  (BKCITY='San Francisco')
```

will result in an internal value of SanbFrancisc for BKCITY.

The only symbolic constant I identified for the baseball standings problem is the special one named BLANK. I gave it a length of 1 and said that it would be given a blank character as a value. This can be accomplished by the statement

```
PARAMETER  (BLANK=' ')
```

9-3 INITIALIZING CHARACTER VARIABLES AND ARRAYS

Character variables and arrays can be given initial values by means of input, assignment, or DATA statements. Character i/o is described in the next section and character assignment statements are fully covered a few sections later; the DATA statement is the subject of this section.

The bank statement problem has one character array that needs to be initialized. The array name is MTHNAM, it has 12 elements of three characters each, and each is to be a common abbreviation for a month of the year. Furthermore, the months should be in logical order, January through December. The DATA statement to accomplish this can be written in at least the following two ways:

```
DATA  MTHNAM /'JAN', 'FEB', 'MAR', 'APR', 'MAY', 'JUN',
    :           'JUL', 'AUG', 'SEP', 'OCT', 'NOV', 'DEC'/
```

or

```
DATA  (MTHNAM(MONTH), MONTH = 1, 12) /
    :      'JAN', 'FEB', 'MAR', 'APR', 'MAY', 'JUN',
    :      'JUL', 'AUG', 'SEP', 'OCT', 'NOV', 'DEC' /
```

Occasionally, it is necessary to initialize a character array so that all the elements have the same value prior to execution. In the baseball program, for example, the array TMNAME could be initially filled with blanks by the statement sequence

```
PARAMETER  (BLANK=' ')
DATA  TMNAME /14*BLANK/
```

Here, 14 is the repetition factor and is also equal to the number of elements in the array. The one blank character of BLANK will be placed in each element of TMNAME, and each element of TMNAME will then be filled to the right with blanks. An alternative way of writing the DATA statement is

```
DATA  TMNAME /14*(' ')/
```

in which the blank character is specified directly.

9-4 I/O FOR CHARACTER VARIABLES AND ARRAYS

Character i/o can be list-directed or explicitly formatted. Either way, the READ, PRINT, and WRITE statements are used in exactly the same manner as they are used for numeric i/o. The primary difference between character and numeric i/o is in the appearance of the i/o data.

9-4-1 List-Directed

When read in list-directed, an input character string has precisely the same form as a character constant; that is, it consists of a group of characters enclosed in apostrophes.

Some of the character input items of the bank statement problem are customer's name (CRNAME), account number (CRACCT), street (CRSTRT), city (CRCITY), state (CRSTAT), and zip code (CRZIPC). These items of data are to be read in and processed for each customer. The list-directed statement for reading the data into memory can be written like this:

```
READ *, CRNAME, CRACCT, CRSTRT, CRCITY, CRSTAT, CRZIPC
```

Then the corresponding data for one customer should be entered in the read iolist order, one or more values per physical record, with each value surrounded by apostrophes. Also, the values should be separated from each other by blanks or commas. Say, for instance, that one of the customers of the Fictitious State Bank is Breezy B. Windmill of Rt. W, Box CW, Countryside, Texas, 75999-9999. If Mr. Windmill's bank account number is 100000001, the corresponding logical input record that will be processed by the READ statement above can have the following appearance.

```
'Breezy B. Windmill', '100000001',
'Rt. W Box CW', 'Countryside', 'TX', '759999999'
```

Observe, in the input record, that only the account number, state, and zip code contain the exact number of characters specified for their lengths in the CHARAC-TER statement given earlier. The name is 12 short of the 30 allowed by its length specifier, the city is one short of the 12 allowed by its length specifier, and the "street" is three short of the 15 allowed by its length specifier. No problem. Each will go into memory left-justified in its respective allocated locations, and the empty positions to the right will be filled with blanks. In memory, all customer names have the same length and all customer streets have the same length. Mr. Windmill's name, in memory will look like this:

```
BreezyƀB.ƀWindmillƀƀƀƀƀƀƀƀƀƀƀ
```

His "street" will look like this:

```
Rt.ƀWƀBoxƀCWƀƀƀ
```

And, as far as the computer is concerned, all the blank characters represented by ƀ in the above are valid and significant.

Any one of the input strings can be longer than its corresponding length specifier and, if so, unexpected results may occur. If the string 'TEXAS', for instance, is entered as input for the state, the variable CRSTAT, which has length 2, would have the value TE in memory; the XAS portion of the input string is lost. What you want to be sure to do is to establish the character data lengths thoughtfully and make sure that the input strings result in valid values being placed in memory.

The list-directed output of a character value is a string without surrounding apostrophes. In other words, the computer writes a character string in the same form that you and I write one—as a group of one or more words. A string's output length is the same as its specified internal length. Given, therefore, that Mr. Windmill's data have been read into memory as exemplified first above, the series of statements

```
PRINT *, CRNAME, ' Account Number: ', CRACCT
PRINT *, CRSTRT
PRINT *, CRCITY, ', ', CRSTAT, ' ', CRZIPC
```

produces output that looks like this:

```
Breezy B. Windmillƀƀƀƀƀƀƀƀƀƀƀ Account Number: 100000001
Rt. W Box CWƀƀƀ
Countrysideƀ, TX 759999999
```

where the ƀ is included only to designate blanks that are created for printing due to the specified lengths of the character entities CRNAME, CRSTRT, and CRCITY.

9-4-2 Explicitly Formatted: The A Edit Descriptor

The form of the edit descriptor to use in a FORMAT statement referenced for the reading or writing of character data is

```
Aw
```

where w is the field width of the character datum in the i/o medium. The field width can be omitted, in which case the default field width is equal to the length (len) specified for the character string in the CHARACTER statement. When w is present in the descriptor, it may be equal to, less than, or greater than len.

   For input, if w is less than len, the w characters in the input field are placed left-justified in the memory location reserved for the string, and the remaining positions of the string are filled with blanks. However, if w is greater than len— pay careful attention to this—if w is greater than len, the rightmost len characters in the input field are placed in memory as the character value; the leftmost (w − len) characters are lost! This means, for instance, that if you use the program segment

```
CHARACTER   LSTNAM*10
       .
       .
       .
110 FORMAT  (A12)
       .
       .
       .
READ 110, LSTNAM
```

with the input record (in which the K is in column 1)

```
Katzenburger
```

then the value of LSTNAM in memory, after the execution of the READ statement, is

```
tzenburger
```

and the Ka is lost—the computer has no access to the first two characters of Katzenburger.

   For output, if w is greater than len, the len characters in memory are placed right-justified in the output field. If w is less than len, the leftmost w characters of the string in memory are placed in the output field.

   Except for the one anomaly existing for input whenever w is greater than len, the use of the A edit descriptor for explicitly formatted character i/o is straightforward. The illustrations given in the next several paragraphs should clarify it for you.

   One use of the student information records described in Figure 9-1 is to print mailing labels for addressing a general mail-out to students. Not all the student information is needed to produce the mailing labels; the only items necessary are the ones having to do with student name and address. Therefore, only these items will be read into memory. Assume, furthermore, that up to 100 of the partial records containing these items are to be in memory at one time. The following segment contains a major portion of the program needed to accomplish the task.

```
INTEGER  MAILOF, NUMSTU, STU, STUIF
CHARACTER  CITY(100)*12, SFNAME(100)*9, SLNAME(100)*12,
:          SMNAME(100)*9, STADRS(100)*15, STATE(100)*2,
:          ZIPCDE(100)*9
PARAMETER  (STUIF=5, MAILOF=6)
       .
       .
       .
```

```
110 FORMAT (A9, A9, A12, A15, A12, A2, A9)
910 FORMAT ('1', A9, 1X, A1, '.', 1X, A12)
912 FORMAT (' ', A15)
914 FORMAT (' ', A12, ', ', A2, 1X, A9)
        .
        .
        .

        NUMSTU = 0
        DO 310 STU = 1, 100
            READ (STUIF, 110, END=320) SFNAME(STU),
    :           SMNAME(STU), SLNAME(STU), STADRS(STU),
    :           CITY(STU), STATE(STU), ZIPCDE(STU)
            NUMSTU = STU
310     CONTINUE
320     DO 410 STU = 1, NUMSTU
            WRITE (MAILOF, 910) SFNAME(STU), SMNAME(STU),
    :           SLNAME(STU)
            WRITE (MAILOF, 912) STADRS(STU)
            WRITE (MAILOF, 914) CITY(STU), STATE(STU),
    :           ZIPCDE(STU)
410     CONTINUE
```

The action code shown is to be executed repeatedly until all the student records in the input file have been processed. If you will trace or actually execute the code using the sample data in Figure 9-1, you will find that the contents of the first two printed labels can be represented as follows:

```
WendybbbbbW.bWindmillbbbb
Rt.bWbBoxbCWbbb
Countrysideb,bTXb759999999

Thomasbbbb A.bTerrificbbbb
9999bSkylinebDr
Megalopolisb,bNYb123459999
```

Observe that only the middle initials, rather than the full middle names, are printed. This is accomplished by specifying an output field width of 1 for the middle name, which has an internal length of 9. Also notice that character constants are used in the output FORMAT statements to "edit-in" periods and commas. Furthermore, you should be aware that the b characters are included merely to designate the actual output field widths for you; they will not be visible on the printed labels.

To indicate the versatility of the A edit descriptor, I point out that the input FORMAT statement can be written in this more general way:

```
110 FORMAT (7A)
```

Clearly, in this statement, the width specifications are omitted. The input values, however, are still read in properly. With the exception of the descriptor for the middle initial, the width specifications can also be omitted in the output FORMAT statements.

In the remaining paragraphs of this section, I will use the baseball standings problem to exemplify formatted i/o. The first-try algorithm and CHARACTER statement of Section 9-1, and the output sample in Figure 9-2, lead almost directly to the coding of the READ, WRITE, and FORMAT statements for the baseball standings program; the only missing item is an input layout. Leaving the specific layout for you to create, I show the sample set of input data in Figure 9-3 for producing the sample report in Figure 9-2.

```
Sundayb̸b̸b̸
AMERICAN
EAST
Baltimoreb̸b̸b̸b̸b̸b̸b̸b̸28b̸b̸b̸b̸15
Milwaukee         26      19
New York          25      19
Cleveland         22      17
Boston            25      20
Detroit           22      24
Toronto           16      31
WEST
Chicago           26      16
Oakland           30      20
Texas             26      18
California        22      27
Kansas City       15      24
Seattle           16      30
Minnesota         13      32
Californiab̸b̸b̸b̸7b̸b̸Chicagob̸b̸b̸b̸b̸b̸b̸4
Oakland            6   Toronto         5
Detroit            5   Baltimore       4
Milwaukee          5   Boston          2
Cleveland          7   New York        2
Minnesota          5   Kansas City     4
Seattle            5   Texas           3
b̸b̸b̸b̸b̸b̸b̸b̸b̸b̸b̸b̸b̸b̸b̸b̸b̸b̸b̸b̸b̸b̸b̸b̸b̸b̸b̸b̸b̸b̸b̸b̸b̸b̸b̸b̸b̸b̸b̸
NATIONAL
EAST
St Louisb̸b̸b̸b̸b̸b̸b̸b̸b̸23b̸b̸b̸b̸16
Philadelphia      26      19
Montreal          25      19
Pittsburgh        20      19
New York          14      27
Chicago           10      32
WEST
Los Angeles       32      15
Cincinnati        27      19
Houston           24      23
Atlanta           22      22
San Francisco     24      25
San Diego         18      29
Montrealb̸b̸b̸b̸b̸b̸b̸5b̸b̸Pittsburghb̸b̸b̸b̸b̸1
Philadelphia       6   St Louis        1
New York           3   Chicago         2
Los Angeles       16   Cincinnati      4
San Diego          5   Atlanta         1
San Francisco      6   Houston         1
```

Figure 9-3. Sample Baseball Standing and Games Input Data

Using SANGIF as the name for the "standings and games" input file, I offer the following groups of statements for discussion of input.

1.   For reading the day of the games:

```
100 FORMAT (A9)
    READ (SANGIF, 100) DAY
```

2.   For the input of a league name:

```
110 FORMAT (A8)
    READ (SANGIF, 110, END=899) LGNAME
```

3.   For reading a division name:

```
112 FORMAT (A4)
    READ (SANGIF, 112) DVNAME(DIVISN)
```

where DIVISN varies from 1 to 2 for the two divisions in each league.

4.   For the input of the standings in a division:

```
114 FORMAT (A13, 3X, I3, 3X, I3)
    DO 310 TEAM = HITEAM, LOTEAM
        READ (SANGIF, 114) TMNAME(TEAM), WON(TEAM), LOST(TEAM)
310 CONTINUE
```

where HITEAM and LOTEAM represent the relative positions of the high team and low team in the division; TEAM, therefore, is the position value of the team for which data are being read; TMNAME is the team name; WON is the number of games won by the team; and LOST is the number of games lost by the team.

5.   For reading the results of the games in a league:

```
116 FORMAT (A13, 1X, I2, 2X, A13, 1X, I2)
    NGAMES = 0
    DO 440 GAME = 1, NTEAMS
        READ (SANGIF, 116, END=899) WINNER(GAME),
    :         WINSCR(GAME), LOSER(GAME), LOSSCR(GAME)
        IF (WINNER(GAME) .EQ. BLANK) GO TO 450
            NGAMES = GAME
            {Won-lost record updating occurs here}
440 CONTINUE
450 {Standings updating begins here}
```

where NGAMES is the number of games played; NTEAMS, the number of teams in the league, is used as an upper-limit on the number of games played; WINSCR and LOSSCR are the respective scores of the winning (WINNER) and losing (LOSER) teams; and the IF statement is used, as explained in the next section, to detect the end of the input data for a league.

6.   For printing the new standings of a division:

```
910 FORMAT ('0', T19, A4, /
    :           '0', T17, 'WON', 2X, 'LOST', 5X, 'PCT', 3X, 'GB', /)
912 FORMAT (' ', A13, 3X, I3, 3X, I3, 3X, F5.3, 3X, F4.1)
    WRITE (SANGOF, 910) DVNAME(DIVISN)
    DO 610 TEAM = HITEAM, LOTEAM
        WRITE (SANGOF, 912) TMNAME(TEAM),
    :                       WON(TEAM), LOST(TEAM),
    :                       PRCENT(TEAM), GMSBHD(TEAM)
610 CONTINUE
```

where PRCENT is the reported "PCT" and GMSBHD is the number of games a team is behind the division leader.

7.   For printing the day and games of the league:

```
914 FORMAT ('0', T6, 'GAMES PLAYED ', A9, /)
916 FORMAT (' ', T6, A13, I3, ',', 5X, A13, I3)
    WRITE (SANGOF, 914) DAY
    DO 710 GAME = 1, NGAMES
        WRITE (SANGOF, 916) WINNER(GAME), WINSCR(GAME),
    :                       LOSER(GAME), LOSSCR(GAME)
710 CONTINUE
```

If you will trace or actually complete and execute the code above using the data in Figure 9-3, you will find that the output looks like that of Figure 9-2 except that the spacing on the games is slightly different. A method for making it the same is explored later in this chapter after substrings are introduced.

9-5   COMPARING CHARACTER VARIABLES AND ARRAY ELEMENTS

The statement

```
IF (WINNER(GAME) .EQ. BLANK) GO TO 450
```

appears in the fifth input segment above for the baseball problem. The purpose of this statement is to detect the blank input record that designates the end of the games for the first league in the input file; the relational expression in it clearly involves a comparison of character strings. For the American League data of Figure 9-3, array WINNER will contain the following strings after the input segment has been executed.

```
Californiabbb
Oaklandbbbbbb
Detroitbbbbbb
Milwaukeebbbb
Clevelandbbbb
Minnesotabbbb
Seattlebbbbbb
bbbbbbbbbbbbb
{remaining elements not defined}
```

Therefore, just after WINNER(7) has been read in, the relational expression is evaluated like this:

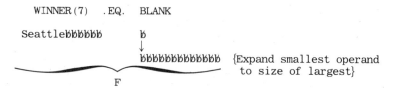

You can see that the comparison is facilitated by the expansion of the shorter string to the size of the longer string by the addition of blanks to the right. This expansion always occurs automatically, if necessary, when strings are compared. Since the evaluated result in this case is false, reading continues. Just after WINNER(8) has been read in, the expression is evaluated like this:

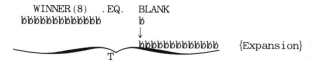

The true result then causes an exit from the read loop into the "standings update" part of the program.

Character string comparisons, therefore, are similar to numeric value comparisons—both are performed in relational expressions. And like numeric values, character strings can be compared by using any of the relational operators; they are not limited to the equality or inequality operators.

Consider how character string comparisons involving relational operators other than .EQ. and .NE. can be made. FORTRAN 77 defines an ordering relationship, known as a *collating sequence*, among the uppercase alphabetic and the numeric characters. The blank character is also included in each defined collating sequence. The alphabetic character collating sequence can be represented by

ƀ<A<B<C< ... <X<Y<Z

Similarly, the numeric character collating sequence can be represented by

ƀ<0<1<2< ... <7<8<9

Furthermore, FORTRAN 77 says that the alphabetic and numeric characters cannot be intermixed in a collating sequence; all the alphabetics must be less than all the numerics, or vice versa. Although FORTRAN 77 defines no collating sequence for the special characters or the lowercase alphabetic characters, every computer has a collating sequence for all characters that it can represent. You can be sure that the lowercase alphabetic characters have the sequence

a<b<c< ... <x<y<z

on all computers; but other than the three sequences specified above, inconsistencies in collating sequence occur from computer to computer.

All the character string comparisons in the baseball program involve equality or inequality comparisons. For instance, comparisons are needed for locating each winner's name and each loser's name in the standings so that their won−lost records can be updated. This "locating" process is commonly referred to as a *search*. The following program segment, which is inserted before statement 440 in the fifth input segment given earlier, can be used for these two particular searches.

```
        DO 420 TEAM = 1, NTEAMS
           IF (WINNER(GAME) .EQ. TMNAME(TEAM)) THEN
              WON(TEAM) = WON(TEAM) + 1
              GO TO 425
           ENDIF
420 CONTINUE
425 DO 430 TEAM = 1, NTEAMS
           IF (LOSER(GAME) .EQ. TMNAME(TEAM)) THEN
              LOST(TEAM) = LOST(TEAM) + 1
              GO TO 440
           ENDIF
430 CONTINUE
```

Interpreted, this segment says: "Search for the winner's name in the standings, adding 1 to the winner's 'WON' record when found; then, immediately, begin the search for the loser's name in the standings, adding 1 to the loser's 'LOST' record when found; then, immediately, quit searching."

An illustrative character string comparison can also be made on the student information records. Notice (Figure 9-1) that the sample records are in no particular order. Record order is important in many applications, such as printing class rolls, updating credit hours and grade points, and producing grade reports. Record ordering by student last name requires the use of statements such as the following:

```
        DO 510 STU = 1, NCOMPS
           IF (SLNAME(STU) .GT. SLNAME(STU+1)) THEN
              . {Interchange last names and other data items;
              .  set interchange indicator}
              .
           ENDIF
510 CONTINUE
```

In this "interchange test" segment, NCOMPS is the number of compares that must be made during the pass. For the data in Figure 9-1, when the value of STU is 1, the relational expression evaluation takes place like this:

```
     SLNAME(1) .GT. SLNAME(2)
     Windmillbbbb .GT. Terrificbbbb
```
                        T

The computer finds the expression true because W is greater than T in the collating sequence; it does not even have to examine the other characters in the two strings. A character string comparison always takes place left to right, and character pairs are compared one by one until the logical value is determined.

This is a good point for you to do some exercises on the material covered so far in this chapter. Just before doing so, however, consider a program control topic that I first mentioned in Chapter 7. It is one that has come into play in this section and is more prominent in Chapter 10 and beyond. The topic is "nested DO-loops."

I stated above that the baseball program search segment is to be inserted into the input segment of Section 9-4 that reads the results of the games in a league. The complete segment, then, ends up with a set of nested DO-loops as shown and explained in Figure 9-4. Study the figure; then go on to the exercises.

1.   The segment:

```
     NGAMES = 0
     DO 440 GAME = 1, NTEAMS
         READ (SANGIF, 116, END=899) WINNER(GAME),
   :           WINSCR(GAME), LOSER(GAME), LOSSCR(GAME)
       IF (WINNER(GAME) .EQ. BLANK) GO TO 450
           NGAMES = GAME
           DO 420 TEAM = 1, NTEAMS
              IF (WINNER(GAME) .EQ. TMNAME(TEAM)) THEN
                 WON(TEAM) = WON(TEAM) + 1
                 GO TO 425
              ENDIF
420        CONTINUE
425        DO 430 TEAM = 1, NTEAMS
              IF (LOSER(GAME) .EQ. TMNAME(GAME)) THEN
                 LOST(TEAM) = LOST(TEAM) + 1
                 GO TO 440
              ENDIF
430        CONTINUE
440 CONTINUE
450 {Standings updating begins here}
```

2.   A general explanation of the nested DO-loops:

   (a) All DO-loops develop logically from the algorithm. Compare the code above to the algorithm given earlier in the chapter.

   (b) All DO-loops are either nested with respect to other Do-loops or they stand alone and have no code in common with other DO-loops.

   (c) "Nested" implies "one or more contained within another." Thus DO-loops are nested if there is an "outer DO-loop" and one or more "inner DO-loops." In the code above, the outer DO-loop begins at "DO 440 GAME =1, NTEAMS" and ends at "440 CONTINUE." Clearly, there are two inner DO-loops inside this one.

   (d) An inner DO-loop must be completely contained within an outer DO-loop; their ranges cannot overlap.

   (e) Only an outer DO-loop can have a portion of its range outside an inner DO-loop. An inner DO-loop cannot have any of its range outside an outer DO-loop.

   (f) DO-loops can be nested to as many levels as are dictated by the logic of the algorithm. This means that the inner DO-loops can contain other inner DO-loops; they, then, are outer DO-loops to only those inner DO-loops.

Figure 9-4. The Baseball Program Segment Containing Nested DO-loops

9-6   EXERCISES

1.   Below, you are given a program segment and two input records. After the execution of the program segment, what values will each of the symbolic constants, variables, and array elements have in memory? (Show all significant blank characters.)

   Program segment:

```
CHARACTER  ABLE*5, BAKER(4)*1, CHARLY*10, DAVID*8
PARAMETER  (CHARLY=' ')
DATA       BAKER /
:          4*(' ') /
  .
  .
  .
READ *, ABLE, BAKER(4), DAVID
IF (BAKER(1) .EQ. CHARLY) READ *, BAKER(1)
```

   Input records:

```
'APPLE' 'ORANGE' 'LEMON'
'CHERRY' 'GRAPE' 'PEACH'
```

2.   Given the following program segment and input records, present a complete layout of the actual results that will be printed when the program segment is executed with the data. Identify the carriage control action for each line, paying particular attention to the first line.

   Program segment:

```
      INTEGER EXIF, EXOF, NB
      REAL  OBS1(5), OBS2(5)
      CHARACTER  BATCH(5)*1, TITLE*80
      PARAMETER  (EXIF=5, EXOF=6)
         .
         .
100 FORMAT (A80)
110 FORMAT (I2)
120 FORMAT (A1, 2F5.1)
900 FORMAT ('0', 5(A4, 3X))
910 FORMAT (1X, 5F7.1)
         .
         .
      READ (EXIF, 100) TITLE
      WRITE (EXOF, 100) TITLE
      READ (EXIF, 110) NB
      DO 210 REC = 1, NB
         READ (EXIF, 120) BATCH(REC), OBS1(REC), OBS2(REC)
210 CONTINUE
      WRITE (EXOF, 900) (BATCH(REC), REC = 1, NB)
      WRITE (EXOF, 910) (OBS1(REC), REC = 1, NB)
      WRITE (EXOF, 910) (OBS2(REC), REC = 1, NB)
      STOP
      END
```

Input records (values begin in column 1):

```
1EXPERIMENT DELTA
03
A1234567890
B2345678901
C3456789012
D4567890123
E5678901234
```

3. Given the declaration

```
CHARACTER  FIRST*7, SECOND*4, THIRD*1
```

and that FIRST='JOHNSON', SECOND='JOHNS', AND THIRD='J', state the value of each of the following relational expressions.

(a) THIRD .GT. FIRST

(b) SECOND .LE. FIRST .AND. THIRD .LE. SECOND

(c) FIRST .EQ. SECOND .OR. FIRST .EQ. THIRD
    .OR. SECOND .EQ. THIRD

4. Complete the planning and writing of the bank statement program exemplified thus far in this chapter. The initial problem is stated as Exercise 12 of Section 7-5. It is modified in Section 9-1. One more modification to add now is to treat each account as an interest-bearing checking account that pays interest on the average balance, provided that it stays above a certain amount, and makes a service charge only if the balance falls below a given minimum. Use the methods and rates of your local bank for accrediting interest and making service charges. Also, use your personal bank statement as an additional output guide. Make up your own test data, and print bank statements for at least five customers.

5. Complete the planning and writing of the baseball standings and scores program exemplified thus far in this chapter (or see the exercise below). Write the program for interactive processing if possible. The problem is stated in full, with a first-try algorithm, in Section 9-1. The reordering of teams to produce new standings in a division should be accomplished by sorting. Use the bubble sort method in Section 8-7, or the selection sort method of Exercise 8 in Section 8-8, or another sort method that you can find in the literature. Be sure that you interchange not only the team names but also the wins and losses.

6. Using the baseball standings and scores example of this chapter as a guide, plan and write a complete Fortran program for one or more of the following sports problems, or choose your own favorite sport. The first four, of those below, are very similar to the baseball standings and scores problem; the last three are similar to each other and have similarities with the baseball problem, but differ enough to offer some additional interesting challenges. The sports section of your daily newspaper—particularly the Sunday edition—

should be extremely useful for this exercise. Before proceeding with it, read Exercise 5.

(a)   Football standings and scores

(b)   Soccer standings and scores

(c)   Basketball standings and scores

(d)   Ice hockey standings and scores

(e)   Golf tournament standings and scores

(f)   Bowling tournament standings and scores

(g)   Major ieague baseball standings for team batting, individual batting, and pitching

9-7 SUBSTRINGS

A *substring* is a contiguous portion of a character string referred to by a character variable name or character array element name. Substrings can be read in, assigned, concatenated (i.e., attached together), compared, and written out. What this means is that portions of character strings can be processed as character entities. Therefore, it is possible to write Fortran program code to refer to, search for, replace, delete, and insert one or more characters within a string.

Every substring that is a part of a character variable value has a name of the form

```
cvar(sel:ser)
```

where cvar is the name of the character variable, and sel and ser are optional substring expressions as explained below. Similarly, every substring that is a part of a one-dimensional array element value has a name of the form

```
carn(loce)(sel:ser)
```

where carn is the name of the character array and loce is the location expression for the array element. Substrings that are part of multidimensional array element values have a name form similar to the one-dimensional form; they are not covered here but follow directly from material presented in Chapter 10.

The substring expressions sel and ser must be integer expressions; they specify, respectively, the leftmost and rightmost character positions of the substring in the string. The defaults are 1 for sel and len for ser, where len is the declared length of the string. The relationship

```
1 <= sel <= ser <= len
```

must hold for the two expressions.

As an initial look at substrings, consider the following progressive illustration.

The statements

```
CHARACTER  MTHNAM(12)*9
DATA  MTHNAM /
  :      'January', 'February', 'March', 'April',
  :      'May', 'June', 'July', 'August',
  :      'September', 'October', 'November', 'December' /
```

describe one character array, and 12 character strings of length 9. The substring names

```
MTHNAM(1)(1:9)
MTHNAM(3)(9:)
MTHNAM(8)(1:3)
MTHNAM(12)(1:1)
```

have the respective values

```
Januaryƀƀ
ƀ
Aug
D
```

Observe that these values vary in length, depending on the left and right character positions specified in the substring names. Add to the code above, the statements

```
INTEGER  FIRSTM, LASTM, MNLGTH, MONTH, SNLGTH
   .
   .
   .
READ *, MNLGTH, FIRSTM, SNLGTH
LASTM = FIRSTM + SNLGTH − 1
PRINT *, (MTHNAM(MONTH − MONTH / 13 * 12)(:MNLGTH), ' ',
  :          MONTH = FIRSTM, LASTM)
```

Then use the input record

```
3 6 3
```

to obtain the printed line

```
Jun Jul Aug
```

The full program segment above has the purpose of printing the names, or abbreviated names, of the months that occur in a given season. Trace the code, for instance, with the input values 3, 9, and 5, and you should obtain

```
Sep Oct Nov Dec Jan
```

A further expansion of this idea results in the program below, which has the purpose of reading the name of a season as well as the other items that are read in above, and then printing an identifying message together with the appropriate months. The program illustrates several of the simpler operations that can be performed on substrings.

```
     INTEGER  FIRSTM, LASTM, MNLGTH, MONTH, SNLGTH
     CHARACTER  MTHNAM(12)*9, SEASON*6, SNMSG*22
     DATA  MTHNAM /
   :         'January', 'February', 'March', 'April',
   :         'May', 'June', 'July', 'August',
   :         'September', 'October', 'November', 'December' /,
   :         SNMSG /
   :         'The season months are ' /

         .
         .
         .
200    READ *, SEASON(1:6)
       IF (SEASON(1:1) .EQ. ' ') GO TO 210
         READ *, MNLGTH, FIRSTM, SNLGTH
         LASTM = FIRSTM + SNLGTH - 1
         SNMSG(5:10) = SEASON
         PRINT *, SNMSG, ' ',
   :         (MTHNAM(MONTH - MONTH / 13 * 12)(:MNLGTH),
   :          ', ', MONTH = FIRSTM, LASTM - 1), ' and ',
   :         MTHNAM(MONTH - MONTH / 13 * 12)(:MNLGTH), '.'
         GO TO 200
210 STOP
     END
```

Given the sample input data

```
'summer'
3 6 3
'school'
9 9 9
'winter'
9 12 3
' '
```

the printed results from the execution of the program are

```
The summer months are Jun, Jul, and Aug.
The school months are September, October  , November ,
December , January  , February , March    , April    , and
May         .
The winter months are December , January  , and February .
```

You can see that the first input season name replaces the word "season" in the message, and subsequent input season names replace the previous season name in the message. You might try a longer or shorter input season name to see what happens; you will find that the code is designed only for six-character fixed-length season names. In the following section I tell you about one approach to handling variable-length substring replacement. Concurrently, I explain how you can eliminate the extra and undesirable blank output characters, like those following some of the month names in the second and third sentences above.

9-8 INTRINSIC FUNCTIONS FOR CHARACTER PROCESSING

If you look in the Appendix at the end of the book, you will find that there is only one character intrinsic function. Its name is CHAR, its one argument is of type integer, and it finds the character that is in the collating sequence position corresponding to the value of the argument. This function is processor dependent; that is, the character found by this function depends completely on the collating sequence of the particular processor that executes the function. If you want to know the collating sequence of your processor, look it up in the processor manuals or execute a code sequence similar to this:

```
        DO 210 CH = 0, NCH
            PRINT *, CH, CHAR(CH)
    210 CONTINUE
```

where NCH is one less than the number of characters that can be represented by your processor, and CHAR(CH) is the function reference that produces the character corresponding to collating sequence position CH.

The integer function ICHAR is just the opposite of CHAR in that it finds the collating position sequence number for a given character that the processor can represent. ICHAR and CHAR are useful for encoding and decoding messages, but because they are processor dependent, any program using them may produce different results on different computers.

The two other useful integer intrinsic functions for character processing have the names LEN and INDEX. Function LEN has the purpose of determining the length of a character string. It is referenced by the form

```
    LEN(ce)
```

where ce is a character expression, often the name of a character variable or array element. The purpose of function INDEX is to locate the starting position of a specified substring within a given character string. Its reference form is

```
    INDEX(ce1, ce2)
```

where ce1 is the character expression that identifies the string and ce2 is the character expression that identifies the substring. If either the substring does not exist within the string or the substring is longer than the string, the function value is defined to be zero.

These two functions, working together, can be used to eliminate the extra and undesirable blank output characters such as those that occur in the following three examples.

Season program output (Section 9-7):

```
The winter months are Decemberb, Januarybb, and Februaryb.
```

Baseball program output (Section 9-4-2):

```
Californiabbb   7,  bbbChicagobbbbbb   4
```

Mailing label program output (Section 9-4-2):

```
Wendybbbb W. Windmillbbbb
Rt. W, Box CW
Countrysideb, TX 759999999
```

where the undesirable and extra blanks are represented by ƀ. The statement used to print the first line of the mailing labels was

```
WRITE (MAILOF, 910) SFNAME(STU), SMNAME(STU),
:                   SLNAME(STU)
```

This statement is now replaced with the sequence

```
LENSFN = INDEX(SFNAME(STU), ' ') - 1
IF (LENSFN .LT. 0) LENSFN = LEN(SFNAME(STU))
PRINT *, SFNAME(STU)(1:LENSFN), ' ',
:        SMNAME(STU)(1:1), '. ', SLNAME(STU)
```

which produces a first mailing label line that has this improved appearance:

```
Wendy W. Windmillƀƀƀƀ
```

Undesirable blank characters can be eliminated from the month names in the season program output by using the same INDEX-LEN function combination, but the application is a little more complicated because of the use of an implied-DO in the statement

```
PRINT *, SNMSG, ' ',
:        (MTHNAM(MONTH - MONTH /13 * 12)(:MNLGTH),
:        ', ', MONTH = FIRSTM, LASTM - 1), ' and ',
:        MTHNAM(MONTH - MONTH / 13 * 12)(:MNLGTH), '.'
```

which prints the season message and the month names. What must be done is to allow the month name length to vary in value rather than having the same value, MNLGTH, for each month referenced in one message. To do this we could use another function that finds the length of a substring up to the first blank character in a string. The PRINT statement could then be written

```
PRINT *, SNMSG, ' ',
:        (MTHNAM(MONTH - MONTH / 13 * 12)
:        (:LENSUB(MTHNAM(MONTH - MONTH / 13 * 12))),
:        ', ', MONTH = FIRSTM, LASTM - 1), ' and ',
:        MTHNAM(MONTH - MONTH / 13 * 12)
:        (:LENSUB(MTHNAM(MONTH - MONTH / 13 * 12))), '.'
```

where LENSUB is the name of the function. Unfortunately, there is no such intrinsic function. But, fortunately, we are not limited to intrinsic functions; with additional knowledge, we can devise an appropriate external function—a function subprogram that is not furnished with the Fortran processor but is written as a separate program unit to perform a specific task when referenced. You will fully gain the requisite additional knowledge when you study Chapter 11, but you can begin to acquire it now by studying the needed external function, presented in Figure 9-5. With the PRINT statement above and the function in Figure 9-5, a representative printed line is

```
The winter months are December, January, and February.
```

```
*II.  NON-BLANK SUBSTRING LENGTH
*
        FUNCTION  LENSUB(STRING)
*        PROGRAMMER:  Jarrell C. Grout
*        DATE:  5/27/81
*
*  A. COMMENTARY
*
*        Given a character string, STRING, find the length, LENSUB,
*        of the non-blank substring that is stored in STRING,
*        beginning in position 1.
*
*           DICTIONARY.
*        INDEX:  Intrinsic function to find the position of the
*                first blank character in STRING.
*        LEN:  Intrinsic function to find the length of STRING.
*        LENSUB:  Length of the first non-blank substring in STRING.
*        STRING:  A given character string.
*
*  B. DECLARATION
*
        INTEGER  INDEX, LEN, LENSUB
        CHARACTER  STRING*(*)
*
*  C. I/O LAYOUT
*        NONE
*
*  D. ACTION
*
        LENSUB = INDEX(STRING, ' ') - 1
        IF (LENSUB .LT. 0) LENSUB = LEN(STRING)
        RETURN
        END
```

Figure 9-5. A Function for Finding Non-blank Substring Length

For practice, you should apply the foregoing ideas directly to the baseball program so that the games can also be printed free of undesirable blanks. You can cause the first game to be printed, for example, like this:

```
California  7,  Chicago  4
```

The LEN and INDEX intrinsic functions as well as the LENSUB external function are also useful for inserting and deleting substrings in strings.

There are four other intrinsic functions available for character processing: the logical functions LGE, LGT, LLE, and LLT. Each produces a logical value. The first L in each one stands for the word "lexically," and the other letters represent "greater than or equal to," "greater than," "less than or equal to," and "less than." Therefore, these functions can be used to compare two character strings in a lexical sense; that is, as to whether or not the two strings are in the order that they would appear in a dictionary.* As long as the two strings in question contain only letters or only digits, the results produced by these functions are the same as the results produced by the corresponding relational expressions. Therefore, for the data considered, the statement

```
IF  (SLNAME(STU)  .GT.  SLNAME(STU+1))  THEN
```

*The order is actually based on the collating sequence described in American Standard Code for Information Interchange, ANSI X3.4-1977 (ASCII). For characters not in the ASCII character set, the result is processor dependent.

taken from Section 9-5, yields the same results as the statement

```
IF (LGT(SLNAME(STU), SLNAME(STU+1)) THEN
```

which uses the "lexically greater than" intrinsic function. Whenever the two strings in question contain letters and digits and other characters mixed together, the relational expression results will vary from computer to computer; the results obtained through the use of these four functions, however, will remain consistent among computers.

9-9 THE CHARACTER ASSIGNMENT STATEMENT

The general form of a character assignment statement is

```
cname = ce
```

where cname is the name of a character variable, array element, or substring, and ce is a character expression. A character expression is either a character constant, the symbolic name of a character constant, a character variable name, a character array element name, or any of these combined with the character operator, which is described in the next section. A character expression identifies a character string and, when an assignment statement is evaluated, the string value of the expression is assigned to cname.

The character assignment statement is needed for moving character strings and substrings around in memory. For example, a direct alphabetic sort for arranging names requires the use of several character assignment statements for the interchange—something like this:

```
TPNAME = NAME(PERSON)
NAME(PERSON) = NAME(PERSON + 1)
NAME(PERSON + 1) = TPNAME
```

where TPNAME and each element of NAME are of character type and of the same length. The statement is also needed to place one string within another, as in the statement

```
SNMSG(5:10) = SEASON
```

from the season message program of the preceding section.

Three rules about character assignment statements should be committed to memory. The first is that if cname is a substring, as in the example immediately above, ce is assigned only to the substring. The second is that none of the character positions being assigned in cname may be referenced in ce. The statement

```
SNMSG(5:10) = SNMSG(6:11)
```

for instance, is invalid. The third is that cname and ce may have different lengths. If cname has more length, the characters of ce are placed in the leftmost positions of cname and the other positions of cname are filled with blank characters. If ce has more length, as many as possible of its characters, beginning with its leftmost, are placed in the positions of cname. For example, the statements

```
CHARACTER  CITY*12, STATE*2
      .
      .
      .
CITY = 'Honolulu'
STATE = 'Hawaii'
```

result in the string values of Honolulu₿₿₿₿ for CITY and Ha for STATE. These rules hold whether the expression ce consists of only one character entity or contains several character entities combined by means of the character operator.

9-10   THE CHARACTER OPERATOR

The character operator consists of two slashes in sequence and it always operates on two character entities in an expression of the form

```
cent1 // cent2
```

Its purpose is to *concatenate*—that is, attach or connect—the values of the character entities. The entities, represented by cent1 and cent2 in the form above, can be character constants, symbolic names of character constants, character variable names, character array element references, character substring references, character function references, and character expressions enclosed in parentheses. Parentheses, however, have no effect on the value of a character expression.

As a first illustration of the use of the character operator, consider a slight modification of the last example in the previous section. The statements

```
CHARACTER  CITY*12
      .
      .
      .
CITY = 'Honolulu'//'Hawaii'
```

result in CITY having the string value HonoluluHawa. Although this is not a particularly practical example, it does illustrate the idea.

A more practical example develops naturally from a desire to further improve the mailing label program given in Section 9-4-2 and first improved in Section 9-8. The printing of the first mailing label line was accomplished originally by the formatted output statement

```
WRITE (MAILOF, 910) SFNAME(STU), SMNAME(STU), SLNAME(STU)
```

which left undesirable blank positions in the print line. The blank positions were eliminated by replacing the WRITE statement with the following three statements.

```
LENSFN = INDEX(SFNAME(STU), ' ') - 1
IF (LENSFN .LT. 0) LENSFN = LEN(SFNAME(STU))
PRINT *, SFNAME(STU)(1:LENSFN), ' ',
:        SMNAME(STU)(1:1), '. ', SLNAME(STU)
```

Notice that the printing is now list-directed rather than explicitly formatted. The information covered since the code above was given can be used to again allow explicit formatting and provide some improvement. First, the declaration

```
CHARACTER  NAME*25
```

is added to the program. Then FORMAT statement 910 becomes

```
910 FORMAT ('1', A25)
```

Finally, the assignment statement, IF statement, and PRINT statement above are replaced by the following two statements.

```
NAME = SFNAME(STU)(1:LENSUB(SFNAME(STU))) // ' ' //
:        SMNAME(STU)(1:1) // '. ' // SLNAME(STU)
WRITE (MAILOF, 910) NAME
```

Then, when the values of SFNAME(STU), SMNAME(STU), and SLNAME(STU) are Wendybbbb, Waterbbbb, and Windmillbbbb, the printed line is

```
Wendy W. Windmillbbbbbbbb
```

9-11   EXAMPLE PROGRAM: MULTIPLE-CHOICE TEST GRADING WITH INDIRECT SORTING

The example problem chosen for complete solution in this chapter appears to be quite different, in nature, from the partial examples covered earlier in the chapter. Yet it provides an opportunity to illustrate most of the FORTRAN 77 character-processing capabilities including operations on substrings. Furthermore, it allows me to show you how to design a sorting procedure that not only performs an alphabetic sort but does so indirectly.

In overview, the problem is to compute and print a report of the grades made on a multiple-choice test. The program here is oriented toward college classes, but it is adaptable to different situations. The input and output layouts (with the exception of an error message that is left for you to depict) are given in Figures 9-6 and 9-7. Explicitly formatted input and output are purposely used so that character input data can be entered free of surrounding apostrophes and, as usual, to provide an organized and readable report. As implied in the input record layout, the input data for one test consist of one header record and one key record, followed by the student response records. On the output layout, strings of identical letters are used to represent character positions in the same way that X's have been used to represent numeric positions.

The program is to read the header record, check the numeric input, read the key record, read and process the student records, and finally, print the report. A first-try algorithm for the solution of the problem is as follows.

Field Name	Description	Location
Header record:		
Department code	Three characters	1−3
Course number	Three numeric characters	4−6
Section number	Two numeric characters	7−8
Exam title	Character	9−19
Number of questions	Integer, XXX	20−22
Key record:		
Correct answers	One character answer per column (up to 100); usually A, B, C, etc.	1−100
Student response record:		
First name	Character, left-justified	1−9
Middle initial	Character, left-justified	10
Last name	Character, left-justified	11−22
Answers	One character answer per column (up to 100); usually A, B, C, etc.	23−122

Figure 9-6. Multiple Choice Test Program Input Record Layouts

```
Read the header record.
If the number of questions is not valid, then
    print an error message and stop.
Otherwise, read the key record.
While there are student response records, do the following:
    read and save a student response record;
    compute the test grade for the student;
    accumulate the test grade for computing the
    class average grade.
Compute the class average grade.
Indirectly sort the student response records by last name.
While there are student response records, do the following:
    if end-of-page, print the headings;
    print the appropriate student response record and
    test grade.
```

As you can see, the solution procedure could be broken into about six separate subalgorithms—one associated with each sentence. However, the only subalgorithm that is considered separately here is the one concerned with the indirect sort.

An indirect sort is beneficial when the sorting involves records that contain several items rather than just one item as in the example program of Figure 8-4. In the current problem, the student response records contain four different items and are to be sorted on the basis of one of them—the last name; therefore, "last name" is the sort key.

Not only are the last names to be sorted, however, but the other items in each record are to be reordered properly. This reordering could be accomplished by interchanging each item in two records every time an interchange occurs. To do so would require an excessive amount of data movement, too much computer time, and extra temporary variables. A better technique is to use a directory through

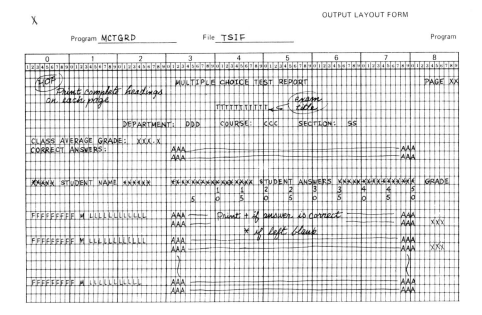

Figure 9-7. Multiple Choice Test Program Output Record Layout

which the sorted records can be addressed. The directory is a one-dimensional array that has as many elements as there are records to be sorted. The value of each element is an address or relative position number for one of the records. Before the sort begins, the directory element values are the successive integers 1 through N, where N is the number of records to be sorted; they, therefore, identify the relative position of the unsorted records. After the indirect sorting process is complete, the directory element values identify the relative positions of the unsorted records in sorted sequence. The records themselves have not been moved; only the directory element values have been appropriately changed. Then the records can be accessed in sorted sequence through the directory. The use of the directory, and of its elements as relative position numbers or relative addresses, leads to the alternative names "directory sort" and "address vector sort" for this technique.

To get a full grasp on the idea, consider the following example. Disregard the test answers for now and consider several data records that each contain three items: first name, middle initial, and last name. From the student records given earlier, and the layout of Figure 9-6, we can depict five records as follows:

```
Wendy      WWindmill
Thomas     ATerrific
Susan      QPrettyface
Johnny     CSkilift
Judy       JJudy
```

The sort objective is to be able to address these records as if they have this order:

```
Judy       JJudy
Susan      QPrettyface
Johnny     CSkilift
Thomas     ATerrific
Wendy      WWindmill
```

This objective is met by establishing a directory through which the records can be addressed. Initially, the directory, set beside the unsorted records for illustration, is established with the values shown below.

Directory	Records	
1	Wendy	WWindmill
2	Thomas	ATerrific
3	Susan	QPrettyface
4	Johnny	CSkilift
5	Judy	JJudy

Thus, before the sort commences, the directory element values are the relative position numbers of the records in their original order. Then the bubble sort method is applied (other sort methods could be used) and the directory element values, rather than the records, are moved around as interchanges occur during sort passes.

Directory, End of Pass 1	Directory, End of Pass 2	Directory, End of Pass 3	Directory, End of Pass 4
2	3	3	5
3	4	5	3
4	5	4	4
5	2	2	2
1	1	1	1

After the last pass, the directory and the records appear as follows.

Directory	Records	
5	Wendy	WWindmill
3	Thomas	ATerrific
4	Susan	QPrettyface
2	Johnny	CSkilift
1	Judy	JJudy

So the directory element values have been moved around but the records remain in their original order. Letting LNAME, FNAME, MIDIN, and DIR represent last name, first name, middle initial, and directory, we find that the reference

```
LNAME(1)
```

Still has the value

```
Windmill
```

just as it did at the beginning. However, the reference

```
LNAME(DIR(1))
```

has the value

```
Judy
```

which happens to be the last name that is first alphabetically. Furthermore, as a group, the references

```
FNAME(DIR(3))
MIDIN(DIR(3))
LNAME(DIR(3))
```

identify the values

```
Johnny
C
Skilift
```

which collectively make up the third name in the alphabetical sequence. You can see that the directory elements are being used as subscripts to address the data records indirectly in alphabetical order by last name.

This indirect sort technique, in which the bubble sort method is used, is incorporated into the final algorithm given in Figure 9-8. You should analyze and study and compare it with the bubble sort procedure devised in Section 8-7. It commences with the comment, "Begin indirect sort procedure: bubble method," and finishes with the comment, "End sort, begin print procedure." The directory elements are initialized in the first DO-loop of the sort procedure. In the second DO-loop of the sort procedure, the test

```
If lname(infirst) > lname(insecnd), Then
```

together with the two lines above it, show that the comparison of last names is made by referring to them through the directory. Then the succeeding three lines represent an interchange of directory element values.

Overall, the algorithm contains more symbolism than the previous algorithms I have given you; that is, the names of variables and arrays are more abbreviated. But they are mnemonic and allow the algorithm to be expressed more succinctly. Notice that substring references, such as

```
corrans(1:numques)
```

which represents "correct answers from 1 through the number of questions," are made in the FORTRAN 77 manner. Note in the print procedure the use of concatenation, and the Fortran-like means of expressing it algorithmically. Also pay particular attention to the way in which the student record elements—fname, midin, lname, ans, and grade—are addressed for printing in sorted order. They are not addressed directly by means of sequential subscripts; they are addressed indirectly through the elements of dir, the directory.

The corresponding program is presented in Figure 9-9, some sample input data are given in Figure 9-10, and the corresponding sample output is shown in Figure 9-11. As indicated in the layout and the algorithm, a + is printed for a correct student answer and an * is printed for an omitted answer. Also observe that the external function LENSUB is referenced in the print procedure. This means that the function must be included with the main program or be in a file that is accessible to the main program.

ALGORITHM MCTest-grading
```
{ Compute and print  a report of  grades made on a multiple-
choice  test.    The   test   can   contain  from  1  to maxques
questions,   and can be  taken by from  1 to maxstu students.
Results  are   sorted  indirectly,  by means of  the bubble sort
method,   and   printed   in   order   by student last name.   The
parameters  maxlines and  ansline  are  the maximum number of
detail  lines  per  printed  page  and the maximum number of
answers per printed line.}

Read dept, course, sect, examtitle, numques
If numques < 0 or numques > maxques, Then
    Write error message {see layout}
Else
    Read corrans(1:numques)
    numstu ← 0
    avg ← 0
    Do stu ← 1 to maxstu by 1
        Read fname(stu), midin(stu), lname(stu),
            ans(stu)(1:numques), at EOF Go To AVG. (Ahead)
        numstu ← stu
        numcorr ← 0
        Do ques ← 1 to numques by 1
            If ans(stu)(ques:ques) = corrans(ques:ques), Then
                numcorr ← numcorr + 1
                ans(stu)(ques:ques) ← '+'
            Else If ans(stu)(ques:ques) = ' ', Then
                ans(stu)(ques:ques) ← '*'
        End Do
        grade(stu) ← NINT[100 * numcorr / numques]
        avg ← avg + grade(stu)
    End Do
AVG.    If numstu > 0, avg ← avg / numstu
    {Begin indirect sort procedure:  bubble method}
    Do stu ← 1 to numstu by 1
        dir(stu) ← stu
    End Do
```

Figure 9-8. Algorithm for Multiple Choice Test Grading

```
              numcomps ← numstu
              intch ← 1
PAS.          If intch = 1 Then
                  intch ← 0
                  numcomps ← numcomps - 1
                  Do first ← 1 to numcomps by 1
                      secnd ← first + 1
                      infirst ← dir(first)
                      insecnd ← dir(secnd)
                      If lname(infirst) > lname(insecnd), Then
                          tdir ← dir(first)
                          dir(first) ← dir(secnd)
                          dir(secnd) ← tdir
                          intch ← 1
                  End Do
                  Go To PAS. (Back)
              {End sort, begin print procedure}
              page ← 1
              lines ← maxlines + 1
              Do stu ← 1 to numstu by 1
                  If lines >= maxlines, Then
                      Write headings {see layout}
                      lines ← 0
                      page ← page + 1
                  next ← dir(stu)
                  name ← fname(next)(1:LENSUB[fname(next)]) // ' ' //
                              midin(next) // ' ' // lname(next)
                  If numques <= ansline, Then
                      Write name, ans(next)(1:numques), grade(next)
                      lines ← lines + 2
                  Else
                      Write name, ans(next)(1:ansline)
                      Write ans(next)(ansline+1:numques), grade(next)
                      lines ← lines + 3
              End Do
          Stop
          END
```

Figure 9-8. (Continued)

```
*I,    MULTIPLE CHOICE TEST GRADING
*
       PROGRAM MCTGRD
*      PROGRAMMER:  Jarrell C. Grout
*      DATE:  6/12/81
*
*  A. COMMENTARY
*
*          Compute and print a report of grades made on a
*      multiple choice test.  The test can contain from 1 to
*      MAXQES questions, and can be taken by from 1 to MAXSTU
*      students.  Results are sorted indirectly, by means of the
*      bubble sort method, and printed in order by student last
*      name.
*
*          Input consists of one Header record and one Key record
*      followed by up to MAXSTU student response records.  All
*      input is explicitly-formatted.  A Header record contains
*      the following:
*
```

Figure 9-9. Multiple Choice Test Grading Program

```
*            Department Code, 3 characters, col. 1-3,
*            Course Number, 3 digits, col. 4-6,
*            Section Number, 2 digits, col. 7-8,
*            Exam Title, 11 characters maximum, col. 9-19,
*            Number of Questions, 1-3 digits, col. 20-22.
*
*       A Key record contains the following:
*
*            Correct Answers, up to MAXQES 1-character answers,
*                             col. 1-100.
*
*       A Student Response record contains these items:
*
*            First Name, up to 9 characters, col. 1-9,
*            Middle initial, 1 character, col. 10,
*            Last Name, up to 12 characters, col. 11-22,
*            Answers, up to MAXQES 1-character answers
*                     corresponding, in order, to the
*                     correct answers above, col. 23-122.
*
*       DICTIONARY.
*
*       ANS:  Student answers, up to 100 1-character
*       ANSLIN:  Maximum number of answers printed per line
*       AVG:  Class average grade
*       CORANS:  Correct answers, up to 100 1-character
*       COURSE:  Course number, 3-digit
*       DEPT:  Department code, 3-character
*       DIR:  Directory for indirect sort
*       EXTITL:  Exam (test) title, 11-character
*       FIRST:  Directory index for first element in sort comparison
*       FNAME:  Student first name, 9-character
*       GRADE:  Test grade
*       INFRST:  Indirect student index for first last name in
*                sort comparison
*       INSECD:  Indirect student index for second last name in
*                sort comparison
*       INTCH:  Sort interchange indicator
*       LENSUB:  Function to find length of non-blank substring
*       LINES:  Line counter for each page
*       LNAME:  Student last name, 12-character
*       MAXLNS:  Maximum number of detail lines per output page
*       MAXQES:  Maximum number of questions on test
*       MAXSTU:  Maximum number of students
*       MIDIN:  Student middle initial, 1-character
*       NAME:  String for compacted student name
*       NEXT:  Student response record and grade index for sorted
*              order
*       NUMCOR:  Number of questions answered correctly
*       NUMQES:  Number of questions on test (1 to MAXQES)
*       NUMSTU:  Number of students taking test (1 to MAXSTU)
*       PAGE:  Page counter
*       QES:  Question index
*       SECND:  Directory index for second element in sort
*              comparison
*       SECT:  Section number, 2-digit
*       STU:  Student index
*       TDIR:  Temporary variable for directory element
*              interchange
*       TSIF:  Test input file
*       TSOF:  Test output file
*  B. DECLARATION
*
*       INTEGER  ANSLIN, MAXLNS, MAXQES, MAXSTU, TSIF, TSOF
*       PARAMETER  (ANSLIN=50, MAXLNS=37, MAXQES=100, MAXSTU=150,
*       :           TSIF=5, TSOF=6)
*       INTEGER  DIR(MAXSTU), FIRST, GRADE(MAXSTU), INFRS, INSEC,
*       :        INTCH, LENSUB, LINES, NEXT, NUMCOR, NUMCPS, NUMQES,
*       :        NUMSTU, PAGE, QES, SECND, STU, TDIR
*       REAL   AVG
*       CHARACTER  ANS(MAXSTU)*100, CORANS*100, COURSE*3, DEPT*3,
*       :          EXTITL*11, FNAME(MAXSTU)*9, LNAME(MAXSTU)*12,
*       :          MIDIN(MAXSTU)*1, NAME*25, SECT*2
*
*  C. I/O LAYOUT
```

Figure 9-9. (Continued)

```
*
  100 FORMAT (A3, A3, A2, A11, I3)
  105 FORMAT (A)
  110 FORMAT (A9, A1, A12, A)
  900 FORMAT ('1', 'FOR EXAM ', A11, 'IN DEPARTMENT ', A3,
       :         ' COURSE ', A3, ' AND SECTION ', A2, /
       :         ' ', 'THE NUMBER OF QUESTIONS, ', I3,
       :         ', IS LESS THAN 1 OR GREATER THAN 100.', /
       :         ' ', 'UNABLE TO RUN.  PLEASE CORRECT AND RETRY.')
  910 FORMAT ('1', T32, 'MULTIPLE CHOICE TEST REPORT',
       :         T83, 'PAGE', I3, //
       :         '0', T40, A11, /
       :         '0', T21, 'DEPARTMENT:  ', A3, 4X, 'COURSE:  ', A3, 4X,
       :         'SECTION:  ', A2, /
       :         '0', T2, 'CLASS AVERAGE GRADE:  ', F5.1)
  912 FORMAT (' ', T2, 'CORRECT ANSWERS:  ', T31, A, /
       :         ' ', T31, A)
  915 FORMAT (/'0', '***** STUDENT NAME ******', 4X,
       :         '**************** STUDENT ANSWERS **************** ',
       :         'GRADE', /
       :         ' ', T40, '1', T45, '1', T50, '2', T55, '2', T60, '3',
       :         T65, '3', T70, '4', T75, '4', T80, '5', /
       :         ' ', T35, '5', T40, '0', T45, '5', T50, '0', T55, '5',
       :         T60, '0', T65, '5', T70, '0', T75, '5', T80, '0', /)
  920 FORMAT (' ', A25, T31, A, T84, I3, /)
  930 FORMAT (' ', A25, T31, A, /, T31, A, T84, I3, /)
*
*  D. ACTION
*
      READ (TSIF, 100) DEPT, COURSE, SECT, EXTITL, NUMQES
      IF (NUMQES .LT. 0 .OR. NUMQES .GT. MAXQES) THEN
         WRITE (TSOF, 900) EXTITL, DEPT, COURSE, SECT, NUMQES
      ELSE
         READ (TSIF, 105) CORANS(1:NUMQES)
         NUMSTU = 0
         AVG = 0
         DO 250 STU = 1, MAXSTU
            READ (TSIF, 110, END=300) FNAME(STU), MIDIN(STU),
       :                              LNAME(STU), ANS(STU)(1:NUMQES)
            NUMSTU = STU
            NUMCOR = 0
            DO 240 QES = 1, NUMQES
               IF (ANS(STU)(QES:QES) .EQ. CORANS(QES:QES)) THEN
                  NUMCOR = NUMCOR + 1
                  ANS(STU)(QES:QES) = '+'
               ELSE IF (ANS(STU)(QES:QES) .EQ. ' ') THEN
                  ANS(STU)(QES:QES) = '*'
               ENDIF
  240       CONTINUE
            GRADE(STU) = NINT(100.0 * NUMCOR / NUMQES)
            AVG = AVG + GRADE(STU)
  250    CONTINUE
  300    IF (NUMSTU .GT. 0) AVG = AVG / NUMSTU
*
*        Begin indirect sort procedure on STU
         DO 310 STU = 1, NUMSTU
            DIR(STU) = STU
  310    CONTINUE
         NUMCPS = NUMSTU
         INTCH = 1
  315    IF (INTCH .EQ. 1) THEN
            INTCH = 0
            NUMCPS = NUMCPS - 1
            DO 320 FIRST = 1, NUMCPS
               SECND = FIRST + 1
               INFRS = DIR(FIRST)
               INSEC = DIR(SECND)
               IF (LNAME(INFRS) .GT. LNAME(INSEC)) THEN
                  TDIR = DIR(FIRST)
                  DIR(FIRST) = DIR(SECND)
                  DIR(SECND) = TDIR
                  INTCH = 1
               ENDIF
  320       CONTINUE
            GO TO 315
         ENDIF
*        End sort procedure
```

Figure 9-9. (Continued)

```
*
*          Begin print procedure
           PAGE = 1
           LINES = MAXLNS + 1
           DO 350 STU = 1, NUMSTU
               IF (LINES .GT. MAXLNS) THEN
                   WRITE (TSOF, 910) PAGE, EXTITL, DEPT, COURSE, SECT, AVG
                   IF (NUMQES .LE. ANSLIN) THEN
                       WRITE (TSOF, 912) CORANS(1:NUMQES)
                   ELSE
                       WRITE (TSOF, 912) CORANS(1:ANSLIN),
        :                                CORANS(ANSLIN+1:NUMQES)
                   ENDIF
                   WRITE (TSOF, 915)
                   LINES = 0
                   PAGE = PAGE + 1
               ENDIF
               NEXT = DIR(STU)
               NAME = FNAME(NEXT)(1:LENSUB(FNAME(NEXT))) // ' ' //
        :             MIDIN(NEXT) // ' ' // LNAME(NEXT)
               IF (NUMQES .LE. ANSLIN) THEN
                   WRITE (TSOF, 920) NAME, ANS(NEXT)(1:NUMQES), GRADE(NEXT)
                   LINES = LINES + 2
               ELSE
                   WRITE (TSOF, 930) NAME, ANS(NEXT)(1:ANSLIN),
        :                           ANS(NEXT)(ANSLIN+1:NUMQES), GRADE(NEXT)
                   LINES = LINES + 3
               ENDIF
       350     CONTINUE
           ENDIF
           STOP
           END
```

Figure 9-9. (Continued)

```
CSC10101 FIRST EXAM 75
ABCDEEDCBAAAAAABBBBBCCCCCDDDDDEEEEEEDCBAABCDEAABBCCDDEEEEEDDCCBBAAAAAABBBCCCD
Wendy      WWindmill    ABCD EDCBAAAAAAABCDECCCCCDDDDDEEEEEEDCBAABCDEAABBCCDDEEEEEDDCCBBAAAAAABB CC D
Calloway   CCaulkenberstABCEDEEDCBAAAAAAABBBBBCCCCCDDDDDEEEEEEDCBAABCDEAABBCCDDEEEEEDDCCBBAAAAAABBBCCCD
Thomas     ATerrific    ABCDEEDCBAAAAAABBBBBCCCCCDDDDDEEEEEEDCBAABCDEAABBCCDDEEEEEDDCCBBAAAAAABBBCCCD
Casey      Strikesout
Susan      QPrettyface  ABCBAABCDEBBBBBCCCCCDDDDDEEEEEEDDDDDAABCDEEDCBAEEEEEEBBBBBAAAAADDDDDCCCCCAAAAA
Majorie    LBenefieldsonABCDEEDCBAABCDEEDBCAABCDEEDBCAEEEEEEDCBAABCDEAABCCDDEEEEEDDCCBBAAAAAABBCCCD
Johnny     CSkilift     ABCDEEDCBAAAAAAABBBBBCCCCCDDDDDEEEEEEDCBAABCDEAABCCDDEEEEEDDCCBBAAAAAABBBCCCD
ElizabethMEwe          ABCDEEDCB A A  BB B CCCCCDDDDDEEEEEEDCBAABCDEAABCCDDEEEEEDDCCBBAAAAAABBBCCCD
Sullivan  AGilbert      AB D  DCBAAAAAABBBBBCCCCCDDADDEEBAAEEDCBAABCDEAA BC DDEEEEEDDCCBBAAAAABBACCCD
Judy       JJudy        ABCDEEDCBAAAAA BBBC CC CCD DDDDE D EEDCBAABCDEAABCCDDEEEEEDDCCBBAAAAAABBCCCC
Jamessir   Bensonmum    EBCDAEDCBAAAAACBBBBBCCCCCEDDDDAEEEEBEDCBCABCDDAABRECDDEABCDECCBBAAAABBBBR
```

Figure 9-10. Sample Multiple Choice Test Input Data

```
                          MULTIPLE CHOICE TEST REPORT                        PAGE

                                    FIRST EXAM
                 DEPARTMENT: CSC    COURSE: 101   SECTION: 01

    CLASS AVERAGE GRADE:  68.2
    CORRECT ANSWERS:        ABCDEEDCBAAAAAABBBBBCCCCCDDDDDEEEEEEDCBAABCDEAABBC
                            CDDEEEEEDDCCBBAAAAAABBBCCCD

    ***** STUDENT NAME *****   ***************** STUDENT ANSWERS *****************   GRADE
                                     1    1    2    2    3    3    4    4    5
                                5    0    5    0    5    0    5    0    5    0
    Majorie L Benefieldson     +++++++++++BCDEED+CAAB+DEE+BCA++++++++++++++++++++
                               +++++++++++++++++++++++++++                         79

    Jamessir   Bensonmum       E+++A+++++++++C+++D++++E+++A++++B++++C++++D++++E
                               ++++ABC+E+++++++++B+++****                          75

    Calloway C Caulkenberst    +++ED+EDCB+++++A++++B++++C++++++++++++++++++++++++
                               +++++++++++++++++++++++++                           88

    Elizabeth M Ewe            ++++++++++*+*+**++*+*+++++++++++++++++++++++++++++
                               +++++++++++++++++++++++++                           92

    Sullivan A Gilbert         ++*+**++++++++++++++++D++++A++++B+++++++++++++*++
                               *+++++++++++++++++B++A++++                          87
```

Figure 9-11. Sample Multiple Choice Test Output Data

```
Judy  J  Judy         ++++++++++++++*+++C*++*+++*+++D+*D*+EDCB+ABCDE+A+B
                      +C+D+++E+D+C+B++++A++B++C                              61

Susan  Q  Prettyface  +++BAAB+DEBBBBBCCCCCDDDDDEEEEEDDDDDAB+DEED+BAEEEEE
                      BBBBBAAAAADDDDDCCCCCAAAAA                              8

Johnny  C  Skilift    +++++++++++++++++++++++++++++++++D++++DCBA+BCDEA+BAC+
                      D+E+++D+C+B+A++++B++C++D*                             69

Casey    Strikesout   ************************************************
                      **********************                                0

Thomas  A  Terrific   ++++++++++++++++++++++++++++++++++++++++++++++++++
                      +++++++++++++++++++++++                              100

Wendy  W  Windmill    ++++*+++++++++++A+CDE++++++++++++++++++++++++++++++
                      +++++++++++++++++++*++*+                              91
```

Figure 9-11. (Continued)

9-12 MORE EXERCISES

1. Below you are given a program segment and some input records. At the points specified, what will be the value, in memory, of each substring identified in parts (a) through (e)? Include significant blanks. Assume that external function LENSUB, as described in the chapter, is available.

   (a) TITLE(:4), immediately after execution of the first READ

   (b) TITLE(12:19), immediately before the first execution of statement 300

   (c) WORD(2)(2:), for its first use, immediately before it is printed

   (d) MESAGE(:22), immediately before its first printing

   (e) MESAGE(:), immediately before its second printing

   Program segment:

```
INTEGER  CH, LET, LOC, NWDS, WDS
CHARACTER  ALFABT*26, MESAGE*100, TITLE*25, WORD(10)*10
DATA  ALFABT /'ABCDEFGHIJKLMNOPQRSTUVWXYZ'/
  .
  .
  .
READ *, TITLE
DO 220 CH = 1, 25
    DO 210 LET = 1, 26
        IF (TITLE(CH:CH) .EQ. ALFABT(LET:LET)) THEN
            LOC = LET - 1
            IF (LOC .EQ. 0) LOC = 26
            TITLE(CH:CH) = ALFABT(LOC:LOC)
            GO TO 220
        ENDIF
210     CONTINUE
220 CONTINUE
300     READ *, NWDS
        IF (NWDS .LE. 0) GO TO 399
        DO 320 WDS = 1, NWDS
        READ *, WORD(WDS)
        DO 310 CH = 1, 10
            DO 305 LET = 1, 26
                IF (WORD(WDS)(CH:CH) .EQ. ALFABT(LET:LET)) THEN
                    LOC = LET + 1
                    IF (LOC .EQ. 27) LOC = 1
                    WORD(WDS)(CH:CH) = ALFABT(LOC:LOC)
                    GO TO 310
```

```
                     ENDIF
305              CONTINUE
310           CONTINUE
320        CONTINUE
           PRINT *, TITLE
           MESAGE = WORD(1)(:LENSUB(WORD(1))) //
      :              WORD(2)(:LENSUB(WORD(2))) //
      :              WORD(3)(:LENSUB(WORD(3))) //
      :              WORD(4)(:LENSUB(WORD(4))) //
      :              WORD(5)(:LENSUB(WORD(5))) //
      :              WORD(6)(:LENSUB(WORD(6))) //
      :              WORD(7)(:LENSUB(WORD(7))) //
      :              WORD(8)(:LENSUB(WORD(8))) //
      :              WORD(9)(:LENSUB(WORD(9))) //
      :              WORD(10)(:LENSUB(WORD(10)))
           PRINT *, MESAGE
           GO TO 300
399 STOP
    END
```

Input records (values begin in column 1):

```
'TPNF DPEFE DMJDIFT: '
4
'ADSSDQ'
'KZSD'
'SGZM'
'MDUDQ'
7
'SHLD'
'ZMC'
'SHCD'
'VZHS'
'END'
'MN'
'NMD'
-999
```

2. Given the following program segment and input records, present a complete layout of the actual results that will be printed when the program segment is executed with the data.

Program segment:

```
      INTEGER   ITEM, LENFNM, LENFVR
      CHARACTER FAVNAM(3)*10, FNAME*11, FRSLIN*60, FVRITS(4)*20,
     :          SECLIN*29, SEX*6
      DATA   FRSLIN /
     :       'Person-name''s favorite food is kind-of-food. ' /,
     :       SECLIN /
     :       'Among h-- other favorites are' /,
     :       FAVNAM /
     :       'color.....', 'sport.....', 'holiday...' /
     .
     .
     .
100 FORMAT (A11, 1X, A6, 2X, A20, /, 3A20)
```

```
900 FORMAT (/'0', A, /)
920 FORMAT (' ', T7, A, A)
        .
        .
        .
210     READ (*, 100, END=299) FNAME, SEX, FVRITS
        LENFNM = INDEX(FNAME, ' ') - 1
        IF (LENFNM .LT. 0) LENFNM = LEN(FNAME)
        FRSLIN(:13) = FNAME(1:LENFNM) // '''s'
        LENFVR = INDEX(FVRITS(1), ' ') - 2
        IF (LENFVR .LT. 0) LENFVR = LEN(FVRITS(1))
        FRSLIN(32:) = FVRITS(1)(1:LENFVR) // '.'
        IF (SEX(1:1) .EQ. 'M' .OR. SEX(1:1) .EQ. 'm') THEN
           SECLIN(8:9) = 'is'
        ELSE
           SECLIN(8:9) = 'er'
        ENDIF
        WRITE (*, 900) FRSLIN, SECLIN
        DO 230 ITEM = 2, 4
           WRITE (*, 920) FAVNAM(ITEM-1), FVRITS(ITEM)
230     CONTINUE
        GO TO 210
299     STOP
        END
```

Input records (values begin in column 1):

```
Helen       female   fried okra
green                sawing logs        Halloween
Joya        female   tacos
orange               tennis             St. Valentine's day
Julie       female   french fries
yellow               football           Christmas
Danny       male     ribs
blue                 hunting            Christmas
Amy         female   turkey
blue                 baseball           Christmas
```

3.   Plan and write a complete Fortran program that will take a given set of student information records, like those in Figure 9-1, and perform an indirect sort by student name. The sort is not, however, to be limited to student last name; it should be performed in such a way that the three different but very similar names,

```
John      Quincy   Adams
Johnny    Apple    Adams
John               Adams
```

occur in the proper sorted order. This means that there are three sort keys, and that the file has to be sorted on each key. One approach is to perform the sort procedure completely for each sort key, beginning with the least significant—in this case, the middle name. Create your own input data file of 10 to 100 records for this exercise using the record description in Figure 9-1.

4.   Plan and write a complete Fortran program to read and print a paragraph of text and then compute and print the frequencies of occurrence of letters in the paragraph. Treat lowercase and uppercase as the same; that is, "A" and "a" represent the same letter. Do not count numeric and special characters. Your program should continue to process paragraphs in this way until a blank input line is read in. Then it should print the overall average frequency of occurrence for each letter.

5. Plan and write a complete Fortran program to read and print a page of text and then compute and print the frequencies of occurrence of individual words on the page. For this purpose, a word is any sequential group of one or more characters that contains only alphabetic letters and is separated from any other such group by at least one blank character. As in Exercise 4, treat lowercase and uppercase letters as the same. Your program should continue to process pages in this manner until a blank input line is read in. Then it should print the overall average frequency of occurrence for each word.

6. A "Big City" TV station has three special phone numbers: 932-6397, 932-8437, and 977-6787. These numbers can be translated—by using the letters on the phone dial—into 932-NEWS, WEATHER, and 9SPORTS; they are used in these forms to allow people to call in for the latest news, weather, and sports summaries. Phone numbers such as these, that spell out familiar words, are used in a variety of commercial and social situations to make it easier for people to place phone calls. Your task, for this exercise, is to plan and write a complete Fortran program that will take a given phone number of the form

```
eee-dddd
```

and find all of the corresponding phone numbers that have the form

```
eee-llll
```

where eee represents the "exchange" digits that are to remain constant, dddd represents numeric digits, and llll represents letters that correspond to the digits.

Since the exchange digits remain constant, you need only find all of the four-character "words" that can be derived from the other four digits. One partial set of printed results could be, for instance,

```
The last four digits of the phone number 932-6397 can be
expressed as MDWP, MDWR, ..., NEWS, ..., OFYR, and OFYS.
```

Chapter

10

Multidimensional Arrays

The array data structure exists not only in one-dimensional form but also in two-dimensional, three-dimensional, and up to seven-dimensional form. Primarily, the forms differ in the number of subscript expressions required to specify an element location. Whereas a one-dimensional array element name requires one subscript expression, a two-dimensional array element name must have two subscript expressions. Similarly, a three-dimensional array element name has to have three subscript expressions, and so on.

The rationale for multidimensional arrays is similar to that for one-dimensional arrays as described in Section 8-1. As a matter of fact, all the concepts covered in Chapter 8, extended in minor ways, apply to multidimensional arrays. The purpose of this chapter is to present the extensions that are necessary to give you an understanding of two-dimensional arrays and a fair amount of insight into three- and higher-dimensional arrays.

10-1 TWO-DIMENSIONAL ARRAYS

Whereas a one-dimensional array can be looked upon as a single column of values, a two-dimensional array can be viewed as a table that contains several columns of values. Specifically, consider the following example.

The merchandise inventory of a company can be represented by a listing of the on-hand quantity of items for sale together with the cost of each item. Assume that a small company sells 10 different items and has three warehouses for storing quantities of the items until they are sold. Figure 10-1 depicts a table that might be used by this company to keep track of its inventory on a periodic basis.

Merchandise Inventory
Date: MM/DD/YY

Item	Units on Hand			Cost
Number	Warehouse 1	Warehouse 2	Warehouse 3	per Unit

(a)

Merchandise Inventory
Date: MM/DD/YY

Item	Units on Hand			Cost
Number	Warehouse 1	Warehouse 2	Warehouse 3	per Unit
101	100	200	300	10.00
102	1000	1000	0	1.00
103	500	400	450	5.00
104	200	200	200	5.00
105	0	0	10	200.00
106	900	1000	1000	4.00
107	400	450	550	6.00
108	50	100	150	5.00
109	40	30	20	50.00
110	300	310	100	7.00

(b)

Figure 10-1. An Example Inventory Table

For discussion purposes, the table is shown in two forms. The first form, containing no data, clearly describes the table organization as well as its contents by name. The second form, in which the data are included, represents a specific use of the table wherein corresponding sets of actual item numbers, units on hand, and costs are recorded. It is easy to see, from this form, that the table not only contains columns whose contents are identified by the column headings, but it also contains rows. Furthermore, although the rows are not identified by row headings, they are related to each other in that each corresponds to one of the items in the inventory. Tables always consist of rows and columns.

A third form of the table, shown in Figure 10-2, comprises only the recorded data and depicts an appropriate arrangement of the data for input into the computer and storage in the computer's memory. The computer, then, must have some means by which to refer to each individual value in the table.

101	100	200	300	10.00
102	1000	1000	0	1.00
103	500	400	450	5.00
104	200	200	200	5.00
105	0	0	10	200.00
106	900	1000	1000	4.00
107	400	450	550	6.00
108	50	100	150	5.00
109	40	30	20	50.00
110	300	310	100	7.00

Figure 10-2. The Example Inventory Table: Data Only

You should be able to see that each column of the table could be treated as a one-dimensional array that is given a name based on its column heading. The first four arrays, then, would be integer arrays, and the fifth—the cost per unit array—would be real. Alternatively, the entire table could be treated as a two-dimensional array known completely by only one name such as INVTRY. If this were done, all elements of INVTRY would have to be real because all elements of an array must have the same data type.

Although either of the two treatments above are programmatically acceptable, neither one is best for this table. The table actually contains three different kinds of data: item numbers, units on hand, and costs per unit. An array should be made up of only one kind of data, and should usually consist of all of that kind of data. Therefore, a better approach is to have a one-dimensional integer array of item numbers, a two-dimensional integer array of units on hand, and a one-dimensional array of costs per unit. References to individual item numbers or costs per unit are then made by giving the appropriate array name qualified by one subscript expression enclosed in parentheses. The value of the subscript expression must be equal to one of the row numbers in the original table—a value that corresponds uniquely to one of the items. For example: ITMNBR(3) refers to row 3 and, specifically, item 103; CSPRUT(3) also refers to row 3 and, specifically, the cost per unit value, 5.00, of item 103.

"Units on Hand" can be viewed as a table within the original table. References to individual units on hand are made by giving the appropriate array name qualified by two subscript expressions separated by commas and enclosed in one set of parentheses. The value of the first subscript expression must be equal to one of the row numbers in the original table, corresponding therefore to an item; whereas the value of the second subscript expression must be equal to one of the column numbers of the "Units on Hand" table—in particular, one of the warehouse numbers. For instance: UNITS(ITEM,WHSE), where ITEM=3 and WHSE=2, evaluates to UNITS(3,2), which references row 3 and column 2 or, specifically, the units on hand value 400, which is the number of units of item 103 on hand in warehouse 2.

10-1-1 Declaration

A two-dimensional array, like a one-dimensional array, is declared in a type state-ment or a type−DIMENSION statement combination.

The declarations for the arrays in the inventory example above can be made in at least the following two ways:

```
INTEGER   ITMNBR(10), UNITS(10, 3)
REAL   CSPRUT(10)
```

or

```
INTEGER   MXITMS, MXWHSE
PARAMETER   (MXITMS=10, MXWHSE=3)
INTEGER   ITMNBR(MXITMS), UNITS(MXITMS, MXWHSE)
REAL   CSPRUT(MXITMS)
```

Here are two other two-dimensional array declaration examples:

1. Exercise 7 of Section 6-5 involves computing the weights of five other planets in the solar system for integral Earth weights from 1 to 100 inclusive. The declarations for storing the weights together in memory could be

```
INTEGER   ERTHWT
REAL   OTHPWT(100, 5), WTFACS(5)
```

where ERTHWT represents the Earth weight, OTHPWT is a two-dimensional array of the weights of the five other planets, and WTFACS is an array of the planet weight factors.

2. Each year, taxpayers receive the publication *Federal Income Tax Forms*. It contains four tax tables of varying sizes that are designated Tax Table A, Tax Table B, Tax Table C, and Tax Table D. Each of these tables has the same basic layout, something like this:

```
If Form 1040,        And the total number
  line XX,           of exemptions claimed
    is—                on line X is—
          But         1     2     3     . . .
          not
Over      Over              your tax is
XXXXX     XXXXX       XXXX  XXXX  XXXX    . . .
  .         .           .     .     .     . . .
  .         .           .     .     .     . . .
  .         .           .     .     .     . . .
XXXXX     XXXXX       XXXX  XXXX  XXXX    . . .
```

Actually, each of these tables consists of two kinds of data. The two leftmost columns are made up of rows of income ranges—lower and upper values; the rest of the columns contain the actual taxes due. The number of tax columns varies from table to table depending on the different numbers of exemptions allowed. The groups of Xs represent whole-dollar amounts.

Since the tables contain two kinds of data, they should each be broken into two tables. If they used Fortran for programming, the IRS might make array declarations something like the following to store the tax tables for checking income tax returns by computer.

```
INTEGER  NIRA, NEXA, NIRB, NEXB, NIRC, NEXC, NIRD, NEXD
PARAMETER  (NIRA=334, NEXA=3, NIRB=692, NEXB=8,
:           NIRC=336, NEXC=3, NIRD=344, NEXD=8)
INTEGER  IRTABA(NIRA, 2), TXTABA(NIRA, NEXA),
:        IRTABB(NIRB, 2), TXTABB(NIRB, NEXB),
:        IRTABC(NIRC, 2), TXTABC(NIRC, NEXC),
:        IRTABD(NIRD, 2), TXTABD(NIRD, NEXD)
```

In the first INTEGER statement, NIRA represents the "Number of Income Ranges in Table A," and NEXA stands for "Number of Exemptions in Table A." The remaining names denote corresponding items for Tables B, C, and D. In the second INTEGER statement, array name IRTABA represents "Income Ranges in Table A," and array name TXTABA designates "Taxes in Table A." The other array names, similarly, stand for income ranges and taxes in Tables B, C, and D. For this example, the given order of names in the statements is more logical than our usual alphabetical ordering.

10-1-2 *Input and Output*

The reading and writing operations for two-dimensional arrays are very similar to the ones for one-dimensional arrays. You must be careful, however, to make sure that your program handles the row and column subscript expressions properly. It will help if you keep in mind that the row subscript expression can be said to correspond functionally to the single subscript expression of one-dimensional arrays.

When values are read into a one-dimensional array they are stored in memory one right after another as if in a column. Similarly, when values are read into a two-dimensional array, they are stored in memory one right after another column by column. This is called column-major ordering. Let arn represent a two-dimensional array name and let locer and locec denote location expressions for rows and columns—the subscript expressions used to identify the location of a particular element in a two-dimensional array. Then the reference without subscript,

```
arn(locer, locec)
```

in an iolist, identifies one array element to be read in or written out. As with one-dimensional arrays, the reference without subscript,

```
arn
```

in an iolist, indicates that all possible array elements—identified in the array dimension declaration—are to be read in or written out. Point of emphasis: If the latter form is used in an iolist, the reading in or writing out will be in a column-by-column fashion because Fortran uses column-major ordering.

With reference back to the merchandise inventory example, and with the input data in the form depicted in Figure 10-2, where one line of data corresponds to one input record, consider the following program segment:

```
INTEGER   ITMNBR(10),  UNITS(10,  3)
REAL   CSPRUT(10)
   .
   .
   .
DO 220 ITEM = 1,  10
     READ *,  ITMNBR(ITEM),  UNITS(ITEM,  1),  UNITS(ITEM,  2),
   :            UNITS(ITEM,  3),  CSPRUT(ITEM)
     PRINT *,  ITMNBR(ITEM),  UNITS(ITEM,  1),  UNITS(ITEM,  2),
   :            UNITS(ITEM,  3),  CSPRUT(ITEM)
220 CONTINUE
```

This segment, which uses the single array element reference form for the one-dimensional and two-dimensional arrays, will cause the data to be read into memory and stored in the same way that it appears in Figure 10-2. It will then cause the data to be printed that same way. In contrast, if the action sequence looked like this,

```
READ *,  ITMNBR,  UNITS,  CSPRUT
PRINT *,  ITMNBR,  UNITS,  CSPRUT
```

the data would not be read in, stored, or printed out properly. Think it over. This READ statement says: "Read values into ALL the elements of ITMNBR; THEN read values into ALL the elements of UNITS; THEN read values into ALL the elements of CSPRUT." Therefore, the first 10 input values encountered will be read into array ITMNBR—an error already, so there is no need to go any further with the read operation. The PRINT statement can be interpreted similarly.

The sequence above will yield correct results if the input data is rearranged to fit the i/o statement interpretations. Here is an arrangement that will work:

```
  101    102   103   104    105   106   107   108    109   110
  100   1000   500   200      0   900   400    50     40   300
  200   1000   400   200      0  1000   450   100     30   310
  300      0   450   200     10  1000   550   150     20   100
10.00   1.00  5.00  5.00  200.00  4.00  6.00  5.00  50.00  7.00
```

By comparing the arrangement above to the one in Figure 10-2 you can see that the rows and columns have been interchanged. In other words, the READ and PRINT operations on entire arrays, like the most recent one above, are column-wise operations (i.e., they process i/o data column by column). Remember, Fortran stores array data in column-major order. This is unfortunate because it means that if you wish to refer to a two-dimensional or higher-order array as an entity in an i/o statement, you will have to arrange the data in a form that you are not used to—one other than the ordinary tabular form. Fortunately, other modern programming languages use row-major ordering that corresponds to the common tabular form. And fortunately, there is a convenient solution in Fortran: the implied-DO.

I introduce you to the implied-DO for two-dimensional arrays by incorporating one into the first merchandise inventory i/o example above. Here is the program segment rewritten in a more general way with implied-Dos:

```
INTEGER  MXITMS, MXWHSE
PARAMETER  (MXITMS=10, MXWHSE=3)
INTEGER  ITEM, ITMNBR(MXITMS), UNITS(MXITMS, MXWHSE),
:        WHSE
REAL  CSPRUT(MXITMS)
.

.

.
DO 220 ITEM = 1, MXITMS
    READ *, ITNMBR(ITEM),
:          (UNITS(ITEM, WHSE), WHSE = 1, MXWHSE),
:          CSPRUT(ITEM)
    PRINT * ITNMBR(ITEM),
:          (UNITS(ITEM, WHSE), WHSE = 1, MXWHSE),
:          CSPRUT(ITEM)
220 CONTINUE
```

The implied-DO in the READ and PRINT statements above is

```
(UNITS(ITEM, WHSE), WHSE = 1, MXWHSE)
```

It specifies the immediate reading or printing of the three units' on-hand values that are in one of the rows of the table. The first subscript expression, ITEM, is also the DO-variable of the DO statement in both sequences; therefore, its values are established in the DO-loop. Each implied-DO can be said to be nested within a DO-loop; each is completely executed every time the DO-loop range is executed.

The implied-DO has the form

```
(arn(locvr, locvc), locvc = aec1, aec2, aec3)
```

where arn is the array name; locvr and locvc are the respective location or subscript variables for the row and column; and aec1, aec2, and aec3 are the implied-DO parameter expressions for establishing the initial, test, and increment values of the implied-DO control variable and column location variable locvc. The value of the row location variable, locvr, must be defined prior to the statement in which this form of the implied-DO appears. Furthermore, this form of the implied-DO can be referred to as a row-wise form; that is, the elements are addressed row by row, and an i/o operation that uses this form will occur in a row-by-row fashion.

A slight modification of the above yields another row-wise form that looks like this:

```
((arn(locvr, locvc), locvc = aec1, aec2, aec3),
                 locvr = aer1, aer2, aer3)
```

This form contains nested implied-DOs. The DO-parameter expressions for the row location variable are defined in the outer implied-DO. This form is interpreted in a manner very similar to the previous one, but it is not appropriate for use with the inventory data, as is, because it implies a continuous reading or writing of the elements of one array, whereas each input record of the inventory data contains elements of three different arrays. However, by using the general implied-DO list form,

```
(idlist, locv = ae1, ae2, ae3)
```

which was given in Section 8-4, it is possible to devise nested implied-DOs to perform the reading and writing of the inventory data. Recall that idlist is an input/output list that may, itself, contain implied-DO lists. Thus nested implied-DOs are intrinsic to this general form and, in fact, both of the previous row-wise forms are subsets of the general form. This information, then, allows the action statements in the most recent program sequence above to be recoded as follows:

```
READ *,   (ITMNBR(ITEM),
  :          (UNITS(ITEM, WHSE), WHSE = 1, MXWHSE),
  :          CSPRUT(ITEM), ITEM = 1, MXITMS)
PRINT *,  (ITMNBR(ITEM),
  :          (UNITS(ITEM, WHSE), WHSE = 1, MXWHSE),
  :          CSPRUT(ITEM), ITEM = 1, MXITMS)
```

In this sequence we still have row-wise read and print operations as before, but the DO statement of the previous sequence has been replaced by implied-DOs. The primary difference between the previous sequence and the one above is in the number of times the READ and PRINT statements are executed. In the previous sequence, the READ and PRINT statements are executed once for each row (item) of data, whereas in the sequence above, the READ and PRINT statements are each executed once—period.

As far as Fortran is concerned, there is no requirement that i/o be performed in a row-wise fashion. The following two implied-DO forms, therefore, are for column-wise i/o:

```
(arn(locvr, locvc), locvr = aer1, aer2, aer3)
```

and

```
((arn(locvr, locvc), locvr = aer1, aer2, aer3),
              locvc = aec1, aec2, aec3)
```

Compare them carefully with the row-wise forms and keep in mind that column-wise i/o requires the data to be in column-wise order.

As you can see, the implied-DO is extremely flexible; you just have to study it and practice with it. To help you study and practice, consider some i/o for the example problems begun in Section 10-1-1.

1. Once the other planet weights of the interplanetary weight problem have been computed and stored, they can then be printed (see the layout in Exercise 7 of Section 6-5). The relevant program statements could be the following:

```
      INTEGER   ERTHWT, HIEWT, INCEWT, IPWTOF, LOWEWT, PLANET
      REAL   OTHPWT(100, 5), WTFACS(5)
      PARAMETER   (IPWTOF=6)
      .
      .
      .
950 FORMAT (' ', 1X, I3, 2X, 5(3X, F6.2))
      .
      .   {Computations; printing of chart headings}
      .
      DO 520 ERTHWT = LOWEWT, HIEWT, INCEWT
          WRITE (IPWTOF, 950) ERTHWT,
      :          (OTHPWT(ERTHWT, PLANET), PLANET = 1, 5)
520 CONTINUE
```

Alternatively, the DO-loop can be replaced completely by this one statement,

```
      WRITE (IPWTOF, 950) (ERTHWT,
      :      ((OTHPWT(ERTHWT, PLANET), PLANET = 1, 5),
      :      ERTHWT = LOWEWT, HIEWT, INCEWT)
```

provided that the FORMAT statement is rewritten like this:

```
950 FORMAT (' ', 1X, I3, 5X, F6.2, 3X, F6.2, 3X, F6.2,
      :          3X, F6.2, 3X, F6.2)
```

It is up to you to decide which alternative suits your situation best. Remember, the primary difference between the two is that the WRITE statement is executed once for each row of the table in the first segment, and precisely once in the second.

2. Given, in Section 10-1-1, the approximate layout for the income tax tables A through D, and assuming that the tables are entered one right after another, the following program segment can be used for reading them into memory:

```
      INTEGER   NIRA, NEXA, NIRB, NEXB, NIRC, NEXC, NIRD, NEXD,
      :          EXEMP, RANGE
      PARAMETER   (NIRA=334, NEXA=3, NIRB=692, NEXB=8,
      :          NIRC=336, NEXC=3, NIRD=344, NEXD=8)
      INTEGER   IRTABA(NIRA, 2), TXTABA(NIRA, NEXA),
      :          IRTABB(NIRB, 2), TXTABB(NIRB, NEXB),
      :          IRTABC(NIRC, 2), TXTABC(NIRC, NEXC),
      :          IRTABD(NIRD, 2), TXTABD(NIRD, NEXD)
      .
      .
      .
      READ *, (IRTABA(RANGE, 1), IRTABA(RANGE, 2),
      :          (TXTABA(RANGE, EXEMP), EXEMP = 1, NEXA),
      :          RANGE = 1, NIRA)
      READ *, (IRTABB(RANGE, 1), IRTABB(RANGE, 2),
      :          (TXTABB(RANGE, EXEMP), EXEMP = 1, NEXB),
      :          RANGE = 1, NIRB)
      READ *, (IRTABC(RANGE, 1), IRTABC(RANGE, 2),
      :          (TXTABC(RANGE, EXEMP), EXEMP = 1, NEXC),
      :          RANGE = 1, NIRC)
      READ *, (IRTABD(RANGE, 1), IRTABD(RANGE, 2),
      :          (TXTABD(RANGE, EXEMP), EXEMP = 1, NEXD),
      :          RANGE = 1, NIRD)
```

10-1-3 Assignment and Comparison

The two-dimensional array element reference of the form

```
arn(locer, locec)
```

can be used anywhere in a program where a scalar variable or one-dimensional array element reference can be used. In the reference, or array element name, arn is the array name, locer is the location expression for rows, and locec is the location expression for columns. A two-dimensional array element name refers to one value just as a variable or a one-dimensional array element name refers to one value. Therefore, the array element names

```
UNITS (ITEM, 2)
UNITS (ITEM, WHSE)
OTHPWT (NEXTWT, PLANET)
TXTABA (RANGE, EXEMP)
```

each refer to one value at a time and each can appear in arithmetic expressions of assignment statements and IF statements. They can also appear to the left of the = sign in assignment statements.

To exemplify: Once the merchandise inventory data of Figure 10-2 is in memory, the individual elements of the UNITS, ITMNBR, and CSPRUT arrays can be utilized to provide answers to any number of questions that might be asked about the inventory. One worthwhile question to answer is: What is the total cost of the inventory? The cost can be determined by multiplying each unit's on-hand value by its corresponding cost per unit value, and then adding the resulting values together. This is simply a summing process of the type we have considered many times before, except that it involves array elements rather than scalar variables. Here is a program segment that uses the variable name TCSINV in determining the total cost of the inventory.

```
INTEGER  MXITMS, MXWHSE
PARAMETER   (MXITMS=10, MXWHSE=3)
INTEGER   ITEM, ITMNBR(MXITMS), UNITS(MXITMS, MXWHSE)
REAL   CSPRUT(MXITMS), TCSINV
    .
    ·   {Row-wise input statements previously given}
    .
TCSINV = 0.0
DO 320 WHSE = 1, MXWHSE
    DO 310 ITEM = 1, MXITMS
        TCSINV = TCSINV + UNITS(ITEM, WHSE) * CSPRUT(ITEM)
310    CONTINUE
320 CONTINUE
```

The outer DO-loop, as you can see, is related to the warehouses, or the columns, of the UNITS array. The inner DO-loop is related to the items, or the rows, of the UNITS and CSPRUTS arrays. The interpretation of this segment can be stated as follows.

1.   Initialize TCSINV to zero.

2.   Initialize WHSE to 1 and begin one execution of the range of the DO-320 loop.

3.   Initialize ITEM to 1 and execute the range of the DO-310 loop until a normal exit from the DO-310 loop occurs.

4.   Complete one execution of the range of the DO-320 loop.

5.   Increment WHSE by 1 and repeat steps 3 through 5 until a normal exit from the DO-320 loop occurs.

If you will use this interpretation to trace through the program segment with the given data, you will see that the final value of TCSINV is 50720.00, the total inventory cost.

   A few minor modifications to the code will allow the costs of the inventory in each individual warehouse to be determined. Let CSWINV be an array of costs of warehouse inventory. Leaving the declarations to you, I write the modified segment below.

```
      TCSINV = 0.0
      DO 320 WHSE = 1, MXWHSE
         CSWINV(WHSE) = 0.0
         DO 310 ITEM = 1, MXITMS
            CSWINV(WHSE) = CSWINV(WHSE) +
      :                         UNITS(ITEM, WHSE) * CSPRUT(ITEM)
310      CONTINUE
         TCSINV = TCSINV + CSWINV(WHSE)
320   CONTINUE
      PRINT *, (CSWINV(WHSE), WHSE = 1, MXWHSE)
      PRINT *, TCSINV
```

The printed results will look something like this:

```
15850.00    16870.00    18000.00
50720.00
```

You should study the action segment and trace it with the data. For further study, consider again the interplanetary weight and income tax problems.

   The program segment below applies the weighting factors to the earth weights to produce the two-dimensional array of interplanetary weights. It assumes that the lower and upper Earth weight bounds, LOWEWT and HIEWT, and the increment on Earth weight, INCEWT, have already been read in and checked.

```
      INTEGER ERTHWT, HIEWT, INCEWT, IPWTOF, LOWEWT, PLANET
      REAL    OTHPWT(100, 5), WTFACS(5)
      PARAMETER  (IPWTOF=6)
      DATA   WTFACS /
      :      0.38, 0.91, 0.38, 2.64, 1.13 /
      .
      .
      .
```

```
         DO 430 PLANET = 1, 5
            DO 420 ERTHWT = LOWEWT, HIEWT, INCEWT
               OTHPWT(ERTHWT, PLANET) = ERTHWT * WTFACS(PLANET)
   420      CONTINUE
   430 CONTINUE
```

Observe that the array element name for the other planet weights, OTHPWT(ERTHWT,PLANET), appears on the left side of an assignment statement, indicating that values are being assigned to the array elements. Also notice that nested DO-loops are used again to step through the array elements; they are arranged so that the operations will be performed in a column-wise fashion. Since array elements are stored in this manner by the Fortran processor, operations specified in this fashion are more efficient than row-wise operations; the opposite is true for some other well-known programming languages.

One more item worthy of mentioning here is that the statement numbers on the nested DO-loop terminals are in numerical order on this and all other program segments. It is easy to make nested DO-loop terminal statement numbers occur in order; just reference larger statement numbers in the outer-DO statements and smaller ones in the inner-DO statements. Be sure, though, to choose statement numbers that are larger than any that have been used in the code up to that point. Now to the income tax example.

Once the income tax tables are in memory, they can be used to check individual income tax returns. To check one return, the filing status, number of exemptions, and taxable income must also be in memory. The first two of these might be read in as input data and the last one might be read in as input data or computed internally. The filing status is used to select the proper table and the other two items are used to locate the taxes due.

Let STATUS denote the filing status; further, let it be 1 for Tax Table A, 2 for Tax Table B, 3 for Tax Table C, and 4 for Tax Table D. Let NMEXEM designate the number of exemptions, and TAXINC stand for taxable income. Assume that a value for each of these variables has been read in and checked. Also, let TAXDUE represent the taxes due. The program segment, then, for the table-lookup process of finding the tax due for one particular tax return is shown below. It involves a linear search through the appropriate table to find the proper range.

```
         INTEGER  NIRA, NEXA, NIRB, NEXB, NIRC, NEXC, NIRD, NEXD,
        :         EXEMP, NMEXEM, RANGE, STATUS, TAXINC
         PARAMETER  (NIRA=334, NEXA=3, NIRB=692, NEXB=8,
        :            NIRC=336, NEXC=3, NIRD=344, NEXD=8)
         INTEGER  IRTABA(NIRA, 2), TXTABA(NIRA, NEXA),
        :         IRTABB(NIRB, 2), TXTABB(NIRB, NEXB),
        :         IRTABC(NIRC, 2), TXTABC(NIRC, NEXC),
        :         IRTABD(NIRD, 2), TXTABD(NIRD, NEXD)
        ·     {Input of tables and other data, including
        ·      STATUS and NMEXEM, occurs here}
        ·
         GO TO (260, 270, 280, 290), STATUS
   *         Table A range search and tax lookup
   260      DO 264 RANGE = 1, NIRA
```

```
          IF (TAXINC .LE. IRTABA(RANGE, 2)) THEN
              IF (TAXINC .GT. IRTABA(RANGE, 1)) THEN
                  TAXDUE = TXTABA(RANGE, NMEXEM)
                  GO TO 300
              ENDIF
          ENDIF
  264   CONTINUE
*       Table B range search and tax lookup
  270   DO 274 RANGE = 1, NIRB
          IF (TAXINC .LE. IRTABB(RANGE, 2)) THEN
              IF (TAXINC .GT. IRTABB(RANGE, 1)) THEN
                  TAXDUE = TXTABB(RANGE, NMEXEM)
                  GO TO 300
              ENDIF
          ENDIF
  274   CONTINUE
          .
    .   {Similar sequences for Tables C & D}
          .
  300 {Tax due determined}
```

In this segment the elements of the two-dimensional arrays IRTABA, IRTABB, IRTABC, and IRTABD, are referenced in IF statements. This allows the taxable income to be compared to the upper and lower income ranges so that the proper range, or tax bracket, can be located. When it is located, the search need not proceed further; so the GO TO 300 statements are used to effect the search termination. The way the code is written assumes that a proper range is found.

10-1-4 Initialization

The elements of two-dimensional arrays can be initialized with executable statements or the DATA statement. The former is preferable if, as is often the case, the element values will be changed by later executable statements. To illustrate: If the elements of a two-dimensional array named ACCUM are to be equal to zero initially and then be assigned other values later, a sequence such as the following should be used for the initialization:

```
      INTEGER  COL, ROW
      REAL   ACCUM(100,5)
        .
        .
      DO 230 COL = 1, 5
          DO 220 ROW = 1, 100
              ACCUM(ROW, COL) = 0.0
  220     CONTINUE
  230 CONTINUE
```

In contrast, if the elements of a two-dimensional array FACTOR are to be initialized with factor values that do not change during execution, a DATA statement such as the one in the following sequence can be employed for the initialization.

```
      REAL  FACTOR(3, 2)
      DATA  FACTOR /
    :       0.1, 0.2, 0.3, 0.4, 0.5, 0.6 /
```

Or, the implied-DO can be made a part of the DATA statement, in the following way, to yield identical results.

```
INTEGER   COL,  ROW
REAL    FACTOR(3,  2)
DATA    ((FACTOR(ROW,  COL),  ROW = 1,  3),  COL = 1,  2) /
:          0.1,  0.2,  0.3,  0.4,  0.5,  0.6 /
```

Or, the row-wise form of the implied-DO can be applied to accomplish the same purpose, like this:

```
INTEGER   COL,  ROW
REAL    FACTOR(3,  2)
DATA    ((FACTOR(ROW,  COL),  COL = 1,  2),  ROW = 1,  3) /
:          0.1,  0.4,  0.2,  0.5,  0.3,  0.6 /
```

Notice the changes that are needed to produce the row-wise form, not only in the implied-DO itself but also in the value list.

10-1-5   Other Names for Arrays

Two-dimensional arrays are also called *rectangular arrays* and *matrices*. Since these terms are mathematical, however, and tend to cloud the issue for many learners, I avoided mentioning them until now. For the same reason I also delayed mentioning that one-dimensional arrays are often referred to as *vectors*. Nevertheless, in the section just completed I illustrated such seemingly complex operations as the addition and multiplication of matrix and vector elements; furthermore, I hesitate no longer to use the terms freely. If you understand the processes described in the preceding and later sections of this chapter, you will have no difficulty developing programs that incorporate vector (one-dimensional array) and matrix (two-dimensional array) operations. Study the processes—making computer runs when necessary—until you understand them well.

10-1-6   Exercises

1. Discuss the correctness of the following code sequence. What will occur during execution?

```
INTEGER   ITEM,  UNITS(10,  3),  WHSE




DO 220 ITEM = 1,  3
    DO 210 WHSE = 1,  10
        UNITS(ITEM,  WHSE)  = 0
210     CONTINUE
220 CONTINUE
```

2. After the following program segment has been executed, what will be the value of each element in array MATRIX?

```
INTEGER  COL, ROW
REAL  MATRIX(2, 3)
   .
   .
   .
DO 220  COL = 1, 3
   DO 210 ROW = 1, 2
      MATRIX(ROW, COL) = 2 * ROW + 3 * COL
210    CONTINUE
220 CONTINUE
```

Are the assignment operations in this segment accomplished in row-wise or column-wise order?

3. Rewrite each of the following, individually, as one statement using nested implied-DOs in the i/o lists. Assume that all items are of integer data type, and that NA and ND are properly defined. State whether each i/o operation is performed row-wise or column-wise on the two-dimensional arrays.

```
(a)  READ *, GAMMA(1, 1), GAMMA(1, 2), GAMMA(1, 3),
     :        GAMMA(1, 4), GAMMA(2, 1), GAMMA(2, 2),
     :        GAMMA(2, 3), GAMMA(2, 4)
(b)  READ *, DELTA(1), BETA(1, 1), BETA(2, 1),
     :        DELTA(2), BETA(1, 2), BETA(2, 2)
(c)      DO 350 DOWN =1, ND
            PRINT *, (GAMMA(DOWN, ACROSS), ACROSS =1, NA)
         350 CONTINUE
(d)  PRINT *, BETA(1, 1), BETA(1, 2), DELTA(1),
     :        BETA(2, 1), BETA(2, 2), DELTA(2)
```

4. Given this program segment:

```
INTEGER  KIND, SWEETS
CHARACTER  PIE(6)*6, CAKE(6, 2)*6
PARAMETER  (SWEETS=5)
   .
   .
   .
100 FORMAT (A6)
   .
   .
   .
DO 310 KIND = 1, 6, 2
   READ (SWEETS, 100) PIE(KIND), CAKE(KIND, 2)
310 CONTINUE
```

and this set of data in the input file (each line beginning in column 1):

```
Apple
Banana
Coconut
Datenut
Egg Custard
Fig
Gingerbread
Huckleberry
```

state the values of each element of the arrays PIE and CAKE following the complete execution of the DO-loop. Give an answer for each array element.

5. Plan and write a complete Fortran program to keep track of the merchandise inventory of a company. Use the inventory information given in this chapter beginning in Section 10-1, including the data in Figures 10-1 and 10-2, as a beginning point. Incorporate the following specifications.

Each item should be identified by a 10-character name as well as by an item number. The input data should be expanded to a maximum number of items larger than 10, and the program should handle the maximum. The program should read, store, and display (print)—with titles and headings—the initial inventory data: that is, item numbers and names, units on hand, and costs per unit. Concurrently, it should also display, appropriately, the total cost of each item, the total cost of all items in each warehouse, and the overall cost of the inventory. As much of the inventory as possible should be displayed on one terminal screen or page. Then, interactively if possible, the program should read batches of updating information and update the inventory appropriately. It should print the total results again after each batch of updating information has been processed. An "updating input record" contains an item number, a warehouse number, and a positive or negative amount to be added to the appropriate units on hand. The end of a batch is designated by a negative number appearing in the item number field of an update record. The end of all data occurs whenever a negative number appears in the item number field of each of two successive update records. After all the batches have been processed, the program should display a final inventory; again, complete results.

6. Plan and write a complete Fortran program that will take, as input, the interest rate of an investment and then compute, store, and finally print several useful investment factors for investment periods from 1 to 48 inclusive, assuming that the interest is compounded each period. The useful factors are the present worth factor (PWF), the future worth factor (FWF), the sinking fund factor (SFF), and the capital recovery factor (CRF).

Letting r be the interest rate and n be the number of periods, the formulas for the factors are as follows.

$$PWF = \frac{1}{(1 + r)^n}$$

$$FWF = (1 + r)^n$$

$$SFF = \frac{r}{(1 + r)^n - 1}$$

$$CRF = \frac{r(1 + r)^n}{(1 + r)^n - 1}$$

For each given interest rate, store the four factors in a two-dimensional double-precision array. Then print the results for that interest rate, including the number of periods, in a tabular fashion. Use interest rates of 10, 15, and 20 percent. Print all factor values to the nearest hundred-thousandth.

7. For this exercise you need to acquire a copy of the IRS publication, *Federal Income Tax Forms*. You are to plan and write a complete Fortran program that computes the income tax and the refund or balance due for a number of income tax returns. The problem is similar to the example initiated in Section 10-1-1.

   Given, as input from an income tax return, a name, address, filing status, number of exemptions, adjusted gross income, and the amount of taxes already paid, the program should locate the income tax in the appropriate tax table, then compute the refund or balance due. Finally, it should print a short understandable report that comprises all the input data and results. To save computer storage and your time, do not store the full-size tax tables; rather, store and use only the portions of the tables that will handle adjusted gross incomes from $19,000 to $20,000 inclusive. Furthermore, allow a maximum of only four exemptions.

   Use a comprehensive set of test input data to check your program. As a part of your program planning, review the descriptions of the income tax example in Sections 10-1-1, 10-1-2, and 10-1-3. Also, become familiar with the process of completing an income tax return as explained in the IRS publication. Learn as much as you can about income tax returns now; it will help you later.

8. Plan and write a complete Fortran program to produce your handwritten initials by means of the line printer. To do this, take a large layout sheet in which the rows and columns are numbered. Write your initials as large as possible on the sheet. Record the row and column number of each location through which your initials pass. These number pairs serve as input to your program. A two-dimensional array of single characters, large enough to hold a full output page of characters, should be established in the program. It should initially be filled with blanks. The program should read in the row−column number pairs of your initials and place an asterisk—or any other character you select—into each of the corresponding positions of the array. Then, it should print the array. You may want to sign-off on all your computer work this way.

9. Plan and write a complete Fortran program to print, via the line printer, a set of X (horizontal) and Y (vertical) axes and a circle on a page. The program will need a two-dimensional array, blanked-out initially, declared with the statement

   ```
   CHARACTER GRAPH(-25:25, -50:50)
   ```

   The axes should be represented by dots which occupy the middle row and middle column of the array. Each should be identified, at its extremes, with an X or a Y as appropriate.

A circle, with centerpoint (c_x, c_y) and radius rad, has the formula

$$\text{rad}^2 = (x - c_x)^2 + (y - c_y)^2$$

Therefore, given rad, c_y, and c_x as input, the values of y can be found from

$$y = \sqrt{\text{rad}^2 - (x - c_x)^2} + c_y$$

for integral values of x that vary from c_x $-$rad to c_x $+$rad. Notice that for all values of x that do not cause the term under the radical to be zero, there are two values of y. Each value of y should be multiplied by the ratio of the vertical-to-horizontal print positions per inch: often 0.6. Call the new value "y-adjusted". All of the nearest-integer values of x- and y-adjusted, then, are column and row positions of the array GRAPH, into which asterisks are to be inserted. Be sure that your program inserts asterisks into valid positions only. When printed, the asterisks in GRAPH form the circle. Do not forget to supply an appropriate title, identifying the circle by its radius and centerpoint at the top of the page.

10. Since Exercises 8 and 9 have to do with using the printer to plot graphs, you might begin to think that the printer can be used to make other graphical plots. Well, you are right; printer plotting is a fairly common computer application that has been done for almost as long as computers have had printers.

Your exercise here is to search the literature for a printer plotting problem to plan and write a complete Fortran program for. To get you started, here are two good references:

Andree, R. V., Andree, J. P., and Andree, D. P. *Computer Programming: Techniques, Analysis, and Mathematics* (Secs. 2-10 and 7-6). Prentice-Hall, Inc. Englewood Cliffs, N. J. 1973.

Maurer, H. A., and Williams, M. R. *A Collection of Programming Problems and Techniques* (Chap. 14). Prentice-Hall, Inc. Englewood Cliffs, N. J. 1972.

11. Plan and write a complete interactive Fortran program (see Exercise 13 of Section 8-8) that allows a person to play the game tick-tack-toe against the computer. Your program should allow the person to select to use Xs or Os and to always make the first mark by specifying row and column. It should then select an appropriate square for its mark. After that, the person and the program should select and mark squares in turn until the game is over. After each pair of marks are made, the program should display the newly marked locations and the current diagram. For instance:

```
Joe placed an X in row 3, column 2.
The computer placed an O in row 2, column 3.
         .   .
   X  .  O  .  X
 . . . . . . . . . . . . . . . .
         .   .
         .  O  .  O
 . . . . . . . . . . . . . . . .
         .   .
         .  X  .
```

At the end of each game, the results of that game as well as all the games played so far by that person should be displayed. For example:

```
Joe placed an X in row 3, column 3 to WIN!
         .   .
   X  .  O  .  X
 . . . . . . . . . . . . . . . .
         .   .
         .  X  .  O
 . . . . . . . . . . . . . . . .
         .   .
   O  .     .  X
Score so far:   Joe        2
                Computer   2
                Draws      2
Joe, would you like to play again (yes or no)?
```

The game should be "friendly" to the person who plays. The program should make certain that it is possible for the person to win, lose, or draw.

12. If you are mathematically adept, you should do this exercise. Expect it to take more time than most, and to reward you accordingly in terms of challenge and learning experience.

Plan and write a complete Fortran program to implement the *least squares* method for fitting a polynomial to a set of x and y data points. The general idea of least squares, which leads to *regression analysis*, is this: Given an observed set of data points that can be plotted on an x- and y-coordinate axis pair, find the polynomial of a given degree that minimizes the squares of the differences between the observed points and corresponding points on the curve. These differences are called *residuals*.

For a polynomial represented by

$$y = a_0 + a_1x + a_2x^2 + \cdots + a_nx^n$$

and a given set of data points,

$$(x_i, y_i), \qquad i = 1, 2, \ldots, m; \quad m > n$$

the $n + 1$ *normal equations* that are used to find the values of the coefficients $a_0, a_1, a_2, \ldots, a_n$, are given by

$$
\begin{array}{ccccccccc}
a_0 n & + & a_1 \sum x_i & + & \cdots & + & a_n \sum x_i^n & = & \sum y_i \\
a_0 \sum x_i & + & a_1 \sum x_i^2 & + & \cdots & + & a_n \sum x_i^{n+1} & = & \sum y_i x_i \\
\vdots & & \vdots & & \vdots & & \vdots & & \vdots \\
a_0 \sum x_i^n & + & \sum x_i^{n+1} & + & \cdots & + & a_n \sum x_i^{2n} & = & \sum y_i x_i^n
\end{array}
$$

where Σ refers to the sum of the identified quantities for $i = 1, 2, \ldots , m$. Once the values of the coefficients are found, the problem is solved. The coefficients can then be used, with values of x, to estimate values of y.

The normal equations above are readily solved if n is fairly small. (For this exercise, limit its value to 3.) Since they consist of a set of $n + 1$ equations in $n + 1$ unknown values, the normal equations can be rewritten in the matrix form

$$
\begin{bmatrix}
n & \sum x_i & \cdots & \sum x_i^n \\
\sum x_i & \sum x_i^2 & \cdots & \sum x_i^{n+1} \\
\vdots & \vdots & \ddots & \vdots \\
\sum x_i^n & \sum x_i^{n+1} & \cdots & \sum x_i^{2n}
\end{bmatrix}
\begin{bmatrix}
a_0 \\
a_1 \\
\vdots \\
a_n
\end{bmatrix}
=
\begin{bmatrix}
\sum y_i \\
\sum y_i x_i \\
\vdots \\
\sum y_i x_i^n
\end{bmatrix}
$$

which can be represented in the more symbolic form,

$$XA = Y$$

To solve the matrix equation above, multiply both sides by the inverse of matrix X, like this:

$$X^{-1}XA = X^{-1}Y$$

which then reduces to this:

$$A = X^{-1}Y$$

Thus the values of the coefficients (the elements of matrix A) can be computed after the matrix X has been inverted. Below is an algorithm you can use for the inversion. It is based on the Gauss−Jordan approach and its efficiency is due to professor Gene Pulley of Texas A&M University, and the late Claude Kelley, as printed in the *Texas A&M University Data Processing Center Newsletter*, vol. X, no. 3, November 1977. It inverts the matrix in place; that is, the original matrix is replaced by its inverse. Because of the complexity of the calculations in a matrix inversion, you should use double precision for the matrix in your Fortran program.

ALGORITHM Matrix-inverse
```
{   Find the inverse of the matrix mat, a
two-dimensional square array of size s x s.   To
facilitate the inversion, mat must have an extra
row and an extra column.   Therefore, it must be
declared with s+1 rows and s+1 columns.}
```

```
c ← s + 1
mat(1, c) ← 1
Do r ← 2 to c by 1
    Do j ← 2 to c by 1
        mat(c, j) ← mat(1, j) / mat(1, 1)
    End Do
    Do i ← 2 to c by 1
        Do j ← 2 to c by 1
            mat(i-1, j-1) ← mat(i, j) -
                            mat(i, 1) * mat(c, j)
        End Do
    End Do
End Do
{Inversion complete}
END
```

For test data, use the following sample set of heights and corresponding weights of male students.

Height, x (Nearest Inch)	Weight, y (Nearest Pound)
67	170
72	210
65	132
67	155
69	156
71	175
72	164
71	180
69	173
67	160

10-2   OTHER MULTIDIMENSIONAL ARRAYS

One- and two-dimensional arrays are sufficient array data structures for most purposes. Occasionally, however, three-dimensional arrays are either needed or convenient. Less frequently, four to seven-dimensional arrays may be called for. The higher-dimensional array forms are merely extensions of the one- and two-dimensional array forms; one additional subscript expression is required for each additional dimension. For purposes of execution efficiency, as well as understandability, arrays of the lowest possible number of dimensions should be employed. Try to stay with two dimensions or less.

In common with one and two-dimensional arrays, three and higher-dimensional arrays are declared by means of type statements or type-DIMENSION statement combinations; read and written individually, or via implied-DO lists; operated on in assignment statements; compared by means of IF statements; and initialized in assignment or DATA statements. The primary feature that distinguishes the arrays of one dimension from those of another is the number of subscript expressions; there must be one for each dimension. Below, a three-dimensional example is used to briefly describe and illustrate the programming concepts for higher-dimensional arrays. The extension of these concepts to four-, five-, six-, and seven-dimensional arrays is straightforward.

One of the examples used earlier in this chapter to illustrate two-dimensional arrays has to do with tax tables for computing federal income taxes. Another kind of table that can be employed in the income tax computation, also included in the *Federal Income Tax Forms* publication, is the "Optional State Sales Tax Table." Actually, there is one of these tables for the District of Columbia and each of the states that has a state sales tax. The Alabama Optional State Sales Tax Table for a recent income tax year, for example, looks like this:

		Family Size			
1	*2*	*3*	*4*	*5*	*Over 5*
93	115	122	121	142	160
109	132	142	153	165	185
124	147	161	173	187	208
138	161	178	191	206	228
152	174	194	209	225	248
164	186	210	226	242	266
176	197	225	242	259	284
188	208	239	257	275	301
199	218	253	271	290	317
210	228	266	285	305	332
221	238	279	299	320	347
231	247	291	313	334	362
241	256	303	326	347	376
251	265	315	338	360	390
261	274	327	350	373	403
271	282	338	362	386	416
280	290	349	374	399	429
14	15	17	19	20	21

With the exception of the last row, the values in the table are amounts that can be deducted from an income before a tax computation is performed; the values in the last row are increments used to figure the deduction for very high incomes. Each row of the table corresponds to an income range; the income ranges are the same for all such tables, but they are not the same as the income ranges for the tax tables used in the earlier example. If an Alabama family of four has an income in the range $24,001−$26,000, for instance, the sales tax deduction of $285 is found in the tenth row, fourth column of the table.

Ordinarily, any one family needs to have access to only one of these tables. The IRS, however, must access the information in all of them. They can, if necessary, all be stored in a computer's memory in the form of a three-dimensional array.

Each table has 18 rows, and each can be established with six columns. Although a very few states have no sales tax, and therefore need no sales tax table, it is reasonable to assume that all states (including the District of Columbia) will eventually have a sales tax. Thus the number of different tables needed can be defined as 51. Since the values in each table are sales tax deductions, the three-dimensional array can be given the name STXDED. It can then be declared with the statement

```
INTEGER  STXDED(18, 6, 51)
```

or the two statements

```
INTEGER  STXDED
DIMENSION  STXDED(18, 6, 51)
```

Values can be read into array STXDED one row at a time by this sequence of statements:

```
DO 420 STATE = 1, 51
   DO 410 INCRGE = 1, 18
      READ *, (STXDED(INCRGE, FAMSZE, STATE),
   :             FAMSZE = 1, 6)
410     CONTINUE
420 CONTINUE
```

where STATE refers to the state and, therefore, the particular table, INCRGE is the income range designator, and FAMSZE denotes family size. One alternative way of accomplishing the input involves eliminating the DO statements and employing a more complicated implied-DO, like this:

```
READ *, (((STXDED(INCRGE, FAMSZE, STATE),
   :          FAMSZE = 1, 6), INCRGE = 1, 18),
   :          STATE = 1, 51)
```

The primary difference between this one and the sequence above it is that the READ statement in the sequence above is executed 51x18=918 times, or one time per table row, whereas this READ statement is executed one time—period.

You can see, then, that the methods for working programmatically with three-dimensional arrays are just extensions of the methods associated with one- and two-dimensional arrays. Simply extend the methods further to work with higher-dimensional arrays. You should also realize that the three-dimensional array STXDED could be handled as 51 two-dimensional arrays of size 18x6 if desired.

10-2-1 Exercises

1.   After the following program segment has been executed, what will be the value of each element in array BOX?

```
INTEGER  BOX(2, 3, 2), COL, FILE, ROW
   .
   .
   .
DO 230 FILE = 1, 2
   DO 220 COL = 1, 3
      DO 210 ROW = 1, 2
         BOX(ROW, COL, FILE) = ROW * COL + FILE
210     CONTINUE
220     CONTINUE
230 CONTINUE
```

2. Are the assignment operations in the segment above accomplished in row-wise or column-wise order?

3. Draw a pictorial representation of the array BOX in Exercise 1.

4. Rewrite the following sequence as one statement that uses nested implied-DOs in the i/o list.

```
READ *, ZETA(1, 1, 1), ZETA(1, 2, 1), ZETA(2, 1, 1),
   :       ZETA(2, 2, 1), ZETA(3, 1, 1), ZETA(3, 2, 1),
   :       ZETA(1, 1, 2), ZETA(1, 2, 2), ZETA(2, 1, 2),
   :       ZETA(2, 2, 2), ZETA(3, 1, 2), ZETA(3, 2, 2)
```

5. Given this program segment:

```
      INTEGER  ALPHIF, COL, FILE, ROW
      CHARACTER  LETTRS(4, 2, 3)*1
      PARAMETER  (ALPHIF=5)
      .
      .
      .
100 FORMAT (3A1)
      .
      .
      .
      DO 430 ROW = 1, 4
         DO 420 COL = 1, 2
            READ (ALPHIF, 100) (LETTRS(ROW, COL, FILE),
         :                        FILE = 1, 3)
420      CONTINUE
430 CONTINUE
```

and this set of data in the input file (each line beginning in column 1):

```
ABC
DEF
GHI
JKL
MNO
PQR
STU
VWX
YZ
```

state the element values, individually or depicted together pictorially, of the array LETTRS following the complete execution of the DO-loops.

6. Revise the program you wrote for Exercise 7 of Section 10-1-6 in such a way that the income tax tables A through D are handled together as one three-dimensional array.

Modularity and Subprograms

By progressing this far successfully, you have acquired the knowledge and ability that enable you to create computer programs to solve virtually any kind of programming problem. Now for the "icing on the cake"—the programming techniques and language features that make programming easier and add elegance to your computer programs. Before this fun begins, however, recall these definitions:

Module: A program unit that is discrete and identifiable with respect to compiling, combining with other units, and loading into the computer.

Program unit: A main program or subprogram.

Main program: A program unit that is executed only when called upon by the operating system of the computer.

Subprogram: A program unit that can be executed only when referenced by another program unit.

Executable program: A collection of related program units that consists of exactly one main program and any number, including zero, of subprograms.

11-1 MODULAR DESIGN

The term "module" can be applied not only to programs but also to algorithms. Whereas *program module* refers to a discrete and identifiable program unit, *algorithm module* pertains to a distinct and definite solution procedure that leads directly to the generation of a particular corresponding program unit. Therefore, every final algorithm presented thus far in this book can be looked upon as an algorithm module.

The derivation of algorithm modules is a natural productive result of top-down design or stepwise refinement: the process of developing a problem solution by decomposing the problem and its component independent subproblems in stages, at levels varying from overview to detail, at which level the subproblems cannot be further decomposed. At each design or refinement level it is usually possible to identify subproblems that are essentially self-contained and whose solution procedures can be expressed in the form of algorithm modules: ultimately, program modules.

Consider an example. Given below is a reproduction of the first-try algorithm for the per capita income problem, involving the bubble sort and median and average, that was solved in Section 8-7.

```
Print the title.
Read the state identifier, number of counties, and
    output option selector.
If either the state identifier
    or the number of counties is invalid, then
    write an error message.
Otherwise, do the following:
    print the state identifier and number of counties;
    read the per capita incomes;
    sort the per capita incomes;
    compute the median;
    compute the average;
    print the median and average;
    if the output option selector is not zero,
        print the per capita incomes.
Stop.
```

This algorithm represents the problem and its solution procedure at an overview level. As pointed out in Section 8-7, at least three subproblems in this algorithm—sort the per capita incomes, compute the median, and compute the average—deserve individual consideration; they are distinct problems whose solution procedures can be expressed as algorithm modules. Furthermore, since these particular subproblems are general in nature, their corresponding algorithm and program modules can be devised and expressed in a general manner.

Here are the three algorithm modules with accompanying explanations:

1. The sort method used in Chapter 8 is the direct descending bubble sort, and the algorithm given there is first expressed in a general form. It is reproduced, with minor modifications, below.

    ALGORITHM Bubblesort.descending [arn, n]
    ```
    {   Values stored in the n > 0 elements of array arn are
    directly sorted into descending order in the array
    by the bubble sort method.}
    ncomps ← n
    intchg ← 1
    ```
    PAS. `If intchg = 1 Then`
    ```
            intchg ← 0
            ncomps ← ncomps − 1
    ```

```
      Do elem ← 1 to ncomps by 1
         If arn(elem) < arn(elem+1), Then
            tempa ← arn(elem)
            arn(elem) ← arn(elem+1)
            arn(elem+1) ← tempa
            intchg ← 1
      End Do
      Go To PAS. (Back)
   Return
   END
```

The modifications include the addition of a list of variable and array names in brackets following the algorithm name and the use of a new primitive, "Return," at the point where sorting is complete. The variable and array names in the added list are called *arguments*; they identify items that must be defined outside the algorithm—prior to its execution—and items that are defined by the algorithm to be used later outside the algorithm. Both "arn" and "n" fall into the first category of arguments; only "arn" is in the second category. The term "Return" serves to designate the completion point of the algorithm, implying a transfer of control to the next major step in the higher-level algorithm; a "Stop" is not appropriate because, although the sorting "stops" there, the higher-level algorithm has subsequent processes that must still be carried out.

You can see that once an algorithm module has been specified in a general form such as the one above, it can be referred to, in a higher-level algorithm, by either the phrase

```
sort the per capita incomes
```

which is already in the first-try algorithm, or a more structured primitive statement such as

```
Sort [per capita incomes, number of counties]
```

where Sort is the generic name of the algorithm module to be executed at that point. The broad form of this second new algorithmic primitive is

```
amname [args]
```

where amname is the generic or specific name of the algorithm module being referenced and args is the list of arguments that corresponds to the argument list in the referenced module.

2. The median computation is also given in a general form in Section 8-7, although not as a complete algorithm. Here it is as a complete general algorithm module:

ALGORITHM Median [arn, n]
```
{ Find the nearest-integer median value of the n > 0
elements of the array arn.}
```

```
m ← INT[n/2]
If MOD[n,2] = 0 Then
    median ← NINT[(arn(m) + arn(m+1)) / 2]
Else
    median ← arn(m+1)
Return
END
```

The primary difference in presentation between this one and the one for the bubble sort is that the name of the algorithm, Median, appears within the algorithm, in an assignment operation, actually assigning the desired value to the algorithm name.

3. The average computation, which is also algorithmically expressed in Section 8-7, can be modularized in a similar fashion as follows.

ALGORITHM Average [arn, n]
```
{ Compute the nearest-integer average of the n > 0
elements of the array arn.}
average ← 0
Do elem ← 1 to n by 1
    average ← average + arn(elem)
End Do
average ← NINT[average / n]
Return
END
```

Here again, the name of the algorithm occurs within the algorithm in such a way as to have a value assigned to it.

The references to the two algorithm modules above can be left as they are in the first-try algorithm; that is,

```
compute the median;
compute the average;
```

or they can be formalized by placing their names and arguments on the right-hand side of an assignment primitive, like this:

```
var ← amname [args]
```

where var is a variable or array element name. The specific references using this form, then, can be :

```
medpci ← Median [per capita incomes, number of counties]
avepci ← Average [per capita incomes, number of counties]
```

Given these algorithm modules and their references, the final overall algorithm for finding the median and average per capita income can be expressed in a simpler fashion than that of Figure 8-2. It is shown in Figure 11-1. Compare the two figures; observe that the algorithms accomplish the same tasks; realize, though, that the one in Figure 11-1 is more flexible because the sort, median, and average modules are specified separately. Notice, too, that the revised algorithm is much shorter than the original. Shorter modules are desirable since they are usually easier to comprehend and are therefore more manageable. Moreover, the debugging and verification tasks for the revised algorithm are greatly facilitated because these separate algorithm modules are universal in nature, can therefore be used in any number of different applications, and yet only need to be verified for their first use. Modules that are not necessarily universal can also be developed by the same approach and presented individually in like manner. A modular design is, indeed, beneficial.

Modules are flowcharted individually. Furthermore, their references are easily depicted in program flowcharts. The reference to a module in which the module name is not assigned a value, such as the one for sorting, is represented by the Subprocess symbol that has the general appearance

This is a revision of the algorithm displayed in Figure 8-2. For simplicity, the variable and array names are more abbreviated yet mnemonic, and separately identifiable modules are referenced rather than being spelled out in detail.

ALGORITHM PCI:median&average.rev 1

```
{ A report of per capita income (pcincome) for a particular
state based on per capita incomes of counties in the state is
created and printed.  Primary items in the report are the
median and average per capita income.  Optionally, the per
capita incomes are printed in descending order.}

Write title {see layout:  Figure 8-1}
Read stateid, ncounties, option
If stateid < 00 or stateid > 99
   or ncounties < 1 or ncounties > maxcounties, Then
   Write invalid-input error message {see layout}
Else
   Write stateid, ncounties
   Do county ← 1 to ncounties by 1
      Read pcincome(county)
   End Do
   Sort [pcincome, ncounties]
   medpci ← Median [pcincome, ncounties]
   avepci ← Average [pcincome, ncounties]
   Write medpci, avepci
   If option <> 0, Then
      Do county ← 1 to ncounties by 1
         Write pcincome(county)
      End Do
Stop
END
```

Figure 11-1. Algorithm for Finding the Median and Average Per Capita Income: Revision 1

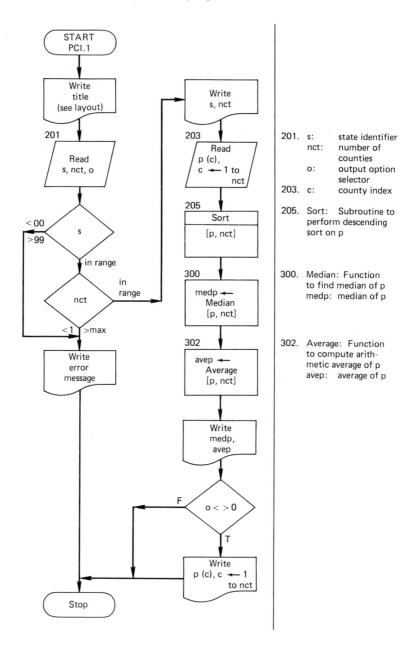

Figure 11-2. Flowchart for Finding the Median and Average Per Capita Income: Revision 1. (A report of per capita income (p) for a particular state based on per capita incomes of counties in the state is created and printed.)

In contrast, the reference to a module in which the module name is assigned a value, such as the ones for finding the median and average, is simply represented as an assignment operation in a General Process symbol. To exemplify, Figure 11-2 contains the program flowchart that corresponds to the algorithm of Figure 11-1. Compare this flowchart with the original, which appears in Figure 8-3. This one is much shorter, less difficult to draw, and easier to understand. Observe, in the annotation, that the modules are referred to as *subroutines* or *functions*. These, their specific programmatic classifications, are described in the coming sections of this chapter.

To complete the program flowchart illustration, a flowchart for the arithmetic average module is exhibited in Figure 11-3. Notice that the word "ENTER" is used in place of the usual "START" in the first symbol to indicate that the execution of this module is invoked by reference in another module. Also, take note that the flowchart concludes with a terminal symbol containing the word "Return."

A modular design also lends itself to a hierarchical depiction that indicates the relationships among the modules. Figure 11-4 comprises a hierarchy chart for revision 1 of the median and average per capita income algorithm. The chart shows that PCI.1 is on a higher-level than the other modules; that the others are on the same level with each other, are distinct, and are subordinate to PCI.1. They therefore represent subprograms. PCI.1, being at the highest level, then, represents a main program.

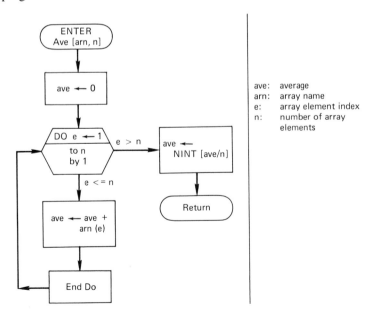

Figure 11-3. Flowchart for Computing the nearest-integer average of the n > 0 elements of the array arn

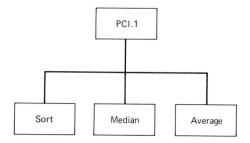

Figure 11-4. A Hierarchy Chart for the Median and Average Per Capita Income Algorithm: Revision 1

11-2 COMMUNICATION AMONG MODULES

Since modules are discrete, yet are expected to furnish values to each other, they are necessarily designed with a communication mechanism. For algorithms, the module name and arguments can serve the purpose. The name given in a reference identifies the particular module that is to be executed; the name may also be assigned a value. The associated variable and array names in corresponding argument lists provide mutual access to the other appropriate items. For instance, the phrase

```
Median [pcincome, ncounties]
```

refers to an algorithm module that has the initial line

ALGORITHM Median [arn, n]

and the corresponding argument lists allow the arrays pcincome and arn, as well as the variables ncounties and n, to be associated with each other. At the time of execution of the Median algorithm, then, the elements of arn are the same as the elements of pcincome; the value of n is the same as the value of ncounties; any changes to the elements of arn are changes to the elements of pcincome; any modification of n would be a modification of ncounties.

Modular communication through arguments is always between two modules at a time—a higher-level or referencing module and a subordinate or referenced module. Additionally, the flexibility of algorithms allows arrays and variables to be shared among several modules by describing them, in commentary, as shared entities.

In Fortran, two program modules can also communicate with each other by means of module names and argument lists. The mechanism is virtually identical to the one described above for algorithm modules. Its programmatic requirements are explained in Sections 11-3 through 11-5. Furthermore, arrays and variables can be shared among several program modules by means of the common block feature that is described in Section 11-6.

11-3 MAIN PROGRAMS

Every executable program has exactly one main program. In a modular design, the main program corresponds to the highest-level algorithm module. Since only highest-level algorithms are shown for the complete program examples given prior to this chapter, all the corresponding programs are main programs. They are identified as such by having a program statement as the first noncomment line.

Whenever an executable program contains one or more subprograms, the main program can reference one or more of the subprograms. A main program can be a referencing program unit but it cannot be a referenced program unit.

Program units that can be referenced by main programs include function subprograms and subroutine subprograms. These program units can also reference each other, subject to the restrictions that are explained shortly. Illustrations of these references are shown and explained in Figure 11-5, which comprises the action section of the main program that corresponds to the revised per capita income algorithm displayed in Figure 11-1. The general forms of the references, as well as of the subprograms themselves, are presented in the next two sections.

11-4 FUNCTION SUBPROGRAMS

In Fortran, the algorithm modules "Median" and "Average" become function subprograms. Ordinarily, a function subprogram comprises one external function and is referred to, simply, as a function. For exemplification, the Median and Average functions are exhibited in full in Figure 11-6.

The primary task of an external function is the same as the main duty of an intrinsic function—to supply a value to an expression in the referencing program unit. A glance back to Figure 11-5 will verify that this duty is the intent of having the Median and Average functions. As shown in Figure 11-6, the external functions, in turn, reference the intrinsic functions MOD, NINT, and FLOAT. In both intrinsic and external functions, the principal value is supplied to the referencing expression by means of the function name.

Each function subprogram must be self-contained and properly constructed in order to be processed successfully by the computer. Whereas the Roman numeral III in the first comment line indicates to a person that the Median function is the third program unit in the executable program, the first noncomment line,

```
FUNCTION MEDIAN (ARN, N)
```

identifies, for the computer, the beginning point of the program unit, the type of program unit, the name of the program unit, and the arguments of the program unit. The required form of a function subprogram with arguments is as follows:

```
FUNCTION fname (dargs)
   .
 ·  {I/O specifications as needed;
```

For Commentary, Declaration, and I/O Layout, refer to the program in Figure 8-4. Add MEDPCI, AVEPCI, and AVERGE to the INTEGER list; do not type BDSORT. For logic, refer to the revised algorithm in Figure 11-1.

```
*   D.  ACTION
         WRITE  (PCIROF,  900)
         READ  (PCIDIF,  *)  STATID,  NOCTYS,  OPTION
         IF  (STATID .LT. 00  .OR.  STATID .GT. 99
      :     .OR.  NOCTYS .LT. 1  .OR.  NOCTYS .GT. MAXCTY)  THEN
            WRITE  (PCIROF,  905)  STATID,  NOCTYS
         ELSE
            WRITE  (PCIROF,  910)  STATID,  NOCTYS
            READ  (PCIDIF,  *)  (PCINC(COUNTY),  COUNTY = 1,  NOCTYS)
            CALL  BDSORT  (PCINC,  NOCTYS)
            MEDPCI  =  MEDIAN  (PCINC,  NOCTYS)
            AVEPCI  =  AVERGE  (PCINC,  NOCTYS)
            WRITE  (PCIROF,  920)  MEDPCI,  AVEPCI
            IF  (OPTION .NE. 0)  THEN
               WRITE  (PCIROF,  930)
               DO 410 COUNTY = 1,  NOCTYS
                  WRITE  (PCIROF,  940)  PCINC(COUNTY)
     410       CONTINUE
            ENDIF
         ENDIF
         STOP
         END
```

The reference

```
CALL  BDSORT  (PCINC,  NOCTYS)
```

calls for the specific sort subroutine BDSORT (Bubble Descending Sort) to be executed using the arguments PCINC and NOCTYS. The function references

```
MEDIAN  (PCINC,  NOCTYS)
```

and

```
AVERGE  (PCINC,  NOCTYS)
```

supply the same arguments and cause their respective functions to be executed, resulting in the assignment of appropriate values to MEDIAN and AVERGE. These values are then assigned, in the main program, to MEDPCI and AVEPCI as shown.

Figure 11-5. Action Section of the Main Program for Finding the Median and Average Per Capita Income: Revision 1

```
      ·   complete declarations;  action}
      ·
   fname = expression
      ·
      ·
      ·
   RETURN
      ·
      ·
      ·
   END
```

Find the median

```
*III. NEAREST-INTEGER MEDIAN
*
      FUNCTION MEDIAN (ARN, N)
*     PROGRAMMER: Jarrell C. Grout
*     DATE:  7/25/81
*
*  A. COMMENTARY
*
*          Find the nearest-integer median value of the N>0 elements
*     of the integer array ARN.
*
*          DICTIONARY.
*
*     ARN:  Array of size N for which the median is to be found
*     MEDIAN:  Nearest-integer median of the elements of ARN
*     MID:  Approximate midpoint of ARN
*     N:  Number of elements in ARN ( N>0 )
*
*  B. I/O LAYOUT
*
*     None
*
*  C. DECLARATION
*
      INTEGER  ARN(N), MEDIAN, MID, N
*
*  D. ACTION
*
      MID = N / 2
      IF (MOD(N, 2) .EQ. 0) THEN
          MEDIAN = NINT((ARN(MID) + ARN(MID+1)) / 2.0)
      ELSE
          MEDIAN = ARN(MID+1)
      ENDIF
      RETURN
      END
```

Compute the average

```
*IV. NEAREST-INTEGER AVERAGE
*
      FUNCTION AVERGE (ARN, N)
*     PROGRAMMER: Jarrell C. Grout
*     DATE:  7/25/81
*
*  A. COMMENTARY
*
*          Compute the nearest-integer arithmetic average
*     of the N>0 elements of the integer array ARN.
*
*          DICTIONARY.
*
*     ARN:  Array of size N for which the average is to be found
*     AVERGE:  Nearest-integer average of the elements of ARN
*     ELEM:  The element index for array ARN
*     N:  Number of elements in ARN ( N>0 )
*
*  B. I/O LAYOUT
*
*     None
*
*  C. DECLARATION
*
      INTEGER  ARN(N), AVERGE, ELEM, N
*
*  D. ACTION
*
      AVERGE = 0
      DO 210 ELEM = 1, N
          AVERGE = AVERGE + ARN(ELEM)
  210 CONTINUE
      AVERGE = NINT(FLOAT(AVERGE) / N)
      RETURN
      END
```

Figure 11-6. Median and Average Function Subprograms

where fname is the symbolic name of the function, dargs is the list of function arguments, called *dummy arguments*, and RETURN is an executable statement that causes control to be transferred back to the referencing program unit. The latter must be a main program, a subroutine subprogram, or a different function subprogram. The general form of a reference to a function subprogram is

```
fname (aargs)
```

where fname is the function name and aargs is the list of referencing program arguments—the *actual arguments* that correspond to the dummy arguments of the function; the reference always appears in an expression in the referencing program unit. Compare the general reference forms above to the specific references and functions in Figures 11-5 and 11-6. Point of emphasis: The main program, a subroutine subprogram, or another function subprogram in an executable program can be the referencing program unit of an external function; but a function cannot reference itself—neither directly nor indirectly through other program units.

Here are some characteristics of function arguments:

1. The actual arguments in the reference to a function and the dummy arguments of the function constitute a communication mechanism for the referencing program unit and the function.

2. The actual and dummy arguments can be completely omitted, in which case the communication among program units takes place through the function name and, if used, through the sharing of storage as explained shortly in Section 11-6.

3. A dummy argument must be a variable name, array name, or the dummy name of a different function or subroutine.

4. An actual argument must be an expression, array name, function name, subroutine name, or the dummy name of a different function or subroutine.

5. There must be as many actual arguments in the reference as there are dummy arguments in the referenced function. The actual and dummy arguments correspond to each other according to their positions in the lists.

6. Corresponding actual and dummy arguments must have the same data type—specified individually in both program units. Take notice of the complete declarations in both the referencing and referenced program units in the examples; *declarations must always be complete in each program unit*.

7. Corresponding actual and dummy arguments can, but need not, have the same spelling.

8. Corresponding actual and dummy arguments must have exactly the same size (specified as constants) unless the dummy argument is an adjustable array or an assumed-size array.

The last item above deserves some immediate explanation. An adjustable array, like ARN in MEDIAN and AVERGE, is one in which one or more variables are used in declaring the array size. If the size of ARN had been expressed with a constant in MEDIAN, the INTEGER statement in MEDIAN would look like this:

```
INTEGER ARN(254), MEDIAN, MID, N
```

where 254 is the exact size of the corresponding array, PCINC, in the referencing program unit. You can see, therefore, that adjustable arrays, specified with variable or adjustable dimensions, provide a great deal of flexibility and program unit independence.

Similarly, assumed-size arrays provide flexibility and independence. An assumed-size array is one for which the dimension declarators are constants or variables except that the upperbound of the last dimension is an asterisk. Thus ARN could be declared as an assumed-size array, in MEDIAN, by the statement

```
INTEGER ARN(*), MEDIAN, MID, N
```

Adjustable arrays and assumed-size arrays can only be present in function subprograms and subroutine subprograms—not in main programs. There are, however, some restrictions on the adjustable and assumed-size features. They are discussed in Section 11-6.

You should now understand not only how functions systematically evolve during the modular design process, but also how they are constructed and referenced in Fortran. You may, however, need to know a little more about the assignment statement

```
fname = expression
```

which must appear somewhere within the action of the function, the RETURN statement, and how functions fit physically into an executable program for computer processing.

The assignment statement provides the means by which the principal value is defined in the function. Its expression must be an arithmetic, logical, or character expression—depending on the data type of the function. More than one such statement can appear. Both MEDIAN and AVERGE, for example, contain two such statements each.

The RETURN statement designates the logical terminating point of the function, but its primary purpose is to transfer control of execution back to the referencing program unit, thereby allowing the referencing program unit to use the function-produced value in the expression, and then proceed. There can be any number of RETURN statements in a function; one can appear anywhere that the algorithm designates as a return point. The RETURN statement can also be omitted. The END statement can then serve to effect the transfer of control. However, since this use of the END statement is totally different from its primary use, I do not use it this way.

In an executable program, a function subprogram can be physically placed anywhere after the main program and before the input data. Since I designate MEDIAN and AVERGE as program units III and IV, I would place them as the third and fourth program units in the executable program file. Alternatively, I might create a file for each program unit and use a separate job control language file to effect their execution, always beginning with the main program. This alternative may be the most desirable approach because it allows universal program modules to be accessible to many different referencing programs but does not require them to be stored in the same file. It is, however, system dependent and you will have to consult your system manuals or computer center personnel or instructor for the specifics of accomplishing it.

Do you remember external function LENSUB of Figure 9-5? LENSUB is an integer function subprogram that deals with character substrings. Reexamine it again and see how it fits the proper form for a function subprogram. It contains the interesting statement

```
CHARACTER STRING* (*)
```

in which the variable STRING is a dummy argument. The asterisk in parentheses indicates that the length of STRING is an "assumed length"; it is assumed to have the length of the associated actual argument. So when LENSUB is referenced in the multiple choice test grading program (Figure 9-9) via the statement

```
NAME  = FNAME (NEXT) (1: LENSUB (FNAME (NEXT) ) )  // ' ' //
  :         MIDIN (NEXT)  // ' ' // LNAME (NEXT)
```

the length of STRING becomes—for that execution—equal to the length of FNAME(NEXT), which is declared to be nine characters in the statement

```
CHARACTER ANS (MAXSTU) *100, CORANS*100, COURSE*3, DEPT*3,
  :         EXTITL*11, FNAME (MAXSTU) *9, . . .
```

LENSUB is, therefore, a generally applicable function subprogram.

An external function, and its reference, can have just as many arguments as necessary—or it can actually have none! You need only make sure that the function is constructed properly and that its actual and dummy arguments are associated correctly.

11-5 SUBROUTINE SUBPROGRAMS

In Fortran, the algorithm module "Bubblesort.descending" becomes a subroutine subprogram. A reference to it appears in Figure 11-5 as the statement

```
CALL BDSORT (PCINC, NOCTYS)
```

Ordinarily, a subroutine subprogram comprises one subroutine and is, therefore, usually referred to simply as a subroutine. As an example, the subroutine BDSORT is displayed in full in Figure 11-7.

A subroutine is a procedure that is specified in a program unit other than the referencing program unit, and that has the purpose of defining a series of opera-

```
*II.   DIRECT DESCENDING BUBBLE SORT
*
*      SUBROUTINE BDSORT (ARN, N)
*      PROGRAMMER:  Jarrell C. Grout
*      DATE:  7/25/81
*
*   A. COMMENTARY
*
*          Values stored in the N>0 elements of the integer array
*      ARN are directly sorted into descending order in the array
*      by the bubble sort method.
*
*          DICTIONARY.
*
*      ARN:  Array of size N to be sorted
*      ELEM:  The element index for array ARN
*      INTCHG:  Interchange indicator; 1 when interchange occurs;
*               0 when sorting is complete
*      N:  Number of elements in array ARN ( N>0 )
*      NCOMPS:  Number of compares in one sort pass
*      TEMPA:  Temporary variable to facilitate interchanging
*               the elements of ARN
*
*   B. I/O LAYOUT
*
*      None
*
*   C. DECLARATION
*
*      INTEGER  ARN(N), ELEM, INTCHG, N, NCOMPS, TEMPA
*
*   D. ACTION
*
*      NCOMPS = N
*      INTCHG = 1
*  210 IF (INTCHG .EQ. 1) THEN
*          INTCHG = 0
*          NCOMPS = NCOMPS - 1
*          DO 220 ELEM = 1, NCOMPS
*              IF (ARN(ELEM) .LT. ARN(ELEM+1)) THEN
*                  TEMPA = ARN(ELEM)
*                  ARN(ELEM) = ARN(ELEM+1)
*                  ARN(ELEM+1) = TEMPA
*                  INTCHG = 1
*              ENDIF
*  220     CONTINUE
*          GO TO 210
*      ENDIF
*      RETURN
*      END
```

Figure 11-7. Subroutine Subprogram for a Direct Descending Bubble Sort

tions that may or may not cause values to be supplied to the referencing program unit. Every subroutine must be named, but the subroutine name is not used to supply a value to the referencing program unit; the dummy arguments are usually employed for that purpose. The subroutine of Figure 11-7 does supply values to the referencing program, shown in Figure 11-5, by means of the associated dummy and actual arguments, ARN and PCINC, in that it rearranges the values in the array.

The subroutine subprogram form that is essential for successful computer processing of a subroutine having arguments is

```
SUBROUTINE sname (dargs)
·
·    {I/O specified as needed;
·    complete declarations; action}
·
```

```
RETURN
     .
     .
END
```

and the corresponding executable referencing statement has the form

```
CALL sname (aargs)
```

where sname is the subroutine name—a symbolic name that has no data type—and dargs and aargs are corresponding dummy and actual argument lists. Compare the forms above to the actual reference and subroutine subprogram in Figures 11-5 and 11-7.

A subroutine can be referenced by the main program, another subroutine subprogram, or a function subprogram in the executable program, but it cannot reference itself—either directly or indirectly. The characteristics of subroutine dummy arguments and their associated actual arguments are identical to those itemized in Section 11-4 for functions. Equally applicable is the explanation of adjustable and assumed-size arrays.

The RETURN statement serves the same purpose in a subroutine that it serves in a function. It is usually written in the same simple form; however, it can be written in a slightly different form that is described in the appendix to this chapter.

The guidelines for physical placement of function subprograms apply also to subroutine subprograms. If BDSORT is to be a part of the file that contains the complete executable program, I would place it immediately behind the main program unit because I designate it as program unit II.

Here is something that you should be mindful of: The statement number 210 appears in both subroutine BDSORT and function AVERGE even though these program units are in the same executable program. This apparent duplication error is not an error at all. The two program units are self-contained; they are devised separately, compiled individually, and executed singly. Therefore, not only statement numbers but also variable names and array names, which do not appear in argument lists or in shared storage can be "duplicated" in like manner without ambiguity. (Symbolic names that are used for items other than variables and arrays, such as program unit names, should not, however, be duplicated.)

It is possible to write BDSORT as a function subprogram. But since BDSORT operates on an entire array and does not supply a value to an expression in the referencing program unit, it should not be written as a function. On the other hand, MEDIAN and AVERGE can, effectively and beneficially, be written as subroutine subprograms. If so, the references to them in the referencing program unit must be rewritten as CALL statements. To demonstrate, I have rewritten the portion of the action section in which they are referenced; I have also rewritten MEDIAN and AVERGE as subroutines. This is all presented in Figure 11-8. Observe that one additional actual and dummy argument pair is required to establish each of the two subprograms as subroutine subprograms. The median is not

```
       .
       .
    CALL BOSORT (PCINC, NOCTYS)
    CALL MEDIAN (PCINC, NOCTYS, MEDPCT)
    CALL AVERGE (PCINC, NOCTYS, AVEPCT)
    WRITE (PCTROF, 920) MEDPCT, AVEPCT
```

(a)

```
*III.  NEAREST-INTEGER MEDIAN
*
       SUBROUTINE MEDIAN (ARN, N, MEDN)
*      PROGRAMMER:  Jarrell C. Grout
           .
           .
           .
*         DICTIONARY.
*
*      ARN:  Array of size N for which the median is to be found
*      MEDN: Nearest-integer median of the elements of ARN
*      MID:  Approximate midpoint of ARN
*      N:    Number of elements in ARN ( N>0 )
           .
           .
*   C. DECLARATION
*
       INTEGER  ARN(N), MEDN, MID, N
*
*   D. ACTION
*
       MID = N / 2
       IF (MOD(N, 2) .EQ. 0) THEN
          MEDN = NINT((ARN(MID) + ARN(MID+1)) / 2.0)
       ELSE
          MEDN = ARN(MID+1)
       ENDIF
       RETURN
       END
```

(b)

```
*IV.  NEAREST-INTEGER AVERAGE
*
       SUBROUTINE AVERGE (ARN, N, AVE)
*      PROGRAMMER:  Jarrell C. Grout
           .
           .
           .
*         DICTIONARY.
*
*      ARN:  Array of size N for which the average is to be found
*      AVE:  Nearest-integer average of the elements of ARN
*      ELEM: The element index for array ARN
           .
           .
*   C. DECLARATION
*
       INTEGER  ARN(N), AVE, ELEM, N
*
*   D. ACTION
*
       AVE = 0
       DO 210 ELEM = 1, N
          AVE = AVE + ARN(ELEM)
   210 CONTINUE
       AVE = NINT(FLOAT(AVE) / N)
       RETURN
       END
```

(c)

Figure 11-8. Median and Average Subroutine Subprograms (a) Referencing Program Action Segment (rewritten from Figure 11-5) (b) Median Subroutine (refer to Median function in Figure 11-6 for omitted portions and comparison (c) Average Subroutine (refer to Average function in Figure 11-6 for omitted portions and comparison)

now supplied as the value of the symbolic name MEDIAN, which is no longer a variable name, but it is supplied via the new dummy argument MEDN and its associated new actual argument MEDPCI. Similarly, the average is supplied through the new dummy argument AVE and its associated actual argument AVEPCI rather than through AVERGE as before.

11-6 SHARING STORAGE

I have said that the argument lists of the subprograms and their references can be omitted. But even so, the referencing and referenced program units must still be able to communicate with each other. Thus an alternative communication method is provided.

The references to all three example subprograms—BDSORT, MEDIAN, and AVERGE—contain the actual arguments PCINC and NOCTYS. Each individual subprogram has the corresponding dummy arguments ARN and N. ARN of BDSORT is "associated" with PCINC through the BDSORT reference, ARN of MEDIAN is "associated" with PCINC through the MEDIAN reference, and ARN of AVERGE is "associated" with PCINC through the AVERGE reference; N is "associated" with NOCTYS in like manner. To be associated means that the storage locations are the same. Thus, by means of a series of argument pairs, it seems that one "ARN" is the same as another "ARN," and so on; but not really so. What is so is that the references to the elements of any particular "ARN" are references to the corresponding elements of PCINC in the referencing program unit during the execution of the particular subprogram. The subprograms share no storage with each other or with the referencing program. In Fortran, the sharing of storage between program units is accomplished by the establishment of common blocks. Program units that declare access to the same common block share the storage of that common block with each other and thereby communicate with each other.

Access to a common block is declared with the nonexecutable COMMON statement, which can be written in the form

```
COMMON /bname/ nlist
```

where bname is the symbolic name of a common block and nlist is a list of variable and array names. The variables and arrays identified in the nlist attached to a particular common block name are the ones that make up that common block; contiguous storage under that common block name is reserved for them by the compiler; in reality, they are not part of any program unit but they can be referenced and modified by every program unit that declares access to that common block. By the very nature of common blocks, a variable or array name can only appear in one nlist within a program unit; furthermore, such a variable or array name cannot also appear in the dummy argument list of that program unit. Additionally, every common block that contains character entities must contain only character entities.

There is an exception to the form of the COMMON statement given above; it is possible to have one unnamed or "blank" common block in an executable program. For an unnamed common block, the bname is omitted.

If desired, we can use a common block to entirely eliminate the argument lists in the per capita income main program and its subprograms. Compare the statements for doing so, given in Figure 11-9, with those in Figures 11-7 and 11-8. (You may also need to look back at the declarations of the original program in Figure 8-4.) Here are some things that you should pay attention to:

1.   Three common blocks are established in Figure 11-9: one for all program units (ALLBLK), another for MEDIAN (MEDBLK), and the third one for AVERGE (AVEBLK).

2.   None of the common block names are present in type statements; they are not to be typed. Nor should they be used for any other purpose.

3.   All three common blocks are necessarily declared for access in main program PCIMA2; only ALLBLK is needed in BDSORT; both ALLBLK and MEDBLK are required in MEDIAN; both ALLBLK and AVEBLK are necessary in AVERGE.

4.   As intended, there are no argument lists.

5.   Associated variables and arrays are spelled the same way whenever practical, but differently whenever appropriate.

6.   The size of the associated arrays PCINC and ARN are declared with the numeric constant 254 rather than with a symbolic constant in the main program and variables in the subprograms as before. This is because symbolic constants and adjustable array declarators cannot be placed in common blocks.

Common blocks can be used to advantage whenever a number of program units in an executable program need to share large groups of constant information that can be defined in DATA statements. In this kind of situation, the DATA statements are placed in a special nonreferenced subprogram which is the subject of the following section.

11-7   THE BLOCK DATA SUBPROGRAM

Block data subprograms are never referenced by other program units; they contain no executable statements. The sole purpose of a block data subprogram is to provide initial values for variables and array elements in named common blocks. I suggest that you use the block data subprogram to establish the value of items that are not modified during execution; otherwise, program reading, debugging, and revision may be more difficult, and errors may creep in undetected.

```
*I.   PER CAPITA INCOME MEDIAN AND AVERAGE:  Revision 2
*
      PROGRAM PCIMA2
        .
        .
        .
*  B. DECLARATION
*
      INTEGER  AVEPCI, COUNTY, INTCHG, MEDIAN, MEDPCI,
     :         NCOMPS, NOCTYS, OPTION, PCIDIF, PCINC(254),
     :         PCIROF, STATID, TEMPIV
      COMMON  /ALLBLK/ PCINC, NOCTYS
      COMMON  /MEDBLK/ MEDPCI
      COMMON  /AVEBLK/ AVEPCI
      PARAMETER  (PCIDIF=5, PCIROF=6)
        .
        .
        .
        READ (PCIDIF, *) (PCINC(COUNTY), COUNTY = 1, NOCTYS)
        CALL BDSORT
        CALL MEDIAN
        CALL AVERGE
        WRITE (PCIROF, 920) MEDPCI, AVEPCI
        .
        .
        .
      END
*
*********************************************************************
*
*II.  DIRECT DESCENDING BUBBLE SORT
*
      SUBROUTINE BDSORT
        .
        .
        .
*  C. DECLARATION
*
      INTEGER  ARN(254), ELEM, INTCHG, N, NCOMPS, TEMPA
      COMMON  /ALLBLK/ ARN, N
        .
        .
        .
      END
*
*********************************************************************
*
*III. NEAREST-INTEGER MEDIAN
*
      SUBROUTINE MEDIAN
        .
        .
        .
*  C. DECLARATION
*
      INTEGER  ARN(254), MEDN, MID, N
      COMMON  /ALLBLK/ ARN, N
      COMMON  /MEDBLK/ MEDN
        .
        .
        .
      END
*
*********************************************************************
*
*IV.  NEAREST-INTEGER AVERAGE
*
      SUBROUTINE AVERGE
        .
        .
        .
*  C. DECLARATION
*
      INTEGER  ARN(254), AVE, ELEM, N
      COMMON  /ALLBLK/ ARN, N
      COMMON  /AVEBLK/ AVE
        .
        .
        .
      END
```

Figure 11-9. Per Capita Income Program With Subroutines and Common Blocks

The overall essential form of a block data subprogram is

```
BLOCK DATA bdsname
·    {Comment lines and declaration statements only;
·    at least one named common block and one DATA
·    statement.}
END
```

where bdsname is the symbolic name of the block data subprogram—a name that must not be typed and should not be used for any other purpose. There can be any desired number of block data subprograms in an executable program, one of which can be unnamed. Each named common block of an executable program can appear in only one block data subprogram; each such block must also be declared in those program units that need to have access to it.

Consider a situation—one encountered in the example program of the next section—in which several program units need to have alphabetical access to the standard two-character abbreviations and names of the 50 United States and District of Columbia. To handle this, two character arrays of 51 elements each can be established in a block data subprogram. However, since the state standard abbreviations and names do not exactly correspond alphabetically, it is necessary to set up an additional array of integer "pointers" which will properly associate the elements of the two character arrays with each other. This pointer array can be established in the same block data subprogram.

The block data subprogram in question is presented in Figure 11-10. Examine the subprogram carefully, observing these items in particular:

1. The character entities (STNABB and STNAME) and numeric entity (STNPTR) are necessarily placed in separate common blocks.

2. Type statements and their corresponding COMMON statements are grouped together for readability.

3. Declarations are completely specified for all items appearing in the subprogram.

4. Only the commentary and declaration sections are present; a block data subprogram has no need for an i/o layout or action section.

11-8   EXAMPLE PROGRAM: PRESIDENTIAL ELECTION ANALYSIS WITH BINARY SEARCH

To keep the public informed as a presidential election day proceeds, a number of different organizations attempt periodic analysis of the vote status of each candidate. The complete example program for this chapter is one that could be used for such a periodic analysis.

The input data are entered into two files, either or both of which can be created for batch processing or for on-line processing while the program is executing. The first input file contains the election year, candidate last names, and abbreviated party names. The second input file contains batches of vote data. The vote

```
*II.  ESTABLISH STATE ABBREVIATIONS, NAMES, AND POINTERS
*
      BLOCK DATA ESTANP
*     PROGRAMMER:  Jarrell C. Grout
*     DATE:  7/28/81
*
*  A. COMMENTARY
*
*        Establish state name abbreviations (STNABB), state
*     names (STNAME), and state pointers (STNPTR) for the fifty
*     United States and District of Columbia.
*
*        DICTIONARY.
*
*     ABNBLK:  Common block for state name abbreviations and
*              state names
*     MXSTAT:  Maximum number of states (including D.C.)
*     PNTBLK:  Common block for state name pointers
*     STNABB:  Standard two-character state name abbreviation
*              vector; alphabetical order
*     STNAME:  State name vector; alphabetical order
*     STNPTR:  State name pointer vector; same order as STNABB;
*              each element identifies the location of the
*              corresponding state name in STNAME
*
*  B. DECLARATION
*
      INTEGER  MXSTAT
      PARAMETER  (MXSTAT=51)
*
      CHARACTER  STNABB(MXSTAT)*2, STNAME(MXSTAT)*16
      COMMON  /ABNBLK/ STNABB, STNAME
*
      INTEGER  STNPTR(MXSTAT)
      COMMON  /PNTBLK/ STNPTR
*
      DATA  STNABB /
     :        'AK', 'AL', 'AR', 'AZ', 'CA', 'CO', 'CT', 'DC', 'DE',
     :        'FL', 'GE', 'HI', 'IA', 'ID', 'IL', 'IN', 'KS', 'KY',
     :        'LA', 'MA', 'MD', 'ME', 'MI', 'MN', 'MO', 'MS', 'MT',
     :        'NC', 'ND', 'NE', 'NH', 'NJ', 'NM', 'NY', 'NV', 'OH',
     :        'OK', 'OR', 'PA', 'RI', 'SC', 'SD', 'TN', 'TX', 'UT',
     :        'VA', 'VT', 'WA', 'WI', 'WV', 'WY' /
      DATA  STNAME /
     :        'Alabama', 'Alaska', 'Arizona', 'Arkansas', 'California',
     :        'Colorado', 'Connecticut', 'Delaware', 'Dist of Columbia',
     :        'Florida', 'Georgia', 'Hawaii', 'Idaho', 'Illinois',
     :        'Indiana', 'Iowa', 'Kansas', 'Kentucky', 'Louisiana',
     :        'Maine', 'Maryland', 'Massachusetts', 'Michigan',
     :        'Minnesota', 'Mississippi', 'Missouri', 'Montana',
     :        'Nebraska', 'Nevada', 'New Hampshire', 'New Jersey',
     :        'New Mexico', 'New York', 'North Carolina',
     :        'North Dakota', 'Ohio', 'Oklahoma', 'Oregon',
     :        'Pennsylvania', 'Rhode Island', 'South Carolina',
     :        'South Dakota', 'Tennessee', 'Texas', 'Utah',
     :        'Vermont', 'Virginia', 'Washington', 'West Virginia',
     :        'Wisconsin', 'Wyoming' /
      DATA  STNPTR /
     :        2,  1,  4,  3,  5,  6,  7,  9,  8, 10,
     :       11, 12, 16, 13, 14, 15, 17, 18, 19, 22,
     :       21, 20, 23, 24, 26, 25, 27, 34, 35, 28,
     :       30, 31, 32, 33, 29, 36, 37, 38, 39, 40,
     :       41, 42, 43, 44, 45, 47, 46, 48, 50, 49, 51 /
*
      END
```

Figure 11-10. Block Data Subprogram to Establish State Abbreviations, Names, and Pointers

data for a state are made up of a record that has the standard two-character state name abbreviation followed by several records that consist of the last names of candidates and the votes they received in the state since the last "batch" was submitted by the state. A batch consists of the vote data for as few as one or as many as 51 states (including the District of Columbia). Because the votes themselves relate to the candidates and the states, they are stored in a two-dimensional array in memory. Special two-character strings are employed as delimiters for the input data in the second file. The strings and their usages are as follows.

String	*Usage*
$S	Denote end-of-state data, each state
$B	Denote end-of-batch, each batch

The desired output consists of a vote tabulation table comprising individual and total votes by candidate and state, and overall vote percentages by candidate. Sample i/o data are given in Figures 11-11 and 11-12.

Here is a first-try algorithm for the program:

```
Establish the initial vote tabulation table, candidate vector,
and party vector.
Process vote update batches, printing an intermediate vote
tabulation table for each, until the end of the vote file
is reached.
Print the final vote tabulation table.
```

This first-try algorithm identifies three modules. It can be rewritten in the following more specific manner prior to refinement.

```
Initialize [vote tabulation table, candidate vector,
   party vector]
Process update batches [vote tabulation table,
   candidate vector, party vector, candidate votes,
   overall total votes, percent votes]
Print final [vote tabulation table, candidate vector,
   party vector, candidate votes, overall total votes,
   percent vector]
```

You can identify the modules more clearly now. The first one can be divided into the following more specific sentences.

```
Initialize the vote tabulation table to zero.
Read the election year.
While end-of-candidate input file has not been reached,
read a candidate last name and a party name abbreviation.
```

The second one can be specified more precisely as follows:

```
Initialize the batch counter to zero.
While the end-of-vote file has not been reached, do this:
   read the abbreviated state name;
   if the abbreviated state name does not denote the
   end-of-batch, then
      using the abbreviated state name, find the location
      of the full state name in the state vector;
      read and process votes for candidates,
      updating the vote tabulation for each,
      until the end-of-state data is reached;
```

(The following data in no way corresponds to any actual data in any real election)

Candidate file: Vote file:

```
19XX                          NH
Freemon    REP                Kingpin    10000
Givers     SOC                Freemon    5000
Kingpin    DEM                Givers     1000
                              $S
                              RI
                              Freemon    5000
                              Kingpin    5000
                              $S
                              ME
                              Kingpin    6000
                              Freemon    4000
                              Givers     500
                              $S
                              FL
                              Freemon    7500
                              $S
                              NC
                              Givers     2500
                              Freemon    7500
                              Kingpin    5000
                              $S
                              DE
                              Freemon    2500
                              Kingpin    5000
                              $S
                              $B
                              SC
                              Freemon    5000
                              Kingpin    4000
                              Givers     3000
                              $S
                              FL
                              Kingpin    10000
                              Freemon    15000
                              Givers     500
                              $S
                              DE
                              Freemon    7500
                              Kingpin    7500
                              $S
                              VA
                              Givers     2000
                              Kingpin    10000
                              Freemon    8000
                              $S
                              ME
                              Kingpin    7000
                              Freemon    3500
                              Givers     100
                              $S
                              CT
                              Givers     1000
                              Freemon    5000
                              Kingpin    7000
                              $S
                              MD
                              Kingpin    10000
                              Freemon    15000
                              $S
                              $B
```

Figure 11-11. Sample Input Data for the Presidential Election Analysis Program

otherwise,
    add one to the batch counter;
    compute vote totals and percents;
    print an intermediate vote tabulation table for
    this batch.

19XX PRESIDENTIAL ELECTION VOTE TABULATION: BATCH   2

STATE	Freemon REP	Givers SOC	Kingpin DEM	STATE TOTALS
Alabama	0	0	0	0
Alaska	0	0	0	0
Arizona	0	0	0	0
Arkansas	0	0	0	0
California	0	0	0	0
Colorado	0	0	0	0
Connecticut	5000	1000	7000	13000
Delaware	10000	0	12500	22500
Dist of Columbia	0	0	0	0
Florida	22500	500	10000	33000
Georgia	0	0	0	0
Hawaii	0	0	0	0
Idaho	0	0	0	0
Illinois	0	0	0	0
Indiana	0	0	0	0
Iowa	0	0	0	0
Kansas	0	0	0	0
Kentucky	0	0	0	0
Louisiana	0	0	0	0
Maine	7500	600	13000	21100
Maryland	15000	0	10000	25000
Massachusetts	0	0	0	0
Michigan	0	0	0	0
Minnesota	0	0	0	0
Mississippi	0	0	0	0
Missouri	0	0	0	0
Montana	0	0	0	0
Nebraska	0	0	0	0
Nevada	0	0	0	0
New Hampshire	5000	1000	10000	16000
New Jersey	0	0	0	0
New Mexico	0	0	0	0
New York	0	0	0	0
North Carolina	7500	2500	5000	15000
North Dakota	0	0	0	0
Ohio	0	0	0	0
Oklahoma	0	0	0	0
Oregon	0	0	0	0
Pennsylvania	0	0	0	0
Rhode Island	5000	0	5000	10000
South Carolina	5000	3000	4000	12000
South Dakota	0	0	0	0
Tennessee	0	0	0	0
Texas	0	0	0	0
Utah	0	0	0	0
Vermont	0	0	0	0
Virginia	8000	2000	10000	20000
Washington	0	0	0	0
West Virginia	0	0	0	0
Wisconsin	0	0	0	0
Wyoming	0	0	0	0
CANDIDATE TOTALS:	90500	10600	86500	187600
PERCENTAGES:	48.2	5.7	46.1	

Figure 11-12. Sample Output Data for the Presidential Election Analysis Program

The third module is fairly straightforward, so I make no attempt to specify it in more detail at this point. In fact, with one significant exception, I leave the further refinement of these modules to you.

The exception, which appears in the second module, is the phrase,

```
using the abbreviated state name, find the location
of the full state name in the state vector;
```

This phrase identifies another module which calls for the establishment of a vector of standard two-character state abbreviations and a corresponding vector of state names, then a search through the vector of abbreviations to find the vector location of the state name that corresponds to the abbreviated name read in from the input file. The vectors are established by means of CHARACTER-DATA statement combinations in a Block Data Subprogram as described in Section 11-7. The search procedure employed is explained and devised below.

We previously used linear search methods to locate key items in arrays, files, and input data sets. A linear search involves the checking of every key value in a data set, beginning with the first key value, until the desired value is found. Linear searches are useful for sets of unordered data. Whenever a data set is ordered, however, it becomes possible to employ search methods that usually require the checking of a lesser portion of the key values in the data set. The *binary search* is one of these methods. It is employed here to find the location of a full state name in a state name vector.

To illustrate the method, I use these subset vectors of the state names, abbreviations, and pointers:

State Name	Abbreviation	Pointer
Alabama	AK	2
Alaska	AL	1
Arizona	AR	4
Arkansas	AZ	3
California	CA	5
Colorado	CO	6
Connecticut	CT	7

The first pointer value, 2, indicates that the second state name, Alaska, corresponds to the first state abbreviation, AK; the second pointer value, 1, indicates that the first state name, Alabama, corresponds to the second state abbreviation, AL; and so on.

A linear search procedure takes a given input abbreviation, say CO, and finds after comparing it to six abbreviations that the corresponding full state name is in location 6 of the state name subset vector. In contrast, the binary search procedure takes advantage of the alphabetical ordering of the state abbreviations by first comparing the given abbreviation to the middle element of the state abbreviation vector. If the input abbreviation is not equal to that element, the binary search procedure repeats the process on the (alphabetical) lower or upper half of the vector, depending on whether the input abbreviation is less than or greater than the middle element. This repetitive process continues until the desired element is found.

Thus, if the input abbreviation is CO, the binary search procedure finds that the location is 6 after comparing it with only two elements: AZ, the middle element, and then CO, the middle element of the upper half. An input abbreviation of CT requires only three comparisons: with AZ, then CO, then CT. But an abbreviation of AK also requires three comparisons: with AZ, then AL, then AK. Therefore, the binary search method does not always result in fewer comparisons than the linear search method; but it does result in fewer compares for all but the first few values in a data set.

Let "stabbr" stand for an abbreviated state name that has been read in, "stnabb" represent an established vector of state name abbreviations, "mid" refer to the location of the middle element of the portion of the vector that contains the input abbreviation, "stnptr" denote the established vector of state name pointers, and "stnloc" identify the location of the desired full state name in its vector. For 51 states, then, the following algorithmic segment expresses the binary search.

```
          low ← 1
          high ← 51
SRH.      If low <= high Then
              mid ← INT[(low + high) / 2]
              If stabbr < stnabb(mid) Then
                  high ← mid − 1
              Else If stabbr > stnabb(mid) Then
                  low ← mid + 1
              Else
                  stnloc ← stnptr(mid)
                  Go To FND. (Ahead)
          Else
              {The input abbreviation is not in the vector;
              take an alternative action-see Exercise 6, Section 11-9.}
          Go To SRH. (Back)
FND.      {stnloc is the location of the state name in its vector.}
```

This segment has been adapted and incorporated, as subroutine BISRCH, into the complete presidential election analysis program displayed in Figure 11-13. The complete program consists of the main program PRELAN, which serves as a "driver" in that its sole purpose is to invoke the execution of the other program units; the block data subprogram ESTANP; the subroutine subprograms INITAL, UPDATE, and PRTFNL, which are referenced by PRELAN; and subroutine BISRCH, which is referred to by UPDATE. The executable module hierarchy can be represented like this:

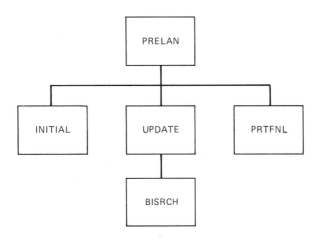

```
*I.  PRESIDENTIAL ELECTION ANALYSIS
*
*    PROGRAM PRELAN
*    PROGRAMMER:  Jarrell C. Grout
*    DATE:  7/28/81
*
*  A. COMMENTARY
*
*
*       Provide a periodic and final analysis of votes during
*    a presidential election in the United States of America.
*    Each analysis consists of a vote tabulation table that
*    contains individual and total votes by candidate and
*    state, and overall vote percentages by candidate.  For
*    this purpose, the District of Columbia is considered to
*    be a state.
*
*       Input data is contained in two files, CANDIF and VOTEIF,
*    the first of which is used in subroutine INITAL and the
*    second of which is used in subroutine UPDATE.  CANDIF,
*    used primarily to set up the candidate vector,  contains
*    the election year, and the last names and abbreviated party
*    names of the candidates.  The election year, a 4-digit
*    character string named ELYEAR, is in columns 1-4 of the
*    first physical record.  This record is followed by one to
*    six additional records, each of which have a candidate's
*    last name (CLNAME) left-justified in columns 1-12 and
*    a three-character party name abbreviation (PARTY) in
*    columns 13-15.
*
*       VOTEIF, an input file used in UPDATE mainly to update the
*    vote tabulation table, consists of batches of vote data.
*    The vote data for a state begins with one record that
*    has the standard two-character state abbreviation (STABBR)
*    in columns 1-2.  This is followed by up to six records,
*    each of which has a candidate's last name (CANDLN) in
*    columns 1-12 and, in columns 13-20, the additional votes
*    (ADVOTE) received by that candidate in that state since
*    the last vote submission by that state.  These records are
*    followed by a record containing the string $S in columns
*    1-2.  A state submits either one or no sets of vote data
*    in a batch.  Any number of different states can submit
*    vote data in each batch.  The last record in a batch has
*    the character string $B in columns 1-2.  It triggers the
*    printing of an intermediate vote tabulation table.  There
*    can be any number of batches; each represents a period of
*    time during the voting day.  An end-of-file on the vote
*    input file signals the completion of voting and triggers
*    the printing of the final vote tabulation table by
*    subroutine PRTFNL.
*
*
*       DICTIONARY.
*
*    ABNBLK:  Common block for state abbreviations and state names
*    ADVOTE:  Additional votes, for one candidate, contained
*             in a 'vote data' input record (file VOTEIF;
*             subroutine UPDATE)
*    CANDIF:  Candidate input file
*    CLNAME:  Candidate last name vector
*    ELYEAR:  Election year
*    INITAL:  Subroutine to initialize vote tabulation table,
*             candidate vector, and party vector
*    MXCAND:  Maximum number of candidates
*    MXSTAT:  Maximum number of states (including D.C.); a
*             parameter that is defined in each program unit
*    NCAND:   Number of candidates in race
*    OTVOTE:  Overall total vote
*    PARTY:   Vector of three-character party name
*             abbreviations
*    PNTBLK:  Common block for state name pointers
*    PRCENT:  Vector of candidate vote percentages
*    PRTFNL:  Subroutine to print final vote tabulation table
*    STNABR:  Standard two-character state name abbreviation
*             vector; alphabetical order
*    STNAME:  State name vector; alphabetical order
*    STNPTR:  State name pointer vector; same order as
*             STNABR; each element identifies the location
*             of the corresponding state name in STNAME
```

Figure 11-13. Presidential Election Analysis Program

```
*      UPDATE:  Subroutine to process vote update batches and
*               print intermediate tabulation tables
*      VOTABL:  Vote tabulation table
*      VOTEIF:  Vote data input file
*      VOTES:   Vector of candidate votes
*      VTABOF:  Vote tabulation output file
*
*    B. DECLARATION
*
       INTEGER  CANDIF, MXCAND, MXSTAT, VOTEIF, VTABOF
       PARAMETER  (CANDIF=4, MXCAND=6, MXSTAT=51,
      :             VOTEIF=5, VTABOF=6)
*
       CHARACTER  STNABB(MXSTAT)*2, STNAME(MXSTAT)*16
       COMMON  /ABNBLK/ STNABB, STNAME
*
       INTEGER  STNPTR(MXSTAT)
       COMMON  /PNTBLK/ STNPTR
*
       INTEGER  NCAND, OTVOTE, VOTABL(MXSTAT, MXCAND+1),
      :             VOTES(MXCAND)
       REAL  PRCENT(MXCAND)
       CHARACTER  CLNAME(MXCAND+1)*12, ELYEAR*4, PARTY(MXCAND)*3
*
*
*    C. I/O LAYOUT
*
*      None
*
*    D. ACTION
*
       CALL INITAL (VOTABL, MXCAND, CANDIF, ELYEAR, NCAND, CLNAME,
      :             PARTY)
       CALL UPDATE (VOTABL, MXCAND, ELYEAR, NCAND, CLNAME, PARTY,
      :             VOTEIF, VTABOF, VOTES, OTVOTE, PRCENT)
       CALL PRTFNL (VOTABL, MXCAND, ELYEAR, NCAND, CLNAME, PARTY,
      :             VTABOF, VOTES, OTVOTE, PRCENT)
       STOP
       END
*
*************************************************************************
*
*II.   ESTABLISH STATE ABBREVIATIONS, NAMES, AND POINTERS
*
       BLOCK DATA ESTANP
*      PROGRAMMER:  Jarrell C. Grout
*      DATE:  7/28/81
*
*    A. COMMENTARY
*
*          Establish state name abbreviations (STNABB), state
*      names (STNAME), and state pointers (STNPTR) for the fifty
*      United States and District of Columbia.
*
*          DICTIONARY.
*
*      ABNBLK:  Common block for state name abbreviations and
*               state names
*      MXSTAT:  Maximum number of states (including D. C.)
*      PNTBLK:  Common block for state name pointers
*      STNABB:  Standard two-character state name abbreviation
*               vector; alphabetical order
*      STNAME:  State name vector; alphabetical order
*      STNPTR:  State name pointer vector; same order as STNABB;
*               each element identifies the location of the
*               corresponding state name in STNAME
*
*    B. DECLARATION
*
       INTEGER  MXSTAT
       PARAMETER  (MXSTAT=51)
*
       CHARACTER  STNABB(MXSTAT)*2, STNAME(MXSTAT)*16
       COMMON  /ABNBLK/ STNABB, STNAME
*
       INTEGER  STNPTR(MXSTAT)
       COMMON  /PNTBLK/ STNPTR
```

Figure 11-13. (Continued)

```
*
      DATA  STNABB /
     :      'AK', 'AL', 'AR', 'AZ', 'CA', 'CO', 'CT', 'DC', 'DE',
     :      'FL', 'GE', 'HI', 'IA', 'ID', 'IL', 'IN', 'KS', 'KY',
     :      'LA', 'MA', 'MD', 'ME', 'MI', 'MN', 'MO', 'MS', 'MT',
     :      'NC', 'ND', 'NE', 'NH', 'NJ', 'NM', 'NY', 'NV', 'OH',
     :      'OK', 'OR', 'PA', 'RI', 'SC', 'SD', 'TN', 'TX', 'UT',
     :      'VA', 'VT', 'WA', 'WI', 'WV', 'WY' /
      DATA  STNAME /
     :      'Alabama', 'Alaska', 'Arizona', 'Arkansas', 'California',
     :      'Colorado', 'Connecticut', 'Delaware', 'Dist of Columbia',
     :      'Florida', 'Georgia', 'Hawaii', 'Idaho', 'Illinois',
     :      'Indiana', 'Iowa', 'Kansas', 'Kentucky', 'Louisiana',
     :      'Maine', 'Maryland', 'Massachusetts', 'Michigan',
     :      'Minnesota', 'Mississippi', 'Missouri', 'Montana',
     :      'Nebraska', 'Nevada', 'New Hampshire', 'New Jersey',
     :      'New Mexico', 'New York', 'North Carolina',
     :      'North Dakota', 'Ohio', 'Oklahoma', 'Oregon',
     :      'Pennsylvania', 'Rhode Island', 'South Carolina',
     :      'South Dakota', 'Tennessee', 'Texas', 'Utah',
     :      'Vermont', 'Virginia', 'Washington', 'West Virginia',
     :      'Wisconsin', 'Wyoming' /
      DATA  STNFTR /
     :       2,  1,  4,  3,  5,  6,  7,  9,  8, 10,
     :      11, 12, 16, 13, 14, 15, 17, 18, 19, 22,
     :      21, 20, 23, 24, 26, 25, 27, 34, 35, 28,
     :      30, 31, 32, 33, 29, 36, 37, 38, 39, 40,
     :      41, 42, 43, 44, 45, 47, 46, 48, 50, 49, 51 /
*
      END
*
**********************************************************************
*
*III.  INITIALIZE VOTE TABULATION TABLE, CANDIDATE AND PARTY
*      VECTORS
*
      SUBROUTINE INITAL (VOTABL, MXCAND, CANDIF, ELYEAR, NCAND, CLNAME,
     :                   PARTY)
*     PROGRAMMER:  Jarrell C. Grout
*     DATE:  7/28/81
*
*  A. COMMENTARY
*
*        Initialize, for program PRELAN, the vote tabulation table,
*     candidate last name vector, and party name abbreviation
*     vector.
*
*        DICTIONARY.
*
*     CAND:  Candidate index
*     STATE:  State index
*
*     These additional terms, used here, are defined in
*     main program PRELAN: CANDIF, CLNAME, ELYEAR, MXCAND,
*     MXSTAT, NCAND, PARTY, VOTABL.
*
*  B. DECLARATION
*
      INTEGER  CANDIF, MXCAND, MXSTAT
      PARAMETER  (MXSTAT=51)
*
      INTEGER  CAND, NCAND, STATE, VOTABL(MXSTAT, MXCAND+1)
      CHARACTER*(*)  CLNAME(MXCAND+1), ELYEAR, PARTY(MXCAND)
*
*  C. I/O LAYOUT
*
  100 FORMAT (A4)
  110 FORMAT (A12, A3)
*
*  D. ACTION
      DO 220 CAND = 1, MXCAND + 1
         DO 210 STATE = 1, MXSTAT
            VOTABL(STATE, CAND) = 0
  210    CONTINUE
  220 CONTINUE
      READ (CANDIF, 100) ELYEAR
      NCAND = 0
      DO 230 CAND = 1, MXCAND
         READ (CANDIF, 110, END=240) CLNAME(CAND), PARTY(CAND)
         NCAND = CAND
```

Figure 11-13. (Continued)

```
     230 CONTINUE
   *     Use extra candidate name position for state total column header
     240 CLNAME(NCAND + 1) = 'STATE TOTALS'
         RETURN
         END

   *****************************************************************************
   *
   *IV.  PROCESS VOTE UPDATE BATCHES
   *
         SUBROUTINE UPDATE (VOTABL, MXCAND, ELYEAR, NCAND, CLNAME, PARTY,
        :                     VOTEIF, VTABOF, VOTES, OTVOTE, PRCENT)
   *     PROGRAMMER:  Jarrell C. Grout
   *     DATE:  7/29/81
   *
   *  A. COMMENTARY
   *
   *        Process vote update batches for program PRELAN.  Print an
   *     intermediate vote tabulation table for each batch until the
   *     end of the vote file is reached.
   *
   *        DICTIONARY.
   *
   *     BATCH:  Vote batch counter
   *     BISRCH:  Binary search subroutine for locating state name
   *     CAND:  Candidate index
   *     CANLOC:  Location in CLNAME of candidate name for whom
   *               votes are submitted
   *     CANDLN:  Candidate last name in a 'vote data' input record
   *     STABBR:  Standard two-character state name abbreviation
   *               in a 'vote data' input record
   *     STATE:  State index
   *     STNLOC:  Location in STNAME of name of state submitting
   *               votes
   *
   *     These additional terms, used here, are defined in main program
   *     PRELAN:  ADVOTE, CLNAME, ELYEAR, MXCAND, NCAND, OTVOTE, PARTY,
   *     PRCENT, VOTABL, VOTEIF, VOTES, VTABOF.
   *
   *     These additional terms, used here, are defined in main program
   *     PRELAN and block data subprogram ESTANP:  ABNBLK, MXSTAT, PNTBLK,
   *     STNABB, STNAME, STNPTR.
   *
   *  B. DECLARATION
   *
         INTEGER  MXCAND, MXSTAT, VOTEIF, VTABOF
         PARAMETER  (MXSTAT=51)
   *
         CHARACTER  STNABB(MXSTAT)*2, STNAME(MXSTAT)*16
         COMMON  /ABNBLK/ STNABB, STNAME
   *
         INTEGER  STNPTR(MXSTAT)
         COMMON  /PNTBLK/ STNPTR
   *
         INTEGER  ADVOTE, BATCH, CAND, CANLOC, NCAND, OTVOTE, STATE,
        :          STNLOC, VOTABL(MXSTAT, MXCAND+1), VOTES(MXCAND)
         REAL  PRCENT(MXCAND)
         CHARACTER*(*)  CLNAME(MXCAND+1), ELYEAR, PARTY(MXCAND)
         CHARACTER  CANDLN*12, STABBR*2
   *
   *  C. I/O LAYOUT
   *
     120 FORMAT (A2)
     130 FORMAT (A12, I8)
     900 FORMAT ('1', A4, ' PRESIDENTIAL ELECTION VOTE TABULATION:  ',
        :          'BATCH ', I3, //)
     910 FORMAT (' ', T24, 7(A12, 3X))
     920 FORMAT (' ', 'STATE', T24, 6(A3, 12))
     930 FORMAT (' ')
     940 FORMAT (' ', A16, T24, 7(I8, 7X))
     950 FORMAT ('0', 'CANDIDATE TOTALS:    ', 7(I9, 6X))
     960 FORMAT (' ', '     PERCENTAGES:', 10X, 6(F5.1, 10X))
   *
   *  D. ACTION
   *
         BATCH = 0
     245   READ (VOTEIF, 120, END=410) STABBR
           IF (STABBR .NE. '$B') THEN
               CALL BISRCH (STABBR, STNLOC)
```

Figure 11-13. (Continued)

```
*              Begin processing votes by candidate
    310        READ (VOTEIF, 130) CANDLN, ADVOTE
               IF (CANDLN(1:2) .NE. '$S') THEN
*                  Begin linear search procedure for locating
*                  candidate name
                   DO 320 CAND = 1, NCAND
                       IF (CANDLN .EQ. CLNAME(CAND)) THEN
                           CANLOC = CAND
                           GO TO 330
                       ENDIF
    320            CONTINUE
*                  End linear search procedure
*                  Perform vote tabulation table update
    330            VOTABL(STNLOC, CANLOC) = VOTABL(STNLOC, CANLOC) + ADVOTE
                   GO TO 310
               ENDIF
           ELSE
*              Increment batch counter, compute overall total votes,
*              state totals, candidate totals, and candidate percents,
*              and print intermediate tabulation table for this batch
               BATCH = BATCH + 1
               OTVOTE = 0
               DO 350 STATE = 1, MXSTAT
                   VOTABL(STATE, NCAND+1) = 0
                   DO 340 CAND = 1, NCAND
                       VOTABL(STATE, NCAND+1) = VOTABL(STATE, NCAND+1) +
                                                VOTABL(STATE, CAND)
    340            CONTINUE
                   OTVOTE = OTVOTE + VOTABL(STATE, NCAND+1)
    350        CONTINUE
               DO 370 CAND = 1, NCAND
                   VOTES(CAND) = 0
                   PRCENT(CAND) = 0.0
                   DO 360 STATE = 1, MXSTAT
                       VOTES(CAND) = VOTES(CAND) + VOTABL(STATE, CAND)
    360            CONTINUE
                   PRCENT(CAND) = VOTES(CAND) * 100.0 / OTVOTE
    370        CONTINUE
               WRITE (VTABOF, 900) ELYEAR, BATCH
               WRITE (VTABOF, 910) (CLNAME(CAND), CAND = 1, NCAND+1)
               WRITE (VTABOF, 920) (PARTY(CAND), CAND = 1, NCAND)
               WRITE (VTABOF, 930)
               DO 380 STATE = 1, MXSTAT
                   WRITE (VTABOF, 940) STNAME(STATE),
                           (VOTABL(STATE, CAND), CAND = 1, NCAND+1)
    380        CONTINUE
               WRITE (VTABOF, 950) (VOTES(CAND), CAND = 1, NCAND), OTVOTE
               WRITE (VTABOF, 960) (PRCENT(CAND), CAND = 1, NCAND)
*              End printing of intermediate tabulation table
           ENDIF
           GO TO 245
    410 RETURN
        END

*
**************************************************************************
*
*IVA. BINARY SEARCH
*
        SUBROUTINE BISRCH (STABBR, STNLOC)
*       PROGRAMMER:  Jarrell C. Grout
*       DATE:  7/29/81
*
*   A. COMMENTARY
*
*           Perform a binary search procedure, for subroutine UPDATE,
*       to find the location (STNLOC) of the state name with abbreviation
*       STABBR in the state name vector (STNAME) using the state
*       name pointer vector (STNPTR).
*
*           DICTIONARY.
*
*       HIGH:   Higher bound on STNABB for binary search
*       LOW:    Lower bound on STNABB for binary search
*       MID:    Mid-point in STNABB bounded by HIGH and LOW in
*               binary search
*       STABBR: Standard two-character state name abbreviation
*               in a 'vote data' input record; defined in UPDATE
*       STNLOC: Location in STNAME of name of state submitting
*               votes
```

Figure 11-13. (Continued)

```
*
*           These additional terms, used here, are defined in main program
*           PRELA1 and block data subprogram ESTANP:  ABNBLK, MXSTAT, PNTBLK,
*           STNABB, STNAME, STNPTR.
*
*       B.  DECLARATION
*
            INTEGER MXSTAT
            PARAMETER  (MXSTAT=51)
*
            CHARACTER  STNABB(MXSTAT)*2, STNAME(MXSTAT)*16
            COMMON  /ABNBLK/ STNABB, STNAME
*
            INTEGER  STNPTR(MXSTAT)
            COMMON  /PNTBLK/ STNPTR
*
            INTEGER  HIGH, LOW, MID, STNLOC
            CHARACTER*(*)  STABBR
*
*       C.  I/O LAYOUT
*
*           None
*
*       D.  ACTION
*
            LOW = 1
            HIGH = MXSTAT
      250   IF (LOW .LE. HIGH) THEN
                MID = (LOW + HIGH) / 2
                IF (STABBR .LT. STNABB(MID)) THEN
                    HIGH = MID - 1
                ELSE IF (STABBR .GT. STNABB(MID)) THEN
                    LOW = MID + 1
                ELSE
                    STNLOC = STNPTR(MID)
                    GO TO 310
                ENDIF
            ELSE
*               The input abbreviation is not in the vector;
*               alternative action to be added by the reader
            ENDIF
            GO TO 250
      310 RETURN
          END
*
*********************************************************************************
*
*V.   PRINT FINAL VOTE TABULATION TABLE
*
      SUBROUTINE PRTFNL (VOTABL, MXCAND, ELYEAR, NCAND, CLNAME, PARTY,
     :                   VTABOF, VOTES, OTVOTE, PRCENT)
*       PROGRAMMER:  Jarrell C. Grout
*       DATE:  7/29/81
*
*       A.  COMMENTARY
*
*           Print the final vote tabulation table for program PRELAN.
*
*           DICTIONARY.
*
*           These terms, used here, are defined in main program PRELAN:
*           CLNAME, ELYEAR, MXCAND, MXSTAT, NCAND, OTVOTE, PARTY, PRCENT,
*           VOTABL, VOTES, VTABOF.
*
*           These terms, used here, are defined in main program PRELAN and
*           block data subprogram ESTANP:  ABNBLK, PNTBLK, STNABB, STNAME.
*
*       B.  DECLARATION
*
            INTEGER  MXCAND, MXSTAT, VTABOF
            PARAMETER  (MXSTAT=51)
*
            CHARACTER  STNABB(MXSTAT)*2, STNAME(MXSTAT)*16
            COMMON  /ABNBLK/ STNABB, STNAME
*
            INTEGER  CAND, NCAND, OTVOTE, STATE, VOTABL(MXSTAT, MXCAND+1),
     :               VOTES(MXCAND)
            REAL  PRCENT(MXCAND)
            CHARACTER*(*)  CLNAME(MXCAND+1), ELYEAR, PARTY(MXCAND)
```

Figure 11-13. (Continued)

```
*
* C. I/O LAYOUT
*
  910 FORMAT (' ', T24, 7(A12, 3X))
  920 FORMAT (' ', 'STATE', T24, 6(A3, 12X))
  930 FORMAT (' ')
  940 FORMAT (' ', A16, T24, 7(I8, 7X))
  950 FORMAT ('0', 'CANDIDATE TOTALS:   ', 7(I9, 6X))
  960 FORMAT (' ', '        PERCENTAGES:', 10X, 6(F5.1, 10X))
  970 FORMAT ('1', A4, ' PRESIDENTIAL ELECTION VOTE TABULATION:  ',
    :             'FINAL RESULTS', //)
*
* D. ACTION
*
      WRITE (VTABOF, 970) ELYEAR
      WRITE (VTABOF, 910) (CLNAME(CAND), CAND = 1, NCAND+1)
      WRITE (VTABOF, 920) (PARTY(CAND), CAND = 1, NCAND)
      WRITE (VTABOF, 930)
      DO 480 STATE = 1, MXSTAT
        WRITE (VTABOF, 940) STNAME(STATE),
    :        (VOTABL(STATE, CAND), CAND = 1, NCAND+1)
  480 CONTINUE
      WRITE (VTABOF, 950) (VOTES(CAND), CAND = 1, NCAND), OTVOTE
      WRITE (VTABOF, 960) (PRCENT(CAND), CAND = 1, NCAND)
      RETURN
      END
```

Figure 11-13. (Continued)

Communication among the program modules takes place by means of common blocks as well as arguments. Observe that one common block necessarily contains only character data; the other comprises numeric data. The values of the common block entities are defined in the block data subprogram; they never change during execution. The COMMON statements, themselves, are placed in the main program, in the block data subprogram, and then only in the subroutines that need to have access to the common blocks.

In the argument lists, only the essential arguments are included. For consistency, the corresponding actual and dummy arguments are spelled the same way. To provide generality, assumed-length declarations are made for character dummy arguments. An example of this kind of declaration is the subroutine INITAL statement

    CHARACTER*(*)   CLNAME(MXCAND+1), ELYEAR, PARTY(MXCAND)

which declares that the length specification of each item in the list is the same as the specification for the actual argument associated with the item.

Also for generality, all dummy arrays are adjustable. Alternatively, assumed-size arrays could have been used. In subroutine INITAL, for instance, the declaration for integer array VOTABL could have been

    INTEGER VOTABL(MXSTAT, *)

and the last dimension declarator would then have been assumed to be the same as the one for the actual argument associated with VOTABL.

The binary search subroutine, BISRCH, is physically placed after UPDATE—its referencing program unit. Its position designation is given as IVA to indicate its relationship with UPDATE, which has the position designation IV. This physical positioning and position designation are part of a personal systematic practice; they are not required by Fortran. As far as Fortran is concerned, a subprogram just has to be accessible by the referencing program unit in order for it to be in the executable program.

11-9 EXERCISES

1. Exercise 6 of Section 5-11 explains how to obtain the factorial of a positive integer. Plan and write a general external function named FACTRL for computing the factorial. Also plan and write a complete main program, which references the function, for finding the number of permutations and combinations of n things taken k at a time. The latter is defined in the aforementioned Exercise 6.

2. Exercise 5 of Section 5-11 and Exercise 4 of Section 7-1-5 have to do with developing an algorithm and main program for finding the square root of a number. Plan and write a general function subprogram that will find the square root of a given nonnegative real number correct to the nearest 0.000001.

3. Plan and write a general external function that will find the sum of the numbers in a real one-dimensional array. The size of the array is known only at the time of execution, and can be furnished by the referencing program unit.

4. The function LENSUB, given in Figure 9-5, finds the length of a nonblank substring. The method that is actually used in the function is to locate the first blank position of the string, if one exists, and assume that the remaining positions are not part of the desired substring. Thus for the string

   ```
   San Francisco
   ```

   it supplys a substring length of 3. Plan and write a general function subprogram to find the length of a substring in which there may be embedded single blanks. The length determined by your function for the string above will be 13.

5. Exercise 6 of Section 8-8 contains an algorithm for printing the change due on a dollar for a purchase price of a dollar or less. Plan and write a general function subprogram for the algorithm.

6. Plan and write a binary search subroutine—similar to BISRCH in Section 11-8—that will find the location of a specific integer in an ordered set of integers. Notice that BISRCH does not specify the alternative action to be taken whenever the input abbreviation is not found in the vector. Your subroutine, however, should specify an alternative action that allows processing to continue whenever an input integer cannot be found in your ordered set.

7. A general bubble sort subroutine is given in this chapter. An indirect sort procedure, in which the bubble sort method is used, is included in the multiple-choice test grading program of Section 9-11. Plan and write a general indirect bubble sort subroutine for sorting data based on an alphabetic key of unspecified length.

8. Plan and write a generally applicable selection sort subroutine using the description given in Exercise 8 of Section 8-8. The sort should be alphabetic.

9. Plan and write a subroutine subprogram named REPLCE that will take a given substring and find and then replace it, in a stored string, with a new substring. The new substring can be longer than, shorter than, or the same length as the old substring. Move the other characters in the stored string appropriately. For instance, in the stored string

   ```
   Different stokes for diffenert folks.
   ```

   the substring

   ```
   strokes for different
   ```

   is to replace the substring

   ```
   stokes for diffenert
   ```

   and, of course, the final result should be

   ```
   Different strokes for different folks.
   ```

   This is an editing exercise. Assume that there are many stored strings and that they are numbered sequentially. Also assume that the maximum length for each stored string is 100 characters.

10. Completely revise the multiple-choice test grading program of Figure 9-9 so that the main program is a driver that references three subroutines. Remember to include the function LENSUB in the executable program. Do not simply sort the student names by last name; rather, sort them by middle initial, then first name, then last name, to ensure that they will be in alphabetical order. Use only one sort subroutine—an indirect one.

11. Plan and write a complete executable program, which has as many subprograms as necessary, to solve the statistical problem assigned in Exercise 11 of Section 8-8.

12. Plan and write a complete executable program to solve the inventory problem described in Exercise 12 of Section 8-8. The main program should be a driver. The reading and printing of the master file, the reading and updating of the transaction records, and the printing of the transaction report should individually be accomplished by means of subroutines.

13. Plan and write a complete executable program for the merchandise inventory problem of Exercise 5 of Section 10-1-6. The main program should be a driver. Use subroutines for the distinct processes in the problem solution.

14. Plan and write a complete executable program to solve the least squares problem described in Exercise 12 of Section 10-1-6. This problem offers plenty of opportunities for using subprograms, including at least these: summation of many quantities (modify the function for Exercise 3 above), creation of the normal equations, inversion of the matrix, and the computation of the coefficients.

APPENDIX: RELATED FORTRAN FEATURES

There are six other subprogram-related features of the FORTRAN 77 language that you should know about. They are itemized and briefly described below. For complete explanations about them, consult reference 2 at the end of Chapter 3, and the Fortran language manual for your computer system.

A1 Alternate Entry

As suggested in Sections 11-4 and 11-5, it is possible to specify more than one external function in a function subprogram and more than one subroutine in a subroutine subprogram. This is accomplished by placing an ENTRY statement among the action statements of a function or subroutine subprogram, just prior to every executable statement that begins a new function or subroutine in that subprogram. The ENTRY statement is nonexecutable. Its form is

```
ENTRY ename (dargs)
```

where ename is the symbolic name of the entry; that is, ename is a function name or a subroutine name, depending on the type of subprogram it appears in. The entry is referenced exactly like a function or subroutine, as appropriate.

You should be aware that the alternate entry violates the recommended structured programming practice of one entry−one exit per module.

A2 Alternate Return

It is also possible to have execution control transferred from a subroutine to one of several statements in the referencing program unit. This is accomplished by using a RETURN statement of the form

```
RETURN iexp
```

where iexp is an integer expression, in conjunction with a SUBROUTINE or ENTRY dummy argument list that contains asterisks and a corresponding CALL statement that contains alternate return specifiers associated with the asterisks. Alternate return specifiers have the form *sn, where sn is the statement number of an executable statement in the referencing program unit. For example, with the reference

```
CALL SUB (A, B, *250, *260)
```

and the subroutine lines

```
SUBROUTINE SUB (A, B, *, *)
.
.
.
RETURN 2
```

control will be transferred to statement 260 in the referencing program unit whenever the RETURN statement is executed.

Clearly, the alternate return feature also violates the recommended structured programming practice of one entry—one exit per module.

A3   The EXTERNAL and INTRINSIC Statements

These statements identify symbolic names as either actual external functions, actual subroutines, dummy external functions, dummy subroutines, or intrinsic functions, and allow the names to be used as actual arguments. The statement forms are

```
EXTERNAL exname, ...
```

and

```
INTRINSIC ifname, ...
```

where ifname denotes an intrinsic function name and exname represents the others mentioned above.

A4   The SAVE Statement

Variables and arrays that appear in a subprogram but do not appear in an argument list or common block in that subprogram normally become undefined upon the execution of a RETURN or END statement in that subprogram. Additionally, such entities that do appear in a common block in that subprogram become undefined on a return if the common block is not declared for access by a program unit that references the subprogram. If it is desired to retain the values of such entities, the SAVE statement can be used in the subprogram. Its form is

```
SAVE item, ...
```

where item is a variable or array that is not in common, or a common block name. The definition status of such variables and arrays is retained for the next reference to the subprogram. The definition status of all entities in such a common block is retained for use by all program units that declare access to the common block.

A5   The EQUIVALENCE Statement

The EQUIVALENCE statement is similar in nature to the COMMON statement, except that it has effect only within the program unit in which it appears. Its purpose is to allow variables, array elements, arrays, or substrings to share storage in a program unit. Its form is

```
EQUIVALENCE (nlist), ...
```

where nlist is a list of sharing variable names, array element names, array names, and substrings. Ordinarily, only like entities should be equivalenced—if any should be equivalenced. Experience indicates that this feature is often used when poor planning has resulted in two or more names being given accidentally to the same entity—an inferior usage. Unless a program is large in storage requirements, and storage is at a premium, equivalencing should probably be avoided. Even then, it should only be done with extreme care.

A6   Statement Functions

Statement functions are defined by a single assignment-like statement and referenced only in the same program unit in which they are defined. Thus a statement function is not a subprogram but is like a function subprogram that has one executable statement. The form of the defining statement, which must appear before any executable statement, is

```
sfname (dargs) = expression
```

where sfname is the symbolic name and dargs is the dummy argument list of the statement function. The statement function name must have a data type and the expression should be of the same type. The items in the expression must be defined or definable through the dummy arguments whenever the statement function is referenced during execution. A statement function reference has the form

```
sfname (aargs)
```

The following is a simple statement function example.

```
REAL   ANUITY, FWF, INTRST, PRIN, RATE
INTEGER   PERIDS, YEARS
FWF (RATE, PERIDS) = (1.0 + RATE) ** PERIDS
  .
  .
  .
ANUITY = PRIN * INTRST / (FWF(INTRST, YEARS) - 1.0)
PRINT *, PRIN, PRIN * FWF(INTRST, YEARS), ANUITY
```

The nonexecutable definition, FWF, has the dummy arguments RATE and PERIDS. Both of the subsequent executable statements refer to the statement function. Upon the execution of each reference, RATE becomes associated with INTRST and PERIDS becomes associated with YEARS; then the expression on the right-hand side of the function definition is evaluated, providing a value for FWF in the referencing expression. For instance, if INTRST, YEARS, and PRIN are previously defined in the action section as 0.15, 5, and 10000, the values printed will be approximately

    10000.00   20113.57   1483.16

Any procedure that can be written as a statement function can also be written as an external function or a subroutine.

File
Input and Output

Clearly, the Fortran language is designed to allow an executable program to accept data from one or more input files and transmit data to one or more output files. In virtually all of the examples and exercises given thus far in this book, each program uses one input file and one output file; each of the input files, purposely kept relatively small for ease of handling as you learn, is stored on an input medium such as punched cards or magnetic tape or magnetic disk; each output file is written, via the printer, on printed pages. In reality, though, many input files are usually very large. Furthermore, they not only provide input data to programs, but they also must be brought up to date by the output from the same or other programs. Therefore, these files can serve as both input and output files. Accordingly, they are usually placed on a secondary storage medium such as magnetic tape or disk, which provides a vast amount of relatively inexpensive storage space and can be used for both input and output.

Files that reside on printed pages, or even punched cards, are usually designed for human beings to read and understand. Therefore, the records of these files are usually formatted and thus contain the letters and digits and other characters that people are used to. In a Fortran program this means that either explicit formats or the implied formats of list-directed i/o are used. Only formatted records have been considered in this book to this point.

Files that reside on magnetic tape or disk can also contain formatted records. But since tape and disk files can only be read and written by the computer, they can be unformatted; that is, the data in the records can have the same binary representation that they have in the computer's main memory. The use of unformatted records in i/o files allows more efficient transfer of data between the i/o device and memory because no data conversion or editing are required during transfer. The primary drawback to the use of unformatted records is that they are processor dependent; they can only be processed by the computer that produced them—or one that is identical to it.

As described above and in earlier chapters, the files referred to are stored outside the program and outside the computer's main memory. In FORTRAN 77 they are called *external files*. FORTRAN 77 also allows data in the form of collections of related records to be placed in main memory for the special purpose of transfer and conversion within memory. These collections are termed *internal files*.

This chapter is intended to expand on what you already know about input and output by familiarizing you with FORTRAN 77's external file processing capabilities, for both formatted and unformatted records, and acquainting you with internal files.

12-1   EXTERNAL FILES

In order for a file to be accessed by a program for either input or output, it must first be connected to a unit. For an external file, this tells the computer that the file either resides on an input device or will reside on an output device.

Once an external file is connected, its records can be accessed either sequentially or directly, depending on the method specified when the connection is made. Also, when the connection is made or when the transfer of data between the file and main memory occurs, certain errors and end-of-file conditions can be detected. Additionally, a file connected for sequential access has a position characteristic—that is, a property that identifies the preceding, current, and next records for i/o—that can be altered during execution. Furthermore, the file can be examined for the presence or absence of certain attributes. Finally, the file is disconnected from the unit.

The procedures and Fortran statements for establishing a connection, specifying an access method, transferring data, positioning, examining, and disconnecting are described, one by one, below.

12-1-1   Connection of a Unit and a File

When connected, a unit refers to a file. When a unit is connected to a file, the file is also connected to the unit. A unit can only be connected to one file at a time. After being connected, a file is accessible to all program units in the executable program until it is disconnected. A file that is not connected is not accessible.

Connection is accomplished either prior to execution by means of system default unit assignments or job control language association of unit and file, or during execution by means of the OPEN statement. The former method is called *preconnection* and is the one employed to this point in the text. For instance, in the presidential election analysis program of Figure 11-13, the values of the symbolic names VOTEIF and VTABOF may identify the system default units for input and output, referring, therefore, to files on the system default devices. In the same program, the value of the symbolic name CANDIF identifies an input unit that may refer to a disk file which is preconnected by means of job control language prior to execution.

The OPEN statement cannot only connect a file to a unit during execution, but it can also create a file or change certain specifiers of a connection. It has the general form

    OPEN (oslist)

where oslist is a list of open specifiers. The specifiers, which pertain only to the identified file, are selected, as needed, from these:

UNIT=u: the unit specifier in which u is the external unit identifier—identical in form and meaning to the one used in READ and WRITE statements. The UNIT= portion is optional.

FILE=fn: the file specifier in which fn is a character expression whose value, excluding trailing blanks, is the name of the file to be connected to the identified unit.

STATUS=st: a file status specifier in which st is a character expression whose value, excluding trailing blanks, is OLD, NEW, SCRATCH, or UNKNOWN. An OLD file is one that already has been created—it already exists. A NEW file is one that is beginning to be created. A SCRATCH file is a temporary one that is created and exists, at its longest, only until execution is terminated—it must not be named. UNKNOWN is the default for this specifier; it means that the status is processor dependent.

FORM=fm: a record-type specifier in which fm is a character expression whose value, excluding trailing blanks, is FORMATTED or UNFORMATTED. If it is omitted, the default is FORMATTED for sequential access files and UNFORMATTED for direct access files.

BLANK=bl: a blank-treatment specifier in which bl is a character expression whose value, excluding trailing blanks, is NULL or ZERO. NULL, the default, causes blanks in numeric input fields of the file to be ignored; ZERO causes trailing blanks in numeric input fields of the file to be treated as zeros. This specifier is for formatted i/o only.

ACCESS=ac: an access method specifier in which ac, the access method identifier, is a character expression whose value, excluding trailing blanks, is SEQUENTIAL or DIRECT. The former is the default. More is said about this in Section 12-1-2.

RECL=rl: a record length specifier, for direct access files only, in which rl, the record length identifier, must be a positive-valued integer expression. If the file records are formatted, the length is stated in characters; if unformatted, in processor-dependent units. More about this one, also, in Section 12-1-2.

IOSTAT=ios: an input/output status specifier in which ios, an integer, becomes defined with a zero if an error condition does not exist or a positive value if an error condition does exist whenever an OPEN statement is executed. More on this in Section 12-1-4.

ERR=s: an error specifier in which s is the statement number of an executable statement in the same program unit. If an error occurs during the execution of the OPEN statement, the statement labeled s is immediately executed and execution continues from there. More on this, also, in Section 12-1-4.

Of the above, only a unit specifier is absolutely required in all OPEN statements; some of the others are required in specific cases that are identified in the following sections. At most only one of each specifier may appear in one OPEN statement; they can appear in any order except that the unit specifier must be first if the UNIT= portion is omitted.

As an initial example, the following OPEN statement could have appeared as the first action statement in subroutine INITAL (or main program PRELAN) of the presidential election analysis program in Figure 11-13.

```
OPEN (UNIT=CANDIF, FILE='FCPCAND', STATUS='OLD',
  :     FORM='FORMATTED', ACCESS='SEQUENTIAL')
```

By including this statement in the program, I would not have had to use job control statements to preconnect the file (though some computer systems might still require some job control statements). Observe that the statement explicitly contains the name of the file, FCPCAND. As an alternative, which provides more flexibility, the file name could be read in as the value of a variable prior to the execution of the OPEN statement. In fact, since file naming methods vary from computer to computer, FCPCAND may or may not be an allowable file name in your computer; you may therefore have to read the file name or define it as a different constant. Assuming, then, that the file name is read in through the system default input device, and that CFNAME is a properly declared character variable, the following two statements could replace the one statement above:

```
READ *, CFNAME
OPEN (CANDIF, FILE=CFNAME, STATUS='OLD')
```

This allows the file name to have any system-dependent form. In addition to reading the file name, the UNIT= portion of the unit specifier, as well as the record type and access method specifiers, were omitted in this second OPEN statement to show you an equivalent alternative form. The latter two specifiers can be omitted because they merely specify defaults in the first OPEN statement. Notice that the file status is OLD in both OPEN statements; this is because it is an input file—a file that already exists.

As a different example, the baseball standing problem, illustrated toward the end of Section 9-4-2 and in Figure 9-3, could have been handled better if each league had two files—a "standings" file maintained in secondary storage and a "games played" file created online each day. This would eliminate the need to manually recreate the standings data each day. Assuming proper definition of the unit identifiers, then, these statements could be used to connect the files prior to reading data from them:

```
READ *, STNDGS, GAMES
OPEN (UNIT=STDIF, FILE=STNDGS, STATUS='OLD')
OPEN (UNIT=GAMIF, FILE=GAMES, STATUS='NEW',
:       BLANK='NULL')
```

The standings file is designated as an existing file because it is updated by the program each day and maintained on secondary storage. It serves, then, not only as an input file but also as an output file for the program. Such a file, which is relatively permanent because it is continually available and shows the up-to-date overall situation for a particular application, is generally called a *master file*. (Consider the similarity of a "baseball standings master file" to a "student information master file," a "personnel master file," a "payroll master file," and so on.)

The games file is designated as a new file because it does not yet exist, but is created by input to the program. It is then used to update the standings file. Finally, it can be saved or deleted. If it is to be deleted, it might just as well have been opened by the statement

```
OPEN (UNIT=GAMIF, STATUS='SCRATCH', BLANK='NULL')
```

which allows the file to be created and used during execution, but results in automatic deletion when the file is disconnected. Inclusion of the blank-treatment specifier causes trailing blanks in game scores to be ignored; since NULL is the default, however, the effect would be the same if the specifier is omitted. Files like the games file, which are created periodically and used on a temporary basis in conjunction with master files, are generally termed *transaction files*.

12-1-2 Methods of File Access

The records of an external file can be accessed either sequentially or directly, depending on the i/o medium used and the value of the access method identifier in the OPEN statement for the file. Sequential access, the method used on all files so far in this book, means that records are read or written consecutively in the sequence that is logical for the file. Magnetic tape is a sequential medium because records are written one by one down the length of a tape. This means, for instance, that in order to read/write the one-hundredth record of a magnetic tape file, or any sequential file, records 1 through 99 must be read/written first. The records in a sequential file are not located by an explicit record number; rather, a particular record is found, when necessary, by the examination of key field values in a linear search process. Punched cards and pages printed by the line printer are other examples of sequential mediums. In contrast, magnetic disks and drums can be used for files that are to be accessed either sequentially or directly.

The direct access method provides a way to read or write a record immediately without first having to read or write any other records. Each record of a file connected for direct access must have a record number—a positive integer. The order of the records in the files is the order of their record numbers; however, the records can be read or written in any order. The record number is specified in the read or write statement as described in the next section.

The OPEN statement examples given so far are for files that are being connected for sequential access. If the baseball standings files were established so that there is one magnetic disk file for each division in each league, random—or direct—inquiries could be made about the standings through an interactive program in which the files are connected for direct access. The OPEN statement in the program might look like this:

```
OPEN (UNIT=STDIF, FILE=STNDGS, STATUS='OLD',
   :      FORM='FORMATTED', ACCESS='DIRECT', RECL=25)
```

where the value of STNDGS, obtained by input, is the name of the file for a particular division in one of the leagues. The records are identified as being formatted and the record length is equal to the number of characters specified in the format statement given in Section 9-4-2, and repeated below, for reading the standings in a division. After the execution of this OPEN statement, the following statements could be used to directly locate and display the name and won−lost record of the team that is in a particular place in the standings.

```
114 FORMAT (A13, 3X, I3, 3X, I3)
    .
    .
    .
    READ *, PLACE
    READ (STDIF, 114, REC=PLACE) TMNAME, WON, LOST
    PRINT *, TMNAME, WON, LOST
```

As you can see, the record number—that is, the value of PLACE—is specified in the second READ statement. This direct access form of the READ statement is explained more fully in the next section. If, for example, the division chosen is the National League East and the input value of PLACE is 3, the results displayed by the execution of the statements above (based on the data in Figure 9-3) would be

```
Montreal      25   19
```

Admittedly, the baseball standings files are rather small, but the concepts presented here are applicable to any size file. For very large files, in which the records need to be located on a random rather than an ordered basis, you can see that the direct access method offers advantages over the sequential access method.

Whereas all of the records in a file connected for direct access must have the same length, the records in a file connected for sequential access can vary in length. However, all the records in both types of files must be either formatted or unformatted, except that the last record of a file connected for sequential access can be an endfile record as described in the section ahead on file positioning. List-directed formatting cannot be used for direct access records.

The baseball standings file exemplified above can just as well be created and processed with unformatted records. The OPEN statement for processing after file creation could then be written as follows.

```
OPEN (UNIT=STDIF, FILE=STNDGS, STATUS='OLD',
    :    FORM='UNFORMATTED', ACCESS='DIRECT', RECL=pdrl)
```

Here, pdrl refers to "processor-dependent record length," indicating that the length identifier units for unformatted records can vary from computer to computer. On my computer, the units are computer words; on yours, they may be bytes. Look in the Fortran language manual for your computer or ask a local computer professional.

12-1-3 Data Transfer

In FORTRAN 77, the transfer of data from a file into memory is always accomplished by a READ statement, and the transfer in the reverse direction is performed by means of a WRITE or PRINT statement. Such transfers can only take place on files that have already been opened either by preconnection or by the execution of an OPEN statement.

The PRINT statement has previously been completely described. However, the READ and WRITE statements have general forms that are more comprehensive than the forms given earlier. These general forms are

```
READ (rslist) iolist
```

and

```
WRITE (wslist) iolist
```

where rslist is a list of read specifiers, wslist is a list of write specifiers, and iolist is—as always—an input/output list that specifies the data to be transferred. The read specifiers are:

UNIT=u: the unit specifier exactly as described for the OPEN statement.

FMT=f: a format specifier in which f is the statement number of a FORMAT statement in the same program unit. The FMT= portion can be omitted. The specifier is included only if a format is used.

REC=rn: a record specifier in which rn, the record number, is a positive-valued integer expression. This specifier is allowed and required only for files that are connected for direct access.

END=s: the familiar end-of-file specifier; allowed only for files that are connected for sequential access.

IOSTAT=ios: an input/output status specifier, as introduced with the OPEN statement and described in the next section.

ERR=s: an error specifier, as introduced with the OPEN statement and described in the next section.

The WRITE specifiers are the same as the above except that the end-of-file specifier is omitted; it cannot appear in a WRITE statement. All READ specifier lists and WRITE specifier lists must contain one unit specifier; a maximum of one of each of the other specifiers can appear in each such list.

The formatted direct access READ statement given in the preceding section is more understandable now. An alternative way of writing it is

```
READ (UNIT=STDIF, FMT=114, REC=PLACE) TMNAME, WON, LOST
```

A program segment that could be used, in a different program unit, to create the baseball standings file from which the statement above extracts one record is:

```
114 FORMAT (A13, 3X, I3, 3X, I3)
      .
      .
      .
    OPEN (UNIT=STDIF, FILE=STNDGS, STATUS='NEW',
   :       FORM='FORMATTED', ACCESS='DIRECT', RECL=25)
    DO 310 TEAM = HITEAM, LOTEAM
       READ *, TMNAME, WON, LOST
       WRITE (UNIT=STDIF, FMT=114, REC=TEAM) TMNAME, WON,
   :                                               LOST
310 CONTINUE
```

provided that all variables are properly declared and defined as necessary. This segment assumes input of the initial data through the system default device (terminal or card reader) to provide values for the creation of the new file. After the new file is opened, its status changes to OLD, indicating that it then exists. Notice, particularly, that the WRITE statement refers to a FORMAT statement that has no carriage control specification. A carriage control specification is only necessary for printing; one is not necessary for writing on devices other than the printer.

The standings file in the form of an unformatted direct access file, as described in the final OPEN statement example of the last section, could be initially created with this segment:

```
    OPEN (STDIF, FILE=STNDGS, STATUS='NEW',
   :       ACCESS='DIRECT', RECL=pdrl)
    DO 310 TEAM = HITEAM, LOTEAM
       READ *, TMNAME, WON, LOST
       WRITE (STDIF, REC=TEAM) TMNAME, WON, LOST
310 CONTINUE
```

where pdrl must be replaced by the actual record length in the correct processor-dependent units. The reason I omitted the UNIT= portion of the unit specifiers is to illustrate an allowed simplification.

Remember this about unformatted files: They allow faster transfer of data between i/o device and memory than do formatted files; however, they, and the OPEN statement used with them, are processor dependent.

12-1-4   I/O Error Detection

You know that errors, such as a numeric value being outside its allowable range, can occur in input data. Accordingly, you build error checks into your programs to detect and identify such errors, and to recover if possible. But other kinds of i/o errors, most of which have been programmatically unchecked to this point, can also occur. Here are a few examples:

1. An attempt to read data from a file after the end of the file has been reached.
2. An attempt to read a character string with a numeric format specification.
3. An attempt to perform i/o on a unit that is not connected.
4. Attempting to read a nonexistent record from a direct access file.
5. Attempting to open an existing file as a new file or attempting to open a nonexisting file as an old file.
6. Attempting to connect a direct access file to a unit that identifies a device which can have sequential files only, such as a magnetic tape drive.
7. Attempting to write unformatted records to a file connected for formatted i/o, or vice versa.

These and other i/o errors usually result in an abnormal termination of execution, or *abend*, unless recovery specifiers are included in the i/o statement being executed when the error occurs.

There are two error recovery specifiers in FORTRAN 77, the end-of-file (END=s) specifier and the error (ERR=s) specifier. You are already familiar with the former because you have used it in READ statements to detect the end of your input files and thus prevent accidental attempts to read beyond the end of those files. This specifier can be used only in READ statements.

The error specifier, on the other hand, can be used in OPEN statements, READ statements, WRITE statements, and some of the other i/o statements covered in later sections, as a general i/o error recovery specifier. It was introduced in Section 12-1-1, and has the simple form

```
ERR=s
```

where s is the statement number of an executable statement in the same program unit. When an i/o error condition occurs during the execution of a statement containing this specifier, execution control is quickly transferred to the statement labeled s. You can include error recovery code beginning with that statement.

Another specifier can be used in conjunction with the error specifier or the end-of-file specifier, to help facilitate recovery. It is the input/output status specifier, which has the form

```
IOSTAT=ios
```

It was also introduced in Section 12-1-1. Whenever an i/o error condition occurs during the execution of a statement that contains this specifier, the integer variable ios becomes defined with a processor-dependent positive value. If an error condition does not occur during the execution, ios is defined with a processor-dependent negative value when an end-of-file condition is encountered, or a zero value when an end-of-file condition is not encountered. The value of this specifier can therefore be checked after the execution of an i/o statement that contains it; appropriate actions can then be taken depending on whether its value is zero, negative, or positive.

To exemplify the error and i/o status specifiers, consider first the most recent example program segment of the preceding section. It is rewritten like this:

```
      IOSOP = 0
      IOSWR = 0
      OPEN (STDIF, FILE=STNDGS, STATUS='NEW',
     :       ACCESS='DIRECT', RECL=pdrl, IOSTAT=IOSOP, ERR=400)
      DO 310 TEAM = HITEAM, LOTEAM
         READ *, TMNAME, WON, LOST
         WRITE (STDIF, REC=TEAM, IOSTAT=IOSWR, ERR=410)
     :          TMNAME, WON, LOST
  310 CONTINUE
  400 IF (IOSOP .NE. 0) THEN
            .
            . {Error recovery code for OPEN error}
            .
      ENDIF
  410 IF (IOSWR .NE. 0) THEN
            .
            . {Error recovery code for WRITE error}
            .
      ENDIF
```

In this segment, if an error condition occurs during the execution of the OPEN statement, IOSOP is set to a positive value, a transfer of control to statement 400 is made, and the OPEN error recovery procedure is executed. If not, but an error condition occurs during the execution of the WRITE statement, IOSWR is set to a positive value, a branch to statement 410 takes place, and the WRITE error recovery procedure is executed. If an i/o error condition does not occur, the tests at 400 and 410 are still performed and then execution proceeds sequentially, bypassing the error recovery procedures.

As a second example, the segment below could appear in subroutine INITAL of Figure 11-13.

```
      OPEN (UNIT=CANDIF, FILE='FCPCAND',
     :       STATUS='OLD', FORM='FORMATTED',
     :       ACCESS='SEQUENTIAL', IOSTAT=IOCAND, ERR=205)
  205 IF (IOCAND .NE. 0) THEN
            .
            . {Error recovery code for OPEN}
            .
      ENDIF
            .
            .
            .
      READ (CANDIF, 100, IOSTAT=IRCAND, ERR=225) ELYEAR
  225 IF (IRCAND .NE. 0) THEN
            .
            . {Error recovery code for first READ}
            .
      ENDIF
```

```
        NCAND = 0
        DO 230 CAND = 1, MXCAND
            READ (CANDIF, 110, END=240, IOSTAT=IRCAND, ERR=228)
       :           CLNAME(CAND), PARTY(CAND)
    228     IF (IRCAND .NE. 0) THEN
       .
       .         {Error recovery code for second READ}
       .
        ENDIF
        NCAND = CAND
    230 CONTINUE
```

Analyze this segment. With a little study, you should be able to interpret it completely.

12-1-5   *File Positioning and Inquiry*

Files connected for sequential access can be positioned, during execution, so that the next record read or written is the first record in the file or even the record that was just read or written. An ordinary use of this "repositioning" is to rewind a magnetic tape so that processing will begin with the first record of the file the next time the file is used. The repositioning can also be used to read or write the same file or one record of the same file again.

Positioning of a file to its initial point is accomplished with the REWIND statement, which has the form

```
REWIND u
```

or

```
REWIND (pslist)
```

where u is the external unit identifier and pslist is a list of position specifiers selected from the previously described UNIT=u, IOSTAT=ios, and ERR=s. The unit specifier is required. A rewind should usually be performed on tape files before they are disconnected. To cause a file to be positioned only one record back, the BACKSPACE statement, having the similar form

```
BACKSPACE u
```

or

```
BACKSPACE (pslist)
```

is employed.

A file may be positioned past its end point by a similar statement that also adds an end-of-file marker, or endfile record, to the file. The statement has the form

```
ENDFILE u
```

or

```
ENDFILE (pslist)
```

Subsequently, the created record is used in detecting the end of the file.

To provide one file positioning example, the program segment below can be added to the last segment of the last section. It causes the input file to be rewound before execution control is returned to the referencing program unit.

```
240 CLNAME(NCAND + 1) = 'STATE TOTALS'
    REWIND (CANDIF, IOSTAT=IRCAND, ERR=245)
245 IF (IRCAND .NE. 0) THEN
        .
        · {Error recovery code for REWIND}
        .
    ENDIF
    RETURN
    END
```

At any necessary point during execution, the properties of a file or its connection to a unit can be ascertained by means of the INQUIRE statement. Its general form is

```
INQUIRE (inlist)
```

where inlist is a list of inquiry specifiers. The list must contain either a file specifier or a unit specifier but not both. It may also contain no more than one of each of the specifiers listed below. Each identifier, except the statement number in the error specifier, is assigned a value when the INQUIRE statement is executed. The values, which can then be checked in the program, indicate the properties of the file or the connection.

IOSTAT=ios and ERR=s, as previously described.

EXIST=ex, where ex is a logical variable or array element that acquires the value true if the file or unit specified exists; false otherwise.

OPENED=od, where od is a logical variable or array element that acquires the value true if the file or unit specified is connected; false otherwise.

NUMBER=num, where num is an integer variable or array element that acquires the external unit identifier value of the unit connected to the file; it becomes undefined if there is none.

NAMED=nmd, where nmd is a logical variable or array element that acquires the value true if the file has a name; false otherwise.

NAME=fn, where fn is a character variable or array element that acquires the value of the file name if the file has a name; undefined otherwise.

ACCESS=ac, where ac is a character variable or array element that acquires the value SEQUENTIAL or DIRECT depending on the access method for which the file is connected.

SEQUENTIAL=seq, where seq is a character variable or array element that acquires the value YES if sequential is in the set of allowed access methods for the file; NO if not; UNKNOWN if it cannot be determined.

DIRECT=dir, where dir is a character variable or array element that acquires the value YES if direct is in the set of allowable access methods for the file; NO if not; UNKNOWN if it cannot be determined.

FORM=fm, where fm is a character variable or array element that acquires the value FORMATTED or UNFORMATTED depending on the file connection; undefined if not connected.

FORMATTED=fmt, where fmt is a character variable or array element that acquires the value YES if formatted records are allowed for the file; NO if not; UNKNOWN if it cannot be ascertained.

UNFORMATTED=fmt, where fmt is a character variable or array element that acquires the value YES if unformatted records are allowed for the file; NO if not; UNKNOWN if it cannot be ascertained.

RECL=rl, where rl is a character variable or array element that acquires the value of the record length of a file connected for direct access; undefined if not connected.

NEXTREC=nr, where nr is an integer variable or array element that acquires a value one greater than the number of the last record read or written on a file connected for direct access; undefined if not connected.

BLANK=bl, where bl is a character variable or array element that acquires the value NULL if null blank control is in effect; ZERO if zero blank control is in effect; undefined if not connected or not for formatted i/o.

12-1-6 Disconnection of a Unit and a File

The disconnection, or termination of connection, of a unit and a file takes place when the unit is closed. An implicit closing of all units occurs whenever the execution of an executable program is terminated. However, it is good programming practice to explicitly close a unit that has been explicitly opened. The explicit closing, which is accomplished with a CLOSE statement, can occur in any program unit of an executable program.

The form of the CLOSE statement is

```
CLOSE (cslist)
```

where cslist is a list of close specifiers selected from

```
UNIT=u
IOSTAT=ios
ERR=s
```

all of which are as defined for OPEN, and

STATUS=st, where st is a character expression whose value, excluding trailing blanks, is KEEP or DELETE. Actually, this specifies the disposition of the file—whether it should be kept stored for future use or eliminated from storage—after the point of execution of the CLOSE statement. The default is KEEP except that scratch files are always deleted.

One and only one unit specifier must be included in cslist and, at most, one each of the other specifiers can be included.

To exemplify the explicit disconnection of a unit and file, the following segment could be inserted between the ENDIF and RETURN statements in the last example program segment of Section 12-1-5:

```
    CLOSE (CANDIF, STATUS='KEEP', IOSTAT=ICCAND, ERR=250)
250 IF (ICCAND .NE 0) THEN
      .
      . {Error recovery code for CLOSE}
      .
    ENDIF
```

Here the file FCPCAND is disconnected from the unit identified by the value of CANDIF, but it is kept in secondary storage for future use.

As another example, the baseball standings file, for which opening is illustrated in Section 12-1-4, can be disconnected from its unit and saved for future use by the statement

```
CLOSE (STDIF)
```

Additionally, the games file exemplified earlier (Section 12-1-1) can be disconnected and deleted by the statement

```
CLOSE (UNIT=GAMIF, STATUS='DELETE')
```

Once disconnected, a unit can be reconnected to the same file or another file within the same executable program. Similarly, a disconnected but still existing file can be reconnected to the same unit or another unit within the same executable program.

12-2 INTERNAL FILES

An internal file exists only in the computer's main memory in the form of a character variable, character array element, character array, or character substring. If the form is that of a character array, the file consists of an array of internal records; otherwise, it comprises only one internal record.

The primary purpose of having internal files is to allow data to be converted from one type to another (e.g., from character to numeric or vice versa) within memory.

Data are transferred from an internal file to another part of main memory by the execution of an explicitly formatted READ statement. Data are transferred to an internal file from another part of main memory by the execution of an explicitly formatted WRITE statement. The writing operation defines one or more of the character entities of the file. Since the records of an internal file are character entities, they may also be defined by other means, such as by data initialization, input from an external file, or character assignment.

Internal files are not opened or closed, nor are they subjected to any other i/o operation except data transfer. Therefore, the only i/o statements used with them are the explicitly formatted READ and WRITE statements. Access is sequential only.

The READ and WRITE statements for internal file processing have the same general forms as those for processing external files except that a format identifier cannot be an asterisk, specifying list-directed formatting, and a record specifier must not be present. Given below are two simple illustrations of the use of internal files.

1. Using an internal one-record file to store a "card-image" for rereading as needed.

    ```
    INTEGER  AGE,
    REAL  HEIGHT, WEIGHT
    CHARACTER  CAGE*3, CARD*80, CHEIT*4, CWEIT*5, LNAME*12
        .
        .
        .
    110 FORMAT (A80)
    120 FORMAT (A12, 1X, A3, 1X, A5, 1X, A4)
    130 FORMAT (13X, I3, 1X, F5.1, 1X, F4.1)
        .
        .
        .
        READ (*, 110) CARD
        READ (UNIT=CARD, FMT=120) LNAME, CAGE, CWEIT, CHEIT
        READ (CARD, 130) AGE, WEIGHT, HEIGHT
    ```

For this program segment, if the first 27 columns of an input record contains

```
KAWALSKIƀƀƀƀƀ030ƀ165.5ƀ69.5
```

the first 27 positions of CARD will comprise the same characters after the execution of the first READ statement. The execution of the second READ statement, in which CARD is referenced as an internal file, results in these character variable definitions:

```
LNAME: KAWALSKIƀƀƀƀ
CAGE:  030
CWEIT: 165.5
CHEIT: 69.9
```

No data conversion takes place in the above. The execution of the third READ statement, in which CARD is again referenced as an internal file, although in a slightly different way for illustrative purposes, causes character-to-numeric conversions and yields these values for the numeric variables:

```
AGE: 30
WEIGHT: 165.5
HEIGHT: 69.9
```

Subsequently, the newly defined values of the character and numeric variables can be used appropriately in character and numeric processing; CARD remains defined as is and, therefore, it can be read as an internal file again and again.

2. Using an internal file in the form of a character array to build a print line or group of print lines before printing.

```
      REAL   NUMBER
      INTEGER   COL, LINE,  INT
      CHARACTER   PAGE(45,  6)*11
      .
      .
      .
910 FORMAT  (F11.1)
920 FORMAT  (1X,  6A11)
      .
      .
      .
      INT = 0
      NUMBER = 0.0
      DO 320 COL = 1,  6,  2
         DO 310 LINE = 1,  45
            WRITE  (UNIT=PAGE(LINE, COL),  FMT=910) NUMBER
            WRITE  (UNIT=PAGE(LINE,  COL+1),  FMT=910)
   :                                        ALOG(NUMBER)
            INT = INT + 1
            NUMBER = INT / 10.0
310      CONTINUE
320 CONTINUE
      DO 330 LINE = 1,  45
         WRITE (*, FMT=920)  (PAGE(LINE,  COL),  COL=1,6)
330 CONTINUE
```

This program segment builds an internal file, PAGE, of real numbers and their natural logarithms. From the point of view of the file as a two-dimensional array, file creation takes place in a column-wise fashion. It is then printed in a row-wise fashion. You can look on this segment as one approach toward solving the natural logarithm table problem posed in Exercise 9(b) of Section 6-5. Compare it to the approach you used, or might have used, after studying through Chapter 6.

12-3 EXAMPLE PROGRAMS: ONLINE INTERACTIVE BOOK INDEX PREPARATION WITH SORT-MERGE

The final problem solved in this book is a very practical problem for the book. The problem solution benefits you because it exemplifies file input and output and it illustrates two additional common techniques—file merging and programming for online interactive processing. It is also useful to the publisher and me because it saves us both some time.

Merging is the process of combining items from two or more ordered sets into one set that has the same order. *File merging*, therefore, involves the combining of the records from two or more sorted files into one file that has the same sort sequence. Online pertains to devices that are connected to the computer and controlled by the central processing unit. *Interactive* refers to a mode of operation in which a human being and a computer communicate back and forth with each other. Computer terminals are used to perform on-line interactive processing.

The specific problem solved in this section, then, is that of producing and printing an ordered file of terms (i.e., important words, expressions, names, etc.) which can be directly used to prepare the index of this book. As in most books of this nature, the index provides a means by which people can locate particular items in the book; the index itself appears at the end of the book. You should examine the index now; it was prepared directly from the results produced by the programs described below.

I divided the problem into these three subproblems: create ordered files of index information for the individual book chapters or parts of chapters, merge the files into one identically ordered index information file, and print the index in a form that can be used by the publisher to set the book index pages. The first two of these three subproblems are solved by means of two separate programs that are presented, described, and illustrated below. The third subproblem is saved as an exercise for you (see Exercise 6 of Section 12-4).

BLDCIF, the program that interactively builds chapter index files, is presented in Figure 12-1. Example input and output for the program are given in Figure 12-2. The commentary of BLDCIF tells you that prompting messages from the program lead the program user through the item-by-item entry of the information that makes up each record of a chapter index file. It also tells you that the information in each record—the information the user enters through a terminal—consists of a major term, a minor term (possibly blank), and a page number or range. Furthermore, it says that after all the items for a file have been entered, the records are sorted indirectly by minor term and major term and then are written, in a formatted manner, to the file. The files are formatted so that, once a file is created, individual records can be directly added, deleted, or edited online without having to use the program to recreate an entire file.

The output, then, from BLDCIF is of two types: prompting messages displayed on the terminal and the files, themselves, stored on an external unit identified by the symbolic name CINDXF, which has the value 1. The unit is a disk drive and, therefore, the file is stored on magnetic disk. Notice that, in one computer run, any number of different files can be created. Each such file is named by the user, following an appropriate prompting message, before the entry of terms for that file begins. The program first opens the file, if possible, then proceeds with the interactive file building, and finally closes the file after adding an endfile record and rewinding the file. If the program cannot open the file, for any reason, it displays an appropriate message and allows the user to start over again.

```
*I.   BUILD CHAPTER INDEX FILES
*
*     PROGRAM BLDCIF
*     PROGRAMMER:  Jarrell C. Grout
*     DATE:  8/26/81
*
*  A. COMMENTARY
*
*          Interactively, create formatted files of index information
*     for individual book chapters or parts of chapters.
*
*          The first item of input for creating a file is an index file
*     name (IFNAME) of up to eight characters.  This is followed by
*     the item-by-item entry of a major term (MAJOR) of up to thirty
*     characters, an optional minor term (MINOR) of up to thirty
*     characters, and a page number or range (PAGE) of up to nine
*     characters, for as many terms as desired - up to MAXREC major
*     terms per file.  Prompting messages, displayed at the terminal,
*     are provided to aid the user in entering the information properly.
*
*          After they are entered, the items are stored internally in the
*     corresponding elements of three arrays - MAJARR, MINARR, and
*     PGEARR.  Whenever all of the terms for a file have been entered,
*     the array elements are alphabetically sorted indirectly by minor
*     term and then by major term.  Then they are written to the file.
*     Each record of the file has this layout:
*
*          major term              positions 1-30
*          minor term (possibly blank)     "    31-60
*          page number or range            "    61-69
*
*     As many files as are needed can be created in one computer run.
*
*          DICTIONARY.
*
*     ADD:  Test input variable to verify addition to a file
*     BUILD:  Test input variable to verify the user's desire
*               to create a new file
*     CINDXF:  Chapter index file unit identifier
*     DIR:  Directory for indirect sort by minor and then major term
*     ELEM:  Array element number for DIR
*     IFNAME:  An index file name (up to 8 characters)
*     INSORT:  Subroutine to perform an indirect alphabetic sort
*     MAJARR:  Array of major terms
*     MAJOR:  A major term (up to 30 alphanumeric characters)
*     MAXREC:  The maximum number of records per file
*     MINARR:  Array of minor terms
*     MINOR:  A minor term (up to 30 alphanumeric characters)
*     NREC:  Number of records placed in a file
*     PAGE:  A page number or range (up to 9 characters having the
*               form PPPP or PPPP-PPPP)
*     PGEARR:  Array of page numbers and ranges
*     REC:  Record number
*
*  B. DECLARATION
*
      INTEGER  CINDXF, MAXREC
      PARAMETER  (CINDXF=1, MAXREC=100)
      INTEGER  DIR(MAXREC), ELEM, NREC, REC
      CHARACTER  ADD*3, BUILD*3, IFNAME*8, MAJOR*30, MAJARR(MAXREC)*30,
     :           MINOR*30, MINARR(MAXREC)*30, PAGE*9, PGEARR(MAXREC)*9
*
*  C. I/O LAYOUT
*
  100 FORMAT (A)
  900 FORMAT (2A30, A9)
*  D. ACTION
*
      PRINT *, 'You can build one or more formatted index files'
      PRINT *, 'of records containing major term, minor term, and'
      PRINT *, 'page number or range, if you follow the instructions'
      PRINT *, 'of the forthcoming prompting messages.  One such file'
      PRINT *, 'can have, at most, ', MAXREC, ' records.  For any files'
      PRINT *, 'of yours that have less than that number of records,'
      PRINT *, 'enter only a $ character, to indicate end-of-file'
      PRINT *, 'when prompted, where you would otherwise enter a'
      PRINT *, 'major term.'
```

Figure 12-1. BLDCIF: A Program That Builds Chapter Index Files

```
 210      PRINT *, ' '
          PRINT *, 'Would you like to build a new file (YES/NO)?'
          READ (*, 100) BUILD
          IF (BUILD .EQ. 'YES') THEN
              PRINT *, 'When ready, please enter the name of your ',
       :             'new file.'
              READ (*, 100) IFNAME
              OPEN (UNIT=CINDXF, FILE=IFNAME, STATUS='NEW',
       :            FORM='FORMATTED', ACCESS='SEQUENTIAL',
       :            IOSTAT=IOS, ERR=220)
 220          IF (IOS .NE. 0) THEN
                  PRINT *, ' '
                  PRINT *, 'Unable to open the file named ', IFNAME
                  PRINT *, 'Please try again.'
                  GO TO 210
              ENDIF
              NREC = 0
              DO 230 REC = 1, MAXREC
                  PRINT *, ' '
                  PRINT *, 'Enter a major term, or $ for end-of-file.'
                  READ (*, 100) MAJOR
                  IF (MAJOR(1:1) .NE. '$') THEN
                      PRINT *, ' '
                      PRINT *, 'Enter a minor term or one blank ',
       :                     'character.'
                      READ (*, 100) MINOR
                      PRINT *, ' '
                      PRINT *, 'Enter a page number or range.'
                      READ (*, 100) PAGE
                      PRINT *, ' '
                      PRINT *, 'You want to add'
                      PRINT *, MAJOR
                      PRINT *, MINOR
                      PRINT *, PAGE
                      PRINT *, 'to file ', IFNAME, ' (YES/NO)?'
                      READ (*, 100) ADD
                      IF (ADD .EQ. 'YES') THEN
                          NREC = NREC + 1
                          MAJARR(NREC) = MAJOR
                          MINARR(NREC) = MINOR
                          PGEARR(NREC) = PAGE
                          PRINT *, ' '
                          PRINT *, 'They have been added.'
                      ELSE
                          PRINT *, ' '
                          PRINT *, 'Then, they have been deleted.'
                      ENDIF
                  ELSE
                      PRINT *, ' '
                      PRINT *, 'You entered $ for end-of-file.'
                      GO TO 240
                  ENDIF
 230          CONTINUE
 240          PRINT *, ' '
              PRINT *, 'Sort and file save in process on file ', IFNAME
              PRINT *, 'Number of records: ', NREC
              DO 250 ELEM = 1, NREC
                  DIR(ELEM) = ELEM
 250          CONTINUE
              CALL INSORT(DIR, MINARR, NREC)
              CALL INSORT(DIR, MAJARR, NREC)
              DO 260 ELEM = 1, NREC
                  REC = DIR(ELEM)
                  WRITE (UNIT=CINDXF, FMT=900) MAJARR(REC), MINARR(REC),
       :                                       PGEARR(REC)
 260          CONTINUE
              ENDFILE (CINDXF)
              REWIND (CINDXF)
              CLOSE (CINDXF, STATUS='KEEP')
              PRINT *, ' '
              PRINT *, 'File ', IFNAME, ' is stored and closed.'
              GO TO 210
          ELSE
              PRINT *, ' '
              PRINT *, 'OK, so long for now.'
              STOP
          ENDIF
      END
```

Figure 12-1. (Continued)

Look at part (a)—the interactive file creation section—of Figure 12-2. Immediately after it begins execution, the program causes the first paragraph in part (a) to be displayed at the terminal. Then it displays the sentence

```
Would you like to build a new file (YES/NO)?
```

The user responds by entering YES or NO (YES in this case) after the processor-created question mark. Subsequently, the program and the user communicate back and forth as the user enters the information requested by the prompting messages and the program acts on the information supplied by the user. Observe that the first file name given by the user is FCP12:01 and the set of record entries consists of the major term "Data," a blank minor term, and the page number 2. The second set of record entries comprise the major term "Computer," the minor term "digital," and the page number 5. These entries, actually entered by me as taken from Chapter 1 of the manuscript of this book, make up the first two records of file FCP12:01 before the file is sorted. The reason the page numbers are from the manuscript, rather than from the book itself, is because I am producing these examples while writing the manuscript and the examples will be printed before I produce the actual book index files. You will find the terms above, and all the example terms, in the book index; their page numbers and ranges, however, may be somewhat different from those shown in these examples.

Only a small portion of the FCP12:01 and FCP12:02 (from Chapter 2) file building interaction is shown in Figure 12-2, but enough is shown to give you the idea. Study it and the program carefully. For the best learning experience, try it yourself on your computer. Rather than using a terminal that prints the interactive information, however, you may want to use a video display terminal to save time and paper. I only used the printing terminal for these examples and your benefit; I used a video display terminal to interactively build the actual index information files.

Figure 12-2(b) and (c) show the exact record-by-record contents of example files FCP12:01 and FCP12:02 after they were sorted and stored by the program. You can locate the terms and page numbers that were shown as being entered in part (a), and observe that they are now in the proper alphabetical positions. You may have noticed that I did not include, with BLDCIF, the sort subroutine, INSORT, that BLDCIF references. I omitted it in order to give you the opportunity of devising it (see Exercise 5 of Section 12-4).

Direct your attention, now, to Figures 12-3 and 12-4. The first of these figures contains program MRGCIF, which interactively merges or combines two sorted index files at a time into one file that is sorted in the same sequence. The input to MRGCIF consists of interactive responses from the program user, as depicted in Figure 12-4, and formatted files created either by program BLDCIF or MRGCIF itself. The output from MRGCIF comprises one merged file for each pair of input files. As indicated in the program commentary, any number of merged files can be produced in one computer run. All such files are kept.

```
You can build one or more   formatted index files
of records containing major term, minor term, and
page number or range, if you follow the instructions
of the forthcoming prompting messages.  One such file
can have, at most,  100   records.  For any files
of yours that have less than that number of records,
enter only a $ character, to indicate end-of-file
when prompted, where you would otherwise enter a
major term.

Would you like to build a new file (YES/NO)?
?YES
   When ready, please enter the name of your
   new file.
?FCP12:01

   Enter a major term, or $ for end-of-file.
?Data

   Enter a minor term or one blank
   character.
?

   Enter a page number or range.
?2

   You want to add
   Data

   2
   to file FCP12:01   (YES/NO)?
?YES

   They have been added.

   Enter a major term, or $ for end-of-file.
?Computer

   Enter a minor term or one blank
   character.
?digital

   Enter a page number or range.
?5

   You want to add
   Computer
   digital
   5
   to file FCP12:01   (YES/NO)?
?YES

   They have been added.




         .
         .
         .
         .
         .


   Enter a major term, or $ for end-of-file.
?$

   You entered $ for end-of-file.

   Sort and file save in process on file
   FCP12:01
   Number of records:   13
```

Figure 12-2. Example I/O for Program BLDCIF. (a) Interactive creation of files FCP12:01 and FCP12:02 (b) File FCP12:01 after being created by BLDCIF (c) File FCP12:02 after being created by BLDCIF

```
File FCP12:01  is stored and closed.

Would you like to build a new file (YES/NO)?
?YES
   When ready, please enter the name of your
   new file.
?FCP12:02

   Enter a major term, or $ for end-of-file.
?Data

   Enter a minor term or one blank
   character.
?Problem

   Enter a page number or range.
?45

   You want to add
   Data
   Problem
   45
   to file FCP12:02  (YES/NO)?
?YES

   They have been added.


        .
        .
        .


   Enter a major term, or $ for end-of-file.
?$

   You entered $ for end-of-file.

   Sort and file save in process on file
   FCP12:02
   Number of records:   21

   File FCP12:02  is stored and closed.

   Would you like to build a new file (YES/NO)?
?NO

   OK, so long for now.
```

(a)

```
Address                                                    19
Byte                                                       23
Computer                       digital                     5
Computer                       primary components          11-20
Computer program                                           28
Computer storage                                           20-28
Data                                                       2
Data                                                       32-36
Data                           problem                     33
Program                                                    28
Programming language           Basic                       29
Programming language           Cobol                       29
Programming language           Pascal                      29
```

(b)

```
Algorithm                                                  65
Algorithm                      guidelines                  68-74
Algorithm                      primitives                  69-72
Algorithm                      relation to programs        65
Algorithm                      symbols                     69-71
Algorithms                                                 65-85
Data                           input                       46
Data                           output                      46
Data                           problem                     45
```

Figure 12-2. (Continued)

(c)

Figure 12-2. (Continued)

```
*I.   MERGE INDEX FILES
*
*     PROGRAM MRGCIF
*     PROGRAMMER:  Jarrell C. Grout
*     DATE:  8/26/81
*
*  A. COMMENTARY
*
*        In an interactive mode, merge two given index files, INF1 and
*     INF2, into one merged index file, MINF.  INF1 and INF2 are chapter
*     index files created by program BLDCIF or merged index files
*     created by this program.  Each record of all three files is
*     formatted, with this layout:
*
*           major term                      positions 1-30
*           minor term (possibly blank)       '    31-60
*           page number or range              '    61-69
*
*     Major term and minor term variables must be character type and
*     and length 30.  Page number or range variables must also be
*     character type, but of length 9.  The program continues to
*     execute, accepting file names and merging files, until the user
*     calls for the termination of execution.  All files are kept.
*
*        DICTIONARY.
*
*     FILE:  File selector; indicates which input file contains the next
*            record to be added to the merge file
*     INDXF1:  Input index file 1 unit identifier
*     INDXF2:  Input index file 2 unit identifier
*     INF1:  Name of index file 1 (up to 8 characters)
*     INF2:  Name of index file 2 (up to 8 characters)
*     IOSO:  I/O status identifier for opening files
*     MAJ1:  Major term from input file 1
*     MAJ2:  Major term from input file 2
*     MAXREC:  One more than the maximum possible number of records
*              that an input file might contain
*     MERGE:  Test variable to verify user's desire to merge files
*     MINDXF:  Merged index file unit identifier
*     MINF:  Name of merged index file
*     MIN1:  Minor term from input file 1
*     MIN2:  Minor term from input file 2
*     PAGE1:  Page number or range from input file 1
*     PAGE2:  Page number or range from input file 2
*     REC:  Record number
*
*        DECLARATION
*
*     INTEGER  INDXF1, INDXF2, MAXREC, MINDXF
*     PARAMETER  (INDXF1=1, INDXF2=2, MAXREC=10000, MINDXF=3)
*
*     INTEGER  FILE, REC, IOSO
*     CHARACTER  INF1*8, INF2*8, MAJ1*30, MAJ2*30, MERGE*3, MINF*8,
*   :           MIN1*30, MIN2*30, PAGE1*9, PAGE2*9
*
*  C. I/O LAYOUT
*
  100 FORMAT (A)
  110 FORMAT (2A30, A9)
```

Figure 12-3. MRGCIF: A Program That Merges Index Files

```
*
*   D. ACTION
*
        PRINT *, 'You can have two index files mersed into a third file,'
        PRINT *, 'for as many pairs of files as you wish, if you follow'
        PRINT *, 'the instructions of the forthcoming prompting messages,'
    210   PRINT *, ' '
        PRINT *, 'Would you like to merse a couple of files (YES/NO)?'
        READ (*, 100) MERGE
        IF (MERGE .NE. 'NO') THEN
            PRINT *, ' '
            PRINT *, 'Please enter the name of one of the files to be'
            PRINT *, 'mersed,'
            READ (*, 100) INF1
            PRINT *, ' '
            PRINT *, 'Please enter the name of the other file to be'
            PRINT *, 'mersed,'
            READ (*, 100) INF2
            PRINT *, ' '
            PRINT *, 'And now, enter the name to be siven to the mersed'
            PRINT *, 'file,'
            READ (*, 100) MINF
            OPEN (UNIT=INDXF1, FILE=INF1, STATUS='OLD',
        :         FORM='FORMATTED', ACCESS='SEQUENTIAL',
        :         IOSTAT=IOSO, ERR=220)
            OPEN (UNIT=INDXF2, FILE=INF2, STATUS='OLD',
        :         FORM='FORMATTED', ACCESS='SEQUENTIAL',
        :         IOSTAT=IOSO, ERR=220)
            OPEN (UNIT=MINDXF, FILE=MINF, STATUS='NEW',
        :         FORM='FORMATTED', ACCESS='SEQUENTIAL',
        :         IOSTAT=IOSO, ERR=220)
    220   IF (IOSO .NE. 0) THEN
            PRINT *, ' '
            PRINT *, 'Unable to open one or more of your files,'
            PRINT *, 'Please recheck and start over,'
            GO TO 210
        ENDIF
        PRINT *, ' '
        PRINT *, 'Hold on, merse in process,'
*
*
*           Prime with record from each input file,
*           Note: Program assumes at least one record in first file,
            READ (UNIT=INDXF1, FMT=110, END=230) MAJ1, MIN1, PAGE1
            READ (UNIT=INDXF2, FMT=110, END=250) MAJ2, MIN2, PAGE2
*
*           Besin merse process
            DO 225 REC = 1, MAXREC
                IF (LLT(MAJ1, MAJ2)) THEN
                    FILE = 1
                ELSE IF (LLT(MAJ2, MAJ1)) THEN
                    FILE = 2
                ELSE IF (LLT(MIN1, MIN2)) THEN
                    FILE = 1
                ELSE IF (LLT(MIN2, MIN1)) THEN
                    FILE = 2
                ELSE
                    FILE = 1
                ENDIF
                IF (FILE .EQ. 1) THEN
                    WRITE (UNIT=MINDXF, FMT=110) MAJ1, MIN1, PAGE1
                    READ (UNIT=INDXF1, FMT=110, END=230) MAJ1, MIN1, PAGE1
                ELSE
                    WRITE (UNIT=MINDXF, FMT=110) MAJ2, MIN2, PAGE2
                    READ (UNIT=INDXF2, FMT=110, END=250) MAJ2, MIN2, PAGE2
                ENDIF
    225   CONTINUE
*
*           File 1 empty; move remaining file 2 records to mersed file
    230   DO 235 REC = 1, MAXREC
            WRITE (UNIT=MINDXF, FMT=110) MAJ2, MIN2, PAGE2
            READ (UNIT=INDXF2, FMT=110, END=260) MAJ2, MIN2, PAGE2
    235   CONTINUE
*
*           File 2 empty; move remaining file 1 records to mersed file
    250   DO 255 REC = 1, MAXREC
            WRITE (UNIT=MINDXF, FMT=110) MAJ1, MIN1, PAGE1
            READ (UNIT=INDXF1, FMT=110, END=260) MAJ1, MIN1, PAGE1
    255   CONTINUE
```

Figure 12-3. (Continued)

```
260            REWIND (INDXF1)
               CLOSE (INDXF1, STATUS='KEEP')
               REWIND (INDXF2)
               CLOSE (INDXF2, STATUS='KEEP')
               ENDFILE (MINDXF)
               REWIND (MINDXF)
               CLOSE (MINDXF, STATUS='KEEP')
               PRINT *, ' '
               PRINT *, 'Files ', INF1, ' and ', INF2, ' have been mersed'
               PRINT *, 'into file ', MINF
               PRINT *, ' '
               PRINT *, 'Again now ... '
               GO TO 210
           ELSE
               PRINT *, 'OK, so long.'
               STOP
           ENDIF
       END
```

Figure 12-3. (Continued)

```
You can have two index files merged into a third file,
for as many pairs of files as you wish, if you follow
the instructions of the forthcoming prompting messages.

Would you like to merge a couple of files (YES/NO)?
?YES

Please enter the name of one of the files to be
merged.
?FCP12:01

Please enter the name of the other file to be
merged.
?FCP12:02

And now, enter the name to be given to the merged
file.
?FCP12:M1

Hold on, merge in process.

Files FCP12:01  and FCP12:02  have been merged
into file FCP12:M1

Again now ...

Would you like to merge a couple of files (YES/NO)?
?NO
OK, so long.
```

(a)

Address		
Algorithm		19
Algorithm		65
Algorithm	guidelines	68–74
Algorithm	primitives	69–72
Algorithm	relation to programs	65
Algorithm	symbols	69–71
Algorithms		65–85
Byte		23
Computer	digital	5
Computer	primary components	11–20
Computer program		28
Computer storage		20–28
Data		2
Data		32–36
Data	input	46
Data	output	46
Data	problem	33
Data	problem	45

Figure 12-4. Example I/O for Program MRGCIF (a) Interactive merging of files FCP12:01 and FCP12:02 into file FCP12:M1 (b) File FCP12:M1 after the merging process is completed

Data	solution	45
Data	test input	48
Design	top-down	53
Diagnostics		59
Flowchart	relation to algorithm	86
Flowchart	relation to program	86
Main program		56
Program		28
Programming language	Basic	29
Programming language	Basic	54
Programming language	Cobol	29
Programming language	Cobol	54
Programming language	Pascal	29
Programming language	Pascal	54
Subprogram		56
Top-down design		53

(b)

Figure 12-4. (Continued)

The entire merging process, which has the ultimate goal of producing one complete index file, involves the repetitive operation of combining two files at a time until the goal is reached. You can understand the process best by studying the program closely, tracing it manually with a portion of the example input data [Figure 12-2(b) and (c)], and actually executing it on your computer. The example output, given in Figure 12-4, is a printout of the exact contents of file FCP12:M1, which is produced by merging files FCP12:01 and FCP12:02. As shown, the output is not quite ready for book index preparation. To make it ready, it should be programmatically edited and arranged in a form that looks more like a book index. I mentioned earlier that this is your task. It is described more completely in Exercise 7 of Section 12-4.

12-4 EXERCISES

1. Plan and write a complete executable program designed specifically to update the standings of major professional baseball, football, soccer, or basketball leagues and divisions within leagues on a daily basis. The standings of each division are to be stored in a file that can be connected for either sequential or direct access. Unformatted i/o should be used for the standings files. Naturally, the standings should be printed in a nicely formatted form, for sports fans, after every daily update. The input of the daily game scores is to be handled separately from that of the standings—preferably read in interactively, in any order, via an on-line terminal.

    This exercise is, of course, closely related to the baseball standings and scores problem introduced in Chapter 9 and discussed further in this chapter. Use the information given in both places and the input data given in Figure 9-3, or data from your local newspaper. For a more challenging exercise, make the program very general so that it can handle the games and standings of any one of the four above-mentioned sports at any given time.

2. Plan and write a complete executable program designed to maintain up-to-date statistics on team batting, individual batting, and individual pitching for the major baseball leagues. One master file of unformatted records should be

maintained for each of the three categories of statistics; they should all, however, be updated by means of only one daily transaction file. Each should be capable of being connected for sequential or direct access. The contents of each master file should be printed weekly in a nicely formatted manner—very similar to the manner in which they are usually printed in the sports section of virtually every U.S. newspaper each Sunday during baseball season.

3. Plan and write a complete executable program to solve the inventory problem referred to in Exercise 12 of Section 11-9. Follow the instructions of that exercise. Additionally, the master and transaction file records should not all be read into memory before updating begins. Rather, file input and updating should take place record by record. This means that the transaction file must be subjected to a sort-merge before updating begins. The files should be capable of being connected for sequential access only. In the sort-merge, use additional files as necessary. In updating, create a new master file and save the old master file. It is common practice to save old master files, particularly in business applications, for a period of time for auditing and protective purposes.

4. Plan and write a complete executable program to solve the merchandise inventory problem referred to in Exercise 14 of Section 11-9. Follow the instructions of that exercise. Additionally, the master file should be stored on a direct access medium and opened for direct access. The item number should be used as the file record number for each item. The transaction file should be stored for sequential access only. It need not be sorted, since master file records are directly accessible.

5. Plan and write the complete subroutine INSORT which is referenced by program BLDCIF, as shown in Figure 12-1, to perform a sort on individual chapter index files before they are stored. You should recall that sorting procedures are given in the multiple-choice test grading program of Figure 9-9 and in Figure 11-7.

6. Plan and write a complete executable program, PRNTBI, which will take a merged file created by program MRGCIF, such as the one presented in Figure 12-4, and produce output from which a book index can be directly prepared. That is, instead of the external file form given in Figure 12-4, the output should have a form that looks more like a book index—a form like this:

```
.... A ....
Address                     19
Algorithm                   65
   guidelines               68-74
   primitives               69-72
   relation to programs     65
   symbols                  69-71
Algorithms                  65-85
.... B ....
Byte                        23
.... C ....
```

```
Computer
     digital                                    5
       primary components                 11-20
   .
   .
   .
```

7. Write and execute a simple Fortran program to read the table of input
    numbers given below, using explicit numeric or list-directed formatting, and
    then print the table as shown under the "output" heading. The program
    should use an internal file to build each print line based on the criterion that
    each zero or positive value is to be printed as is and each negative value—
    representing missing data—is to be replaced by a field that contains a series
    of periods.

    Input:

5. 6	6. 3	−9	7. 7
3. 3	−9	4. 6	5. 2
−9	1. 0	2. 0	2. 4
11. 3	−9	12. 7	13. 7
0. 4	1. 0	−9	1. 8
0. 5	0. 0	0. 3	0. 5

    Output:

5. 6	6. 3	....	7. 7
3. 3	....	4. 6	5. 2
....	1. 0	2. 0	2. 4
11. 3	....	12. 7	13. 7
0. 4	1. 0	....	1. 8
0. 5	0. 0	0. 3	0. 5

8. Write and execute a simple Fortran program to read the table of input
    numbers given below, using explicit numeric or list-directed formatting, and
    then print the table as shown under the "output" heading. The program
    should use an internal file to build each print line based on the criterion that
    each zero or positive value is to be printed as is and each negative value—
    representing missing data—is to be replaced by a field that contains a series
    of periods.

    Input:

5. 6	6. 3	−9	7. 7
3. 3	−9	4. 6	5. 2
−9	1. 0	2. 0	2. 4
11. 3	−9	12. 7	13. 7
0. 4	1. 0	−9	1. 8
0. 5	0. 0	0. 3	0. 5

    Output:

5. 6	6. 3	....	7. 7
3. 3	....	4. 6	5. 2
....	1. 0	2. 0	2. 4
11. 3	....	12. 7	13. 7
0. 4	1. 0	....	1. 8
0. 5	0. 0	0. 3	0. 5

Appendix: Fortran Intrinsic Functions

Intrinsic functions are referenced by specifying the function name and arguments in the form

        fname(args)

The value of the function is returned through its name. The data type of the value is the same as the function type.

In the following tables, the data types of arguments are designated symbolically by I for integer, R for real, D for double precision, Co for complex, and Ch for character.

A. Real Functions with One Argument (a)

Function Name	Argument Type	Value Supplied
ABS	R	Absolute value of R
ACOS	R	Arccosine of R
AIMAG	Co	Imaginary part of Co
AINT	R	Truncated equivalent of R
ALOG	R	Natural logarithm of R
ALOG10	R	Common logarithm of R
ANINT	R	Nearest whole number to R
ASIN	R	Arcsine of R
ATAN	R	Arctan of R
CABS	Co	Absolute value of Co
COS	R	Cosine of R
COSH	R	Hyperbolic cosine of R
EXP	R	Exponential of R
FLOAT	I	Real equivalent of I
REAL	I	Real equivalent of I
SIN	R	Sine of R
SINH	R	Hyperbolic sine of R
SNGL	D	Real equivalent of D
SQRT	R	Square root of R
TAN	R	Tangent of R
TANH	R	Hyperbolic tangent of R

B.   Real Functions with Two Arguments (a1, a2)

Function Name	Argument Type	Value Supplied
AMOD	R	Remainder of a1/a2
DIM	R	Transfer of sign, a2 to a1
ATAN2	R	Arctangent of a1/a2

C.   Real Functions with More Than Two Arguments (a1, a2, . . .)

Function Name	Argument Type	Value Supplied
AMAX0	I	Largest argument
AMAX1	R	Largest argument
AMIN0	I	Smallest argument
AMIN1	R	Smallest argument

D.   Integer Functions with One Argument (a)

Function Name	Argument Type	Value Supplied
IABS	I	Absolute value of I
ICHAR	Ch	Integer equivalent of Ch
IDINT	D	Integer equivalent of D (truncated)
IDNINT	D	Integer equivalent of D (rounded)
IFIX	R	Integer equivalent of R (truncated)
INT	R	Integer equivalent of R (truncated)
LEN	Ch	Length (bytes) of Ch
NINT	R	Integer equivalent of R (rounded)

E.   Integer Functions with Two Arguments (a1, a2)

Function Name	Argument Type	Value Supplied
IDIM	I	Positive difference, a1 − a2
INDEX	Ch	Starting position of a2 in a1
ISIGN	I	Transfer of sign, a2 to a1
MOD	I	Remainder of a1/a2

F.   Integer Functions with More Than Two Arguments (a1, a2, . . .)

Function Name	Argument Type	Value Supplied
MAX0	I	Largest argument
MAX1	R	Largest argument
MIN0	I	Smallest argument
MIN1	R	Smallest argument

G. Double Precision Functions with One Argument (a)

Function Name	Argument Type	Value Supplied
DABS	D	Absolute value of D
DACOS	D	Arccosine of D
DASIN	D	Arcsine of D
DATAN	D	Arctangent of D
DBLE	I,R, or C	Double precision equivalent of a
DCOS	D	Cosine of D
DCOSH	D	Hyperbolic cosine of D
DEXP	D	Exponential of D
DLOG	D	Natural logarithm of D
DLOG10	D	Common logarithm of D
DNINT	D	Nearest whole number to D
DSIN	D	Sine of D
DSINH	D	Hyperbolic sine of D
DTAN	D	Tangent of D
DTANH	D	Hyperbolic tangent of D
DSQRT	D	Square root of D

H. Double Precision Functions with Two Arguments (a1, a2)

Function Name	Argument Type	Value Supplied
DATAN2	D	Arctangent of a1/a2.
DDIM	D	Positive difference, a1-a2
DMOD	D	Remainder of a1/a2.
DPROD	D	Double precision product, a1*a2.
DSIGN	D	Transfer of sign, a2 to a1.

I. Double Precision Functions with More Than Two Arguments (a1, a2, . . .)

Function Name	Argument Type	Value Supplied
DMAX1	D	Largest argument
DMIN1	D	Smallest argument

J. Complex Functions with One Argument (a1)

Function Name	Argument Type	Value Supplied
CCOS	Co	Cosine of Co
CEXP	Co	Exponential of Co
CLOG	Co	Natural logarithm of Co
CMPLX	I, R, or D	Complex equivalent of a
CONJG	Co	Conjugate of Co
CSIN	Co	Sine of Co
CSQRT	Co	Square root of Co

K. Logical Functions with Two Arguments (a1, a2)

Function Name	Argument Type	Value Supplied
LGE	Ch	Lexically greater than or equal, a1 >= a2
LGT	Ch	Lexically greater than, a1 > a2
LLE	Ch	Lexically less than or equal, a1 <= a2
LLT	Ch	Lexically less than, a1 < a2

L. Character Functions with One Argument (a)

Function Name	Argument Type	Value Supplied
CHAR	I	Character equivalent of I

Answers to Selected Exercises

SECTION 1-7

5. Given below is one possible revision. Yours may be different, as long as it accurately specifies the solution.

    (1) Let the total initially be zero.
    (2) Repeat instruction 3 below until all of the numbers have been added to the total; then stop.
    (3) Add the next number to the total.

SECTION 2-1-9

2. This problem involves finding the area of a circle. The distance around the traffic loop is the circle circumference which can be squared and divided by 4π to yield the area. One top-down procedure is this:
    Overview statement:

    ```
    Find square miles in city-within traffic loop.
    ```

    First refinement:

    ```
    Find traffic loop circumference in miles.
    Find area within traffic loop in square miles.
    ```

    Second refinement:

    ```
    Drive automobile around traffic loop.
    Note miles driven.

    Compute square of miles driven.
    Divide result by 4π to obtain area.
    ```

Third refinement:

```
Get into automobile.
Drive to a point on traffic loop.
Write down beginning odometer reading.
Drive around traffic loop, back to starting point.

Write down final odometer reading.
Subtract beginning reading from final reading
to obtain circumference in miles.

Compute square of circumference.

Divide square of circumference by 4π to obtain
number of square miles in city.
```

Further refinement can be performed if desired. As you will soon see, a computer-oriented solution procedure can easily be developed from this beginning.

SECTION 2-2-3

3. The left-pointing arrow, ←, represents the assignment of a value on the right to a variable on the left; the equal sign, =, represents equality of values on the left and right.

4. In the first algorithm, change the $>=$ operator in the "If" rule to $<$. In the second algorithm, perform the interchange only if a $>$ b.

7. The algorithm prints the input values of a, b, and c, in order from largest to smallest.

9. One possible alternative algorithm:

```
        ALGORITHM Study:1:alternative.1
        {   Print the values of a, b, and c, in order from
        largest to smallest.}
        Read a, b, c
        loop ← 1
INT.       If b >= a Then
                h ← a
                a ← b
                b ← h
            If loop <= 1 Then
                If c >= b Then
                    h ← b
                    b ← c
                    c ← h
                loop ← loop + 1
                Go To INT. (Back)
        Write a, b, c
        Stop
        END
```

SECTION 2-3-3

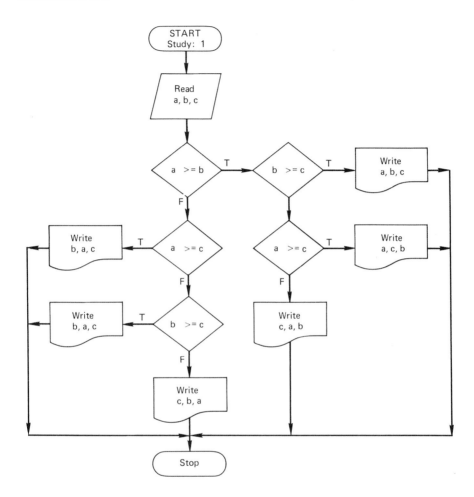

SECTION 2-5

3. One possible algorithm and corresponding flowchart (sans annotation):

ALGORITHM Sq-inches:Sq-centimeters

```
{Develop and print a table of square inches and
corresponding square centimeters for values of square
inches from lowin to highin, inclusive, in increments
of 0.5.}
Write title:   'SQUARE INCHES TO SQUARE CENTIMETERS',
       headings:  'SQUARE INCHES', 'SQUARE CENTIMETERS'
Read lowin, highin
If lowin > highin Then
```

```
              Write 'THE GIVEN LOWEST NUMBER OF INCHES', lowin,
                    'IS LARGER THAN THE GIVEN HIGHEST', highin,
                    'PROCESSING TERMINATED. '
        Else
              sinchs ← lowin
EOD.          If sinchs <= highin Then
                    scenti ← sinchs / 6.4516
                    Write sinchs, scenti
                    sinchs ← sinchs + 1
                    Go To EOD. (Back)
        Stop
        END
```

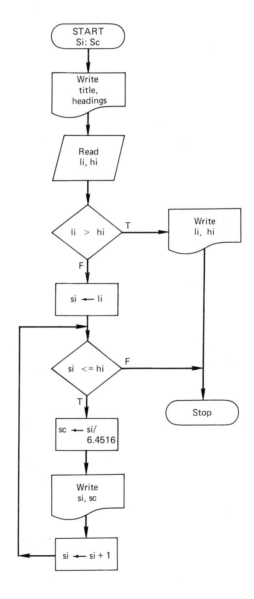

SECTION 3-6

1. (b) Add the value of COST to the current value of SUMCST and assign that sum to the variable SUMCST as its new current value.

3. (b) The first noncomment line of a program unit that identifies the program unit as a subroutine named DEDUCT.

SECTION 4-10

1. (b) The values of OUTGO and INCOME are compared. If the value of OUTGO is greater than the value of INCOME, the assignment LOSS=GREAT is executed; otherwise, it is not executed.

    (e) Program execution terminates and control is given to the processor.

2. The first two printed lines are:

```
SALES LIST
4200   100   100   10.5000
```

7. To accomplish this task in the program, add these lines right before the STOP statement:

```
RANGE  = MAX − MIN
PRINT *, 'RANGE:  ', RANGE
```

Make corresponding additions to the algorithm and flowchart. Be sure to declare RANGE properly in the program. Fully test the modified algorithm, flowchart, and program.

9. Refer to PROGRAM AVRAGE in Chapter 3 to help you answer this one. In program AVRAGE, the variable COUNT is used for the purpose of counting the number of valid input observations.

11. One possible program (Action only):

```
            READ *, AGRINC, PRMIUM, DGCOST, OTHMED
    *       BASIC INSURANCE PREMIUM DEDUCTION
            IF (PRMIUM .LT. 150.0) THEN
               BASDED = PRMIUM * 0.5
               PREBAL = BASDED
            ELSE
               BASDED = 150.0
               PREBAL = PRMIUM − 150.0
            ENDIF
    *       DRUG DEDUCTION
            DGBASE = 0.01 * AGRINC
            IF (DGCOST .LT. DGBASE) THEN
               DRUGDN = 0.0
            ELSE
               DRUGDN = DGCOST − DGBASE
            ENDIF
```

```
*         M&D EXPENSES, EXCLUDING BASIC INS. DEDUCTION
          BASEMD = 0.03 * AGRINC
          DEDMDE = PREBAL + DRUGDN + OTHMED
          IF (DEDMDE .GT. BASEMD) THEN
              DEDMDE = DEDMDE - BASEMD
          ELSE
              DEDMDE = 0.0
          ENDIF
*         M&D DEDUCTION TOTAL
          DEDMDE = DEDMDE + BASDED
          PRINT *, 'THE MEDICAL AND DENTAL EXPENSE DEDUCTION IS ',
          :            DEDMDE
          STOP
          END
```

SECTION 5-2-3

1. Items (a), (e), (j), and (l) are invalid. Item (c), a real number, and item (i), an integer, may be invalid for your processor because of the respective number of significant digits and size.

2. Items (b), (d), (f), and (g) are invalid.

SECTION 5-5

INCDAY is declared to be a whole number constant with a value of 1; YEAR becomes a whole number-valued variable with an initial value of 1900. INCSEC is specified as a real number constant equal to 0.001; SECOND is declared as a real-valued variable, initially equal to 0.0.

SECTION 5-7-1

1. (b) Missing operator between right parenthesis and PRIN.
    (d) Two operators, ** and −, next to each other.
2. (a) 12.6.
    (c) 1
3. (a) Any variable beginning with a letter in A−H or O−Z.
    (c) Any variable beginning with a letter in I−N.
4. (a) 12
    (c) 1.0D0

SECTION 5-8-1

1. All can be evaluated.
    (b) 89
    (d) 90
    (f) 1.001
    (i) 0

2. (b) NEWLOC=10

3. One possible algorithm:

ALGORITHM ABS(VAR)
```
{Find the absolute value of the variable VAR.  The
value of VAR is assumed to be supplied through the
argument list of a referencing algorithm.}
ABS ← VAR
If ABS < 0   ABS = −ABS
Return    {to the referencing algorithm}
END
```

In the above, VAR is in parentheses next to ABS as an argument. This allows the algorithm to obtain the value of VAR from the referencing algorithm argument list. Rather than using an argument list, you may have read in the value of VAR. Also, you may have used a "Stop" rather than a "Return." The Return simply means that the execution control is given back, with the absolute value, to the referencing algorithm rather than execution being terminated as with a Stop.

SECTION 5-11

2. Only the Action is given here; list-directed i/o is used. The algorithm given in answer to Exercise 3, Section 2-5, is employed as a guide.

```
*   D.  ACTION
*
        PRINT *, 'SQUARE INCHES TO SQUARE CENTIMETERS'
        PRINT *, ' '
        PRINT *, 'SQUARE INCHES     SQUARE CENTIMETERS'
        READ *, LOWIN, HIGHIN
        IF (LOWIN .GT. HIGHIN) THEN
           PRINT *, 'THE GIVEN LOWEST NUMBER OF INCHES, ',
        :          LOWIN
           PRINT *, 'IS LARGER THAN THE GIVEN HIGHEST, ',
        :          HIGHIN
           PRINT *, 'PROCESSING TERMINATED.'
        ELSE
  220      SINCHS = LOWIN
  225      IF (SINCHS .LE. HIGHIN) THEN
              SCENTI = SINCHS / 6.4516
              PRINT *, SINCHS, '        ', SCENTI
              SINCHS = SINCHS + 1
              GO TO 225
           ENDIF
        ENDIF
        STOP
        END
```

5. One possible algorithm:

ALGORITHM SQRT(VAR)
```
{Find the square root of VAR, if nonnegative, using
Newton's method.  The computed square root is
accurate to 0.000001xVAR.}
```

```
            If VAR < 0 Then
                Write message: 'NEGATIVE SQUARE ROOT ARGUMENT', VAR
            Else If VAR = 0 Then
                SQRT ← 0
            Else
                SQRT ← VAR / 2
    ITR.        SQRT ← 0.5 * (SQRT + VAR / SQRT)
                acc ← ABS[VAR / (SQRT * SQRT) - 1.0]
                If acc >= 0.000001, Go To ITR. (Back)
            Return
            END
```

7.   (a)   *Hint:* Rearrange the given formula to obtain the angle in radians.

$$\text{radians} = (\text{angle in degrees})\,\pi\,/\,180$$

Then, in the program, use Fortran statements such as the following for the desired trigonometric computations:

```
SINE   = SIN (RADANS)
COSINE = COS (RADANS)
TANGNT = SINE / COSINE
```

(b)   *Hint:* The Fortran statement

```
RTKVAR = EXP  (ALOG(VAR)  / K)
```

will yield root k of VAR.

8.   Here is an "early-try" algorithm to get you started:

```
            Read principal, rate, months
                                 months            months
            factor ← rate*(1+rate)      / ((1+rate)      -1)
            payment ← principal * factor
            ending debt ← principal
            month ← 1
    NXM.     If month <= months Then
                 begin debt ← ending debt
                 interest ← begin debt * rate
                 prin pay ← payment − interest
                 ending debt ← begin debt − prin pay
                 If month = months, prin pay ← prin pay +
                                                ending debt
                 month ← month + 1
                 Write month, begin debt, interest,
                       prin pay, ending debt
                 Go To NXM. (Back)
            Stop
```

SECTION 6-1-4

4.   The input data for all the problems mentioned in this exercise can, and should be, read in list-directed. Therefore, the input values on each input record need only be separated by blank columns or commas. A possible input layout for the quadratic roots problem in part (c) is given in the FORMAT STATEMENT section, Section 6-3-3. A possible input layout for the Fahrenheit-to-Celsius conversion program is

Field Name	Data Description	Columns
Lowest Fahrenheit temp. Highest Fahrenheit temp.	Integer Integer (Up to machine-allowed size)	List- directed, one blank between

5. *Suggestion:* Prepare and run it on your computer to check your answer; actual columnar alignment may vary from processor to processor.

SECTION 6-5

1. The second formulation would result in the truncation of the GPA because both GPRCVD and HRSTRI are integer variables.

2. (b) DELTA=1234.5, MU=6789, RHO=1.0
    (d) ZETA=1.0, ETA=5.55555, THETA=−0.01

4. {Double space: one blank line}
    ```
    WHEN THE AMOUNT INVESTED IS $ 1000.00
    AND THE INTEREST RATE IS   .055
    THEN, IF COMPOUNDING IS QUARTERLY,
    THE AMOUNT OF INTEREST GAINED WILL BE $   56.14
    AND THE FINAL BALANCE WILL BE $   1056.14.
    ```

5. {Head-of-form: new page}
    ```
    ANALYSIS PROGRAM ANSWERS
    ```
    {Double space: one blank line}
    ```
        1     1000.00    .10      1       1010.00
    ```
    {Double space}
    ```
        2     1000.00    .10      1       1010.00
    ```
    {Double space}
    ```
        3    10000.00    .00      1      10000.00
    ```
    {Head-of-form: new page}

6. *Hint:* Given the proper variable usage (which you should be able to determine from the variable names), the Fortran statement

    ```
    CRSAVG = GRDEXA * PCTEXA + GRDEXB * PCTEXB +
    :        GRDEXC * PCTEXC + GRDHWK * PCTHWK +
    :        GRDFIN * PCTFIN
    ```

    can be used to find the course average for each student.

8.   *Hint:* Since you have not yet learned to use arrays (Chapter 8), the factor for-
     mula will actually have to appear in the program one time for each output
     column—five times as indicated by the output layout. The factor-computing
     statements can be written like this:

```
FACT1 = RATE1 *  (1.0 + RATE1)**N /
:           ((1.0 + RATE1)**N - 1.0)
FACT2 = RATE2 *  (1.0 + RATE2)**N /
:           ((1.0 + RATE2)**N - 1.0)
      .
      .
      .
FACT5 = RATE5 *  (1.0 + RATE5)**N /
:           ((1.0 + RATE5)**N - 1.0)
```

where RATE1, RATE2, ..., RATE5, are the interest rates corresponding to
the five output columns (RATE2 = RATE1 + increment, RATE3 = RATE2
+ increment, etc.). Then, to print one of the detail lines, use a statement
pair like this:

```
930 FORMAT (' ',  4X, I2,  12X, F8.6)
    WRITE (PO, 930) MONTHS, RATE1, RATE2, RATE3,
:                       RATE4, RATE5
```

SECTION 7-1-5

1.   One likely IF statement:

```
IF  (BCOEF**2  .GE.   4.0 * ACOEF * BCOEF)  es
```

where es is an appropriate executable statement leading to the computation
of the real roots.

3.   One possible segment:

```
REAL  ACOEF, BCOEF, CCOEF
LOGICAL  RLROOT
    .
    .
    .
RLROOT = BCOEF**2 .GE.  4.0 * ACOEF * CCOEF
IF (RLROOT)  es
```

where es is as in Exercise 1.

5.   `.NOT. (OBS .GE. LOWOBS .AND. OBS .LE. HIOBS)`

7.   (a)   True

     (b)   False

8.   One possible segment:

```
POSLYR = MOD(YEAR, 4) .EQ. 0
IF (POSLYR) THEN
```

```
      ORDLYR = .NOT.   MOD(YEAR, 100) .EQ. 0
      CENLYR = MOD(YEAR, 400) .EQ. 0
      IF (ORDLYR .OR. CENLYR) THEN
         PRINT *, YEAR, ' IS A LEAP YEAR'
      ELSE
         PRINT *, YEAR, ' IS NOT A LEAP YEAR'
      ENDIF
   ENDIF
```

SECTION 7-5

3. (b) The Fortran DO-loop is established by the initialization, incrementation, and testing of a loop control variable, whereas the loop in AVRAGE is based upon the repetitive performance of an input operation until an end-of-file condition is encountered. Although a "counter" is used in AVRAGE to count the valid input values, it is not, and cannot be, employed as a loop control variable. The loop in AVRAGE is, however, a DO-while loop having this intepretation: "Perform the statements in the loop as long as there are values of OBS in the input file."

6. The computed GO TO portion (where c is CLASS, w is WTDSCR, r is RAWSCR, f is FRSFAC, sp is SPHFAC, j is JNRFAC, and s is SIDNUM) can be flowcharted as follows:

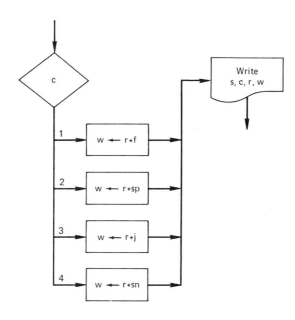

15. With all variables declared as integers:

```
*   D. ACTION
        READ *, NUMBER
        DUMMY = NUMBER
        REVRSE = 0
        DO 300 DIGIT = 1, 10
            IF (DUMMY .LE. 0 ) GO TO 310
                REVRSE = MOD(DUMMY, 10) + REVRSE * 10
                DUMMY = DUMMY / 10
    300 CONTINUE
    310 PRINT *, NUMBER, ' REVERSED IS ', REVRSE
        STOP
        END
```

SECTION 8-8

2. One likely revision:

```
INTEGER  NU
PARAMETER  (NU=75)
INTEGER  ALPHA(NU), BETA(2*NU), ELEM, LAM
REAL  DELTA, GAMMA(5)
        .
        .
        .

DO 210 ELEM = 1, NU
    ALPHA(ELEM) = 0
210 CONTINUE
    BETA(1) = 0
    DELTA = 0.001
    READ *, (GAMMA(LAM), LAM = 1, 5)
    {where appropriate input values are entered for
    GAMMA; alternatively, construct a DO-loop and use
    assignment statements.}
```

3. (b) `READ *, (LENGTH(NEXT), WEIGHT(NEXT), NEXT=1, 3)`

(c) ```PRINT *,   (HEIGHT(NEXT),   NEXT = 1, 3),
     :   (LENGTH(NEXT),   NEXT = 1, 3),
     :   (WEIGHT(NEXT),   NEXT = 1, 3)```

4. (a) `PRINT *, (ALPHA(NEXT), BETA(NEXT), NEXT=1, NIR)`
{This statement, however, will cause several values of ALPHA and BETA to be printed on each line.}

5. Partial answer: XOBS(1) = 0.3, YOBS(2) = undefined, IN = 5 upon completion.

7. *Hint:* Consider the test that is used to determine whether or not an interchange is to be made.

9. One likely algorithm:

ALGORITHM Bowling:scoring.1

```
{ Find the score of one or more bowling games, for
as long as game  data is entered.  The first input
record  for each  game contains  a game identifier
(gameid)  and  the  number  of  times the ball was
rolled  (rolls)  in that  game.  Individual counts,
ranging from 0 to 10,  are entered for the rolls on
as many succeeding records as necessary.}
NXG.    Read gameid, rolls, at EOF Go To QIT.(Ahead)
            Do ball ← 1 to rolls by 1
              Read count(ball)
            End Do
            score ← 0
            ball ← 1
            Do frame ← 1 to 10 by 1
              If count(ball) = 10, Then
                {strike}
                score ← score + 10 + count(ball+1) +
                                      count(ball+2)
                ball ← ball + 1
              Else If count(ball) + count(ball+1) = 10 Then
                {spare}
                score ← score + 10 + count(ball+2)
                ball ← ball + 2
              Else
                {open}
                score ← score + count(ball) +
                                count(ball+1)
                ball ← ball + 2
            End Do
            Print title:  {as appropriate}, gameid, score
            Go To NXG. (Back)
QIT.    Stop
        END
```

13. *Hint:* Binary numbers are converted directly to decimal numbers by summing the positional values of all 1s in the binary number. The binary number 110000111, for instance, has 1s in these positions (right to left): 0, 1, 2, 7, and 8. The corresponding positional values are 1, 2, 4, 128, and 256; that is, in each case, 2 raised to the position number as a power (exponent). The sum of the positional values in this example is 391—as indicated in the problem statement. *Additional note:* For interactive program references you may want to go ahead and examine the programs and i/o in Section 12-3.

SECTION 9-6

1. Some of the answers are: ABLE=APPLE, BAKER(1)=C, CHARLY=ƀƀƀƀƀƀƀƀƀƀ.

2. {Head-of-form: new page}
    EXPERIMENT DELTA

{Double space: one blank line}

A	B	C
1234.5	2345.6	3456.7
6789.0	7890.1	8901.2

3.   (b)   True.

SECTION 9-12

1.   (b)   CLICHES:

      (d)   BETTER LATE THAN NEVER

2.   Printed results for the second pair of input records only:

```
Joya's          favorite food is tacos.
Among her other favorites are
        color.....orange
        sport.....tennis
        holiday...St. Valentine's day
```

SECTION 10-1-6

1.   UNITS is being referenced as if it had 3 rows and 10 columns instead of 10 rows and 3 columns as declared. Thus the processor will not be able to calculate the correct location for any elements beyond the first three [i.e., UNITS(1,1), UNITS(2,1), and UNITS(3,1)]. Some of the incorrectly calculated locations will be inside and others will be outside of the established array bounds. The reaction, if any, will differ from processor to processor. Some processors will not detect the error. Try it on your computer, printing some of the array elements, to see what happens.

2.   Column-wise assignment.

3.   (b)
```
READ *, (DELTA(COL), (BETA(ROW, COL), ROW = 1, 2),
    :        COL = 1, 2)
{column-wise on BETA}
```

      (c)
```
PRINT *, ((GAMMA(DOWN, ACROSS), ACROSS = 1, NA),
    :           DOWN = 1, ND)
{row-wise on GAMMA}
```

4.   Some of the answers: PIE(1) = Appleḃ, PIE(4) = (undefined), CAKE(5,2) = Figḃḃ, entire column 1 of CAKE undefined.

11.   Additional information: Two interactive programs, with sample i/o, are given in Section 12-3. You may want to go ahead and examine them now.

SECTION 10-2-1

2. Column-wise order.

3.

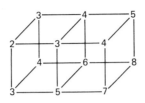

4. READ *, ((((ZETA(ROW, COL, FILE), COL=1,2), ROW=1,3),
: FILE=1,2)

5. Some answers: LETTRS(1,1,2) = B, LETTRS(2,2,2) = K, LETTRS(4,2,3) = X.

SECTION 11-9

1. One possible function:

```
*I.    FACTORIAL OF N
*
       FUNCTION FACT(N)
*      PROGRAMMER:  Jarrell C. Grout
*      DATE:   10/3/81
*
*   A. COMMENTARY
*
*          Given a nonnegative integer N, find its
*      factorial, FACT.  A negative value of N will
*      return an invalid negative FACT value of -1.
*
*          DICTIONARY.
*
*      FACT:  Factorial of N
*      I:  Loop index for computing factorial
*      N:  A nonnegative integer
*
*   B. DECLARATION
*
       INTEGER FACT, I, N
*
*   C. I/O LAYOUT
*
*      None
*
*   D. ACTION
*
       IF (N .LT. 0) THEN
          FACT = -1
       ELSE
          FACT = 1
```

```
        IF (N .GT. 1) THEN
            DO 300 I = 2, N
                FACT = I * FACT
300         CONTINUE
        ENDIF
    ENDIF
    RETURN
    END
```

4.   *Hint:* Search for a two-blank sequence.

6.   One likely subroutine, in part:

```
*n.   INTEGER BINARY SEARCH
*
      SUBROUTINE INBSCH (NUMBER, ARRAY, SIZE, LOC)
         .
         .
         .
*   B. DECLARATION
*
      INTEGER  ARRAY(SIZE), HIGH, LOC, LOW, MID, NUMBER,
      :              SIZE
         .
         .
         .
*   D. ACTION
*
      LOW = 1
      HIGH = SIZE
250   IF (LOW .LE. HIGH) THEN
          MID = (LOW + HIGH) / 2
          IF (NUMBER .LT. ARRAY(MID)) THEN
              HIGH = MID - 1
          ELSE IF (NUMBER .GT. ARRAY(MID)) THEN
              LOW = MID + 1
          ELSE
              LOC = MID
              GO TO 310
          ENDIF
      ELSE
*         Number not in set (ARRAY);
*         designate negative location:
          LOC = -1
          GO TO 310
      ENDIF
      GO TO 250
310   RETURN
      END
```

SECTION 12-4

6.   One likely solution:

```
*n.   INDIRECT ALPHABETIC BUBBLE SORT
*
```

```
        SUBROUTINE INSORT (DIR, ARR, N)
*       PROGRAMMER:  Jarrell C. Grout
*       DATE:  9/3/81
*
*  A. COMMENTARY
*
*          Values stored in the N>0 elements of the
*       character array ARR are indirectly sorted into
*       alphabetical order in the array by the bubble
*       sort method.  Each value in ARR should contain
*       only alphabetic letters or proper ordering may
*       not occur.
*
*          DICTIONARY.
*       ARR:  Array of size N to be sorted
*       DIR:  Directory for indirect sort; element values
*             supplied by referencing program unit
*       FIRST:  Directory index for first element in sort
*               comparison
*       INFRS:  Indirect student index for first element
*               in sort comparison
*       INSEC:  Indirect student index for second element
*               in sort comparison
*       INTCH:  Sort interchange indicator
*       N:  Number of elements in array ARR
*       NUMCPS:  Number of compares in one sort pass
*       SECND:  Directory index for second element in
*               sort comparison
*       TDIR:  Temporary variable for directory element
*              interchange
*
*  B. DECLARATION
*
        INTEGER  DIR(N), FIRST, INFRS, INSEC, INTCH, N,
      :          NUMCPS, SECND, TDIR
        CHARACTER  ARR(N)*(*)
*
*  C. I/O LAYOUT
*
*       None
*
*  D. ACTION
*
        NUMCPS = N
        INTCH = 1
  315 IF (INTCH .EQ. 1) THEN
            INTCH = 0
            NUMCPS = NUMCPS - 1
            DO 320 FIRST = 1, NUMCPS
               SECND = FIRST + 1
               INFRS = DIR(FIRST)
               INSEC = DIR(SECND)
               IF (LGT(ARR(INFRS), ARR(INSEC)) THEN
                  TDIR = DIR(FIRST)
                  DIR(FIRST) = DIR(SECND)
                  DIR(SECND) = TDIR
                  INTCH = 1
               ENDIF
```

```
320    CONTINUE
          GO TO 315
       ENDIF
       RETURN
       END
```

7. A copy of the program that produced the index preparation output can be purchased from the book's author.

8. One solution, without header and commentary:

```
*   B.  DECLARATION
*
       INTEGER  MAXCOL, MAXROW
       PARAMETER   (MAXCOL= 4, MAXROW=6)
       REAL   TABLE(MAXROW, MAXCOL)
       INTEGER  COL, ROW
       CHARACTER  LINE(MAXCOL) *12
*
*   C.  I/O LAYOUT
*
  900 FORMAT (F12.1)
*
*   D.  ACTION
*
       DO 210 ROW = 1, MAXROW
          READ *, (TABLE(ROW, COL), COL = 1, MAXCOL)
          WRITE (UNIT=LINE, FMT=900)
     :            (TABLE(ROW, COL), COL = 1, MAXCOL)
          DO 205 COL = 1, MAXCOL
             IF (TABLE(ROW, COL) .LT. 0)
     :          LINE(COL) = '        ....'
  205     CONTINUE
          PRINT *, (LINE(COL), COL = 1, MAXCOL)
  210 CONTINUE
       STOP
       END
```

Index